English Social History

* *

*PROTESTANT
ISLAND*

Arthur Bryant

PROTESTANT ISLAND

Collins
ST JAMES'S PLACE, LONDON

First Impression September, 1967
Second Impression December, 1967
© *Introduction Sir Arthur Bryant, 1966*
© *Text, in this edition, Sir Arthur Bryant, 1966*
Printed in Great Britain
Collins Clear-Type Press
London and Glasgow

"The Bishop of Rome hath no jurisdiction in this Realm of England."

Book of Common Prayer

"Upon the Bible stood both Anglicanism and Nonconformity. . . . Without it we can scarcely imagine English constitutionalism or English imperial expansion. . . . It provoked and rationalized the theory and the action of those three great centuries during which Britain placed her stamp upon world history."

A. G. Dickens,
The English Reformation

Contents

Contents

The Breach with Rome

"They ordered his bones . . . to be taken out of the ground and thrown far off from any Christian burial . . . and cast into Swift, a neighbouring brook . . . This brook conveyed his ashes into Avon, Avon into Severn, Severn into the narrow seas, they into the main Ocean. And thus the ashes of Wycliffe are the emblem of his doctrine, which is now dispersed all the world over."

Thomas Fuller, Church-History of Britain

A CENTURY AND A HALF after Wycliffe denounced the corruptions of the medieval Church and sixteen years after Luther nailed his theses against papal indulgences to the door of Wittenberg church, Henry VIII and his parliament repudiated the authority of the Pope and constituted the king Supreme Head of the English Church. "By divers sundry old authentic histories and chronicles," the Act of Appeals laid down, "it is manifestly declared . . . that this realm of England is an Empire . . . governed by one supreme head and king." It was the culmination of a process begun in the fourteenth century with limitations on the rights of ecclesiastical courts and of appeals to the Roman *curia*—one which had derived increasing popular support from the resentment felt by property owners and taxpayers at papal interference with native rights and the provision of English benefices for the *curia*'s nominees and creditors. It was with the threatened penalties of life imprisonment and total confiscation imposed by an act of Richard II's reign—Praemunire—on those who removed legal cases out of the king's jurisdiction into that of a foreign court that Henry VIII browbeat Convocation into submission and the surrender of its independence and, three years later, procured the dissolution of the monasteries and the confiscation of their wealth.

Unlike that which had preceded it on the continent, the English

Reformation began purely as an act of State. Rewarded, before his breach with Rome over his divorce, with the papal title of Defender of the Faith, Henry VIII by his apostasy let loose anti-clerical forces greater than even he could control. During his last years a radical but powerful minority of his subjects, inspired by their reading of the printed scriptures and the polemics of continental theologians, denounced as idolatrous superstitions many of the leading tenets of the medieval Church—transubstantiation, the confessional, the efficacy of indulgences and papal remission of sin, of pilgrimages, relics and the intercession of the saints. All that Wycliffe and the Lollards had sought were now openly acclaimed and demanded: communion without the Mass, congregational worship, a married clergy, and the acceptance of the scriptures as the sole authority for Christ's teaching and Christian doctrine. After Henry's death and during the brief reign of his son the floodgates opened wide, and the attempts to close them of the devout Mary Tudor—daughter of Henry's divorced Spanish wife—only strengthened the flood's force. The popular reaction against the Smithfield fires, and the accession in 1558 of Anne Boleyn's daughter, Elizabeth, enrolled England permanently among the nations that had rejected Rome.

This momentous and tragic breach in the religious unity of Europe had been preceded only a generation before by the discovery of the ocean trade-routes round the Cape of Good Hope and across the Atlantic. It had been the little kingdom of Portugal that during the fifteenth century, under the aegis of a grandson of John of Gaunt, paved the way to this transformation of the globe. By breaking in 1497 into the Indian Ocean her seamen achieved what the crusaders had failed to do. Outflanking Turkish and Arab land-power from the rear, they ended the Islamic blockade that had so long barred European traders from the Orient. At the very time that, fresh from their capture of Constantinople and the destruction of the Byzantine empire, Moslem fleets and armies were advancing westwards across the Mediterranean and up the Danube valley against the surviving half of Christendom, the tables were turned on them by ocean sea-power. It was to prove a second and vaster Salamis.

In that at first unrealised victory for Europe—for it took nearly a century before its full effects were felt—the Protestant maritime nations with Atlantic seaboards followed where the Catholic ones had led. During the reign of Elizabeth the seamen of London and the West Country challenged the monopoly of the Indies that a papal decree had given to Spain and Portugal. Throwing down the gauntlet to the former—the world's greatest empire and the militant champion of the Roman Church and Counter-Reformation—they plundered the Spanish Main and, under Drake, broke into the closed Pacific and, following in the sea-steps of Magelan, circumnavigated the globe. When, with the Pope's blessing, Philip of Spain launched his invincible Armada against England, aided by her stormy seas they destroyed it, leaving Parma's army of invasion stranded on the Netherlands shore. During the maritime war, which continued, first in an unofficial and then in an official form, for the greater part of Elizabeth's reign, the Protestant minority in England became a majority. By the beginning of the seventeenth century, their crown joined on the queen's death with that of Scotland—a country which had also repudiated Rome and embraced a Presbyterian system of Church government and a Calvinist theology—the English were a Protestant people who had turned their backs on the social institutions of their Catholic past—monasticism, the Latin liturgy, the worship of the Host, shrines, relics, the pilgrimage, and the chantry chapel's *obits* for the dead. Instead, the reading and individual interpretation of the Bible—made available in a series of great English translations, culminating in the beautiful Authorised Version of 1611—made them, with their growing love of individual liberty, a people, not of one, but of many sects and creeds. And though the episcopalian national Church—of which the king was Governor—claimed an unbroken succession from the early Christian Church, purged by the breach with Rome of what it deemed false and superstitious accretions, so strongly did many of the English resent even this tenuous link with their Catholic past and the support given to that Church by their Stuart kings, that in the middle of the century they took up arms against both the hereditary monarchy and the Anglican Church and, after a bloody civil war, abolished both.

Yet in 1660, only nine years after the execution of Charles I, the monarchy and Anglican Church were restored in a revulsion of public feeling against the doctrinaire excesses of the sectarian enthusiasts and the despotism of their standing army which had virtually abolished parliament and the independence of the courts of law. Though once more a monarchy presiding over an episcopalian Church, outside a small minority at Court and in the remoter provinces the England of Charles II was whole-heartedly Protestant in feeling, habit and thought. It was this, even more than the growth of its capital, maritime trade and new industries—themselves largely by-products of its vigorous Protestantism—that differentiated its social life from that of the Catholic England of the Plantagenet and Lancastrian past.

*   *   *   *   *

During her first century as a fully-committed Protestant nation, out of the native stock schooled by a thousand years of Catholic civilisation England produced the world's greatest seaman, Drake, its greatest poet, Shakespeare, and its greatest scientist, Newton. Under a queen descended on her father's side from a line of petty Welsh squires and on her mother's from East Anglian clothiers, her people laid the foundations of their future maritime ascendancy and, under her Stuart successors, founded beyond the Atlantic the thirteen colonies which were to become the United States of America. What is remarkable is how much, with their material limitations, this little nation of five millions achieved.

Like their Catholic ancestors these English of the first Protestant generations believed implicitly that the world was governed by moral law. Released from the international bureaucratic and doctrinal strait-jacket of Roman orthodoxy, they differed, often violently, as to the character of that law. But they still believed that God—its embodiment and enforcer—was all-seeing and that men and nations who transgressed it would be punished. The civil wars which convulsed England in the middle of the seventeenth century, with all their heroism, nobility and tragic waste, were a witness, not only to their pugnacity and factiousness, but to the intensity of their religious feelings and striving for moral betterment. And when their fanatic enthusiasms in religion and politics provoked, as they were bound to do, a reaction, they embarked with equal enthusiasm on the task of making human existence more comfortable and intelligible. By their energy, curiosity and good sense they helped to lay the foundations of the modern world.

CHAPTER I

Approach to the Capital

ONE USUALLY APPROACHED her from the French shore, travelling in the packet-boat from Calais. The drawbacks were much as to-day, only more acute, for not only was conversation apt to be interrupted, as one disgusted traveller put it, by the disorder to which those who are not accustomed to the sea are subject, but such interruption was more prolonged. Adverse winds might hold up the boat for several days, and it was fortunate if the delay occurred in harbour rather than in mid-Channel. In reasonably fair weather the crossing took seven hours.

Even before landing the sensitive traveller was made aware of the island, for if the wind blew from off her cliffs scents of thyme and sheep on the uplands were borne out to sea. Other scents, too, for the little town of Dover was as innocent of the art of sanitation as any in Europe. Nestling beneath its castle, it presented an inviting appearance, which closer acquaintance modified. Both castle and harbour works were much decayed, and the shingle was constantly drifted by storms into the fairway, so that on more than one occasion the mayor was forced to summons reluctant householders with shovels to the beach for the customary labour of clearing the harbour. And once—it was in 1662—the authorities in London were aroused from lethargy by the arrival from the storm-beleaguered town of a missive fearfully endorsed: "In haste, post haste, or all's lost; port, town and people."

Landing was attended by formalities: by the officers of the Customs with prying eyes, by those of the castle on watch for undesirable entrants—a constant succession of whom were lodged in its dungeons and who, aided by bribery, almost as constantly escaped—and, in the case of very distinguished visitors, by the royal Deputy Master of Ceremonies sent down from London to do the honours.

For more ordinary mortals welcome was accorded by the younger inhabitants of the town, who, leaving their games or their loafing, accompanied them to their inns with such affronts as seemed appropriate to the species of foreigner before them. Of these the most common was the cry of "A Monsieur, a Monsieur," accompanied by a certain mocking and dandified gait. It was best to accept this with a smile, for opposition to the island proletariat quickly brought out its more quarrelsome traits, and jeers would then give way to angry growls of "French dogs" and threats of worse. But those of the educated class were not averse to criticism, and, as they sat around the newcomer over the inn fire, they invited him to express his views on their customs and character and even seemed to take pleasure in hearing the truth; only if it were adverse they showed by their laughter that they did not believe it. They appeared to have plenty of leisure and to be in no particular hurry about anything, spending much of their time drinking, taking tobacco and talking, disapprovingly for the most part, about the Government; nor, for all this apparent laziness, did they seem to suffer from the flagrant destitution noticeable in continental towns. And when, after the night's stay, they presented the bill, it was obvious that they were accustomed to gentlemen with well-lined purses.[1]

From Dover the traveller climbed the hill and rode over the downs to Canterbury—"a pleasant champaign country with the sea and the coast of France clear in view." There was wide choice of transport. Those in a hurry might gallop the twelve miles in an hour's time on the excellent post-horses in which the island abounded, for the English, though leisurely in the ordinary concerns of life, were rapid in travelling; the very country people rode to market"as it were for a benefice". Or, if one shirked the heavy post-horse charge of threepence a mile—with an extra fourpence for the guide at each stage—and did not mind being made a little

[1] Sorbière 3-8, 46-7, 54; Cosmo 116, 202; R. Kilburne, *Topography of the County of Kent*; Rawlinson MSS. A 172. ff 5, 113, 127, 133, 137, 139; Statham, *History of Dover*, 114.

sick, one could travel more slowly in a swaying wagon drawn by six horses and directed by a man with a whip who walked beside bandying personalities with his passengers.

The sights of the road revealed England. Gentlemen's coaches, with six horses drawing them and much colour and gilt of emblazonry, travellers, carriers and drovers passing and repassing, country-folk going to market and, in the fields or on the open downs beside the grass highway, haymakers and shepherds at their business. Occasionally there would be some special excitement: a royal courier riding post, or, if it were assize time, the splendid inconvenience of being jostled out of a narrow lane by the coaches and horses of the judges and lawyers pressing forward to the next circuit town.

Beyond the road the landscape stretched into blue horizons. "The country and the grass here," wrote one who saw them for the first time in 1670, "seemed to me to be finer and of a better colour than in other places." Trees were everywhere, stirred to life by sea-breezes that blew perpetually across the island, carrying with them clouds which gave changing lights and shades to every contour. And in the weald beyond the downs there were orchards of apple and cherry, so many that from an eminence it looked as though the whole land was given over to forest. Here, too—and this was unlike the greater part of the country, which was still open —there were enclosures with quickset hedges surrounding the meadows; parks, too, with smooth parterres and bowling-greens before houses which, though inferior in grandeur to the châteaux of France, had with their homely timbering and long peaked roofs a trim and intimate dignity of their own. The general effect was that of a planted garden.[1]

Of the weather one was made conscious from the first, for it was much as it is to-day. All that could be predicted for certain was that it would never be for long the same. Summers of rare loveliness, when the fruit and corn ripened to a bumper harvest and July flowers were out in May, and Christmases bright with snow and holly, lived as now in the consecrated memory of old

[1] Sorbière 3-8, 7, 9-10; Blundell 183; Defoe 27, 122, 388; Fiennes 194; H.M.C. Portland II 302-3; *Verney Memoirs* II 311.

men; more usually the climate showered down its variegated blessings with humorous inappropriateness. "A verie tempestious slabby day" would be succeeded by a night of "brave moonshine"; "a good misling morning" by an afternoon gale; and a hard frost by "a monstrous great thaw" that sent everyone unexpectedly skidding down the streets. One January it was so fine that the dusty roads were haunted by flies and the rose-bushes were full of leaves—"glorious and warm, even to amazement, for this time of year"; in the May of the same year, after two months of almost continuous rain, the bishops declared a fast; only when the time came the weather had changed to drought, so that they were forced to compromise according to Anglican wont by keeping the day half as a fast and half as a feast. Yet though they hated the white fogs which haunted the country ditches and crept even into the towns, foreigners praised the general salubrity of the climate: there was pure air, plenty of wind and an absence of anything that enervated. And the soft moisture of the atmosphere gave the land ever-changing beauty and colour—the blues and greys and silver whites that enchanted every horizon.

Canterbury was the first town reached. At a distance, its cathedral rose majestic above the surrounding walls; nearer at hand it was seen, like the town itself, to be in that decay which, since the days of the Reformation, had befallen the cathedral cities of England, and which the desecrations of the Commonwealth men in recent years had only intensified. Still the general air of ruin was qualified, as in all things English, by a certain pleasant and intimate charm. There were ancient prebendal houses of crumbling stone set in gardens of blossom and fresh green, and in the narrow streets of the city the houses, so low that occupants of middle height were forced to stoop perpetually, nestled together till their eaves almost touched. To a foreigner it seemed remarkable that most of the windows were glazed instead of being shuttered; those of the lower rooms had curtains and iron bars for privacy and safety, and those of the upper casements which opened in the middle, throwing at night an air of candle-lit intimacy on to the street below. Another peculiarity were the bay windows, which, set in little angles and projections of the houses, enabled a householder to overlook the street in both directions without being observed. And behind each house, which was thus in itself a small castle, were gardens and meadows; for *rus in urbe* was the English rule.[1]

Leaving Canterbury on the Faversham road, the traveller entered a land of apples, hops and cherries. High two-wheeled carts drawn by oxen, bearing hops for the local maltsters or Kentish pippins and russets for the Medway and Three Cranes Wharf, herds of red bullocks with crumpled horns from the Weald pastures, and troops of labourers with scythe and sickle tramping for refreshment to the next village, showed the agricultural interests of the neighbourhood. Indeed, Kent was a kind of agriculturist's Mecca, with its great hop gardens, its orchards of cherries, pears and apples, its tidy habits of cultivation and high wages. Its only drawback for the labourer, who in harvest time could earn as much as two shillings a day—almost double what he could hope for elsewhere —were its notorious agues.

Faversham, a long, straggling town, encompassed the road for over a mile. Beyond the town, coast and road ran for a time within sight of one another, until from the higher ground west of Sittingbourne the traveller caught the gleam of the Medway. A few miles later he entered the twin towns of Chatham and Rochester. Here were the king's naval arsenals, with lanes of storehouses going down to the water's edge, and a main street which stretched for half a league along the Medway until it crossed it by a stone bridge, adorned by a parapet of iron balusters set there by the authorities to catch suicides and hats.

After Rochester the way divided. Here experienced travellers left the main London road through Dartford and bore riverwards to Gravesend. In doing so they were wise to seek each other's company, for the road passed over Gad's Hill, notorious since the days of Falstaff for its robberies. Here on a summer's dawn in 1676 a highwayman on a bay mare robbed a gentleman as he came over the brow of the hill; then, setting spurs to his horse, crossed the ferry to Tilbury—where the delays attendant on tide and a leisurely waterman kept him champing for nearly an hour—and hastened through the Essex lanes to Chelmsford and thence over the

[1] Sorbière 11; Defoe 118; Hasted, *History of Kent*.

downs to Cambridge and Huntingdon, where he rested his horse. An hour later he was mounted again and, galloping up the Great North Road, miraculously reached York the same afternoon, where, after changing his clothes, he repaired to the bowling-green and, singling out the Lord Mayor, made a small wager with him on the fortunes of the game, being careful to ask the time as he did so. All of which subsequently proved an irrefutable alibi, and not only earned the highwayman, whose name was Nicks, a triumphant acquittal but a private interview with His Sacred Majesty King Charles II who was entranced by the whole story and endowed his prudent subject with the sobriquet of "Swift Nicks."

At Gravesend, a little snug town of watermen's houses, one took the ferry to London. Here outgoing ships were forced to anchor for a last visit from the Customs officials, and there was always a fleet of vessels riding in the road. With the tide in one's favour, one could reach London in four hours, either by wherry or, if one chose to be less exclusive and more economical, by the common tilt boat which carried up to sixty passengers at eightpence a head. One had one's money's worth, not only in the passage, but in the sights—fleets of colliers beating up the river with Newcastle coal, Barking smacks with mackerel, sailing under such clouds of canvas that it seemed they must at any moment upset, hoys from Deal and Sandwich bringing the produce of Kent to London, and merchantmen bound for the Indies or Mediterranean. As one proceeded, the chalk-pits and marshes near Gravesend gave way to almost continuous villages and yards busy with ships' carpenters making vessels to take possession of the watery realms which the Navigation Acts were giving England. For those who loved the sight of busy mankind it was the most beautiful river in Europe.

At Woolwich travellers crowded to the port gunwale for a statelier sight, where in the deep water against the shore the king's gilded yachts lay against the wall of the dockyard. A mile beyond, under the trees of its sloping park, lay royal Greenwich, with its old, rambling palace, sadly plundered in the late troubles, lying in ruins, and, on the lawns that stretched before the Queen's House which Inigo Jones had built under the hill, a new palace of white stone rising by the waterside. Then, in a moment, one was in the grey, windswept waters of Long Reach, with one unbroken arsenal stretching along either shore—the greatest shipbuilding centre in the world, save the yards at Schiedam by Amsterdam. Yet within living memory what was a continuous street of buildings along the water had been a lonely tract of marsh, broken only by the gallows on which condemned pirates had been wont to hang till three tides had covered them. And so, at the bend by Limehouse, one came to London. Before lay the Tower, and the many-arched, house-crowned bridge, and the Thames flowing out to meet the sea between a hundred spires and a hundred thousand roofs.[1]

[1] Rawlinson MSS A 188 114-19; Cosmo 197; H.M.C. Dartmouth III 3; Defoe 94-5, 101-3, 123, 249-51; Fiennes 99; Ogg 233-4; H.M.C. Portland II 276; Sorbière 12.

21

Pepys's London

AROUND THE LONDON of 1660 there were still walls, thirty-five feet high in places, with bastions and gates through which King Hal had ridden two and a half centuries before on his return from Agincourt. But the suburbs had long outgrown the city's medieval confines and were spreading tentacles in every direction over the fields. At the Restoration, London housed anything from half a million to six hundred thousand, or about a tenth of the total population of the kingdom, and stretched from Westminster to All Hallows, Barking, and from Shoreditch to St. George's Fields. But there were as yet no buildings north of St. James's Park or west of St. Martin's; St. Giles was still in the fields, and grass meadows fringed the inns along the northern side of Holborn; Southwark was bordered by marshy dikes, and Kensington, Islington and Hackney were country villages. Less than half a century later the population numbered a million, and the houses stretched from Blackwall to Chelsea. Throughout Charles II's reign, despite the destruction wrought by the Fire of 1666, "this great and monstrous thing called London" grew perpetually. It was hard, therefore, to say exactly where one entered it, but the traveller knew by the old formula, "So soon as the coach was got upon the stones."[1]

For it was then that the rattle began. Of wooden and iron wheels rumbling on cobbles, of apprentices standing before every shop bawling, "What d'ye lack?", of hawkers crying, "Lilly white vinegar!" and "White-hearted cabbages!" and "Kitchen stuff, ha' you maids"; and, as the warm months drew on and rich folk

[1] Brown I 202; Bell, *Fire* 11, 17; Clark 39; Cosmo 396; Defoe 316-18, 324; Ogg 94-5; Pepys, 21 March 1663; Sorbière 15; Thurloe II 670.

wished themselves on their country estates, "Cherry Ripe!" "Peas!" and "Fine strawberries!" There were custard mongers—forerunners of the costers—hawking apples; old clothes men and small coals men with sacks of Newcastle cobbles on their backs, milkmaids rattling pails and intoning, "Any milk here?", tinkers with loud, "Have you any brass pots, iron pots, skillets or frying-pans to mend?" and mouse-trap men with "Save alls!" and "Buy a mouse-trap, a mouse-trap, or a tormentor for your fleas!" One sensed the context of these incitements to commerce by their music rather than by their words; by the lilt and rhythm of

> "Here's fine herrings, eight a groat,
> Hot codlins, pies and tarts,
> New mackerel I have to sell.
> Come buy my Wellsfleet oysters, ho!
> Come buy my whitings fine and new."

Nor were these the only sounds. In narrow streets crowded with coaches and carts, traffic control tended to be a matter of vocal adjustment "till the quarrel be decided whether six of your nobles sitting together shall stop and give way to as many barrels of beer." Every nobleman's coach was preceded by a footman calling on the commonalty to make way for his master, a claim which the draymen and the drivers of hackney coaches were quick to dispute. These last, which waited for their fares in ranks at street corners, were to be had at a shilling a mile or eighteen pence an hour. To travel in them was to be involved in frequent turmoil. There were traffic blocks which, lasting sometimes half an hour, set whole streets swearing and shouting; accidents when wheels came off or bolts broke so that the horses went on and the passengers remained stationary; Jehu-like incidents, such as set splashed and endangered pedestrians screaming with rage or brought down in some narrow thoroughfare the wares hanging from hooks outside the shops.[1]

Even at night the noise of London persisted, the constable and his watch brawling with midnight revellers, the watchman's cry

[1] Pepys, 15 Dec '62; 6 Feb, 13 June '62; 6 Feb, 13 June '63; 26 Oct '64; 12 Jan, 12 Nov '66; Aubrey 153; Cosmo 401; H.M.C. VIII (House of Lords) 157; H.M.C. Verney 469.

of "Past one of the clock and a cold frosty windy morning," and the sounds which bespoke the agricultural undertakings hidden behind London's urban exterior, like that "damned noise between a sow gelder and a cow and a dog" which woke Pepys up one sultry summer's night. For the country's capital was still rural at heart, and the rich earthy smell of the fruits and beasts of the home counties lay about it.

One did not only hear London, one smelt it. The lack of sanitation, comparatively innocuous in a country village, was appallingly noticeable in the metropolis. Rivers of filth coursed down the centre of the streets, and, at the time of the emptying of slop-pails, the passer-by nearest the wall had cause to be grateful for the over-hanging stories. Around the city stretched a halo of stinking, steaming lay-stalls, haunted by flies and kites, while in its densest quarters the graveyards, piled high above the surrounding ground, repeopled themselves. Even on a spring evening, when the air was full of scents of sap and blossom from the trees that shaded every court and alley garden, the citizen taking the air on the leads of his house was sometimes driven indoors by—in Pepys's graphic phrase—"the stink of shying of a shitten pot." The most cultured, however nice in their tastes, were utterly innocent of public sanitary sense, the refined Lord Guilford installing a pump to drive the piled ordure from his cellar into the street.

Public conveniences there were none. The polite would step aside to an alehouse, those less so to the street wall. Mrs. Pepys, taken ill at the theatre, unconcernedly went out into Lincoln's Inn Walks and "there in a corner did her business." Even in their homes their possessors did not always employ the houses of office that the richer among them tucked away in cellar or on leads; Pepys himself occasionally made use of the bedroom chimney. Country mothers wrote anxiously to their sons bidding them have a care of the close, crowded air, and members of parliament, when the end of the session released them to their country homes, recalled with horror the smells descending into the House from the small apartments adjoining the Speaker's chamber. Smallpox and fevers, nd more periodically bubonic plague, haunted the town, subse-uently spreading all over the kingdom. They were the price

England had to pay for the wealth which its growing capital made for it.[1]

Other signs of Mammon's presence attended the city. Between it and the sky visitors frequently noted a pall of smoky vapour, arising from the furnaces of the brewers, soap-boilers and dyers, who, unhindered by State or Corporation, carried on their trades in its heart. Evelyn, the most fastidious observer of his day, wrote indignantly of the "horrid smoke which obscures our churches and makes our palaces look old, which fouls our clothes and corrupts the waters." In winter this coal vapour sometimes descended on the streets in a blanket of fog, so that "horses ran against each other, carts against carts, coaches against coaches." Yet in summer the rays of the sun reached the trees and flowers of the city courts without hindrance, and the Thames, for all its unseen load of filth, still sparkled brightly as in the Middle Ages.

For if the London of Charles II was dirty, it was also beautiful. Colour and the pomp of life, moving in gilded majesty, had come back with the king; the streets were full of bright garments. Pepys clothed his footboy in green lined with red and went abroad himself in a summer suit of coloured camelot, with a flowered tabby vest, very rich, and gold lace sleeves. And on May Day, when he drove in Hyde Park in his new coach, the horses' tails were tied with red ribbon, the standards were gilt and all the reins were green.

Until the Great Fire the background of this pageantry was the medieval city which Chaucer had known and in which Shakespeare had worked. The houses were still framed in oak, with walls of lath and plaster, and their overhanging stories were painted and heavily carved. Compared with Paris London spread outwards rather than upwards; the buildings were low and in the better quarters inhabited by only one family apiece, save round the Court and the New Exchange, where furnished rooms and lodgings could be had at easy rates. But in the outer suburbs, in hovels pent to-

[1] Pepys, 30 Jan, 20, 25 Oct, 8, 27 Nov '60; 1 April '62; 7, 8, 26 July '63; 21 April, 28 Dec '64; 28 Sept '65; 30 April '66; 5 Sept '67; Aubrey 107; Brown I 13; H.M.C. Cowper 411; Dartmouth I 129; Portland II 308; Wood III 68; Wynn Papers 357.

25

gether of weather-boards smeared with pitch, the poor were crowded together in indescribable congestion.

Along the southern side of the Strand were the palaces of the nobility. These had gardens running down to the Thames, with private stairs on to the water. Other great mansions, standing in parks and gardens, were scattered round the western outskirts—Bedford, Wallingford, and Burlington Houses and the vast mansion which Lord Chancellor Clarendon built himself after the Restoration in the fields beside Piccadilly and was never suffered to inhabit. More manageable in size were the substantial houses which rich merchants raised and country magnates, in attendance at parliament or Court, rented. Such was Sir Nathaniel Hobart's fine new house in Chancery Lane "near the 'Three Cranes', next door to the 'Hole in the Wall'," with "a very handsome garden with a wash house in it," carrying a rental of fifty-five pounds a year.

Rising above the houses of rich and poor alike were the churches. The sky of the city, as one saw it from the southern bank, was pierced by over a hundred spires and, dominating all, the nave and tower of St. Paul's. The spire of the cathedral had fallen many years before, and the nave had been half ruined by generations of decay and the depredations of the Interregnum. Cromwell's troopers had used it as a stable, and there had been an unsuccessful attempt to sell part of it as building material for a Jewish synagogue. Yet it was still, after St. Peter's in Rome, the greatest church in Europe.

The streets between the crowded buildings were narrow, cobbled with egg-shaped stones, with posts at the sides of the broader thoroughfares to protect pedestrians, and made fantastically crooked by the uneven frontage of the houses. Above them painted signs, projecting on creaking iron branches, proclaimed to an illiterate age the addresses of their occupants—the "Three Pigeons" in Great Queen's Street, the "Crooked Billet" "over against Hill, the Quaker cook's, upon the Mall Bank, Westminster." Behind the streets were courtyards and lanes, sometimes giving access on to a hundred others, sometimes ending in nothing, like that "blind alley, on the backside of Mr. Trice's house, just at the close of the evening," where Dryden's wild gallant was wont to make his rendezvous. Here, too, were gardens with fruit and flowers, and here the innumerable stables which the coaches and horses of the capital required. "Now for the stables," wrote a London friend to Buckinghamshire Sir Ralph Verney, "I have my choice of two. One is in Magpie Yard. There is a pond on the yard to wash the horses in and very good water. It will hold four horses, and the hay loft will hold four loads of hay. There is bins for oats. They say they are very honest and civil people; Judge Atkins's coach has stood there this fourteen years. Now there is another at the 'Red Harp' in Fetter Lane; 'tis one turning more beyond the 'Magpie', but it has the same conveniency. The 'Magpie' is sixteen pounds a year if they lodge a man; the other I can have for fourteen pounds."[1]

On winter nights the principal streets were lit until ten or eleven by lanterns placed at regular intervals, and, more spasmodically, by the uncertain efforts of householders who were expected between the feasts of All Saints and Candlemas to expose a light to the street—a civic obligation often compounded for or evaded. More useful were the link-boys who waited at every corner with torch and lantern to light travellers home. These poor urchins—recruited from the ragged company of homeless strays who lodged in doorways and disused penthouses—assailed the passer-by with cries of "Do you want light?" Grander citizens, like Pepys, who went out to supper with the wench carrying a lanthorn before him, provided their own street lighting.

At intervals London was lit by a brighter illumination. The houses were built "as if formed to make one general bonfire", and whenever a careless householder supplied a spark and the wind was in the right quarter, they obliged. The parish authorities with leather buckets, hatchets and iron crows for removing thatch, the enthusiastic Lord Craven and his amateur fire-fighters, and the fire-engines of the early insurance companies—who, however, confined their efforts to the houses of their own clients—did something to

---

[1] *Verney Memoirs* II 197; Blundell 140-1; Dryden, *Wild Gallant* Act II Scene II; Pepys 22 June '63; H.M.C. Portland III 269; Powell 151; Sorbière 302.

keep this perpetually recurring nuisance within bounds. But in September 1666, with a summer gale blowing from the east after long drought, they met their match. In four days a third of the city perished, including the cathedral, the Guildhall, and eighty-four churches.

For nearly a generation after the Fire a man could stand in Cheapside and gaze through bare ruins at the boats on the river and the wooded Surrey slopes beyond. In that dismal desert of calcined stone and ashes, where more than thirteen thousand houses had been burnt, there were nothing but islands of scaffolding rising from the rubble lines of familiar streets, dotted with wretched huts and cabins of board and canvas and the gaunt skeletons of burnt churches. Over all towered the open roof and glassless windows of old St. Paul's, its beautiful portico rent in pieces. This devastated area, into which the Londoner passed as he came out of the populous streets of Tower Hill or left the prosperous western faubourgs at Temple Bar, was the key to the political feelings of a generation which, twenty-two years later, swept away, in a frenzy of Protestant hysteria, the last English sovereign who dared to avow the Catholic faith. It was a reminder of all that an ultra-Protestant England had suffered since the restoration of the Stuarts—Plague, Fire and the shameful sound of Dutch guns on the Medway. It spelt a legend of nightmarish fears, of popes and red cardinals, priests and foreign dragoons threatening stake, massacre and wooden shoes to the free people of England. And even when a new city of warm coloured brick and pleasant, ordered streets had risen out of the ruins, the legend persisted. On the wall of the house in Pudding Lane on the site where the Fire began, the Lord Mayor of the most bigoted city in the world inscribed the words:

"Here by the permission of Heaven Hell broke loose upon this Protestant City from the malicious hearts of barbarous papists."

Popery was the bugbear with which seventeenth century English children were brought up by their mothers and nurses: a terror they never outgrew. They had learnt their religion from the crude woodcuts of Protestants burning at the stake in Foxe's *Book of Martyrs* and their history from tales of the Massacre of St. Barthol-

28

omew, the Gunpowder Plot and the Irish Rebellion of '41. The
Great Fire seemed to them but one more page in that bloodstained
mythology, a prelude to some gruesome Popish plot of assassin-
ation, midnight massacre and foreign invasion.

Yet this great calamity, far from holding up London's growth,
stimulated it. The new brick houses that arose in the devastated
areas were so much more handsome and commodious than the old
that property owners whose houses had not been burnt became
anxious to rebuild. Moreover, many, who had gardens round their
houses in the old London, recouped themselves for their losses by
building houses and shops where formerly had been grass and
trees. Mr. Swithin's spacious garden by the Royal Exchange
reappeared as Swithin's Alley, with twenty-four houses upon it,
and what had been the stable yard of the "King's Arms" in Cole-
man Street became Copthall Court. This example of building on
open spaces was followed in the unburnt portions of the town, and
one by one the great houses of the nobility disappeared, to be
replaced by squares and terraces bearing the names of their former
owners. Of the palaces along the Strand only three remained by the
end of the century—Somerset House, the Savoy (itself divided
into apartments), and Northumberland House—while the names
Essex, Norfolk, Salisbury, Worcester, Exeter, Hungerford and
York passed into a new chapter of London's topographical nomen-
clature. And since, while the town was rebuilding, the dispossessed
shopkeepers opened their booths on Moorfields and other public
open spaces outside the city, these latter also tended to disappear
and grow into streets and squares. For where London had once
encroached it never receded.

Yet the old divisions remained. The new houses rose on the
same lines as the old, the strength of the foundations and walls
undestroyed by the fire making it difficult for them to do otherwise. The merchants and shopkeepers went back to their old
haunts: Thames Street once more stank of oil, tallow and hemp,
the goldsmith bankers rehung their signs in Lombard Street, mercers
and ladies' tailors spun their costly webs in Paternoster Row, and
drapers and booksellers in Paul's Churchyard. And the fashionable
folk of the West End continued to inhabit the stately porticoed

houses of Covent Garden and Lincoln's Inn Fields—both spared the fire. Before the end of the reign there was a tendency to migrate farther west to the new houses which Lord St. Albans had laid out on his property to the north of St. James's Palace. For in the new London as in the old, birds of a feather flocked together. Even the street-vendors returned to their ancient haunts, and nuts, gingerbread, oysters and night-caps were sold as of old from the barrows by Fleet Bridge at the foot of Ludgate Hill.

The wares which Londoners purchased came to them through the great markets—meat from Hungerford and Queenhithe, fish and coal from Billingsgate, cloth from Blackwell Hall, herbs from Covent Garden and the Stocks Market, horses and livestock from Smithfield, and fish, butter, poultry, bacon, raw hides, leather and baize from Leadenhall. The shops were small, consisting generally of the open door and front downstairs room of the house in which the shopkeeper's family and apprentices lived and worked. But though the multiple shop was unknown, the bazaar already flourished. Great ladies with their husbands and "servants", as their admirers were called, flocked to the New Exchange in the Strand, which, with its rows of shops along double galleries of black stone conveniently adjacent to the fashionable quarter of the town, had long ago outdistanced its Elizabethan rivals—the nave of St. Paul's cathedral and the old Royal Exchange in Cornhill. And here were those elegant young women, the sempstresses and milliners of the Exchange, who, with their ogling eyes and pretty chirpings of "Fine linens, sir, gloves or ribbons," made gentlemen customers buy more than they had intended, and who sometimes, unless they have been maligned by their contemporaries, were not averse to selling their persons as well.[1]

All this business required refreshment, and it was easily to be had. Eating-houses ranged from grand taverns like the "Sun" in Fish Street or the "Dolphin"—beloved by Pepys—in Seething Lane, to little cookshops where one might feast on a chop of veal, bread, cheese and beer for a shilling or buy a joint or sirloin of roast ready cooked for consumption at home. A common mode

[1] Brown III 33; Clark 39-40; Cosmo 296; Defoe 345-7; H.M.C. Dartmouth 120; H.M.C. Gawdy 186; Sorbière 14; Ward II 74; *Varney Memoirs* II 315.

of dining was to take the "ordinary" at the long table of a tavern, each man contributing his share of the conversation and paying his club. At one such Pepys and a friend had "very good cheer for 18d. a piece, . . . and an excellent droll, too, my host, and his wife so fine a woman and sung and played so well that I stayed a great while and drank a great deal of wine." A month later, revisiting it, the same diner-out had another tale to record of "great wrangling with the master of the house when the reckoning was brought, he setting down exceeding high everything."

Places of purely liquid refreshment were innumerable; had one tried to count all the ale-houses between the "Hercules Pillars" by Hyde Park gate and the "Boatswain" in Wapping, one might have counted for ever. In these, men of all classes congregated to smoke, drink and talk—much to the astonishment of foreigners, who could not accustom themselves to the way in which they left their work at all hours of the day for this purpose. Later in the reign the place of the ale-house was partly taken for the middle classes by the coffee-house. This was a novel institution and a great place for the latest tattle of Church and State, derived as likely as not by the loquacious master of the house from the barber or tailor of some courtier's valet. So popular did the coffee-houses become and so seditious their conversation, that successive Governments were forced to issue proclamations against them and subject them to the same licensing restrictions as their rivals, the ale-houses. Out of the coffee-house evolved the club, already, in an informal and not too exclusive way, in its genesis.[1]

In public buildings other than churches London was not rich. There was the Guildhall and the Royal Exchange, where merchants met for news and business, the Customs House and the Navy, Victualling and Pay Offices, the Old Bailey, and the prisons of King's Bench, Fleet, Bridewell and Marshalsea, and the halls of the City Companies. There were also seven beautiful, though for the most part crumbling, gates. And just outside the city walls was the Temple, which escaped the Great Fire only to enjoy a

[1] Aubrey 26; Brown III 15; Harleian Miscellany VI 465; H.M.C. VI (Ingilby 381); North I 66; Ogg 100-2; Ponsonby, English Diaries 136; Sorbière 62; Wycherley, Plain Dealer Act II Scene I.

private fire of its own in 1677—rendered legally memorable by the pedantry of a young barrister who, in the midst of flames, sternly warned the Duke of York, the future James II, and his fellow fire-fighters that they were rendering themselves liable to an action for trespass. That he was subsequently hit over the head with a crowbar does not detract from his professional glory. One other important London building escaped the fire—the Tower—thanks to the forethought of Pepys and Admiral Penn, who fetched up the men from the royal dockyards to fight the flames. The old Norman fortress was the chief landmark of eastern London and a great resort for country visitors. Here were the Mint, the Ordnance, the national archives and the royal armoury, and here, displayed behind an iron grill, the crown jewels which Colonel Blood, the Irish outlaw, attempted to steal in 1670. There were also lions. These, named after the kings of England, were much gaped at by hordes of country cousins and children, and shared their captivity with a number of mangy leopards and eagles.

Other sights were Westminster Hall, the Court at Whitehall, the tombs and effigies in the Abbey, the lunatics at Bedlam and the penitent prostitutes who beat hemp under the lash at Bridewell. There were also the wooden figures that struck the quarters on St. Dunstan's church to the delight of a crowd of country fellows daily congregated in rapt attention before them, and the monsters of the animal world who were nearly always on show in street or tavern—the bearded woman of Holborn, the calf with six legs and a top-knot, and the rhinoceros on which the enemies of Lord Chief Justice North so irreverently declared they had seen him riding. Grander spectacles were the regular events of the London round—the Lord Mayor's Show and its pageantry by land and river, the drills of the City Trained Bands in Artillery fields, and the great September saturnalia of Bartholomew Fair.

But finest of all the sights of old London was its river. For nearly eight miles it bordered the houses, nor, so dependent were its citizens upon it, did the town at any point stray far from its shores. There was no embankment, but the buildings came down to the waterside, where a succession of slippery stairs joined the city lanes to the life of the water. This winding blue canal was the Londoner's highway and the ceaseless background of his life. It was governed in theory by the Lord Mayor and his water bailiff, whose jurisdiction as Thames Conservator stretched from Staines Bridge to the Medway. In practice it was ruled by a corporation of jolly swearing Wapping watermen, who brooked no competition and whose ribaldry was proverbial; though what it was they shouted to the western bargemen about the women of Woolwich which made them so mad we shall never know. For fear of them, though at any hour of the day coaches, drays and cattle were mingled in profane confusion on London's single bridge, no other bridge could be built, and the king, who called them his nursery of seamen, supported them.

It was by these one was greeted as one approached the waterside. From the wooden benches that fringed the stairs there started up a clamorous multitude of grizzly Tritons in sweaty shirts and short-necked doublets with badges on their arms, hallooing and hooting out, "Next oars" or, if their prospective clients were of the black-coated fraternity, "Scholars, scholars, will you have any hoars?" Their boats were of two kinds—sculls with one rower, and the faster "oars" with two, in which one could travel with a favourable tide from one end of London to Westminster in a quarter of an hour.

The boats were not uncomfortable. Passengers sat on cushions and had a board to lean upon. But there was no covering save a cloth spread over a few rough hoops in the stern, generally soaked before there was time to raise it—a fact which caused Pepys when Secretary of the Admiralty to have his open boat converted into a barge with a cushioned cabin, painted panels and windows that slid up and down in sashes like those of a coach.

The bridge was one of the wonders of Britain. Guarded by piles or "starlings" to protect the stonework, it stood on eighteen arches and was crowned by a double row of shops and houses, six stories high. Nervous passengers, frightened by the foam and roar of its cataracts, were wont to land at the "Old Swan" on the northern bank and rejoin the boat below bridge. Save that one was apt to get "soundly washed," shooting the rapids was not so bad as it looked; in flood-time one could take up haddocks with one's hands as they lay there blinded by the thickness of the waters.[1]

To those who took the foul language and rough humour of the watermen as part of the game, the river was full of delight. There were the gilded barges of the king and nobility with gorgeous liverymen, the long, shallow boats that bore malt and meat to feed London from the upper reaches, the picturesque and very dirty vendors of fruit and strong waters, who with wheedling shouts brought their unlicensed skiffs alongside. When the weather was hot, one might pull off one's shoes and stockings and trail feet and fingers in the stream; at flood-tide see the water coursing over the mill banks opposite Vauxhall and boats rowing in the streets of Westminster, or at low-tide watch a daring boy wading through mud and pebbles from Whitehall to Lambeth. Boys and young men swam in the river naked, barristers like Roger North kept yachts on it to while away briefless days, and shopkeepers sought its cool breezes on summer evenings. Pepys was always using the river for recreation. He would "on a sudden motion" take up his wife and his maids in a frolic and, with cold victuals and bottled ale, sail down to Gravesend to see the king's ships lying in the Hope, or, more usually, take the evening air as far as Greenwich or the Chelsea "Neat House." At Barn Elms ladies and courtiers came on June afternoons with bottles and baskets and chairs to sup under the trees by the waterside. Higher up beyond Hammersmith and Putney were gentlemen's villas and gardens and pleasant villages. Small wonder that the seventeenth century Londoner loved his river and went abroad on it whenever he could to look on "the sun, the waters and the gardens of this fair city."[2]

He could take his pleasure if he chose in other ways. As the working day began before dawn, and most well-to-do folk left their business not long after midday, there was plenty of time in the long summer afternoons for recreation. For those whose views

[1] Brown I 148; II 136-7; Chamberlayne 203; C.S.P.D. 1662-3, 86; Cosmo 297, 401; Fiennes 247; Hatton I 231; Howell 13-22; Newdegate, *Cavalier and Puritan* 239; Misson 21; Pepys, 2 Feb, 22 July, 14 Oct, 26 Dec '60; 24-5 March, 13 April, 18 May '61; 2, 8 April '68; Sorbière 14; J. R. Tanner, *Further Correspondence of Samuel Pepys* 297; Thurloe II 670; Ward 50.

[2] Cosmo 320; H.M.C. VII (Corporation of Trinity House 251) H.M.C. Fleming 49; H.M.C. V (Sutherland 196); North III 27-32.

were not too rigid there were the two licensed theatres, with their circular tiers of boxes to which admittance cost four shillings or more, their half-crown pit and upper galleries where, for a shilling, footmen and other humble, but by no means silent, spectators could obtain admittance. The King's Theatre was in Drury Lane, and the Duke of York's or Opera House in Lincoln's Inn Fields. Though decidedly smart, the theatres were informal and friendly; ladies and gentlemen, much to the horror of foreigners, sat side by side in the boxes, and sometimes, it would appear, on one another's knees. In the pit women selling oranges shoved and wheedled their way between the spectators; while the king and queen with Castlemaine and the great ladies of the Court sat without state in the boxes above. In all this the licensed playhouses were the microcosm of a new age, which demanded fare less rough and imaginative, better mannered and more intimate than had been afforded by the older pre-Commonwealth drama. From their little picture stages, with their green baize coverings, their scenery screens "embellished with beautiful landscapes," their tall wax candles and velvet curtains, dainty actresses, with impudent alluring ways, looked down on bewigged, approving gentlemen.[1]

For less sophisticated folk there were still the unlicensed theatres of the Red Bull and Sadler's Wells, where a good deal of rather extravagant noise and ranting amid rough surroundings could be enjoyed at a moderate charge. Far wider in popular appeal, suppressed in name under the Commonwealth though never quite in fact, were the bear and bull gardens, and the cock pits in which the proletariat—and its betters—took their rough pleasures. Pepys left a picture of one of their cock fights: "After dinner . . . directed by sight of bills upon the walls, I did go to Shoe Lane to see a cock-fighting at a new pit there . . . But Lord, to see the strange variety of people, from parliament men to the poorest 'prentices, bakers, butchers, brewers, draymen and what not; and all these fellows one with another in swearing, cursing and betting.

[1] *Roscius Anglicanus*; Cosmo 191; Evelyn, *Diary* 26 Nov '61; Feb '62; 18 Oct '66; H.M.C. Fleming 29; L. Hotson, *The Commonwealth and Restoration Stage*; A. Nicoll, *History of Restoration Drama*; Pepys, *passim*; Orrery, *Letters* I 81; De Witt, *Lady of Lathom* 283; Wycherley, *Love in a Wood* Act III Scene II.

I soon had enough of it, and yet I would not but have seen it once, it being strange to observe the nature of these poor creatures, how they will fight till they drop down dead upon the table, and strike after they are ready to give up the ghost, not offering to run away when they are weary or wounded past doing further, whereas a dunghill brood . . . will, after a sharp stroke that pricks him, run off the stage, and they wring his neck off without more ado, whereas the other they preserve, though both eyes be out, for breed only of a true cock of the game." The more squeamish Evelyn, at the Bear Garden, saw a bull toss a dog into a lady's lap many feet above the arena; saw also two dogs killed and the show end, amid applause, with an ape on horseback.

Through all this rough texture ran a thread of beauty. Perhaps it was because the fields were never far away; trees invaded the streets and squares; there were gardens lurking behind the houses, and nightingales in Lincoln's Inn. And since the fields were so near, the recreations of the citizens were still in part rural. On May Day the milkmaids, with garlands and silver on their pails, danced down the Strand with a fiddler playing before, while Nell Gwynn, in smock sleeves and bodice, stood at the door of her lodgings and watched them go by. All round the town were the green places to which the Londoners repaired whenever their occasions allowed them: Hyde Park, with its balustraded ring round which the coaches drove the rich and fashionable; Moorfields with its mulberry trees; the meadows and milk of Hackney for the apprentice, the farthing pie-houses of Hoxton for the mechanic, and Epsom waters for "Steeplehat", the burgher, and his mincing lady. One might sit in one's coach and drink ale at a tavern door or take a morning mess of cream and sillabub at "The World's End" in Knightsbridge, or visit the Mulberry Gardens—a pretty place by moonlight, and a vast contrast, with its "rascally, whoring, roguing sort of people," to the nineteenth century Buckingham Palace which in due season rises in its place. Further afield, lay Kensington's grotto, the cheroie of Rotherhithe and the cakes of Islington; the Jamaica House at Bermondsey, where Pepys's maids ran races on the bowling-green; or, best of all, wooded Vauxhall, with its spring blossoms, where one could listen to the nightingale and other birds, and "here fiddles and there a harp, and here a Jew's trump, and here laughing, and there fine people walking."

Yet if the London of Charles II seems rural to us, it was metropolitan enough to our forefathers. Such a one would visit it in an Easter term to sample its towny joys—to the destruction of tarts and cheese-cakes—to see a new play, buy a new gown, take a turn in the park. He would sup at the "Hercules Pillars" in Fleet Street or at the sign of "Old Simon the King"—or, if he wished to be very fashionable, at the new French house in Covent Garden, Chatelin's, with its fricassees, ragouts and salads, its music and gay company and unforgettable bills. And everywhere for his delight were sociable little taverns in blind corners, "The Trumpet," "The Sugar Loaf" or "The Green Lettuce"; "The Old House" at Lambeth Marsh, where Pepys on his unlawful occasions wheedled the wives of his naval subordinates; the little bawdy house behind the House of Lords, where he went to drink wormwood; and the fair, frail ladies whom Mother Temple and Madam Bennet in Drury Lane and Moorfields vended to all and sundry.[1]

[1] Brown I 105, 211; III 44; Cosmo 175, 303; Evelyn, 2 July '61; Patrick Gordon, Diary, 85-6; North, I 66 II 237; Pepys, 29 May '62; 23 July '64; 13 March, 22 April '68; Powell 179n; H.M.C. Rutland II 21; Sorbière 15.

CHAPTER 3

Country Faith and Habit

"I wish I were with you a little
in the sweet country."
Elizabeth Shakerley to Mrs. Dobson, Shakerley MSS

THIS WAS LONDON—the rich foam on the surface of the national brew—but England was the country. And, as the population did not much exceed five millions, there was space in it—elbow-room for liberty, and solitude for thought and unsullied imagination. The French ambassador, travelling westwards, was surprised to see how empty it was, passing in a distance of thirty leagues of fine land, very few villages and scarcely a soul on the road. Yet how lovely this open, lonely land was! In Devon the folk clotted their cream with sugar to crown their apple-pies, and, in the fields beside the Ouse in Huntingdonshire, the milkmaids bore home their pails with music going before. In that county, so rich was it in corn, it was the custom, whenever a king of England came, to meet him with a hundred ploughs.

Here in the country quiet the old ways of life persisted. Parson Moore of Horsted Keynes did his shopkeeping by barter, receiving a box of pills and sermons in return for a ribspare and hog's pudding, and in remote parts of Lancashire boon-services were still unsuperseded by rents. The colliers of the Tyne rowed on their holy days by verdant flats and woods, with trumpeters and bagpipes making music in the stern, and west of the Pennines the country-people went bare-footed, leaping as if they had hoofs. Rich and poor alike talked and spelt in the dialect of their county, Cheshire Mrs. Dobson writing to tell her husband:

"I leve here tow and twenty milke cous and a boll, three big

38

hefers and a boleke and seven which are yer old bests; and one boll calfe which runs upon one of the coues and seven other calves which are this year rered, and one fat tegg."

It was a world of hedge squires and parsons, of yeomen, cottagers and ragged squatters, making their wares and pleasures after the manner of their forbears with little news of or regard to what was happening elsewhere. For "that great hive, the city," its vices and graces, country-folk had nothing but pity. To cousins there imprisoned they sent vast cheeses and pies of game; "there was two very fat geese, eight wild ducks, and eight woodcocks, and in the box a pair of stockings" in one such that Lady Shakerley sent her son in London. "When I came home," wrote Robert Paston, "which is the sweetest place in the world, I found my children and Mrs. Cooper pretty well, and she and the gentleman are taking their pleasure to see an otter hunted in the pond."[1]

In the summer of 1667, after the Dutch fleet sailed up the Medway, seeking a respite from overwork and clamour the Clerk of the Acts of the Navy, Samuel Pepys, took his family by coach for a day's outing to Epsom. Here on the downs, only fifteen miles from London, "far from any houses or sight of people," he encountered an old shepherd listening to his boy reading the bible. "He did content himself mightily in my liking his boy's reading and did bless God for him, the most like one of the old patriarchs that ever I saw in my life, and it brought those thoughts of the old age of the world in my mind for two or three days together."

That age was nearer than the rising young official from London realised. For, though England had broken her last links with Rome a century before and was, politically speaking, militantly Protestant, her simple country folk were still instinctively rooted in the faith the medieval Church had taught them. Faith was the air its people breathed. To them it explained everything; even affliction was a visitation sent to test the spirit and teach patience and resignation. "If you be taken away by this dreadful pestilence," a correspondent

[1] H. M. C. Rep. 6 (Ingilby 375-6); Aubrey 154; Shakerley MSS, 16 May '79; Fiennes, *passim*; Chamberlayne 6-11, Jusserand 168; H.M.C. Portland II 263-314; Savile 135-6, 165, 179; North, I 37-8, 175, 183.

wrote during the plague of 1665, "you have had a fair warning and a very long time to prepare yourselves for Heaven. It seems that every day at London is now a day of judgment and that all our thoughts are placed on death, on Hell, on Heaven and upon eternity. Thy will be done on earth as it is in Heaven is the balsam that cureth all."[1]

Such faith sustained men in all the major crises of life, nerved them to bear pain worse than modern medical science permits us to know, and buoyed them in the hour of deprivation which, with early mortality and constant epidemic disease, was so often their lot. "For the world," the Norwich physician, Sir Thomas Browne, wrote, "I count it not an inn but a hospital, not a place to live but to die in." Death still seemed the climax of existence—the hour when a man reaped what he had sown.

In an age when religious feeling was so strong as to amount to an obsession, men saw the hand of God in every happening. "It was an hideous and portending thing", wrote Sir Edward Harley of a gale, "I pray God we may learn the voices of these things". Even the most ordinary occurrences seemed "providences." "I got home," a country parson recorded in his diary, "and found my wife pretty hearty, having taken physic this day and it working very easily with her: a great mercy!"[2]

Behind all this lay the universal reading of the Bible. Educated and uneducated alike spoke its direct and inspired English; official jargon had still to turn the phraseology of administration into a mystery, though Pepys in his vast and laborious naval memoranda was paving a way. An ambassador related in an official dispatch how, when a mob chased its victims to the water-front, "it pleased Him who bridges the sea with a girdle of sand to put bounds to the fury of the people." Familiarity with the Bible was the first step in all seventeenth century education. The very children's alphabets were biblical, one beginning,

> "In Adam's fall
> We sinned all,"

and ending ingeniously,

[1] Blundell 108.   [2] See also Aubrey lxvii; Powell 87.

> "Zaccheus he
> Did climb a tree
> Our Lord to see."

The national religion as re-established by law in 1660 was Anglicanism—that temperate and homely blend of ancient Catholic ritual and Church government with Protestant tenet which expressed the English genius for compromise. During the Interregnum the Anglican Church had suffered severely—its priests expelled, its estates alienated, its cathedrals desecrated. With the Restoration it entered upon a golden period. Its parsons, in their black gowns, square hats and vast white bands, enjoyed a revenue which, though only a fraction of that of the rich "possessioners" of the medieval Church, gave its incumbents an assured place in society. And in the cathedral towns comfortable and dignified colonies of the higher clergy made themselves as much at home as the rooks in the elms above the prebendal houses they inhabited. At Wells there dwelt under the shadow of the cathedral no less than seven and twenty prebends and nineteen canons, besides a dean, a preceptor, a chancellor and an archdeacon. Here the high pomps of Anglicanism—for a generation banished as idolatry— were revived in all their glory. At Exeter the bishop sat beneath a crimson canopy in a seat covered with red cloth. It almost seemed to Catholic observers as though they were in the presence of their own ancient rites: only there was a difference. For as one of them observed, "under the tabernacle, on a level with the floor of the church, in an enclosure of wood, stood the wife of the bishop and his children, no less than nine in number." "I have seen," wrote another witness, "the bishop and the bishopess, the little bishops and the little bishopesses."

In the parish churches neither vestments nor images had any place: the royal arms, the tables of the Decalogue and the sepulchral monuments of the landed gentry were the only idols permitted. Everyone went to church once a week, many two or three times. Here the *pièce de résistance* was the eloquence of the clergy. A priesthood was still as essential to social life as in the Middle Ages, but it was now a Protestant priesthood teaching by sermons, the translated scriptures and a vernacular liturgy, instead of a

Catholic one using images, dramatic representations and Latin incantations. Two sermons a day was the normal Sabbath fare[1] and an hour apiece not thought too long. Sermons were much read by the laity, and many a carrier's cart as it lumbered into the shires bore a folio of good Dr. Sanderson's or Dr. Cosin's sermons for the delectation of some country lady. "The bishop this week," wrote a London correspondent, "comes down to you in the wagon, and I hope brings his blessing with him."

In the towns and the rich eastern and south-western counties, Puritanism had taken root. After the Restoration it was christened by new names—fanaticism by its Anglican opponents, nonconformity by the State. The rules and ritual of the established Church proved too narrow for many who had embraced the intense, though diverse, beliefs of Puritan revelation. To foreigners these presented a bewildering variety. There were Anabaptists who believed in the extinction of rank, Libertines who held that sin was only an opinion, Adamites at whose weddings bride and bridegroom wore only a girdle of leaves, Brownists who regarded church bells as popish inventions and broke into prophecy after sermons, and Sabbatarians who believed that divine revelation had been exclusively vouchsafed to Robert Dogs, the London coal-man. "The common people," observed an astonished foreigner, "enjoy a liberty which is incredible, every man following that religion and those rites which most suit his fancy." Yet the followers of all these varied creeds had two things in common: all loathed the Church of Rome and all believed implicitly that they alone were in the right.[2]

Most powerful of the Nonconformist sects were the Presbyterians, whose quarrel with Anglicanism centred round the question of Church government. At the Restoration it was hoped that they might be induced to conform to a creed which in its essential beliefs differed little from their own, but their dislike of bishops proved too strong. In 1662 over a thousand clergy laid down their livings rather than conform to episcopal government and read the

[1] Pepys would sometimes drop into three or four City churches on a Sunday to sample the sermons.
[2] Sorbière 17; Cosmo 143, 400; H.M.C. Gawdy 195; Ogg 134-5; Wood II 44.

liturgy. Setting up as private teachers, some at least did rather better for themselves than had the Anglican clergy whom they had dispossessed during the Interregnum; for their congregations were drawn largely from the thriving middle class of the towns, who were ready to pay handsomely for their oratory. In London, Mr. Cotton in the Great Almonry, Baxter in Great Russell Street, and the famous Manton in Covent Garden, preached to packed and fashionable congregations every Sunday.

The unlicensed preachers were a great thorn in the side of the royal Government, whose practices they constantly, and not unnaturally, attacked in their sermons. It seemed to loyal subjects as though they were planning a new revolution and second republic. But, to do them justice, they were probably quite unconscious of any ulterior purpose but a divine one; their gloomy and awful prognostications on the fate of Church and State seemed in their eyes as inspired and disinterested as the prophesying of Balaam. "I preached," recorded honest Oliver Heywood, "to a pretty full congregation at the house of Jeffrey Beck; the Lord made it a refreshing night to many souls, though our adversaries watched and gnashed their teeth when they saw so many coming together. I had great liberty of speech in preaching and praying, though," he added a little sadly, "not such melting of heart as sometimes I have enjoyed."

Yet the narrowness and pride that at times showed itself in the Puritan leaders was redeemed by the humility and seemly lives of their followers. Readers of the *Pilgrim's Progress* will remember the song the shepherd boy sang in the Valley of Humiliation. Less familiar is the description of the boatswain, Small, in John Sheffield's *Memoirs*. Small had been captured with the rest of the crew of the *Royal Katherine* at the battle of Southwold Bay, and, after the captain and officers had been sent off, had been stowed under hatches with the remaining survivors. Unarmed and urging them on with his whistle, he led them in a surprise assault on the Dutch guard and almost miraculously recaptured the ship. "He was a Nonconformist," added Sheffield, "always sober, meek and quiet (even too mild for that bustling sort of employment) and very often gave me an image of those enthusiastic people who did such brave things in our late Civil War; for he seemed rather a shepherd than a soldier and was a kind of hero in the shape of a saint."[1]

Two Christian creeds were outside the pale of English public opinion—the Quaker's and Roman Catholicism. The Quakers had few friends. Despite the ultimate gentleness of their tenets, their outrages against contemporary manners won them enemies in all places. One of them, a woman, rose in the middle of the sermon in Windermere church and, "with a loud inarticulate noise," shouted down the preacher; another made a practice of visiting market-places and rich men's houses, stark naked and smeared with excrement, informing all and sundry that the Lord God would besmear their religion as he was besmeared. Inevitably the poor man was subjected to "many grievous whippings with long coach whips, stonings and diverse imprisonments." Such excesses, though unfairly, were universally attributed to the Quakers. Until their sturdy integrity of life and constancy of purpose had won them the honoured place they later took in the national life, they suffered unceasing persecution.

The Catholics, or papists as they were called, were even more universally detested. They were suspected, quite erroneously, of perpetual machinations against the Government and people of England. Among the upper and middle classes no reading was more popular than that which exposed, usually at devastating length and with no mincing words, the fallacies of Rome. As for the common people, any demagogue who was unscrupulous enough to play on their anti-Catholic feelings could loose a murderous wild beast. Once a year the London mob processed through the city with effigies of pope, cardinals and devils stuffed with live cats to make them squeal realistically when burnt, amid shouts of delight, at Smithfield.

Composed almost entirely of members of certain ancient families and their tenantry, the English Catholics had shown conspicuous loyalty to the king's cause during the Civil War and Interregnum. After the Restoration they received little reward, for, however

[1] Sheffield, Duke of Buckingham, *Memoirs* I 15; Wynn Papers 385. Baxterianæ 231-6; Clark 17-32; H. M. C. Fleming 58; Leeds 15-16; Ogg 214-18; Ponsonby 132.

much the king might incline to them, he was powerless in face of the universal hatred in which they were held. Fines for "recusancy," which during the "bad times" had sometimes reached as much as twenty pounds a month, were still imposed, though at a milder rate, and priests were forbidden to minister the rites of their religion under pain of death. Even the most common rights of justice were denied to Catholics, who dared not resort to litigation when an unscrupulous opponent could always enforce on them an oath incompatible with their faith or win the case by default. In times of national panic their lot became still more precarious, for then their houses were searched for arms and their liberty restricted by "chains," which forbade them to travel more than a mile or two from their homes. During the "Popish Plot" of 1678, the best advice a friendly Westmorland justice could give to a Catholic widow was to marry a Protestant who could protect her property and person. Yet persecution only strengthened their constancy. The sons mostly of ancient English Catholic houses, their priests were trained abroad at St. Omer or one of the other English Catholic colleges, and then returned to their own country to pass secretly from house to house, ministering to their flocks in attics and secret oratories and faithfully discharging their duty in constant peril of death. Their epitaph was written by one of their flock, William Blundell of Crosby. " 'We'll hang them,' sayeth a Lancaster jury. 'We'll crown them,' sayeth Christ."[1]

Intolerance was the ugly reverse of seventeenth century piety. It could hardly be otherwise when heresy was still supposed, as in Catholic days, to involve eternal damnation. A neighbour of another religion seemed as great a peril to a man's children as the plague. All the political struggles of the age, culminating in the Revolution of 1688 and the triumph of parliament over crown, sprang partly from the attempt of the last two Stuart kings—the one secretly, and the other publicly, a Roman convert—to grant to the Catholics a greater degree of tolerance than their other subjects would countenance.

. . . .

[1] Blundell 71, 80-1, 172-7, 234. See also Powell 176.

The government of this bigoted land rested on triple supports—Crown, Law and People. The Crown was the executive and provided the element of decisive power. Yet it was a carefully tempered power. Its seat was the old Tudor palace of Whitehall. For nearly half a mile it stretched along the river, a warren of galleries, apartments and gardens, the home not only of the king but of the ministers of State, servants high and low, courtiers, chaplains, ladies and all the gilded army which encompassed the throne. One entered it either from the river or "the lane"—that "long dark dirty and very inconvenient passage"—which, spanned by two gateways, linked Charing Cross with Westminster. Its buildings were of all sizes and ages, from Inigo Jones's classic Banqueting Hall to the little octagonal Cockpit.

The centre of this courtly city was the long Stone Gallery, the hub of the Stuart government of Britain. On its walls hung the pictures which Charles I had collected and his enemies dispersed, and which his son had partly reassembled. Here they made a kind of national picture gallery, for the place was open to all comers. Yet few in the crowd that walked continuously up and down the galleries came for the pictures; places, preferment, sightseeing, above all, news, were the business of that place of rumours. "It runs through the galleries," was the prefix which sped the national gossip.

Well it might, for those who waited here saw the outward stir of all that was moving the wheels of State. The velvet curtains across the doors would part and the king himself pass through the crowd, followed by a group of ministers and suitors from Bedchamber or Council Room, still contending for that royal ear whose retention was at once the hardest and most precious achievement of a careerist's life. Here in the Gallery, for a moment, opportunity flitted by.

From the Stone Gallery guarded doors opened into the royal apartments. In the Robe and Council Chambers the principal committees of State sat in debate, while in the Withdrawing-room waiting gentlemen warmed their hands before the fire. Beyond was the holy of holies, the Bedchamber. In this great room, with its windows looking on to the tides and shipping of the river, the most secret affairs of State were transacted at all hours of the day "between the bed and the wall".

It was not here, or in his closet, that England saw the king, nor even in the Ante-room where the Foreign Ministers daily awaited his return from the park, but in perfumed banqueting hall and chapel. He dined in state, a little after midday, before a background of tapestry, while the massed lords of the household served him on bended knee and all England came and went in the galleries above to share the pageantry. The mysteries of State were performed against a setting of crimson and gold, with the royal trumpeters and kettledrummers marching in scarlet cloaks faced with silver lace, before fringed hangings, gilt mirrors and a world of gleaming fabric.[1]

A few hundred yards down the muddy lane called King Street and across the cobblestones of Palace Yard was the Parliament House. Here sat the watchdog set by the nation to prevent the royal executive from overriding the law. At least that was how people saw it, for the theory of parliamentary sovereignty, first put forward by the extremists of the iron time, had been abandoned at the Restoration as repugnant to English Constitution and habit; the old view of England was that parliaments met, not to govern, but to prevent others from misgoverning. The age of Charles II was the last age in which this was so; after 1688, when the people's representatives became themselves the rulers of the nation, the people, whatever else they gained, lost this traditional buffer between themselves and the executive.

Parliament represented not the masses but the privileged estates of the realm—those who were best able to safeguard ancient legal rights against an encroaching executive. The House of Commons was composed mainly of country magnates, with a sprinkling of merchants, officials and courtiers. They were chosen by a curious blend of nomination and limited election which varied from locality to locality; it was never easy to say who had the right to

[1] Ailesbury 15, 85, 93; H.M.C. Buccleuch II 105; Chamberlayne 155-90, 207-9; Evelyn, 14 May, 3 Oct '61; Ogg, 139-40, 450-60; 13 Sept '66; Halifax 203-4; Lauderdale III 28; Newdegate 23, 27; H.M.C. Ormonde IV 277; VII 27-31; Sutherland 199.

vote and who not. Their sittings were still spasmodic; twice in Charles II's reign long periods passed without any session at all, and there is little evidence that the people as a whole, as distinct from the politically interested minority, much resented the omission. It was only when the nation was in trouble or its religion threatened that parliament was ardently desired by everyone. Its power lay in its right to withhold those additional aids to the customary income of the Crown without which the executive could not afford to embark on any new policy. Throughout the seventeenth century, owing to the continued decline in the value of money, the Crown was generally in need of such aid. This and the fear of Catholicism were the chief causes of national dissension.

* * * * * * * *

Dwarfed by its neighbour France, with her 19,000,000 inhabitants, the population of England stood at about 5,000,000 at the beginning of Charles II's reign, and perhaps 500,000 more at the end. The statistician, Gregory King, reckoned that all but a million and a half lived in the country. According to him nearly a fifth of the heads of the nation's 1,360,000 households were yeomen owning their own land either by freehold or copyhold. More than half were agricultural labourers and cottagers, many of whom, though working for others, had a small stake in the land, if only a commoner's right of grazing and turfage. But the greater part of the soil—formerly vested in the Crown and the medieval Church— was now the hereditary property of a few thousand landowners. The primogenitary system evolved by the Plantagenet lawyers, the erosion of feudal tenures and the spoliation of the monasteries had combined to create an aristocracy of dynastic landed families whose estates and traditions were transmitted unbroken by the partition that occurred in other European countries. Though less than two hundred of the heads of such families were peers and, as such, hereditary legislators, it was from the general body of landed gentry that the Crown drew the unpaid local leaders who represented the shires in parliament, enforced as justices of the peace the law in their native place, and in their courts of Quarter Sessions administered the counties.

Many of these county families had been founded by some yeoman, merchant or court official who had risen to wealth and power
in the fifteenth and sixteenth centuries on the ruins of the medieval
State and the dissolution of the monasteries. Others had grown
rich from the expanding cloth-trade, as often as not marrying their
heirs into aristocratic or knightly families. Yet, though the
occupant of the Tudor manor house was frequently a hard man
who had nails in his boots for those who climbed beneath him, as
the magic of the English countryside closed around him and his
children good humour revived and the grasp of greedy fingers
relaxed. The courtier, merchant or lawyer, who had invested his
gains in a country estate, oppressed his tenantry and harried his
neighbours with lawsuits, was transmuted in a generation or two
into the chivalrous loyalist who gave his life for a king with whose
cause he had little sympathy but whom he supported because, as
one squire put it, he had eaten his bread and would not do so base
a thing as to desert him in his need. He was still often quarrelsome,
but that was because most Englishmen at the time were. "If you
said any such thing," wrote one of his kind, "I would advise you
to eat your words immediately, else—by the living God—I'll cram
them down your throat with my sword—and that very shortly."
But when his temper was not aroused, the typical squire, like
Addison's Sir Roger de Coverley, was good humoured and
friendly: the kind of man who saluted everyone who passed him
with a good morrow or good night and, "when he entered a house,
called the servants by their names and talked all the way upstairs to
a visit."

After religion—belief in the all-importance of which he shared
with his contemporaries of all classes—the squire's ruling passions
were the chase and the enlargement of his estate. He sought the
latter in parliament, in the courts of law and in matrimony—especially in matrimony. Few things, even the king's favour, could do
so much to advance a dynastic family's fortunes as a rich and in-
fluential marriage. For this reason—though most seventeenth century marriages occurred no earlier than those of to-day—the heirs
and heiresses of large properties were sometimes contracted at a
very early age. Thus Sir Ralph Verney wrote of "a young wedding

between Lady Grace Grenville and Sir George Cartwright's grandson"—a Buckinghamshire family uniting with a Northamptonshire one—"she is six years old and he a little above eight years,
therefore questionless they will carry themselves very gravely and
love dearly." Occasionally an heir kicked over the traces and chose
for himself; when this happened, the defrauded father was justly
indignant. "Sir," wrote Lord Cork to his son, "I am informed
that you are so miserably blinded as to incline to marry and so with
one wretched act to dash all my designs which concern myself and
house." Few parents, however, expected a son or daughter to
marry anyone who aroused active aversion. A right of veto was
allowed, such as John Verney used when he had his prospective
bride paraded up and down Drapers' Garden so that he might
see if there were "nothing disgustful" about her.[1]

The marriage of daughters was seldom a profitable business.
Young ladies with fortunes were, of course, easily disposable;
"Sir Ambrose Crawley's daughters go off apace, but £50,000
ladies will never stick on hand." But no father would allow a son
with expectations to marry a girl, however attractive, without a
portion proportionate to his estate, and in the correspondence of
the time the girls of landed families often present a somewhat
pathetic picture, nervously anxious to marry and doomed to a life
of dependence as companion to some rich relative if they failed.
"I think," wrote one young lady in despair, "my marrying very
unlikely in any place and impossible in this." Shortly afterwards
she made a runaway match with a penniless curate; anything she
felt was better than being left an old maid.[2]

All this made a marriage settlement a complicated business. The
parties' legal advisers would engage in interminable correspondence,
and learned counsel in London would be feed, so that children and
grandchildren unborn might be provided for and remote con-
tingencies anticipated. Months, sometimes years, would pass before
the final details were complete and the young people free to wed.
In one case, when the latter took matters into their own hands and
married before the legal formalities were completed, the father of

[1] *Verney Memoirs* II 176, 272, 316. Shakerley MSS; Blundell 85, 139, 240.
[2] *Verney Memoirs* II 177-8, 188; *Postman's Horn* 79-108.

the bride—who gained greatly by the bridegroom's impatience—wrote to his discomfited opposite, "And to show you he is your own son, we had much ado to keep him from kissing his bride before matrimony was all read."

Though occasionally genuine tenderness sprang up between the young people before the wedding, a conventional phraseology of courtship was *de rigeur*. They called themselves one another's "servants" and wrote such letters as young William Blundell with his father's aid wrote to Mary Eyre: "Oh! my most honoured dear lady, how shall I count those unkind hours that keep me from so great a joy? I told you once before (as I hope I did not offend) that your goodness hath cause to pardon what your virtue and beauty hath done." Most of the love-letters of the time were written after, not before, marriage. There were exceptions like those of Dorothy Osborne. Forbidden to see her love, she wrote to him: "I think I need not tell you how dear you have been to me, nor that in your kindness I placed all the satisfaction of my life; 'twas the only happiness I proposed to myself, and had set my heart so much upon it that it was therefore my punishment to let me see that, how innocent soever I thought my affection, it was guilty in being greater than is allowable for things of this world." She waited for him for seven years and had him in the end without breaking any of the commandments of God or man.

The courtships and betrothals of the yeomanry and merchantry were of a simpler kind. "Usually the young man's father or he himself writes to the father of the maid to know if he shall be welcome to the house. . . . If the motion be thought well of and embraced, then the young man goeth perhaps twice to see how the maid standeth affected. Then if he see that she be tractable and that her inclination is towards him, then the third time that he visiteth, he perhaps giveth her a ten-shilling piece of gold or a ring of that price. . . . So soon as the young folk are agreed and contracted, then the father of the maid carrieth her over to the young man's house to see how they like of all, and there doth the young man's father meet them to treat of a dower and jointure."[1] As for the

---

[1] Henry Best of Elmswell, *Rural Economy in Yorkshire in 1641, Surtees Society* No. 33 (1857) p. 116-17. cit. Laslett 96-7.

poor, whose marriages usually took place much later than those of the well-to-do owing to the necessity of finding a home and the wherewithal to support a family, all that was required was a verbal contract before witnesses, sealed by a kiss and the presentation of a ring.

From courtship and the making of settlements one passed into marriage through the ceremonies and junketings of an English wedding. On the bridal day in a well-to-do home the company put on coloured scarves, love-knots and ribbons, and fine gloves and garters. After the sack posset had been eaten and all were "high-flown," the bride was undressed by her maids and the bridegroom by his male friends, the company coming up from their junketings below to see them to bed, scramble for ribbons and garters, fling the bride's stocking and draw the curtains on them. "We saw Sir Richard and his fine lady wedded," wrote Buckinghamshire Edmund Verney, "and flung the stocking, and then left them to themselves, and so in this manner ended the celebration of this marriage à la mode; after that we had music, feasting, drinking, revelling, dancing, and kissing; it was two of the clock this morning before we got home."

Honeymoon there was none, and among the landed gentry for the first few weeks after marriage the bride usually had the comfort of being surrounded by her own folk and friends. Then she passed into the possession of her husband's family and became as much the daughter of her father and mother-in-law as if she had been their own child. In most cases she was received with love and kindness, for in the seventeenth century the tie of kinship was very strong.

   •   •   •   •   •   •   •   •

Whether the parties were rich or poor, marriage marked the beginning of a new household and the enrolment in the community of a new householder. The household was the economic and legal unit of life, and seventeenth century society was organized in households. "I am a wise fellow," said Dogberry, "and, which is more an officer, and which is more, a householder." The poorest household might consist of no more than the householder, his wife and children, but a large proportion accommodated more than the householder's family. A craftsman or shopkeeper when he set up house would have a journeyman and apprentices to share his root and board, a schoolmaster pupils and an usher, a farmer "servants-in-husbandry"—a farm boy "to plough and hoe and reap and sow", a dairy maid or maids to milk the kine and ewes, and a serving one to help his wife prepare meals and make butter, cheese and whey. In days when everything had to be done by hand, probably as many as a quarter or even a third of England's families enlarged themselves in this way in order to earn their livelihood and get the work of the community done, while poorer families sent their children to serve in them and learn their trade until they, too, could marry and form households of their own. The cash wages of such servants was often minute, but they shared the same food and living conditions and, in the average decent Christian home, the affections of those for whom they worked. So did the day labourers who slept in their own cottages but worked on the land of their better-to-do neighbours and took their daily place at the family table. It was a patriarchal system that had existed from time immemorial, in which the father was the "master" and the "master" the father-figure of the household. Though subject to obvious abuse, so long as there was food for all—which there usually was unless the harvest failed for several seasons in succession—it made for a more contented and humane organisation of economic activity than was to exist later under factory conditions.[1]

Once married, even into the richest family, a bride had plenty to do. The management of a country house called for all a woman's energies. The smallest manor house was forced to maintain a large household in an age when public services were non-existent and even letters had to be fetched by a servant from the nearest post-town. A country house was a factory for living, making its own food and drink from seeding to brewhouse and kitchen, its own fuel and candles, spinning flax and wool for clothing and up-holstery, and even curing feathers to make mattresses and pillows. Of all this work the lady of the house was priestess and her maids

[1] See Peter Laslett's remarkable work, *The World we have Lost* (Methuen 1965), based on group study and analysis of seventeenth century parish registers.

the acolytes. "I hear she looks to her house well," wrote Lady Hobart of a newly wedded niece, "and grows a notable housewife and delights in it."

The end of seventeenth century marriage was the procreation of children. "I hope," a husband wrote, "that I shall yet live to see my little round wife come tumbling home to her brats with a brat in her belly." For economic reasons the poor married and bred late, but better-to-do parents were always praying that God would "fill the cradle with sweet brave babes." "Your mother," wrote a ruined cavalier to his son, "was well delivered of her tenth daughter (the thing is called Bridget), so that now you have had three sisters born in the space of thirty-two months. You may well think that is not the way to get rich."

Few mothers were too grand to nurse their young. "I wish you could see me sitting at table with my little chickens one on either side," wrote one great lady; "in all my life I have not had such an occupation to my content to see them in bed at night and get them up in the morning." "My boy is now undressing by me," wrote another, "and is such pretty company that he hinders me so I cannot write what I would."

Education began early. Life was too uncertain to prolong childhood unnecessarily; the sooner boys stood on their own feet and girls were married the better. Rich and poor alike learnt their catechism from the parson after Sunday morning service, while those who were taught to read studied the alphabet from the hornbook—a printed page pasted on a small wooden bat covered with talc, framed in horn and hung round a child's neck; it could also be used for battledore and shuttlecock. For most, however, there was no book-schooling save such as was given, at best, for a year or so in childhood at the village dame-school. The majority of the population was illiterate; Pepys tells of a mayor of Bristol who pretended to read a pass upsidedown. But there was education in craftsmanship and vocation, taught by father to son or master to apprentice; a master tailor's son became a tailor, and a carpenter's a carpenter. It was a training that, at best, utilised the imitative instinct in a boy, taught him to do one thing thoroughly, and that the trade which he was to follow, and to take pride in doing so.

For those destined for positions in Church and State—a minority, though by no means confined to a single class—a classical education afforded the mental discipline needed to make decisive minds. Bred on brown bread, cheese and small beer—drunk from a stone jar into which careful mothers would sometimes drop a little rhubarb—while the girls were set to sampler work and the arts of deportment and household management, the sons of the gentry, armed with goose-quill, slate and ink-horn, advanced against the first entrenchments of the classics. Leaving aside such prodigies as little Richard Evelyn, who could, before his fifth year, decline all the nouns, conjugate the verbs, regular and most of the irregular, and recite the entire vocabulary of Latin and French primitives, the average of attainment was surprisingly high. Thirteen-year-old Richard Butler, who had been brought up at home in the wilds of Ireland and was regarded as backward, could read Caesar's *Commentaries* in Latin to his grandfather with ease. "You may find us now and then," wrote the latter, "up to the ears in Plutarch, in a hot dispute whether Alexander or Caesar was the braver man, and perhaps within an hour or two this gallant young disputant will be up to the knees in the brambles, at the head of a whole regiment of pitiful tatterdemalions beating to start a hare."[1] For, reared in a communal household drawn from every rank in rural society, a seventeenth century country gentleman was in little danger of growing up out of touch with those whom he was called upon to govern.

"In all your letters," wrote a squire during a political crisis, "I find not one word of horse, hawk and hound." It needed a time of exceptional stress to cause such an omission. The country was still largely unenclosed and game was plentiful. Shooting, which was taking the place of the older sports of fowling and hawking, was becoming a science, and most squires kept and trained pointers, setters and retrievers. As for horse dealing, it provided a means of sport, travel and profit, as well as entertainment, for the whole nation. "Had you seen or heard how Mr. H. V. and Mr. J. O. Risley cheated one another in the exchange of two admirable jades," wrote one countryman to another, "and with what con-

[1] Blundell 176-7. H.M.C. Fleming 373; North III 10-11; Ponsonby 12.

fidence and craft it was carried, 'twould make you intermit a little of your serious thoughts." Hunting was universally practised, but was still rather a miscellaneous sport, where every hedge squire kept his own hounds and went after anything that ran. The main pursuit was hare-hunting.

Love of field sports gave the nation bluff, cheerful, healthy rulers —men such as Lord Shaftesbury's friend, Squire Hastings of Woodlands in Dorset. Long, thin, fiery-haired, in aged clothes of green which even when new had never cost more than five pounds, he kept all manner of hounds that ran—buck, fox, hare, otter and badger—and his house was full of hawks, hounds and terriers. His walls were hung with gamekeepers' poles and the skins of foxes and martens, and the floor of his hall strewn with marrow-bones. "He was well-natured, but soon angry, calling his servants bastards and cuckoldry knaves, in which he often spoke truth to his own knowledge, and sometimes in both, though of the same man. He lived to be a hundred and never lost his eyesight, but always wrote and read without spectacles and got on horseback without help. Until past four-score he rode to the death of a stag as well as any."

Yet, despite their passion for field sports, the country gentry were far from all being gross, boorish nimrods. Their letters give a very different picture of their tastes and interests than those of contemporary plays and lampoons. Educated, the best of them, at famous Latin schools like Westminster, Eton and Winchester—"the best nursery for learning for young children in the world"—and at Oxford or Cambridge colleges which drew their revenues from their native shires, they built commodious classical houses, filled them with artistic treasures and, encompassing them with walled gardens to catch the sunlight, made fountains, parterres and grottoes and walks of beech and sycamore. They stocked their libraries with finely printed editions of the classics and of history, theology and literature, and bound them in the seemly russet and gold of their age. And since there was no other secure form of investment but land, they looked after their estates with industry and good sense.

· · · · · · · ·

After the Civil Wars the value of land began to rise steadily as a result of agricultural improvements. Everywhere the gentry were experimenting with new methods. Even a poor Catholic squire, half ruined by decimations for his loyalty, could not resist the ruling passion and overspent his slender income making new outbuildings. In the barren places of Lancashire William Llundell of Crosby laid out £5 an acre for marling, while Essex squires brought chalk from the Kentish cliffs to enrich their waste lands. Such enterprise was needed if England was to maintain a larger population, for the prevailing peasant system of agriculture, though sound, was ancient and unprogressive. In Midland counties, like Oxfordshire and Leicestershire, the ploughs were still wheel-less and drawn by oxen.

Where the innovators were successful they reaped a rich reward. In some cases the rentals of lands enclosed increased threefold; those of one Cambridge college rose during the last half of the century from £140 to £537 per annum. Farms in the prosperous south-west sold in good times at twenty-eight years' purchase; in the eastern counties at twenty or twenty-one; in the turbulent, barren north, with its peel-towers, moss troopers and parish blood-hounds, at only sixteen. The average rent for good arable land was 5s. or 6s. an acre; for pasture-land perhaps 3s. more. Lord Arlington let his farms in Sussex at 6s. an acre, payable half yearly, giving his tenants full liberty to use land for plough or pasture or sublet it as they chose; less enlightened landlords were inclined to oppress their tenants with restrictive covenants. But rack renting was seldom employed; with the difficulty of finding good tenants, the squire who opened his mouth too wide was soon left with nothing but men of straw for tenants or with his farms thrown useless on his hands. As usually in England, with its familial organisation of rural society, it paid to be reasonable.[1]

The most remarkable thing about English agriculture was its diversity. The corn lands were mostly in the east—in Cambridgeshire with its hedged fields and rows of willows, in Norfolk where

[1] *Verney Memoirs* II 195-6; J. Blagrave, *Epitome of the Art of Husbandry*; Blundell 41, 100; Cosmo 219; Ernle, *passim*; Defoe I 100, 131; Fiennes 135; *Historical Essays* 181; North I 31; Ogg 55-65; Shakerley MSS.

the gentry exported their surplus wheat to Holland, and in Bedfordshire and Huntingdonshire where every village was under the
plough. Much of the wheat of the southern home counties was
sold at Farnham, whence it was borne on vast wagons to mills on
the Wey and thence by barge to London; that of Oxfordshire and
Bucks passed through Aylesbury to be ground on the hill streams
between Wycombe and Thames. There was good wheat, too,
in the west, notably in Hertfordshire and Monmouth. The
north grew little wheat or rye, but barley, peas, oats, beans and
lentils.

The finest grazing lands were in Leicestershire, Lincolnshire and
the Vale of Aylesbury. Norfolk was famous for the black cattle
that browsed in the meadows by Yare and Waveney, while its
eastern marshes fattened the runts of the north which were driven
there on their annual trek to the London markets. The dairy-lands
were Cheshire—the vale royal of England—High Suffolk, which
sent its butter to the capital in small firkins, North Wilts and South
Gloucestershire, famous for soft, rich green cheese. The valleys of
Severn and Wye, where fruit was so plentiful that any passer-by
could pick it unhindered, were given over to hops and cider-apples,
and those of northern Kent to hops and cherries. Sussex and
Hampshire were rich in timber, drawn thence by oxen or floated
down the southern rivers to the sea.

Sheep were still England's richest agricultural product. Though
Leicestershire bred the largest for mutton, Cotswold, Wiltshire and
Dorset upland, with their sweet, aromatic plants, raised the flocks
whose wool fed the fine cloth trade of the south-west. In 1669 it
was reckoned that 40,000 sheep grazed within three miles of Dor-
chester alone, while once a year graziers travelled from every part
of the country to the great sheep fair on lonely Weyhill above
Andover. And beside every road that crossed the chalk downlands
of southern England were shepherds tending their flocks.

These were the high-lights, but the glow from English farming
was diffused over the whole land. Black dray- and coach-horses
from Leicestershire, turkeys and geese from Essex and Suffolk that
marched every autumn Londonwards in armies along the eastern
highways, poultry from sandy Surrey commons, and hogs fattened

for bacon on the surplus whey and skimmed milk of Hampshire, helped to make England as prosperous as she was beautiful. More than any European land she was famed for good fare: Besseleigh turnip and Derby ale, Hampshire honey, Tewksbury mustard, and Warwickshire ram.[1]

. . . .

Yet England was no longer a purely agricultural country. Fostered by the Puritan virtues, trade was steadily growing. The poverty that followed in the train of the Civil Wars stimulated this expansion, for it drove many, whose early upbringing had accustomed them to a high standard of living, to seek a return on their reduced capital that only enterprise could give. The costly tastes which the restored Court imported from France furthered this process. "Venturing" was in the air. When young Dudley North made his first voyage to the Levant as apprentice to a Turkey merchant, his lawyer brother invested the whole of his slender savings with him, while his father gave him a hundred pounds and bade him live on it and make his fortune. He did so, peer's younger son though he was; a life of poverty would have been the only alternative. So also William Blundell of Crosby, struggling to keep his estates together under the pressure of fines and decimation scraped together £40 and risked it in a small share of "an adventure to the Barbadoes in the good ship *Antelope* of Liverpool," to receive a year later a hundred per cent return on his investment. "Keep your shop and your shop will keep you," was the prudent motto of the London trader; and this sober integrity was enhanced by a capacity for taking risks. A city merchant told Pepys how by doing so he had had credit for £100,000 at a time when his total wealth in hand was not more than £1,000.

Though the growth of luxurious tastes offered a premium to the trader who had the capital or credit to lay out on remote returns, there was scope for the small man with pluck and initiative.

[1] Clark 39-40; Cosmo 147, 700-1; Defoe I 14, 53, 68-9, 81, 129, 218, 284-6, 290, 430, 447-8, 448-9, 451, 471, 550; Evelyn 31 Aug '54; Fiennes 133, 158; Ogg 42-7, 65-66; H.M.C. Portland II 270, 275-6, 283, 304, 309.

A universal spirit of enterprise prevailed, everyone seeming ready to supplement his earnings by setting up in some sort of trade. A foreign visitor in 1669 reported that there was not a rustic's cottage in Devon or Somerset that did not manufacture white lace; in Suffolk every housewife plied her rock and distaff at the open cottage door and in Gloucestershire the old women knitted stockings while they smoked their pipes and baked their puddings.

With industry went integrity of workmanship. Throughout the world the English were building a reputation for quality. It was symptomatic of their genius that they excelled in the making of instruments of precision. Every parish had its subsidiary population of masons, carpenters, smiths and wheelwrights, who made its houses and furniture, supplied its agricultural implements, shoed its horses and did its repairs. This rustic proximity of client to craftsman set a premium on thorough workmanship, which, handed down from father to son, survived in newer crafts where the local check was wanting. The typical English craftsman of the seventeenth century was old Jonas Shish, that plain, honest ship's carpenter whom Evelyn knew, and who, though he could hardly read and never could explain his trade to another, built many a fine ship, as his forbears had done before him.

The quiet years of Charles II's reign were marked by steady mercantile and colonial expansion. Men were laying up for themselves and their children treasure for the future. On every sea the adventurous ships of England sailed, returning with riches in their holds to enhance the wealth of a little island of squires, yeomen and homely merchants, and bringing silks and scents and delicate fabrics for their ladies. In a quarter of a century Evelyn's £250 invested in the stock of the East India Company multiplied threefold. Pennsylvania, where Charles dispatched the Quaker Penn in 1682; the Carolinas, New York and the shores of the Hudson; treaties with the Turks and Moors to make Englishmen free of the Mediterranean; trading settlements at Bombay and Fort William, and dusky ambassadors bringing gifts from the Great Mogul; companies to trade with Africa, Guinea and the coasts of Barbary; expeditions to find a new road to the East through the Arctic ice or discover the wonders of the South Seas: all these were milestones in the country's commercial and imperial development. "This part of Africa is very fertile," a pioneer, reported "and wants nothing but English industry to improve it." There was immeasurable confidence in what an outward-looking maritime community of five million could achieve. "The thing which is nearest the heart of this nation," wrote the king to his sister, "is trade and all that belongs to it."

The atmosphere of adventuring and experimenting was favourable to scientific discovery. During the Interregnum a little group of learned men had begun to meet in Wadham College at Oxford to discover something of the world they lived in. They were the nucleus of the Royal Society, which was founded in Christopher Wren's room in Gresham College shortly after the Restoration. At their weekly meetings the conversation was philosophical and cheerful, and the experiments ranged all nature. They employed an itinerant, who every year made a report of his discoveries, bringing back, not tales of new Messiahs or godly judgments on the wicked, but dried fowls, fish, plants and minerals. When Prince Rupert was about to lead a fleet against the Dutch on the Guinea coast the virtuosos requested him to employ his leisure in sounding the depths and fetching up water from the bottom of the sea. In their boundless curiosity they were blue-printing a new design for living. Even, when the plague of 1665 was at its height, Evelyn, calling at Durdans, discovered Dr. Wilkins, Sir William Petty and Robert Hooke contriving chariots, new rigging for ships, a wheel to run races in, and other mechanical inventions.

Pneumatic engines, aeolipiles for weighing air, calculating machines, quench-fires, even a "new fashion gun to shoot off often, one after another, without trouble or danger, very pretty," all came alike to this remarkable generation. And with all this achievement these men were not specialists, but versatile beyond imagination. Wren, at twenty-four, was a professor of astronomy and the wonder of Europe for mechanical invention, and was over thirty before he ever thought of architecture. The learned Lord Keeper Guilford, beside attaining to an exquisite skill in music, devoted much time to the Torricelian experiments; his youngest brother, Roger North, barrister, musician, author and architect, mastered the theory of light. 'The very remembrance of these things," he wrote in after years, "is delight, and while I write methinks I play. All other employments that filled my time go on account of work and business: these were all pleasure."[1]

. . . .

Mercantile enterprise was backed by the country's natural resources. With plenty of coal, iron, lead, lime and timber, and an easily accessible littoral, rich in harbours, England was ideally equipped for world trade. Her chief commodity was her woollen manufactures, but she also exported tin, pewter, brass, horn, leather, glass and earthenware. In return, her merchants brought home tobacco from the plantations of the New World, wine from France, Spain and Portugal, sugar and rum from Barbados and Jamaica, spices and silks from the Levant, timber and tar from the Baltic and cotton goods from India.

The Navigation Acts gave the carriage of most of these commodities to English shipowners. Those who manned their vessels served a rough and varied apprenticeship, often beginning their sea-life in the fishing trade before they took service in the merchantmen or, more occasionally, in the king's ships of war. All round the coasts the shipbuilders were busy—at Newcastle, Sunderland, Hull, Yarmouth, Aldeburgh, Harwich, Shoreham, Portsmouth and Bristol—while the whole of the Thames from London Bridge to Blackwall was a vast shipbuilding yard. And to feed the yards the rivers were filled with timber floating seawards from the more accessible woods.

This sea-borne trade was paid for by a heavy price in human suffering. The merchant captains and seamen who trafficked with the Mediterranean ports took their lives in their hands, and suffered more perils than those of the Atlantic waves. From Sallee, Algiers and Tripoli issued the Moorish corsairs, with whose governments

---

[1] North, I 153-4, 320, 387-93; II 243-5; III 63-6; Aubrey 37, 158, 165-7; H.M.C. Beaufort 49-50; T. Birch, *History of the Royal Society*; Clark 40-2, 359-61; Evelyn, 7 April '60; 9 March '61; 10 July '67; H.M.C. Hodgkin 175-6; Ogg 720-33; Pepys, 4 March '64; 14 March '68; Petty Papers; Plot, *Oxfordshire* 227; T. Sprat, *History of the Royal Society*; Williamson II 7.

the English Crown lived, at best, in a state of precarious peace, and whose swift vessels were a match for all but the strongest merchant-man. Many English seamen captured by them passed the rest of their lives in loathsome captivity. Others, after years, were ransomed by the funds raised by the charitable in England for the redemption of slaves. So a tender-hearted gentleman wrote to the Secretary of the Admiralty to tell him how Captain Spurrill, who had endured nine years' cruel usage at Tangier, had been redeemed by his efforts. "And now this poor suffering man is free," he added, "if you will thrust him into his Majesty's service that he may know how to live, I will publish your generosity to everybody."

Of the freights that English ships bore outwards, cloth was still king. The three great districts of its manufacture were East Anglia, the south-west and Yorkshire. From the first came the baizes and serges of Colchester and Sudbury, all the villages round which span wool for Portugal and Italy. Colchester in 1662 boasted eight churches and employed 10,000 workers. As one travelled from Suffolk to Norfolk the signs of industry and prosperity became still more marked, a face of diligence being spread over the whole county, till the spires of Norwich rose before one, the greatest town in England for the making of stuffs and worsted stockings.

In the south-west was the quality trade. This was the broadcloth manufacture which clothed the fine gentlemen of half Europe. Fed by the wool of Salisbury Plain and the Cotswolds, almost every parish between upper Thames and Exe was learning to make fine cloth. From the towns of four counties—Somerset, Wiltshire, Dorset and Gloucestershire—the master-clothiers sent out wool to the villages, where women and children spun the yarn which later their packmen collected for their looms. Here a union of nascent capitalism and cottage industry was enriching a whole community. In the pleasant valleys of the Stroud and Wiltshire Avon the sides of the hills were covered with the paddocks of clothiers, each man in "his fair stone house" and spending his £500 a year. Bristol for drugget and cantaloon, Taunton for serges, Wells for fine Spanish stockings, Frome for medley cloth, and

Bradford-on-Avon and Stroud for dyes, were the household names of the west-country trade that Bristol, Barnstaple and Blackwell Hall exported to all the world. And farther west was Exeter of the serges, where thousands of artisans and all the country folk for twenty miles round were continuously employed in making baizes and light cloths for Spain, France, Italy and the Levant.

The cloth trade of the West Riding was as yet only concerned with the coarser manufactures. The Yorkshire kerseys of Leeds, Halifax, Huddersfield, Bradford and Wakefield supplied the needs of common folk who could not afford the fine medley and broadcloth of the west. The wool market at Leeds, which appeared miraculously twice a week down the broad main street of the town, was already resorted to by factors with letters from customers in places as distant as Russia and North America. It was fed by the industry of the Yorkshire clothiers, whose houses and stony enclosures lined the slopes of the West Riding valleys, so that, as one gazed down them, the eye was caught by the pale gleam of innumerable pieces of white cloth stretched upon the tenters. With coal and running water at their doors, they were able to complete in their own houses almost all the processes required for their trade.

All this manufacturing was rural in its setting, and most of those who practised it were also engaged in agriculture. The merchants and shopkeepers of the provincial towns kept farm and orchard in the adjacent meads. Only giant London, and to a lesser degree Bristol, were urban entities. The latter, with its crowded Tolsey, its tall bridge across the Avon, lined like London's with continuous houses, and its cobble-stones worn smooth by sledges, was the only place in England beside the capital which could market unaided the goods which its merchants brought home. Its carriers supplied all South Wales, the south-west, and the western midlands with sugar, wine, oil and tobacco. Liverpool, which with the development of the industrial north was to outdistance Bristol in the next century, was still only in process of transition from a ragged fishing-village to a brick town, while Southampton was apparently dying of old age and London competition.

Straw hats from Dunstable, saddles from Burford, buttons and thread from Maidstone, salt from Worcester, Chester and Newcastle, were some of the lesser manufactures which rustic England produced in the last age before the Industrial Revolution. The geographical distribution of industry is best indicated by the annual excise returns; that for 1665 shows that while London, Middlesex and Surrey were together farmed for £140,000, the yield for Yorkshire, Kent, Norfolk and Devon was £16,000, £15,000, £13,800, and £9,500 respectively, and for Essex, Gloucester, Suffolk and Lincolnshire from £8,600 to £7,200. None of the other counties was farmed for more than £4,600, with little Huntingdonshire, which was almost entirely rural, bringing up the rear with an excise rental of only £1,400.

In all this activity of the English breadwinner there was little hindrance from the State. Most of the old medieval restraints operated in theory rather than in practice, and were everywhere falling into disuse. After the crushing exactions of the Interregnum, taxes were low, and direct taxation, save in time of war, almost negligible. Most of the revenue was raised by the indirect impositions of Customs and Excise, and the former protected English industry as much as the latter penalised it. And wherever Customs duties proved excessive they were mitigated by the wholesale smuggling that immediately sprang up, for in those policeless days the laws of supply and demand easily overrode the paternal intentions of governments. On Romney Marsh the illicit export of wool, which was called "owling", and the import of brandy, wine and tobacco proved so profitable that it maintained a whole population of armed smugglers, usually more than capable of intimidating the occasional soldiers sent to suppress them.

. . . .

The domestic trader's chief handicap was the state of the roads. Subjected to an ever-growing volume of wheeled traffic, they were worse than they had been in the Middle Ages. So deep were the ruts on the main highways that in the spring it was customary for the parish authorities to plough them up with the road-plough kept under the church-porch. In some parts of the country, notably in the heavy midlands and the deep clays of Sussex, teams of oxen were used to draw carts and coaches, and in the west the hills were so full of rolling stones and the lanes so narrow that corn was carried, not in carts, but on the backs of horses, corded on wooden frames. The demands of the metropolis turned every highway near it into a quagmire, sodden with the ordure of a never-ceasing procession of beasts—cattle, sheep, pigs, turkeys, geese—marching to the London slaughter-houses. And on every heath and moor suspicious-looking men, muffled up in great-coats and with pistols at their sides, might be observed speculating on the possible strength of passing travellers. Those who seemed to have small capacity for resistance they would approach and travel beside for a while, until opportunity offered for even closer acquaintance.

On such roads it was easy for travellers to lose their way. Signposts were almost unknown, and on the lonelier stretches travellers hired guides. Riding from Huntingdon to Biggleswade, Pepys had to employ the services of two countrymen to lead him through the waters. Every few miles travellers were forced to ford a stream, and every few hundred yards a watercourse. Bridges were few, and many of the broader rivers could only be crossed by ferry, an unpleasant proceeding which necessitated maddening delay and often, in winter, a severe cold.[1]

For those who wished to travel quickly the post-horse was the surest medium. Post-horses could be hired from the Government postmasters along the main roads at threepence a mile, with an extra fourpence for the guide at each stage. But, though a single man riding post might cover the distance from Huntingdon to London in the inside of a day or from Chester to London in two, anything on wheels travelled far more slowly. Private coaches, drawn by teams of shire horses or Flemish mares, were an uncertain and expensive form of travel, especially when they began to grow old. "I wish the new wheels had come up with my coach," complained one magnate, "for these old wheels break every time they go out." "I had a sad mischance coming from London with my wife and servants," wrote another, "for the coach overturned and fell on the side I sat on, and those in the coach fell on me and thereby

[1] J. Parkes, *Travel in England, passim*; Blundell 179, 183; Defoe 129, 493, 517, 521,; Fiennes 7, 9, 11, 32, 66, 116, 128, 159, 169, 189, 197, 216; H.M.C. Kenyon 83; Pepys, 20 Sept. '63; H.M.C. Portland II 32-3; Shakerley MSS.

put one hip out of joint and mightily strained the joint of my other hip and my back bones are displaced."

Stage coaches were the chief contribution of the time to the amenities of travel. Clumsy, boxlike vehicles, usually made of black leather and swung on leather straps, with wooden shutters or flaps for windows, they jolted at thirty or forty miles a day up and down the main roads. To those who remembered the country before the Civil Wars they appeared almost unbelievably fast: "in four days and a half from Garswood to London," wrote Lancashire William Blundell, "it seems to be almost incredible." Yet the printed bills advertising the "flying coaches" which accomplished the journey from Oxford to the "Greyhound" in Holborn in a single day, never failed to end with the cautious proviso, "If God permit."

Every coach had its inns of call in the towns along its route, where horses were changed. Innkeeping in England was regarded as a respectable profession; at the "Crown", Mansfield, the landlord and his wife were gentlefolk. More often the former was "an honest ingenious man" of the middle rank, who distilled "incomparable strong waters" and kept good wine, a bowling-green and perhaps a cockpit for his neighbours. In many places after the Restoration he was an old soldier, who had fought for King Charles and loved to regale travellers with tales of Prince Rupert and Marston Moor. And since horses and inns went together, he was generally something of a jockey, and, like good Mr. Hunt of the "Three Cranes," Doncaster, was fond of talking horses. And with good fare for mind and body, it mattered little if an odd frog or two croaked in one's chamber, or if mine host, anxious not to foul more sheets than necessary, was over-apt to assume that his guests were ready to share a bed.[1]

Heavy goods, if they went by land, did so without reference to time. Perishable wares could only be moved at heavy expense. Mackerel, which could be bought at a penny a hundred on the beach at Bridport, fetched twice as many shillings in the London market. Long strings of pack-horses, travelling in file with a bell

[1] Cosmo 202; Brown I 137; Fiennes 128, 185; Ogg 102-4; H.M.C. Portland II 267, 289, 292-7 298,, 300, 303, 305, 308, 310.

tinkling from the leading horse, were the goods trains of the age; unless they went by water, coal, iron, wool and crates of clay for the potteries all travelled in this way. In many parts of the country narrow stone causeways, raised above the morass of the surrounding highway, were built to accommodate such traffic.

Since the roads were so bad, much of the heavier merchandise went by river. The wharves of Reading, Maidenhead and Henley shipped Berkshire and Oxfordshire malt and meal on to barges which fed London, taking in return oils, groceries, salt and tobacco for the neighbouring countryside. Every sizable river bore its share of freightage, and, as the century drew to a close, scheme after scheme came before parliament for making navigable some provincial river and opening up new trade.

One commodity in England travelled quickly—his Majesty's mails. Ever since the Crown had taken over responsibility for a postal service at the beginning of the century the speed at which letters moved had been increasing. Each of the main roads radiating from London had its regular service, with post-houses at all the principal towns. Here letters were distributed to the local carriers or fetched by the messengers of the country gentry. They were charged on delivery, and by the sheet and distance: a single sheet travelled from London for twopence for the first eighty miles, and a double sheet for twice as much. Envelopes being unknown, letters were elaborately folded, sealed and addressed on the outside, as

> "To my honourable Friend
> Sir Jeffrey Shakerley
> at his house Hulme
> Stone bag."

Sometimes, especially in the case of Government dispatches, they were further superscribed with directions to local postmasters and postboys. "Haste, haste, haste," was scrawled across one letter which must have aroused much excitement as it travelled down the Great North Road, "for his Majesty's most important service. Ride for your life."

The chief drawback of the postal service was its cost. An unsuccessful private scheme of 1659, and a successful one of 1680, attempted to overcome this by the establishment of a penny post in the capital. That of 1680, which conferred immortality on a not too reputable speculator named Dockwra, introduced the principle of dated postmarks. As, however, it infringed the Government's monopoly, the scheme was taken over by the State, which incorporated most of its other features, yet characteristically doubled the cost. But the high cost of postage was in part overcome by the privilege of franking, allowed to members of both Houses of Parliament. As legislators were exceedingly generous in providing their friends and constituents with signatures, few merchants of importance had any difficulty in getting their letters franked.

. . . .

Apart from the post there was no national public service except the courts of law, the revenue, the Navy and the newly formed standing Army of royal guards. All other administration was left to the parish, whose humble officers preserved the peace, enforced public order, maintained the highways and administered the poor law and public relief under the supervision of the justices of the peace, the sheriff and lord lieutenant. Those who did the dogs-body work of government at the lowest level were still drawn from the general body of the people. Except in the towns, where their duties were performed by paid deputies, they were unpaid. Every householder who was not a member of one of the classes specially exempted by parliament was expected to serve his turn in the parish offices or provide a substitute. Service was usually for a year; failure to perform its duties was punishable at law by fine and imprisonment. The principal parish officers were the churchwardens, the overseers of the poor, the overseers of the highways. and the petty constables. The first, in addition to the duties of church maintenance, still in theory exercised some of the moral functions of the medieval church, such as visiting ale-houses during the hours of divine service and driving malingerers to worship. The duties of the overseers of the poor were much more onerous. Appointed by the justices from a rota of householders, it was their business to give weekly relief to the aged and impotent, to keep a stock of raw material on which to set the able-bodied unemployed to work,

to build houses on the common land for the houseless, to educate
poor children and bind them as apprentices and to administer
any lands or moneys left by the charitable for the poor of the parish.
To provide such services they were empowered to levy a poor
rate under cover of the signature of the local justices; for failure
to perform them adequately they could be indicted at Quarter
Sessions. Neglect of a destitute person might even bring them to
the dock for manslaughter, while extravagance in the use of parish
funds exposed them to the wrath of their neighbours.

The surveyor of the highways, sometimes called the boonmaster
or waywarden, was appointed by the court of Quarter Sessions
from a list of agricultural holders submitted by the vestries. It was
his business to see that all whose property adjoined the public highways kept clear their gutters and drains, trimmed their hedges and
refrained from stacking manure, timber or hay on the road. If they
proved refractory it was his duty to name them in the parish church
after the sermon, giving them thirty days' grace in which to make
amends, after which he was entitled to do it himself at their expense.
It was also his duty to waylay passing carts and wagons with more
than the statutory number of horses or with wheels of less than the
statutory width, and generally enforce the transport enactments of
parliament and Privy Council. And three times a year he had to
"view" every road, watercourse, pavement and bridge in the parish
and report their state to the justices, subsequently, with the latter's
authority, levying a highway rate to bear the cost of repairs. His
most arduous duty was the supervision of the statute labour which
every householder, either in person or by deputy, was compelled
by law to perform for six days in the year.

Apart from the small fry of parish officialdom—clerk, sexton,
beadle and bellman—most of whom were paid, the oldest of the
parish officers was the constable. He was appointed at the court
leet and sworn by the justices. First and foremost it was his duty
to preserve the king's peace. If any affray was made he had to proceed to the spot and, bearing his staff of office, call upon the offenders
to desist. "Christopher Stubbs of Wath," ran the record of a
north-country court, "presented at Richmond for making an
assault and affray, on Christmas last in John Tanfield's house, on

one John Stapleton and also for abusing James Harrison, constable of Wath, reviling him and pulling away a great part of his beard, when commanding the said Christopher to keep the peace." In pursuance of his duty the constable could call on any citizen to assist him, and it was an indictable offence to refuse. For in the village community, democracy was not a right but an obligation.

The constable's functions were so many that it must have been difficult for him during his year of office to earn his livelihood. It was his duty to enforce the statutes which a puritanically-minded parliament periodically passed against cursing and swearing, tippling in ale-houses, profaning the Sabbath and eavesdropping at neighbours' windows. In such matters, however, custom and the remoteness of central authority allowed him wide discretion. If in the execution of his duties he exceeded the law or trespassed on some private liberty, an action lay against him at the suit of the injured person; if he allowed a malefactor committed for trial to escape from the parish cage or lock-up, or his own house, he could be imprisoned. It must sometimes have been a relief to his feelings to execute the punishments meted out by the justices to erring citizens—to put a nagging woman in the ducking-stool or affix such a notice as Robert Storr and Christopher Smith, constables of Bedale, were ordered to attach to the person of Margery Metcalf of Crackall: "I sit here in the stocks for beating my own mother."

Most educative of all the constable's tasks was his attendance at the courts—to present an offender at petty sessions, to wait on the head constable of the hundred, to present a return or pay in the parish taxes, to journey to the county town to answer an indictment brought against his village for failure of some statutory duty. It brought him into contact with a wider world, showed him how public business was executed and taught him the practical difficulties of administration.

. . . .

Such was the nursery of England's democracy. Her people were proud and independent, accustomed to manage their own affairs and resentful of interference. When a Court official tried to keep the common folk of Windsor out of the royal park they assembled in force, broke the gates and pales and announced that the park was their own. Foreign visitors were always testifying to the rude strength of English democracy; the king, wrote Sorbière, had to be free and easy with the nobility, the officers of the army with their soldiers, landlords with their tenantry.

For there could be no ruling such a people on any other terms. Fighting was their favourite pastime. In Moorfields, on holidays, the butchers, out of hereditary hatred, fell upon the weavers till they were glad to pull off their aprons and hide them in their breeches; or sometimes it would be the weavers who won, wounding and bruising all their rivals and calling out round the town: "A hundred pounds for a butcher!" The very Inns of Court were riotous, and when the lord mayor elected to go to dinner in the Temple with his sword borne before him, the students pulled it down and besieged him all day in a councillor's room. Even in Oxford a learned antiquary belaboured one of his fellow-dons whenever he met him, giving him many a bloody nose and black eye.

This pugnacity the English carried into the concerns of State. In this they astonished foreigners; a Frenchman reported that the very boatmen wanted the milords to talk to them about State affairs while they rowed them to parliament. With those who disagreed with their views they had a short way. When the French ambassador omitted to light a bonfire at his door to celebrate an English victory over the Dutch, the mob smashed his windows and all but grilled him on his own furniture. His successor, after describing an attempt to kill the first Minister of the Crown in his own bedroom, could only comment: "When I reflect that this land produces neither wolves nor venomous beasts, I am not surprised. The inhabitants are far more wicked and dangerous."

Yet, widespread though the instinct for liberty was, the exercise of authority was equally so. If England was libertarian—even, within its aristocratic framework, democratic—it was also sternly and practically authoritarian. From time immemorial the Crown had ruled by delegating its authority at every level to local worthies and representatives whom it supervised through the instrument of

72

royal functionaries and the law—privy councillors, judges of assize and eyre, sheriffs, high constables, coroners, lord lieutenants and deputy lieutenants, justices of the peace and many more. Few Englishmen of whatever rank to whom authority was entrusted seemed afraid of exercising it; those who failed to do so were little accounted. Part of the immense respect in which Cromwell was held by his countrymen—for all the opprobrium he suffered as a usurper and regicide—was that he was not afraid to use the full authority of a king. One sees the men of that age through the mists of time—the hot-blooded gentry who fought in their cups, the country tenants twisting words in their manor courts to cheat their lords, the unpoliced Londoners who plundered the very sweet-meats from the feasts of the great. Proud and unbending, their natures were tinged by melancholy and deep feeling that sometimes turned their pugnacity to strange enthusiasms and stranger oddities. "Everywhere in England," wrote a foreigner, "you will meet with gloomy and fanatical humours, presumption and extravagance of thought." Yet, there was something in them, he added, that was great and which they seemed to inherit from the old Romans. It was from their freedom that they derived it.[1]

[1] Sorbière, 7, 46-7, 50, 54; Cosmo 378, 396-9; C.S.P.D. 1663-4, 919; H.M.C. Kenyon 88; North I 30; III 108; Ogg 120-3, 486-95; Pepys (28 Sept '60; 12 April '69) Rawlinson MSS A 94 f,268; H.M.C. Rutland II, 11; Shakerley MSS; Somerset Quarter Sessions' Records, I 36; Trotter, *passim*; Webb, *The Parish and the County* Vol. I, *passim*; Wood II, 11, 114, 313, 341.

CHAPTER 4

Heart of Oak

IN THE *Spectator* papers, published in the reign of Queen Anne, two writers of genius described the pride that Englishmen felt in the expanding commerce and wealth of their country's capital at the beginning of the eighteenth century. "As I moved towards the city," wrote Steele, "gay signs, well disposed streets, magnificent public structures and wealthy shops, adorned with contented faces, made the joy still rising till we came to the centre of the city and centre of the world of trade, the Exchange of London." "Our ships," Addison boasted, "are stored with spices and oils and wines; our rooms are filled with pyramids of china and adorned with the workmanship of Japan; our morning's draught comes to us from the remotest corners of the earth; we repair our bodies by the drugs of America and repose ourselves under Indian canopies."

For beyond the island mists, within reach of a little nation which was learning to use its vantage-point at the ocean gates of Europe, lay the future outlines of a wealth and maritime power such as no people had ever enjoyed. "He calls the sea the British common," Addison wrote of his imaginary merchant, Sir Andrew Freeport: " there is not a point in the compass but blows home a ship in which he is an owner." In the century after the fall of the Stuarts, the English—and the Scots with whom their throne and parliament were now joined—seized their opportunity.

For, divided since the death of Elizabeth by violent religious and political controversies, with the Revolution of 1688 the English achieved a working compromise and, with it, national unity. The essence of that Revolution and of the settlement that followed it was that Englishmen should cease to destroy one another for the sake of abstract theories and seek a working compromise upon

74

which they could agree to differ. Its philosopher was the grandson of a Somerset clothier, John Locke, who grew up during the Civil War and Interregnum and lived to hear the news of Blenheim. He was the first—and English—prophet of the Age of Reason and the Rights of Man. His two cardinal principles were that it was an error to entertain "any proposition with greater assurance than the proofs it is built upon will warrant," and that no man should "be subject to the inconstant, uncertain, unknown arbitrary will of another." Moderation, toleration and liberty, preserved by rational laws and the sanctity of private property, were his recipe for human well-being. He voiced the experience of a generation that had seen all its religious and political ideals discredited by fanatics. His attitude was enshrined in the urbane *Spectator* essays of Joseph Addison whose self-proclaimed mission was to wean his country-men from party rancour and spleen and teach them to co-exist with "good-nature, compassion and humanity." In his portraits of the slightly absurd but lovable old Tory squire, Sir Roger de Coverley, and his Whig adversary and fellow clubman, Sir Andrew Freeport—types of the rival landed and moneyed interests—he showed how arguments between fellow countrymen, which a generation earlier had been resolved only by sword and cudgel, need "proceed no further than to an agreeable raillery" between friends. In this capacity for good-humoured controversy, in which political opponents could differ and yet remain friends, lay the key, not only to the English eighteenth century, but to the next two hundred and fifty years of peaceful parliamentary evolution.

Given permanence by an alliance between the Whig nobility and the City merchants and bankers, the Revolution of 1688 placed a Dutch, and later a German prince, on the throne, but gave the controlling direction of the kingdom to the greater owners of land. Wiser than the Stuarts they had overthrown, they exercised power by shunning its outward forms. They governed in the king's name and legislated through an assembly of country gentlemen, lawyers and placeholders, more than equal to their own hereditary chamber in political status but indirectly subject to their social and territor-ial influence. In this they showed their shrewdness. For the English people did not like the appearance of power.

Nor did these supremely fortunate creatures exercise power for its own sake—these Russells and Grenvilles, Cavendishes, Talbots and Howards with their scores of thousands of acres, their hereditary titles and offices, their State sinecures and pensions for their younger sons and cousins and retainers.[1] They sought honours and riches with avidity and retained them with firm grasp, securing their continued enjoyment by elaborate entails on their elder children. But they valued them almost entirely for what they brought in freedom and ease to themselves. They extended and improved their domains and cheated the king's Exchequer for the glorious privilege of being independent.

The countryside was dotted with their lovely palaces and noble avenues, the fields and woods of the whole kingdom were open to their horses and hounds, the genius of man, past and present, was brought to decorate their houses and gardens, to fill their libraries with the masterpieces of the classical and modern mind, to cover their walls with paintings and tapestries and adorn their tables with exquisite silver and porcelain. Theirs was an ample and splendid design for living. Nor was it a purely material one. For such was the subtlety of their intelligences that they instinctively refused to be chained by their possessions and comforts. They encouraged freedom of expression and diversity of behaviour, preferring a vigorous existence and the society of equals to a hot-house tended by serfs. They sent their sons to rough, libertarian schools where strawberry leaves were no talisman against the rod[2] and afterwards to the House of Commons where men used plain words and likewise suffered them. And if by their English law of primogeniture they transmitted to their firstborn a wealth and freedom equal and if possible superior to their own, the same law endowed their younger sons with incentive and scope for action and adventure. They left the doors of opportunity open.

Nor did they ignore nature. They made no extravagant attempt to secure exclusive privilege for their blood, but frankly recognised

---

[1] As late as 1760, at the beginning of George III's reign, there were only 174 British peers.

[2] At Harrow, according to school tradition, the Duke of Dorset was always beaten twice—once for the offence and once for being a duke.

the principle of change. They were realists. Though possessing almost unlimited power, the English aristocracy never attempted to make itself a rigid caste. The younger sons of a duke or marquis were by courtesy entitled lords; the younger sons of a viscount or baron, honourables. There their transmitted dignities ended. Save for the eldest male their grandchildren were all commoners with the same prefix as groom and gamekeeper. Kinship with them, though a social asset, was no defence to breach of the law: a man might be hanged though he were cousin to a marquis with 80,000 acres. The great lords looked after themselves and their immediate kin: they refused to endanger their privilege by extending it too widely.

Within the confines of their sensible ambition and the law there was no limit to their personal power and enjoyment. They did as they pleased. The world was their park and pleasance, and they never doubted their right to make themselves at home in it. "Mr. Dundas!" cried the Duchess of Gordon to the Home Secretary at an Assembly, "you are used to speak in public—will you call my servant"; Lord Stafford paid a Home Secretary a private retaining fee of £2000 a year to do his accounts.[1] And if they chose to be naughty, naughty they were: his Grace of Norfolk—"Jockey of Norfolk"—who looked like a barrel and reeled like a drunken faun, broke up a fashionable dance he was attending by ringing the church bells and distributing cider to a mob under the ballroom windows to celebrate a false rumour that a fellow "radical" had won the Middlesex election.

Because they enjoyed life and seldom stood deliberately in the way of others doing the same, they were popular. They took part in the nation's amusements and mixed freely with their neighbours. They were healthy, gregarious and generous and had little fear in their make-up. They governed England without a police force, without a Bastille and virtually without a civil service, by sheer

---

[1] "If I were a great nobleman I should come at once to a distinct understanding with my steward, auditors, etc., that they should upon no account take places in the Cabinet under pain of not being received again in my service, since such a practice, if encouraged, might occasion to me great loss and hindrance of business."—John Ward to Mrs. Dugald Stewart, Oct., 1809, *Dudley*, 85.

assurance and personality. When the Norfolk Militia refused to march to a field day unless a guinea a man were first distributed, their colonel, William Windham, strode up to the ringleader and, ignoring their oaths and raised muskets, carried him to the guard-house, standing at the door with a drawn sword and swearing to the mob about him that while he lived the man should not go free.

Wishing to be *primi inter pares* and not solitary despots, the higher aristocracy merged imperceptibly into the country gentry. The Marquis of Buckingham in his white pillared palace at Stowe was only the first gentleman in Buckinghamshire, the social equal, if political superior, of the Verneys, Chetwodes, Drakes, Purefoys and other humbler squires. They went to the same schools, sat round the same convivial tables, rode together in the hunting field and took counsel with one another at Quarter Sessions. In each family the elder son was the independent lord of his own little world, whether it was a couple of thousand homely acres or a broad province such as fell to the lot of a Fitzwilliam or a Percy. The younger sons and their younger sons after them quickly shaded off into the general body of lawyers and clergymen, Navy and Army officers, bankers and merchants. Proud blood and breed-ing flowed in a broad unimpeded current through the nation's veins.

So did the desire to live well: to dine and hunt and lord it like an elder son. Despite inequalities of wealth and status the English preserved a remarkable unity of social purpose. Even in their most snobbish occasions—and in their veneration for the "quality" they seemed snobs to a man—there was something of a family atmos-phere. On the continent, where noble blood was a fetish and caste a horizontal dividing line, a nobleman's house tended to be a vast barracks rising out of a desert and set against a background of miserable hovels in which ragged creatures of a different species lived an animal, servile existence. In England even the costliest mansion soon mellowed into something cosy and homely: more modest, more human than anything dreamed of by Polish count or German baron. French princes and princesses at Versailles built themselves sham cottages in their grounds and dressed up as shep-herds and shepherdesses to feed their starved palates on homely pleasures; in England simplicity, with sturdy mien and broad bucolic joke, was never far off. The cottage, snug and thatched, with its porch, oven and tank and its garden warm with peonies and rambler roses, stood four-square against the mansion gates.

The thing that first struck foreign travellers about England was its look of prosperity. "As always," wrote the young Comte de la Rochefoucauld of a Norfolk journey in 1784, "I admired the way in which in all these little villages the houses are clean and have an appearance of cosiness in which ours in France are lacking. There is some indefinable quality about the arrangement of these houses which makes them appear better than they actually are." In *The Deserted Village* Goldsmith, by describing what sweet Auburn had been before the east wind of enclosure struck its Christian polity, idealised yet painted from a still living model common to England alone:

"How often have I loitered o'er thy green
Where humble happiness endeared each scene!
How often have I paused on every charm,
The sheltered cot, the cultivated farm,
The never-failing brook, the busy mill,
The decent church that topped the neighbouring hill,
The hawthorn bush, with seats beneath the shade
For talking age and whispering lovers made."

Poverty there was and injustice—in many cases harsh, bleak and grinding. With the coming of large-scale enclosure in the last quarter of the century they began to increase fast, for the new methods of farming and land-tenure brought wealth to the few but debasement and suffering to the many. But though men were everywhere being dispossessed by mysterious parliamentary and legal processes beyond their understanding of rights their forbears had enjoyed, the countryside as a whole retained the air of well-being that had pervaded it for the past hundred years. The predominant type, soon to become a minority, was the cottager who laboured three or four days a week on his richer neighbour's land and two or three on his own. He still regarded the larger farmer who was beginning to be his employer as an equal: had lived in his house in his bachelor days as an unmarried farm ser-

vant, had perhaps aspired to his daughter, and shared his bread
and cheese at the long oaken board and drunk his home-brewed
beer or cider round his winter ingle-nook. In an unenclosed village
he farmed three or four acres of his own in the common fields,
holding them by a tenure—a copyhold or perhaps a lease for the
longest survivor of three or more lives—which made him something more than a cap-touching tenant dependent on another man's
will.

Such men could afford to feel independent: they were. "If
you offer them work," wrote an improving farmer, "they will tell
you that they must go to look up their sheep, cut furzes, get their
cows out of the pound or, perhaps, say that they must take their
horse to be shod that he may carry them to the horse-race or a
cricket-match." It was, indeed, this independence[1] that caused
their better-to-do neighbours to disregard them in their attempt
to enlarge their own freedom by opening new avenues to wealth.
The tragedy of the enclosures was not that they changed the older
basis of farming and land tenure, which was ill-suited to the needs
of a growing country, but that they did so without making provision for that continuing stake in the soil for their neighbours
which had made the English a nation of freemen. When the
Parliamentary Commissioners offered a poor commoner a few
years' purchase for his hereditary rights of grazing and turfing, they
were depriving unborn generations of their economic liberty. This
was forgotten by a vigorous gentry exercising untrammelled legislative power and possessed by an enlightened, if selfish, desire to
improve on the wasteful and obstructionist farming methods of the
past. In their impatience they overlooked the fact that freedom—
their own most prized privilege—usually appears inefficient in the
short run.

Yet, though decline and decay had set in and during the last
forty years of the century nearly three million acres were subjected
to Enclosure Acts, the typical village was still a microcosm of the

[1] The great agricultural innovator, Jethro Tull of Hungerford, complained that
improved farming was often made impossible by the independence and excessive
conservatism of the English peasant. "It were more easy to teach the beasts of
the field than to drive the ploughman out of his way." *Horse-hoeing Husbandry.*

greater England of which it was a part, whose members included
every social type from the squire who administered the law to the
barber who cupped veins and drew the rustic tooth. Here was the
blacksmith whose smithy was at once the ironmongery of the
community and the wayside repair-station of an equestrian age, the
wheelwright with his cunning craft, the clockmaker, the tailor
seeking orders from door to door, the upholsterer, glazier, miller,
cobbler, farrier, maltster, reddleman and tranter. Arthur Young,
writing in 1789, enumerated in a Norfolk parish of 231 families
38 husbandmen, 26 spinners, 12 farmers, 12 publicans, 8 carpenters,
with a total of 57 different classes of employment. Such employments were intricately interwoven. The farrier, the miller and the
maltster generally also held or rented farms; each village craftsman had his garden and, in an unenclosed village, his holding in
the common fields. Few were solely dependent on their craft. The
rustic world, by geographical measure, was narrow, but there was
choice in it.

In many counties a subsidiary form of employment was afforded
by the cloth industry. Like other local crafts, such as the cottage
lace industry and straw plaiting of Buckinghamshire, it afforded
domestic occupation and employment not only to men, but to
women and children. The wealth thus acquired, as Wilberforce
said, was not obtained at the expense of domestic happiness but
in the employment of it. Such trades had their ups and downs, and
with the expansion of machinery it was soon to be mostly downs.
But in the last decades before the Napoleonic Wars, the weavers,
especially in the North, were doing well, often employing journey-
men and apprentices in addition to their families. The new mechanical spinning frames gave them cheap and plentiful supplies of
yarn. They enjoyed well-furnished dwellings bright with clocks,
prints, oak and mahogany furniture and Staffordshire ware, and
plenty of butcher's meat, oatmeal and potatoes.

Good fare was regarded as an Englishman's birthright. Every
cottage had its flitch of home-cured bacon hanging from the smoky
beam and its copper for brewing ale. Eggs, geese, poultry and
rabbits abounded, though the wild game which in earlier days had
come easily to the peasant's pot was disappearing with enclosures

and the growing passion of the rich for the chase. But although a term was being set to all this prosperity and a stormier horizon lay in the path of the poor, the age of comparative rustic plenty lingered into the 'eighties of the Hanoverian century. Rochefoucauld in 1784 noted how much greater the consumption of meat was in England than in any other country and even claimed that in East Anglia the labourer enjoyed butcher's meat every day.[1] This was probably an exaggeration, but in contemporary France and Germany such a claim would have seemed fantastic.

With transport still dependent on the beast and the soft cart-track, the bulk of what was raised could only be consumed locally. Every place and season had its peculiar delicacies. "My dinner (I love to repeat good ones)," wrote John Byng over his slippered ease in his inn at nightfall, "consisted of spitchcock'd eel, roasted pigeons, a loin of pork roasted, with tarts, jellies and custards." Woodforde, a Norfolk parson with a modest living, entertained his neighbours to "fish and oyster sauce, a nice piece of boiled beef, a fine neck of pork roasted and apple sauce, some hashed turkey, mutton stakes, salad, etc., a wild duck roasted, fried rabbits, a plum pudding and some tartlets, desert, some olives, nuts, almonds and raisins and apples." Nor was such feasting confined to the days when the good parson entertained. He and his niece Nancy did themselves almost equally well on ordinary days. "We returned home about three o'clock to dinner. Dinner to-day boiled chicken and a pig's face, a bullock's heart roasted and a rich plum-pudding." Small wonder that Nancy sometimes felt ill of an afternoon "with a pain within her, blown up as if poisoned"; that the parson was forced to complain after a somewhat restless night, "mince pie rose oft."

They drank as deep, even when it was only tea. Miss Burney's mother once made Dr. Johnson twenty-one cups in succession. After dinner, bottles of spirits—brandy, rum, shrub—moved in ceaseless procession round the table. At Squire Gray's—"a fine jolly old sportsman"—the cloth was not cleared until a bottle of port had been laid down before a mighty silver fox's head, out of which the squire filled a bumper and drank to fox-hunting pre-

[1] Rochefoucauld 230.

paratory to passing it about.[1] Parson Woodforde did not scruple
to entertain five fellow-clergymen with eight bottles of port and
one of Madeira, besides arrack punch, beer and cider.

It was the hallmark of your true Englishman that he "loved his
can of flip." In London alone there were more than five thousand
licensed houses within the Bills of Mortality. From the royal
family to the poor labourer "being in beer"—a state so habitual
that it was ordinarily held to excuse almost any excess—there was
a general contempt for heeltaps. George III's sailor son, the Duke
of Clarence, whenever one of his guests stopped drinking, would
call out, "I see some daylight in that glass, sir: banish it." "We
made him welcome," wrote Ramblin' Jack of the fo'c'sle, "as all
Englishmen do their friends, damnabell drunk, and saw him safe
home to Dean's Square, Ratcliffe way."[2]

Foreigners were much impressed, if sometimes appalled, by all
this exuberant grossness. These robust islanders, with their guzzling
and swilling, seemed like so many pieces of animated roast beef
with their veins full of ale. It appeared a point of pride with them
—a mark of their superiority to other starveling nations—to fill
themselves up. A farmer at the "Wheel" at Hackington Fen ate for
a wager two dozen penny mutton pies and drank half a gallon of
ale in half an hour: then, remarking that he had had but a scanty
supper, went on for the sheer love of the thing and consumed a
3d. loaf, a pound of cheese and a leg of pork. "Sir," said the great
Dr. Johnson, the very embodiment of eighteenth century England,
"I mind my belly very studiously, for I look upon it that he who
will not mind his belly will scarcely mind anything else."

.   .   .   .

The foundation of this good living was the wealth of the English
soil. Throughout the century a succession of remarkable men—
aristocrats, hedge squires and farmers—devoted their lives to the improvement of crops and livestock. Bakewell's new breed of
Leicester sheep in the 'sixties and 'seventies gave his country two
pounds of mutton where she had one before. From the king—
"Farmer George"—who contributed to the *Agricultural Magazine*

[1] Dyott I 17.   [2] *Ramblin' Jack* (ed. R.R. Bellamy) 204.

under the pseudonym of Robinson and carried a copy of Arthur Young's *Farmer's Letters* on all his journeys—to Parson Woodforde, who recorded daily his horticultural activities and observations on the weather, the pursuit of husbandry gripped the English mind. Great lords would pay £400 or more for the hire of one of Mr. Bakewell's rams, and yeomen would club together to establish cart-horse and ploughing tests. The country gentleman who did not look after his estate lost as much caste as he who shirked his fences in the hunting field. Hardy and realist, the landowners of England were a source of astonishment to continental neighbours, who did not know at which to wonder more: aristocratic absorption in clovers and fat cattle or the intelligence with which farmers and peasants, who abroad would have been regarded as no better than beasts of burden, conversed on the principles of their calling.[1]

This common passion was one of the influences that tempered the aristocratic government of the country. By accustoming men of all classes to act together, it gave them national cohesion. It was not that the political constitution of the country was democratic: it was on the face of it overwhelmingly aristocratic. The House of Lords was hereditary. Of 558 members of the House of Commons, 294—a majority—were returned by constituencies with less than 250 electors. Many of the newer and larger centres of population had no representation at all, while an under-populated county like Cornwall still returned a tenth of the English and Welsh members. 157 M.P.s were nominated by eighty-four local proprietors, mostly peers, and 150 more on the recommendation of another seventy. Yet the power of the great lords, who regarded the Whig rule of England as something permanently ordained by Heaven, did not prevent the younger Pitt from carrying the country against the prevailing parliamentary majority in the election of 1784. The effect of corruption, openly acknowleged and shamelessly displayed, largely cancelled itself out. Those who sought entry to parliament were often childishly sensitive to what their fellow-

[1] "It is only in this country that one may see a man like Mr. Wenar, who is visited and courted by dukes and peers, dines at their table and returns their dinners, and all this because he can fatten oxen better than his brethren, the other farmers. A German baron could hardly believe this." *Wynne Diaries* III 72.

countrymen—and particularly their neighbours—thought of them. The very illogicality of the electoral system inclined them to bow to any unmistakable expression of public opinion; they felt the intellectual weakness of their position and claimed no sanctity for their point of view.

The ninety-two knights of the shire were the elite of the House and carried far more weight than could be explained by their numbers. When they were united—an event however which only happened in a time of national emergency—no Government could long withstand their opposition. This was because their election by forty-shilling freeholders gave them a real right to speak for England: they represented the substance of her dominant interest and industry. They were no placemen or carpet-baggers but independent gentlemen openly competing with their equals for the suffrages of their neighbours—of those, that is, best fitted to judge their character and stewardship. Before a county election sturdy freeholders rode into the shire town from every side to hear speeches from the rival candidates, to be canvassed by them in market hall and street, to march in bannered and cockaded processions behind bands of music, and to eat and drink at their expense in the leading inns and taverns. The most important of all county elections— because it represented the largest constituency—was that of the great province of Yorkshire: on the result of this the eyes of Ministers and even of European statesmen were fixed.

In such contests, and even in those of the close boroughs, there was a wealth of homely plain speaking and even homelier conduct. The candidates, however splendid their lineage and estates, had to take their turn of lampoons, brutal jests and rotten eggs and run the gauntlet of a fighting, drunken, cheering, jeering crowd before they could hope to enter the portals of Westminster. One did not have to be an alderman or an hereditary burgess or even a forty-shilling freeholder to fling a dead cat at the hustings. The right to do so during an election was regarded as an inalienable privilege of every Englishman: the only check the right of every other subject to return the compliment. At the Wycombe election in 1794 Lord Wycombe was thrown down in the mud and Squire Dashwood, another candidate, lost his hat and almost his life.

"Elections are certainly of some use," wrote radical John Byng, "as affording lessons of humility and civility to a proud lord and a steeped lordling."

The rowdiest of all elections was that of Westminster. Here, by one of the incalculable illogicalities of the English constitution, something approaching manhood suffrage prevailed. Every adult male with his own doorway and a fireplace on which to boil his pot had the right to record his vote. Like Yorkshire, Westminster was regarded by statesmen as a political test: in its noisy humours—its riots, its stuffed effigies, its grand ladies cajoling porters and draymen with kisses—one could feel the pulse of England.

Perhaps the most startling manifestation of English licence was the power of the mob. England had no police force, and it was regarded as a mark of effeminate namby-pambyism to wish there to be one. Facing a mob was like facing a fence or standing up to an enemy in the ring: a thing a gentleman took in his stride. One did it with courage and good humour, and then the monster —which, being English itself, respected courage and good nature— did no great harm. True in 1780 the London mob surrounded the Houses of Parliament, took drunken control of the capital for four days and burnt down about a tenth of it. But even this excess was regarded as part of the price of popular freedom. And in its crude, barbarous way the mob did—under guidance—act as a kind of rough watchdog of the national liberties. Thus, when the House of Commons, in its dislike of the disreputable John Wilkes, outraged the principles of freedom of choice and speech which it was its duty to uphold, it was the constancy of the mob to the cause which had brought Strafford to the scaffold that shamed and finally defeated the advocates of despotism.

Liberty outside parliament was reflected by liberty within. For all the power of the great nominating lords and borough-mongers and the allurements of the Treasury, there were more independent members in the House than is possible under the rigid Party machinery of to-day. In a major issue it was not the Whips but men's consciences that turned the scale in the lobbies. Minorities could make themselves felt. A great speech could decide a hard-fought debate: members were not the tied advocates of particular interests obeying mandates issued in advance. They gave their constituents unfettered judgment.

Nor did the complexion of the House discount the rise of talent. Within its narrow range the old parliamentary system fostered it. Again and again it recruited to the country's service the strongest motive power in the world—the force of genius untrammelled by the rule of mediocrity. A young man of brilliance, who had the good fortune to attract the notice of some great peer, might be set on the high road to the Front Bench; Pitt with £300 a year was Prime Minister at twenty-four, and Burke, a man of genius without any of the arts of the demagogue and lacking both birth and independent fortune, entered parliament by the back door of a rotten borough and a discerning aristocrat's approval.

Behind every English exercise of liberty was the conception of law. It did not coerce a man from acting as he pleased: it only afforded redress to others if in doing so he outraged their rightful liberty or the peace of the community. Every man could appeal to the law: no man could legally evade it. Not even the king: perhaps it would be truest to say, least of all the king. The squire who rebuked George III—a very popular monarch—for trespassing on his land became a national legend.

In England there was no *droit administratif*; no sacred principle of State with which to crush the cantankerous subject. The official had to produce the warrant of law to justify his action. If he exceeded his authority, whatever his motives, he suffered the same penalty as though he had acted as a private citizen. There was no escape from the law: it was like divine retribution and might overtake the transgressor at any moment of his life. Joseph Wall, for all his fine connections, was hanged at Newgate in front of a cheering mob for having twenty years before, while Governor of Goree, sentenced a mutinous sergeant to an unlawful flogging that caused death.

Trial by law was conducted in public. Judges were appointed for life and were irremovable save for gross misconduct. Issues of fact were decided by a jury of common citizens. Any man arrested could apply to the courts for an immediate writ of *Habeas Corpus* calling on his custodian to show legal cause why he should be detained. In all doubtful cases the prisoner was given the benefit of the doubt and acquitted. These were the main pillars of English justice, together with an unpaid magistracy of local worthies, the absence of a paid constabulary,[1] and a traditional distrust of the standing army which was always kept by parliament—alone capable of voting funds for its maintenance—at the lowest strength compatible with national safety, and often a good deal lower.

There was another safeguard for freedom—the legal sanctity of property. It was individual ownership, it was held, that enabled a man to defy excessive authority. Without a competence of his own to fall back on, the subject could be bribed or intimidated: a John Hampden without an estate seemed impracticable to the English mind. The guardians of her liberties were the gentlemen of England whose hereditary independence protected them from the threats and guiles of despotism. They were tyrant-proof.

Any interference with a man's property by the State—that infringed what an eighteenth century correspondent called "the sweet majesty of private life"—was regarded as pernicious. Free men were supposed to be free to do as they liked with their own. Taxation had to be kept as low as possible and the extent of a man's contribution to the kingdom's upkeep left, wherever practicable, to his own choice. Direct taxation was regarded as repugnant to English principles both on account of its compulsion and of the power of inquisition it involved. The taxpayer had the option of declining to purchase the taxed article and so avoiding the tax. For this reason many antiquated tariff barriers which would otherwise have been swept away in the rising tide of free trade were retained for revenue purposes.

"No taxation without representation" was the oldest battle-cry in the armoury of English freedom; it dominated the constitution. Those assembled in parliament did not represent numbers but

[1] In London a small patrol of less than fifty mounted men was maintained to guard its highwayman-infested approaches, while a handful of professional Bow Street runners—popularly known as "redbreasts" on account of their scarlet waistcoats—occasionally patrolled the more lawless districts. For the rest the public order of the capital was left to the medieval constables of the parishes assisted by a race of venerable watchmen or "Charlies" with traditional staffs, lanterns and rattles.

property: the greater landowners in the House of Lords, the lesser in the Commons, side by side with the burgesses who represented the nation's mercantile interest. Such an assembly was tender to the taxpayer, unsympathetic to the executive. Eighteenth century England had been saved from a recurrence of the seventeenth century struggles between Crown and parliament by vesting power in a Cabinet of Ministers who commanded the support of a majority in the House of Commons. Because of this, administration and justice were supported more cheaply than in any other country of equivalent size and importance. The cost of administration in Prussia was twice as much, in France many times that of Britain. The chief civil expenses were the sinecures and pensions which the ruling aristocracy, usurping the former perquisites of the Court, lavished on their relations and supporters. Even the Navy, in peacetime, was pared to the bone, particularly in the matter of seamen's pay. Yet economy on the Navy was at least kept within limits. For experience had taught the English that their commercial wealth depended on their fleet.

. . . .

"Trade," Addison had written, "without enlarging the British territories has given us a sort of additional empire; it has multiplied the number of the rich, made our landed estates infinitely more valuable and added to them the accession of other estates as valuable as the lands themselves." The development of commerce under the Hanoverians was prodigious. In 1720 the value of the country's imports was just over £6,000,000; by 1760 it was nearly £10,000,000, by 1789 over £37,000,000. During these years East Indian tea and West Indian sugar became part of the staple dietary of the people.[1] Everything conspired to further this process: natural health and vigour, free institutions, aptitude for seamanship and colonisation and a unique geographical position.

In the half century after Addison's death it also brought the British a great empire, acquired not by design of imperial conquest but through the individual's search for trade. The fight to main-

[1] Rochefoucauld noted that an English peasant had tea twice a day like the rich man. Rochefoucauld 23.

tain that trade against their rivals, the French, placed them on a pinnacle of unprecedented glory During the Seven Years War, under Chatham's leadership they gained supremacy in India and a new dominion in Canada. Before Clive's victory at Plassey in 1757 they had only been casual factors trading from isolated coastal ports in the anarchical Indian peninsula by leave of native princes and in armed rivalry with other European trading companies. But in the second half of the century the East India Company of London found itself administering possessions many times the size of England. At first it merely regarded this unlooked-for dominion as a windfall for its factors and shareholders; the imagination of Leadenhall Street could stretch no further.

It was not only in India that a race of farmers and shopkeepers failed to visualise the magnitude of their political opportunity. Along the eastern seaboard of North America, now freed from fear of French aggression by the conquest of Canada, lived two million British settlers. These a patronising Court and parliament treated as if they lacked the stubborn independence of their kinsfolk at home. The result was a quarrel, persisted in with all the ferocious obstinacy and moral rectitude of the race until no alternatives remained but either a systematic conquest of the colonies by British soldiers or the end of the imperial connection.

The issue was still undecided when Britain's outdistanced competitors in the race for empire seized their opportunity for revenge. France, Spain and Holland—the three chief maritime powers of the continent—supported by Russia, Sweden and Denmark, joined hands with the colonists. With her fleets outnumbered and her finances in ruin, Britain seemed beaten. Then the brilliance of her seamen and the stubborn defence of Gibraltar turned the scale. A disastrous war dwindled away into stalemate. The British faced the facts and in 1783 made peace. Their former colonies became the United States of America.

Yet unperceived by the islanders, who thought their imperial heritage lost for ever, the process which had made the first empire continued and at an accelerated pace. What had happened before happened again. In every corner of the world where ships could sail enterprising Britons appeared, begging concessions, planting factories and on occasion hoisting the imperial flag as a protection for their ventures. No sooner, in the poet Cowper's phrase, had the jewel been picked from England's crown, than new jewels blazed in the empty sockets. Within five years of the final loss of the American colonies, Captain Phillip had established the first British settlement on the continent of Australia. An even vaster new Britain in America took embryonic shape amid the snows of Canada where 140,000 defeated French, 60,000 migrant loyalists from the United States and a few thousand rough Scottish emigrants contrived to live together under King George's writ. Elsewhere a chain of forts, naval bases and sugar and spice islands continued to afford British traders springboards of opportunity.

For the moment the chief imperial field for the aspirant to wealth was India, which was beginning to take the place of the West Indies. From this oriental El Dorado flowed an ever-widening stream of spices, indigo, ivory, sugar, tea, ebony, sandalwood, saltpetre, cotton, silks and calicoes and fabulously rich merchants who bought up English estates and rotten boroughs, married their children into the aristocracy and received from their less fortunate countrymen the envious name of nabob. It was due to them that Britain first became conscious of her eastern possession and began to assume a direct responsibility for its government, The India Act of 1784, subordinating the political power of the Directors of the East India Company to a Board of Control appointed by the Crown, and the impeachment of Warren Hastings in 1787 were symptoms of this new interest, half-humanitarian and half-imperial.

The commercial success of the nation was beginning to change its character; already it was setting out on its long trek from country to town. London by now had more than three-quarters of a million inhabitants within a circuit of twenty miles from Millbank in the west to Limehouse and Poplar hamlet in the east and from Islington in the north to Newington in the south.[1] Elsewhere population was concentrating itself in urban entities of a kind unknown to the civic culture of the past. By 1790 Manchester

---

[1] Gouverneur Morris reported in 1790 that from the western gateway of Hyde Park Corner to Chiswick village there was an almost continuous suburban highway running through the Middlesex meadows and market gardens. Morris I, 556.

had 80,000 inhabitants, Liverpool and Birmingham over 70,000 and Leeds 50,000. The population of Lancashire, hitherto one of the most barren areas of England, had grown to 600,000.

For here on the humid western slope of the Pennines a new industry arose during the second half of the century to rival the cloth trade of Yorkshire. It grew out of the demand for the bright cottons of India. Raw cotton, it was found, could be grown with slave labour on the plantations of the southern American colonies. The Lancashire climate, the traditional skill of English spinners and weavers and the astonishing ingenuity of British inventors did the rest. In 1771 Richard Arkwright, a Bolton barber, improving on the earlier work of the handloom weaver, Hargreaves of Blackburn, set up the first water-propelled spinning frame in Derbyshire. Eight years later Samuel Crompton, a Lancashire farmer and weaver, invented his spinning mule. These changed the entire nature of the industry and ultimately of British domestic life. The factory with its myriad turning machines took the place of the cottage spinning wheel. In 1741 Britain exported £20,000 worth of cotton goods; in 1790 £1,662,369 worth.

The northern deserts with their water power and coal-seams became transformed. Gaunt buildings with rows of windows rose like giant wraiths on the wild Matlock hills and in misty Lancashire valleys, and around them rows of cheerless, squalid little houses. Within a few years quiet old market towns like Rochdale swelled into noisy, straggling cities, filled with unwashed, pagan spinners and weavers: they seemed to a Tory of the old school "insolent, abandoned and drunk half the week." The capital of this area, now given over to the service of Mammon, was the old Jacobite town of Manchester, whose new population huddled together in damp, stinking cellars. Its port, importing corn and raw cotton, was upstart Liverpool, home of the West Indian trade and its scandalous offspring, the slave trade, with windmills and warehouses full of flies, rum and sugar, crowding for a mile along the northern bank of the Mersey.

Farther south in a formerly wild countryside another industrial area was growing up round the coal and iron-fields of Staffordshire and north Warwickshire. This was the Black Country—by 1790 a land of forges, collieries and canals with grimy trees and hedges. The traveller, venturing into this little-trodden, satanic region, saw rows of blackened hovels swarming with ragged children, and, instead of church spires, tall chimneys belching metallic vapours and at night lit by flames. At its southern extremity was Birmingham—a squalid village afflicted with elephantiasis, where "crusty knaves that scud the streets in aprons seemed ever ready to exclaim, 'Be busy and grow rich!' " and where the head grew dizzy with the hammering of presses, the clatter of engines and the whirling of wheels. Here almost every man in the cobbled streets stank of train-oil, and many had red eyes and hair bleached green by the brass foundries.

A few miles from Birmingham, the "toyshop of Europe," lay the great Soho manufactory of Boulton & Watt. Here over his own works lived the princely capitalist who in the course of thirty virtuous and laborious years turned the creative genius of a Scottish engineer, James Watt, into a dynamic force to refashion the world. Here the first practical cylindrical steam-engines were placed on the market, and manufacturers, statesmen and princes flocked to see the first wonder of Europe and buy the commodity which all the world of Mammon needed—"power." Such men as Boulton were pioneers of a new race, serving and exploiting the needs of their fellow-creatures with an energy and disregard for all other objects that make them loom through the mists of time like Titans. John Horrocks, the Quaker spinner, beginning work in a horse quarry, within fifteen years amassed a fortune of three-quarters of a million and entered parliament as member for his native town. Josiah Wedgwood of Etruria, exploiting the contemporary love for the ceramic art, made £500,000 out of pottery and transformed a wild moorland into a hive of smoking ovens trodden by thousands of horses and donkeys laden with panniers and by men and women with faces whitened with potter's powder. Far below them in the social scale but travelling the same adventurous road were newer and ever newer capitalists: dispossessed yeomen venturing their little all in the fierce industrial hurly-burly, or spinners earning, perhaps 35s. a week, working what would be regarded to-day as inconceivable hours and denying themselves every comfort to purchase a mill where others should work as hard for them in their turn.

Moralists deplored what was happening and, in the spread of depravity and atheism, predicted revolution. Instead of thinking of national well-being, statesmen and men of substance, they argued, were becoming obsessed with sordid considerations of profit-making. By 1798 there were 100,000 men and women and 60,000 children working in the cotton mills, many of the latter indentured by Poor Law Guardians to masters who treated them little better than slaves. Yet the national conscience was not asleep but only bemused by a multiplicity of new activities and openings for money-making. A great people, firmly launched on the ocean of untrammelled enterprise, was bound to commit errors, even crimes. Liberty had her economic gales as well as political. Yet the sea of endeavour was wide, and it was open. There was room to correct mistakes.

For all the while an eternal transformation was taking place. As popular energy, overwhelming the barriers of restriction, swept away obstructions to the free flow of trade and talent the competition of ruder types tended to out-produce and undersell those already established. The genteel merchants of Bristol, mellowed by a hundred years of wealth and refinement, were no match for the products of pushing, hungry Liverpool, whose merchant captains were content with a moiety of the wages paid to their haughtier rivals. Those who had their way to make by a natural process caught up and ultimately outdistanced those with an inherited start. At first sight this seemed to threaten a progressive debasement of culture and social standards: the tough and the shover tending to shoulder out the gentleman and the fair dealer. Yet, as one bucket in the well of commerce fell, the other rose. The national passion for emulation constantly replanted the standards of quality in fresh soil; the greasy, aproned, clog-footed mechanic of one generation became the worthy merchant of the next. And if the process of cultural rise was not so quick as that of fall, the artistic and intellectual reserves of society were so vast that they could afford a good deal of dilution.

For in culture England had never stood higher, not even in the

age of Shakespeare or that of Wren and Newton. Samuel Johnson
died in 1784 and Goldsmith ten years earlier. But in 1788 Reynolds,
Romney, Gainsborough, Opie, Rowlandson, Stubbs and the young
Lawrence were all painting, Cowper, Crabbe and Blake were
writing poetry, Boswell was putting the last touches to the greatest
biography in the language, and Gibbon had just finished its most
majestic history. Wordsworth was born in 1770, Coleridge in 1772,
Turner, Jane Austen and Charles Lamb in 1775, Constable in 1776,
Hazlitt in 1778, de Quincey in 1785 and Byron in 1788. North of
the border, where Adam Smith of Glasgow had established an
international reputation as the first political economist of the age,
Edinburgh was entering upon her brief but glorious flowering of
native wit as the northern Athens. Raeburn was beginning to
paint, Dugald Stewart to lecture, Walter Scott was studying the
romantic lore of his country, and an Ayrshire ploughman, Robert
Burns, had published his first volume. And in the realm of science
Britain's achievements were equally remarkable. Joseph Black, the
chemist, Hunter the founder of scientific surgery, Priestley the
discoverer of oxygen, and Jenner who conquered the scourge of
smallpox are among its great names. It was an age of gold that
had the Adam brothers as its architects, Cosway as its miniaturist,
Hepplewhite and Sheraton as its cabinetmakers. In the drawing
rooms of London and of the lovely pastoral mansions that looked
out on to the dreaming gardens of Repton and Capability Brown
a society moved, brocaded, white-stockinged and bewigged, more
gracious, more subtle, more exquisitely balanced than any seen on
earth since the days of ancient Greece.

Yet this society was governed by no fixed and absolute laws,
confined by no insurmountable barriers. Under its delicate polish
lay a heart of stout and, as the event was to prove, impenetrable
oak. Its people were tough to the core. "I shall be conquered, I
will not capitulate," cried Dr. Johnson as he wrestled with death,
guiding the surgeon's blade with his own hand. The Duke of
Portland at 68 underwent an operation for the stone and was seven
minutes under the knife without a murmur. Diminutive Jacob
Bryant, the great classical antiquary, asked by his sovereign what
branch of activity he was most noted for at Eton, answered to the

astonishment of his auditor: "Cudgelling, sir, I was most famous for that." Young girls wore sticks of holly in their bosoms to teach them to hold their heads high, old Edge of Macclesfield at 62 walked 172 miles in under fifty hours for a bet; the king rose daily at 4 a.m. and spent three hours on his dispatch boxes before taking his morning ride in Windsor Park. And the common people were tougher, if it were possible, than their betters. At Shirley village in Bedfordshire the penny barber told a traveller that he never used a brush since his customers, complaining of the tickling, preferred to be shaved dry.

They were fighters to a man: a race as game as the cocks they backed in the crowded, stinking pits of Jewin Street and Hockliffe. "Look you, sir," cried old General Sherbrooke to a fellow-officer who had offended him, "my hands are now behind my back, and I advise you to leave the room before they are brought forward, for, if they once are, I will break every bone in your body." "Why, my little man," asked one of the East India Directors of twelve-year-old John Malcolm at his interview for a commission, "what would you do if you met Hyder Ali?" "Cut off his heid," came the instant reply.

Yet, though passionately addicted to barbarous sports like bull-baiting and cock-fighting, the English led the world in humanitarian endeavour. It was an Englishman who, at extreme risk and personal inconvenience, travelled 50,000 miles visiting the putrid, typhus-ridden jails of Europe; and it was Englishmen who at the close of the century first instituted organised opposition to cruelty to children and animals. Nothing so well illustrates the slow but persistent national impulse to mitigate inhumanity as the popular condemnation of the slave trade. This movement ran directly counter to the immediate material interests of the country; it none the less steadily gained strength from its inception by a handful of Quakers in the 'sixties until at the end of the century it was espoused by the Prime Minister himself and the overwhelming majority of thinking Englishmen.

The transatlantic slave trade had grown up to meet the needs of Britain's plantations in the West Indies and American colonies. Its headquarters was Liverpool, whose merchants imported seven-eighths of the negroes brought from Africa to America. In return for the slaves sold to the planters, they brought back to England sugar, rum, cotton, coffee. Thus the whole of the country indirectly benefited from this horrible traffic. The slaves, many of whom were kidnapped and who were sold to the traders by their African chiefs and neighbours, were taken from the West African coast across the "Middle Passage" to the West Indies in crowded slavers, loaded three slaves to a ton, the poor chained wretches being packed so tightly between decks that they were often forced to lie on top of one another. The mortality both of human cargo and seamen was appalling but, the smaller the consignment of slaves that arrived, the better the price paid for the remainder.

Every reason was sought to justify the continuance of the traffic. Liverpool merchants and their parliamentary representatives declared that, were a measure passed to regulate the miseries of the "Middle Passage", the West Indian trade would be ruined, Britain's commercial supremacy lost and the Navy be denuded of trained seamen. Yet having once been brought to the notice of the British people, the slave trade was doomed. For, with all its barbaric survivals, Britain was a land of decent folk: of men and women with conscience. And because of the blend of freedom with order in her political institutions, the dictates of that conscience, though slow to mature, were ultimately given effect. Barbarous laws and customs[1]—men hanged in public for petty crimes, lunatics chained to the wall knee-deep in verminous straw, animals tortured at Smithfield and in the bull-ring—of these and their like there were plenty, but they were continually being ameliorated by the advancing pressure of public opinion. Instinctively a nation of freemen turned towards the light. That age-long process was the justification of their freedom.

For by freedom the English meant something more than freedom for themselves, though they certainly meant that. Conventional and conservative in their prejudices, often thoughtless and mentally lazy, they yet genuinely valued freedom for its own sake: for

[1] Rochefoucauld (p. 31) noted with astonishment that the sideboards of the most aristocratic houses were furnished with chamber-pots which, after the ladies' departure, were resorted to freely as the drink circulated.

others, that is, as well as for themselves. And their ideal of liberty was never an abstraction. It was based not on generalising but on measuring: on a calculation of the comparative rights and wrongs of every individual case. Burke's dictum, "If I cannot reform with equity, I will not reform at all," was, for an Irishman, a curiously English saying. It expressed the intensely personal interpretation of the national idea of freedom.

Heretics in Catholic eyes, backsliders in those of Geneva, since ridding themselves of the Catholic Stuarts the English, while remaining stubbornly Protestant, had grown far more tolerant. Except for Holland, theirs was the only European country in which men might worship God in any way they pleased. It was true there was a State Church to which the majority of Englishmen belonged and whose membership conferred civic privilege. But the Church of England was supported by parliament less because it had a monopoly of truth as because it seemed the most suitable medium for promulgating Christian and Protestant teaching.[1] With their genius for evolving institutions capable of withstanding the erosion of human nature the English had rejected both the Catholic and Calvinist conceptions of religious society. In place of a priesthood uncontaminated by the ties of marriage but in danger of undermining the mutual trust of the home, they had licensed a sobermarried clergy with the same family responsibilities as other men. In place of a theocratic caste untrammelled by secular obligations and therefore a source of political intrigue, they had established a Church subordinate to and allied to the State. But in their desire to give its ministers independence and social status, they had endowed many of them with more of the world's goods than was readily compatible with their spiritual vocation. After a century's monopoly of the loaves and fishes there was a good deal of pluralism, in cases amounting to downright scandal,

---

[1] "Gentlemen," said Lord Chancellor Thurlow to the deputation of Nonconformists which waited on him in 1788 to ask for a repeal of the Corporation and Test Acts, "I'm against you, by God. I am for the Established Church, damme! Not that I have any more regard for the Established Church than for any other church, but because it is established. And if you can get your damned religion established, I'll be for that too!" Crabb Robinson, *Diary* I 378.

much neglect of church and parishioner, and a general atmosphere of comfortable complacency. Almost a quarter of the country's nine thousand parishes were without resident incumbents, and in many churches there was an atmosphere of damp and decay: weeds grew in the graveyard and small boys played fives in the shady corner under the belfry.

Yet those whom the Church neglected, the rejected of the Church cared for. The missionary journeys of the early Methodists among the pagan outcasts of industrial Britain did God's work where well-endowed complacency had failed. Preaching a crusade, Wesley's disciples carried the Gospel into the dark corners of what, but for them, might have ceased to be a Christian land. In its remoter parts there sprang up a new Protestant religion of passion and poetry attuned to the simplicities and superstitions of the poor. Among the roughest of the rough—the lonely weavers of Yorkshire and Lancashire and the miners of Durham and Cornwall—thousands were to be found practising a faith as pure as that taught by Christ to the fishermen of Galilee. This noble work of conversion —the supreme triumph of eighteenth century English individualism —served not only spiritual but political ends. As much as any single factor the faith and discipline of Methodism helped in the last terrible decade of the century to save Britain from the fate of revolutionary France.

· · · · · · · ·

Yet, with her solid heart of sober, quiet folk, England had such reserves of strength that it was hard to estimate her breaking point. To comprehend her secret one must probe beneath the variegated surface—the splendours of aristocratic salons and provincial parks and palaces, the gambling dens and cockpits of the metropolis, the grim sores of factory and foetid slum—and seek it in the calm continuity of family life. The lessons handed down from mother to daughter, the hereditary craft taught the boy at his father's knee, the sturdy children playing together in the orchard, the clean-dressed, home-spun village people taking the road to church on Sunday morning, here were the enduring roots of national life. In the pages of John Nyren's *The Cricketers of My Time*, published in

1833, the author recalled the men of Hambledon with whom he had grown up in the 'seventies and 'eighties of the previous century. In his gallery of cricketing heroes we can see the fathers of the men who tended the guns at Trafalgar and manned the squares at Waterloo making their way with curved bat and eager eye up the woodland road from Hambledon village to the downland pitch on Broad-Halfpenny on the first Tuesday in May. The dew is still on the grass and the sun is shining high over "Old Winchester" as they take the field against All England. Here is little George Lear the famous long-stop, so sure that he might have been a sand-bank, and his friend, Tom Sueter, the wicket-keeper who loved to join him in a glee at the "Bat and Ball"; Lambert, "the little farmer", whose teasing art, so fatal to the Kent and Surrey men, had been mastered in solitude by bowling away hours together at a hurdle while tending his father's sheep; and "those anointed clod-stumpers, the Walkers, Tom and Harry" with their wilted, apple-john faces and long spidery legs as thick at the ankles as at the hips. "Tom was the driest and most rigid-limbed chap; . . . his skin was like the rind of an old oak, and as sapless. . . . He moved like the rude machinery of a steam-engine in the infancy of construction and, when he ran, every member seemed ready to fly to the four winds. He toiled like a tar on horseback."

What Wellington became to his Peninsular veterans and "Daddy" Hill to Wellington, Richard Nyren was to the Hambledon cricketers and John Small to Nyren. "I never saw," his son recorded, "a finer specimen of the thoroughbred old English yeoman than Richard Nyren. He was a good face-to-face, unflinching, uncompromising independent man. He placed a full and just value upon the station he held in society and maintained it without insolence or assumption. He could differ with a superior, without trenching upon his dignity or losing his own." And his *fidus Achates*, yeoman Small, was worthy of him. He loved music, was an adept at the fiddle and taught himself the double bass. He once calmed a bull by taking out his instrument and playing it in the middle of a field. His fellow cricketer, the Duke of Dorset, hearing of his musical talent, sent him a handsome violin and paid the carriage. "Small, like a true and simple-hearted Englishman, returned the compliment by sending his Grace two bats and balls, also paying the carriage."

In the English memory there are few more endearing scenes than that famous pitch on the Hampshire down. When "Silver Billy" Beldham—the first bat of the age—was in or runs were hard to get and the finish close, Sir Horace Mann, that stalwart patron of the game, would pace about outside the ground cutting down the daisies with his stick in his agitation, and the old farmers under the trees would lean forward upon their tall staves, silent. "Oh! it was a heart-stirring sight to witness the multitude forming a complete and dense circle round that noble green. Half the county would be present, and all their hearts with us—little Hambledon, pitted against All England, was a proud thought for the Hampshire men. Defeat was glory in such a struggle—victory, indeed, made us only 'a little lower than angels.' How those fine brawn-faced fellows of farmers would drink to our success! And then what stuff they had to drink! Punch!—not your new *Ponche à la Romaine*, or *Ponche à la Groseille*, or your modern cat-lap milk punch—punch be-deviled; but good, unsophisticated, John Bull stuff—stark! that would stand on end—punch that would make a cat speak! . . . Ale that would flare like turpentine—genuine Boniface!

"There would this company, consisting most likely of some thousands, remain patiently and anxiously watching every turn of fate in the game, as if the event had been the meeting of two armies to decide their liberty. And whenever a Hambledon man made a good hit, worth four or five runs, you would hear the deep mouths of the whole multitude baying away in pure Hampshire—'Go hard!—Go hard!—Tich and turn!—tich and turn!' To the honour of my countrymen . . . I cannot call to recollection an instance of their wilfully stopping a ball that had been hit out among them by one of our opponents. Like true Englishmen, they would give an enemy fair play. How strongly are all those scenes, of fifty years by-gone, painted in my memory!—and the smell of that ale comes upon me as freshly as the new May flowers."

From the high hill which rose out of the woods beyond the pitch one could see on clear days half southern England—valley and down and forest. Over that wide countryside the sea winds never ceased to blow from every point of the compass, free as the hearts of oak the land bred. Waving trees and smoke fluttering like a ragged banner, feathery heath, lonely cottages at the edge of moor and forest, ragged cows and geese and ponies pasturing in the wild by ancient prescribed rights. Tidal rivers flowing through marshes to the ocean with black cattle grazing at their salt edges and wooden cobles and crab-boats tossing on their silver bosom; land of semi-nomads, gatherers of shellfish, fowlers, longshore fishermen and armed smugglers—of Slip-jibbet and Moonshine Buck tip-trotting by in the dark with tubs of Geneva for the parson and "baccy for the clerk." Sometimes travellers and shepherds near the coast would see the fleet of England riding at Spithead in one of the broad bays of the Channel shore; "pleasant and wonderful was the sight as seen from Ridgeway Hill, with the West Bay and the Isle of Portland and Weymouth and Melcombe Regis, all lying in the calm sunshine," wrote Elizabeth Ham in after years, "I see it now."[1]

Further inland were the familiar objects of the country scene: the reapers in the golden field, the cottages of wattle and timber with their massive brick chimneys and deep thatch, the mill with its weather-boarded walls and throbbing wheel amid willows and alders, the saw-pit with sweating craftsmen and stacked timber, the leafy lane with the great hairy-footed horses drawing home the wain laden with hay and laughing children. Along the high roads bright, liveried postilions glinted like jewels before swaying postchaises, and postmen, riding or mounted high on coaches, passed in the scarlet livery of England. With infinite slowness, soon overtaken by these fast-moving ones, a vast tilted stage-wagon crawled like a snail behind its eight horses, their neck-bells making discordant music while the carrier trudged beside idly cracking his whip in the air. Along the road were haymakers at their work, mansions with ancient trees and cropping deer, and at every village the blacksmith's forge with old Vulcan looking out from his open door, "grey and hairy as any badger." And perhaps as it grew dark and the lights were lit on the coaches, the traveller might overtake a neighbouring gentleman's hounds, as

[1] *Elizabeth Ham by Herself* (ed. Eric Gillett).

John Byng did one May evening, coming home from an airing.

Within the candle-lit windows of the wayside cottage and the farmhouse on the hill, old John Bull would sit dozing with his pot beside the kitchen fire, the dog and cat asleep at his feet, the good wife at her wheel, the pretty maid his daughter coming in with her pail, the children playing with the caged bird, the tinder-box on the shelf, the onions and flitches hanging from the ceiling. From this home he was presently to go out to face and tame a world in arms. For the moment he was content and at his ease, perhaps more so than was good for his continuing soul. In the tavern down in the village old England still lived on where over their pipes and bowls, gathered round the bare rude table, the local worthies, with russet, weather-beaten faces, cracked their joke and trolled their song. Though their summer was brief before winter aches and penury encompassed them, they knew how to be merry. Cricket matches and fives playing, the crowd at the fair gathered round the cudgellers' high wooden stage, the squeak of a fiddle or the shrill cry of a mountebank with his Merry Andrew on the village green on a warm summer evening, the carollers and the mumming players coming out of the Christmas snows, these were the outward symbols of a race of freemen taking their pleasures in their own way as their fathers had done before them. It seemed a far cry from these peaceful scenes to the rough humours and turbulent racket of London—the butchers of Shepherd's Market and May Fair elbowing their way through the dirty streets to a hanging at Tyburn, the footpads in the shadows of Park Lane, the foetid cells of Newgate —or the restless, sullen money-making of Manchester and Birmingham. Yet all were part of an English whole whose meaning it was hard to compass in a word, but whose people were in a greater or lesser degree adherents of two dominant ideals—justice and their own freedom.

> "The nations not so blessed as thee
> Must in their turn to tyrants fall,
> While thou shalt flourish great and free,
> The dread and envy of them all."

So sang the islanders in their favourite "Rule Britannia," and the words expressed their firm, unalterable conviction. Their very versatility was part of their heritage of liberty. "Now in as hot a climate as that of the East or West Indies and sometimes in winter feel the cold of Greenland," wrote John Byng, "up and down; hence we are precarious, uncertain, wild, enduring mortals. And may we so endowed continue, the wonder and balance of the universe."

CHAPTER 5

The Coloured Counties

AFTER twenty-two years of war, much of the time alone, Britain emerged in 1815 victorious from her struggle against the revolution in arms and the military dictatorship of Napoleon. By her use of sea-power and the constancy and resolution of her people, she had withstood a martial State with nearly three times her population. Even when all Europe was mobilised against her by the greatest military conqueror of all time she had continued to fight on and, in the end, with the allies she had financed, armed and helped to liberate, had utterly broken him and his power.

Yet for all her immense sacrifices, she had grown richer than ever before. Though it had cost her seven hundred millions, the long struggle doubled her export trade and trebled her revenue. The carrying trade of the world was in her hands. Despite her enemies' efforts to break her stranglehold of the seas, her merchant tonnage had risen from a million to two and a half million tons, while her commerce with the Spanish and Portuguese colonies in South America had increased fourteenfold. By her occupation of the Cape, Ceylon and Malta, her voyages of trade and discovery and her continued conquests in India, she had extended her tentacles into every part of the globe and raised the population of her overseas empire from twenty to seventy millions.

Yet, while withstanding tyranny abroad, she had preserved liberty at home. The Revolutionary dream of a new birth of freedom founded on resounding phrases had proved, it seemed, a bloody and destructive delusion. The French under their military dictatorship had shown themselves incapable of the liberty they proclaimed. The authoritarianism of Prussia had broken, Austria had become a byword for defeat, the antique chivalry of Spain had dissolved under the hammer-blows of the armed Revolution. Even the triumphant Russians had proved barbarians in the grain. Only one kingdom had emerged victorious while assuring her people social order and freedom of choice. Britain might not be the utopia of the philosophers, but she seemed nearer it than anything mankind had yet achieved.

At the time of her victory the United Kingdom consisted of two islands—a dominant one with a population of ten million English, two million Scots and half a million Welsh, and a subordinate one inhabited by five million Catholic Irish peasants and a million Protestants of Anglo-Scottish descent who alone held the right to sit in parliament and enjoy high office. The condition of the two islands was thus dissimilar: the one a closely-knit commonwealth pursuing its own interest, the other a dependency garrisoned by a ruling caste, foreign in religion and mainly so in race. The gulf between them had been widened rather than lessened by the Act of Union of 1801, which had abolished the Irish Parliament in favour of minority representation in the imperial legislature at Westminster, where its members could always be outvoted.

For except in Protestant Ulster, the Irish were a very different race from the sober, law-abiding English and the thrifty, tenacious Scots. The difference was partly one of climate, partly of religion, economics and history, partly of diet. The English lived on meat, beer and wheaten bread, the Irish on potatoes and whisky. They were at once a tragic, reckless, kind-hearted, superstitious and, by English standards, lawless and unreliable race, always doing wild things and in so gay and absurd a manner that their irresponsibility was a jest rather than a reproach. Their only point in common with the English, apart from their courage, was their passion for horses. Ireland's vivid green Atlantic landscape, with its mournful bogs and misty mountains, its stinking hovels and elegant, filthy, drunken capital, seemed to belong to a foreign country. Here women, half-naked, with matted hair hanging over their bosoms, sat at cabin doors smoking pipes and staring at melancholy horizons, and men in blue cloaks and slouching hats, carrying shillelaghs, stood jesting at street corners in sinister groups. In this other island the most savage crimes were constantly being committed for religious, patriotic or agrarian reasons by a peasantry whom Harry Smith found the lightest-hearted, kindest, most generous creatures he had ever known.[1]

Ireland was not the only part of the British Isles which presented a contrast to the wealth and splendour of London and the garden of Kent and Sussex. There were the marshes and fens with their half-animal fishermen and fowlers; poor primitive villages along the rocky, western coasts with mud walls and blackened, ragged thatch; the northern moors and the Welsh valleys where a sturdy people—almost as broad as they were high—talked in a strange tongue, wore traditional dress and lived a life apart.[2] Scotland, too, though its wealth had increased immeasurably in the past half century, was a poor land compared with England. The country women still went about bare-footed, except on Sundays when they attended kirk in fine shawls, black velvet bonnets and looks of ineffable piety. They lived in bare, unfloored cottages, mostly of one room, with dung piled against sodden turf walls. Even in its noble capital—"Auld Reekie"—with its labyrinth of crooked closes and tall medieval houses, the cry of "gardy loo" still warned the passer-by that the ordure of the past twelve hours was about to descend into the roadway. For all the fine new farms of the Lothians and the Lanarkshire cotton mills, Scotland's chief wealth was still the frugality and honesty of its deeply religious people.

Beyond the Lowlands were the feudal Highlands—the primitive land of mountain and flood made fashionable by Walter Scott's poems and novels. Here, in poor shepherds' huts full of animals and peat-smoke, lived a race whose splendid physique and proud

---

[1] Smith, I, 337. See Mrs. Arbuthnot, *Journal*, 5th Jan. 1822; Ashton, II, 201-2; Bell, I, 181, 187, 192; Bury II, 109, 112, 115-16; Colchester, II, 591-2; Farington, VIII, 64, 121; Granville II, 456-7, 458; Grattan, 327-8; Gronow, II, 87; Keats, *Letters*, 6th July, 1818; *Lavengro* 57-9; Lockhart, V, 179; Nevill, 56-60; Newton, 193; Peel, I, 206-7, 231, 236-7; Simond, I, 65; II, 135, 259, 324-6, 332, 339; Woodward, 314-24.

[2] When Richard Ayton landed in the Pwllheli peninsula in 1814, Cymric amazons emerged from filthy wigwams and proceeded to twist and pull about his umbrella with cries and grunts of amazement. Daniell, I, 167. See *idem*, 69 *et seq.*; Festing, 159-60; Marlay Letters, 256; Simond, I, 210-37.

bearing recalled the soldiers of ancient Rome or the noble savages of North America. There were only 300,000 in all, but, their former loyalty to the House of Stuart having been gloriously expiated on England's battlefields, their kilts, pipes and sporrans had lately become a national institution.[1]

Of the English people more than three-quarters still lived in villages and small market-towns. Though a new industrial population was growing up in the north and midlands, it was as yet an insignificant fraction of the national community, hidden out of sight in lonely Pennine valleys and remote heaths. Set against "Britain's calm felicity and power," the helot settlements beside the Irk and Swayle seemed accidental and unimportant. Only a prophet could have foreseen that the England of the future lay there and not in the pastoral and feudal south.

Here, Washington Irving wrote, everything was the growth of ages, of regular and peaceful existence, conveying an impression of "calm and settled security, an hereditary transmission of home-bred virtues and attachments that spoke deeply and touchingly for the moral character of the nation." That traditional life could be seen on Sunday in the villages: the well-dressed family groups converging through the fields and lanes as the church bells pealed —a continuous chain of sound at that hour across the country— the spacious pews of the gentry, the old peasants in the aisle, the choir with their strings, clarinets and serpents in the gallery, the old men and girls in white gowns on either side of the chancel, the dignified high-church rector and parish clerk intoning "England's sublime liturgy," the happy neighbours meeting afterwards in the churchyard that Harry Smith and his fellow soldiers recalled with such nostalgia on a Sabbath morning in the little Spanish town of Villa Alba.[2] One saw it in the market towns with their beautiful houses—Georgian, Queen Anne, Tudor and Gothic— the romantic eaves and latticed windows of the old and the classical

---

[1] Simond, I, 273-4, 301, 302-24; Bewick, 74-7; Clapham I, 28-9, 37; Keats III, 163, 164, 166, 170-1, 191-213; Letts, 247; Lockhart, IV, 218; Lady Shelley, II, 57-8.

[2] *Autobiography of Sir Harry Smith* I 108. Cooper, 161; Farington VIII 125; Howitt 570-3.

cornices and pediments of the new, the broad high streets with driven cattle and umbrellaed market tables, the fine trees casting their shade over garden walls, the pillared market-halls. Such towns crowned nearly a thousand years of unbroken civilisation. From their upper windows one looked across gardens to fields, woods and clear rivers whose waters carried trout and crayfish. "One of those pretty, clean, unstenched and unconfined places," Cobbett called Huntingdon, "that tend to lengthen life and make it happy." At Winchester, when Keats stayed there in 1819, nothing ever seemed to be happening in the still, cobbled streets; nothing but the sound of birds in the gardens, the echoing, unhurrying foot-steps of passers-by, the roll of market carts flooding in or out of the city with the tides of the encircling shire.

Everywhere, as one travelled this rich, ancient land, one saw the continuity and natural growth of a community that had never known invasion and where the new, not confined as on the con-tinent by fortifications, had been free to develop without destroying the old. At Norwich, capital like York and Exeter not of a shire but of a province, the city was grouped round an episcopal tower, a Norman castle and a vast market square from whose stalls poured that abundance of foodstuffs which so astonished the German, Meidinger. "The most curious specimen at present extant of the genuine old English town," Borrow called it, "with its venerable houses, its numerous gardens, its thrice twelve churches, its mighty mound."

England still preserved a pageantry, beautiful and impressive though homely, that educated men in the meaning of society. The mayor with his laced cloak, sword-bearer, maces and aldermen, the gentlemen of the shire dining together in lieutenancy uniform, the humble beadles and criers in their cocked hats, flaxen wigs and silver lace, the very postmen in red and gold were unconsciously teaching history. At Assizes the judges drove into the county towns in scarlet and ermine, with outriders, javelin men and halberdiers, while the bells pealed and the streets were thronged with gentlemen in dark-blue coats, glossy hats and shining boots, and misses in white muslin and their prettiest bonnets. In Edinburgh the Lord Justice Clerk and judges passed through the city to their daily tasks in robes of red and white satin; in the grey streets of university and cathedral cities there was usually a flutter of gowns and a glimmer of wands and maces.[1] The sense of history had not yet been dulled by the impersonal segregation and ugliness of an industrial society; men understood something of the march of their country through time, of its traditions and culture. When the Guards' band played the old martial airs of England outside the palace, a visitor noted that many in the crowd had tears in their eyes. It was not, Paley wrote, by what the Lord Mayor felt in his coach that the public was served, but by what the apprentice felt who gazed on it.

Though by 1815 all this pageantry was beginning to wear a little thin, and sophisticated folk to sneer and denigrate, it still served its purpose of enriching the imagination of successive generations. Men felt at one with their native place, loved its beauty and took pride in its history. Old castles and monastic ruins were sources not only of intellectual interest to the few but of wonder and poetry to the many. So were the rude signs in bright colours swinging over the tavern doors, of Admiral Keppel or Vernon braving the battle and the breeze, the Marquis of Granby in scarlet coat, or St. George busy, with plumed helm and shield, slaying dragons. Unlettered lads from Tyneside colliers stood "beneath the wondrous dome of St. Paul's with almost awful surprise," and Bewick's neighbours, the Northumbrian peasants, spent their winter evenings listening to the tales and ballads of the Border. The earliest rhymes that Thomas Cooper, the Chartist leader, remembered were those of Chevy Chase. He used to repeat them until they made him feel as warlike as the sight of Matthew Goy riding into the town with news of a victory in the Peninsula or the scarlet-coated volunteers marching through Gainsborough on exercise days to the sound of fife and drum. "As I came down here to-day," wrote Lady Bessborough, "I met a procession that I thought quite affecting— numbers of men without an arm or leg or variously wounded, with bunches of laurel in their hats, and women and children mingling

[1] Ackermann, *Microcosm* I 11; Ashton I 215; Dixon 61-2; Howitt 83-5; Letts 200; Lockhart IV 188, 204; Newton 206-7; Pyne, *Costume of Great Britain*; Simond I 3, 255, 269, 299, 361; II 67, 72, 115.

with them. I inquired what it was and found it to be the anniversary of the battle of Talavera."

So, too, the English commemorated their faith and the seasons of the pastoral year. Before Christmas the weavers of South Lancashire sang all night at their looms to keep themselves awake as they prepared for the holiday. In the West the yule-log was brought home and tales told over posset and frumenty, and the carollers and string-choirs went their frosty rounds. With the farmhouses and cottages full of greenery and the kissing-bush hanging from the rafters, the traditional roast beef, plum pudding, mince-pie and roasted crab were eaten, while the mummers in painted paper and floral headgear—King George, the Doctor and the Turkey Snipe—banged one another with their wooden swords. On New Year's Eve the wassailers came round with garlanded bowls, cleaving the wintry skies with their song:

> "Here's to our horse and to his right ear,
> God send our master a happy New Year;
> A happy New Year as e'er he did see,
> With my wassailing bowl I drink to thee!"

and neighbours, made kindly by the season, sat in one another's houses, "fadging" over cakes and wine. The same gatherings were repeated with differences on Twelfth Night, when fires were lit and the farm beasts and apple trees carolled. On Distaff's Day and Plough Monday the resumption of work was celebrated by labourers going round the parish in animal masks, blowing cows' horns and cracking whips.[1]

Such feasts succeeded one another throughout the year, hallowed by memory yet sources of recurring excitement and activity. On Shrove Tuesday the miners of the north visited one another's houses to turn their pancakes and "stang" whoever had not eaten theirs, carrying the laggards with laughter to the midden. Mothering Sunday was commemorated with a simnel cake, Good Friday by children going round with a fiddler "peace-egging." There were rituals that commemorated remote historical events, like the riding of the black man through the streets of Ashton-under-Lyne on Easter Monday, the torchlit procession of ropemakers at

[1] *British Calendar Customs* II 97; Howitt 466-71.

Chatham to celebrate the benefactions of Catherine of Aragon, the Pack Monday Fair at Sherborne on the anniversary of the completion of the abbey nave. There were other days when the bonds of law were loosed, as at Michaelmas in Kidderminster when the gentry bombarded the bailiff and corporation with apples and for a "lawless hour" everyone threw cabbage stalks in the streets; St. Luke's Day in Cheshire when parsons were pelted with fruit; Tandering Day when school-children barred out their teachers and men and women spent the evening drinking hot elderberry wine in one another's clothes; and the Mischief Meet on May Day when, so long as one was not caught, it was lawful to pay off old scores: to throw a neighbour's gate off its hinges, upset his cart or let out his cattle.

There were occasions, too, when the poor had a right to largesse and the hungry were filled with good things. There were rituals that marked the course of the farm year; the Whitsun Ale and the sheep-shearing festival, the Holy Night at Brough, when a burning ash was carried in front of the town band with everyone dancing and firing squibs behind, the hiring fairs when the markets were full of toys and ginger-bread stalls and young men and women stood in the streets wearing the emblems of their craft to sell their services for the next year. The greatest of all the farm feasts was Harvest Home when the Kern Dolly or Ivy girl, fashioned from the corn, was set upon a pole and borne home in the last cart, with music playing and the farmer and his men shouting in procession while the good-wife dished up the supper that was to crown the rustic year. There, at the long wooden tables, the reapers— "with sunburnt hands and ale-enlivened face"—rejoiced over their beef, beer and pipes, singing familiar songs and tossing down sconces with double forfeits for every drop spilt, until the time-honoured chorus was reached:

"Here's a health unto our master, the founder of this feast!
I hope to God with all my heart his soul in Heaven may rest,
And all his works may prosper that ere he takes in hand,
For we are all his servants and all at his command—
So drink, boys, drink, and see you do not spill,
For if you do, you shall drink too, for 'tis our master's will!"

After which those able wound their way home, and those who could not slept where they lay, well content, in barn or stable.

Other dates in the calendar linked craft or calling to the Christian faith: the Spinners' Feast at Peterborough when workhouse children in white dresses and scarlet ribbons marched through the streets singing the spinning song; the processions of wool-combers on St. Blase's Day in the cloth towns of Yorkshire and East Anglia, with their heralds, banners and bands: wool-staplers on horseback, spinners in white stuff-waistcoats and silver sashes, wagoned pageants of Jason with Golden Fleece, Castor and Pollux, shepherds and shepherdesses, and good Bishop Blase in mitre and gown. Before the Lancashire wakes, proclaimed by the bellmen in the churchyards on successive Sundays, every fold and hamlet vied in preparing the rush cart, decking its ornamental sheet with ribbons, streamers and silver ornaments. With lanes resounding with fife, drum and fiddle, the girls all flounces and frills in new kirtles and bonnets, the lads in jingling horse-collars and bright with ribbon and tinsel, the whole community followed the cart to the parish church, while the morris dancers leaped and spun before:

> "My new shoon they are so good,
> I cou'd doance morrice if I wou'd,
> An' if hat an' sark be drest
> I will doance morrice w' the best."

When Keats, in his *Ode to a Grecian Urn*, asked

> "What little town by river or sea-shore . . .
> Is emptied of its folk this pious morn?"

he may have recalled the customary rites—doomed by the advance of an iron economy—of the Lancashire villages through which he had recently passed on his way to Scotland.[1]

The English poor loved to voice their patriotism in a song. Bob Johnson, the jockey, after his victories on the turf, would climb on the table and strike up his favourite:

---

[1] *Keats* IV 119-21. For an account of the Wakes see Bamford I 130-5, 146-7, 188 and Howitt 493-4. See also for a detailed account of English social and ritual custom before it was destroyed by the Industrial Revolution, A. R. Wright's great compilation, *British Calendar Customs*.

> "If ye ax wheer oi comes fra,
> I'll say the Fell side;
> Where fayther and mither
> And honest folk bide."

Having to make their own music, many Englishmen knew how to perform vocally and instrumentally; at a homecoming, a wedding, a gathering of neighbours, a man would take down his fiddle or send for his neighbour's. Bamford's weaver father could read from the book and play both fiddle and flute, and even compose. The yeomen of Cranborne Chase gathered weekly at an inn on Salisbury Plain for instrumental music and part singing; the artisans of Lincoln formed a choral society to render Handel's Oratorios.

This love of singing came out in the folk songs which, despite enclosure, lingered on in the villages like the string choirs and morris dancers. In the alehouse or the fields over the midday cheese and ale, countrymen would sing of their craft and skill, prizing them the more for the singing:

> " 'Hold, gard'ner, says the ploughman, 'my calling don't despise,
> Since each man for his living upon his trade relies,
> Were it not for the ploughman both rich and poor would rue,
> For we are all dependent upon the painful plough.' "

Often such songs, with their scope for character, would be acted, some elder piping up,

> "O true love, have you seen my gold?
> And can you set me free?
> Or are you come to see me hung
> All on the gallows tree?"

and the hearer, to whom the words were so familiar as to be automatic, joining in. They voiced the sentiment, honour, memory, poetry and robust coarseness of the race. "So fleet runs the hare," chanted the drovers at the Weyhill alehouse:

> "and so cunning runs the fox,
> Why shouldn't this young calf live to grow an old ox?
> O! for to get his living among the briars and thorns
> And drink like his daddy with a large pair of horns."

The seamen, roughest and hardest-used of men, had their traditional songs and shanties, whose rhythm served their work and
whose poetry sprang from the element they sailed:

> "Then a-weigh our anchor, my jolly, jolly tars,
>   For the winter star I see."

Deep down a vein of poetry, simple, sensuous and strangely
delicate, ran through this healthy, courageous, cohesive people.
"Rosy apple, lemon and pear," sang the children of the Dorset
villages at their traditional games:

> "A bunch of roses she shall wear,
>   Gold and silver by her side,
>   I know who'll take her as his bride;
>   Take her by her lily-white hand
>   And lead her to the altar;
>   Give her kisses one, two, three,
>   Mrs So-and-so's daughter."

And in the sturdy north—the land of Bobby Shaftoe—the wives
of Tyneside dandled their babies to the lilt:

> "Dance ti thy daddy,
>   Sing ti thy mammy,
>   Dance ti thy daddy,
>   Ti thy mammy sing!
>   Thou shall hev a fishy
>   On a little dishy,
>   Thou shall hev a fishy
>   When the boat comes in."

There were songs that kept England's history bright; of ships with
names like poems, of pastoral duties transformed by imagination
into acts of significance and beauty; of courtship, tender, tragic or
bawdy, but always shot with the haunting loveliness of the green,
peaceful land that gave them birth; of wild rovers and the mis-
fortunes that befall poor men when passion sounds and the reckless
heart tries to transcend the iron bars of destiny; of indignation
against cruel laws and injustice and foul play; and, underlying all,
the moral sense of a great people and their perception of the sweetness of love, courage and loyalty to wife and home, and of the
unchanging goodness of laughter and comradeship, striking, as the

pewter pots beat time on the dark, dented, malt-stained alehouse table, chords that rose from the very depths of the English heart.[1]

. . . .

Because of these things humble men respected learning and culture. It was still natural for English artisans to admire the best: to distinguish civilisation from barbarism. Good taste was widespread; it was no coincidence that both the artisan radical leaders to whose autobiographies we owe much of our knowledge of working-class outlook in the transitional stages of the Industrial Revolution, acquired in youth a love and knowledge of engraving. Farington, the academician, staying in Norwich in 1812 was introduced to a house-painter and a coachmaker who were connoisseurs of the arts; the former, he thought, was more devoted to pictures than anyone he had ever met. The unspoilt countryside of Britain, its songs and folklore created a natural instinct for poetry; more than one of the rustic giants whose mechanical and scientific genius charted the course of mankind's industrial future wanted in youth to become poets. Burns was no isolated phenomenon; he sprang from the conditions of his age. So did Hogg and Clare, both peasants, Keats the liveryman's son, Lamb the serving man's, Wordsworth the petty yeoman's, Blake the poor artificer. Such a man as Bamford the weaver might lack their literary gifts, but he was cast in the same mould. Such simple folk thought there was no country like theirs; they felt, as Lord Dudley put it, that "abroad was a poor place compared with England." A Wiltshire peasant, sitting at his door on a summer's evening, recalled how, having heard the parson preach of Paradise, he had made up his mind that "if there was but a good trout-stream

[1] Proceedings of the Dorset Natural History and Antiquaries Field Club, XXXVIII, Rev. H. Pentin, *Dorset Children's Doggerel Rhymes*, 112-52. See also Francis Collinson and Francis Dillon, *Songs of the Countryside*; Ashton, 213-18; Bamford, I, 27, 87, 91, 97; II, 262, 274; Bewick, 52; Broughton, II, 153; Colchester, II, 503; Cooper, 107-10; *Cranbourn Chase*, 107-10; Dixon, 70, 201, 204; Espriella, I, 167; Fowler, 253, 264; H. Lea, *Thomas Hardy's Wessex*, 86; Leigh Hunt, *Autobiography*, II, 15, 207; Keats, IV, 91-2; Lamb, VI, 510-12; VII, 828; Lockhart, IV, 167; V, 16, 40; Dudley, 293-4; Mitford, *Our Village*, 67, 146; *Old Oak*, 187; *Real Life in London*, I, 158; Simond, II, 34, 83, 240.

running down Chicken Grove Bottom, Fernditch Lodge would beat it out and out." Even where the dark mists of industrialism were settling on the northern fells and moors, the love of England's beauty remained strong; the young lovers in Manchester in the early years of the century would seek out and walk together in Tinker's Garden, "then a sweet bowery place."[1]

The first thing that struck every visitor to England was the beauty of the landscape. It derived from her exquisite turf and foliage and soft, aqueous atmosphere: what Leigh Hunt, pining among the Apennines for the buttercup meadows and elms of the vale of Hampstead, called the grassy balm of his native fields. Everywhere was the sense of peace, wealth and security: the avenues of huge elms, the leafy Middlesex landscape, the great trees on Hampstead's airy height, the blue horizons, the farmhouses of beautifully fashioned brick and stone, the pastoral Thames still set, as Horace Walpole had pictured it, amid enamelled meadows and filigree hedges, with brightly-painted barges, solemn as Exchequer barons, moving slowly up to Richmond or down to Syon, the sculptured, classical bridges, the wayside alehouses with placid drinkers under their spreading oaks and chestnuts, the old grey churches and barns, the ghostly trees in the evening twilight, the drinking cattle and homing rooks, the mystery and the mist.

Though England's forests had long been shorn to feed her fleets and furnaces, the sense of fine trees was all-pervading. She was still, as Constable painted her, carpeted with her native hard-woods, which gave moisture to her soil, shade to her cattle and depth and mystery to every horizon. From the terrace at Richmond, or from Harrow hill, one looked across a vast plain from which trees rose in endless waves of blue. Every commentator dwelt on the same phenomenon: the great oaks, the hedgerows of elm and ash, the forest trees scattered about the meadows. Cobbett, stumbling for the first time on the Hampshire hangars, sat motionless on his horse, gazing down on that mighty flood spilling into every valley.

[1] Bamford, I, 102, 187, 195, 199, 209, 219; II, 187, 267; Bewick, 12-13, 31-2, 37-8; Brownlow, 21; Cowper, 22-3; *Cranbourn Chase*, 85-6; *Fraser's Magazine*, XXXI (1845), 192; Granville, I, 436; Haydon, I, 205, 282; Leslie, 228; Dudley, 309; Smith, I, 335.

In Sherwood Forest avenues stretched for miles in every direction, the solitude broken only by the whirring of partridges and pheasants. Cranborne Chase in Dorset had still nearly ten thousand deer; Windsor Forest, Burnham Beeches and Epping, close to the capital, almost as many. In the Berkshire woodlands south of Reading, Mary Mitford described the forest-like closeness—a labyrinth of woody lanes, crossroads and cartways leading up and down hill to farmhouses buried in leaves and wreathed to their clustered chimneys with vines, and little enclosures so closely set with grow-ing timber as to resemble forest glades. One could scarcely peep, she wrote, through the leaves.[1]

Probably at no period was England so beautiful. Man had every-where civilised nature without over-exploiting and spoiling it. The great landscape-painters and water-colourists—Gainsborough, Morland, de Wint, Cozens, Rowlandson, Crome, Cotman, Girton, Turner, Bonington and Constable, the Suffolk miller's son who revolutionised European painting—were the human products of that countryside. Like the poets they were not isolated phenomena but men inheriting, though in expression they transcended, the common feelings of their countrymen. Cobbett, who prided himself on being a plain man with no nonsense about him, travelling from Redbourne to Chesham described how in every field the haymakers had left a closely-mown strip between the hedgerow and the corn; "this," he wrote, "is most beautiful. The hedges are full of shepherd's rose, honeysuckles and all sorts of wild flowers, so that you are upon a grass walk with this most beautiful of all flower-gardens and shrubberies on your one hand and with the corn on the other. And thus you go on from field to field, the sort of corn, the sort of underwood and timber, the shape and size of the fields, the height of the hedgerows, the height of the trees, all continually varying. Talk of pleasure-grounds, indeed!

[1] Mitford, *Our Village* 74-5, 115; *Cranbourn Chase*; Grote, *passim*; Bamford II 98; Cobbett I, 10, 25, 53, 57-9, 91, 121; Cundall, *Byegone Richmond*; Edlin, *Woodland Crafts in Britain*; Howitt 366-92; Old Oak 2-3; Raumer III 136-7; De Selincourt II 886; Simond I 16, 150-3, 201, 335; II 98, 103, 230, 255, 282. Raumer thought that, though England might not be the richest land in forests, she seemed the fullest of trees.

What that man ever invented under the name of pleasure-grounds can equal these fields in Hertfordshire?"

This landscape was constantly being enriched. It was ditched, hoed and hedged to an extent elsewhere unknown. Stacks over forty feet high, meticulously finished and roofed with straw, barns built to outlast the centuries, outhouses, windmills and watermills which were miracles of fine workmanship, sturdy gates and fences made by men who were masters of their craft, were the common-places of the English scene. The thrifty and loving use of nature's resources and the spirit of active and methodical enterprise seemed almost universal. "The white farms, . . . the well-stocked rickyards behind," wrote Mary Mitford, "tell of comfort and order."

Yet every shire, every parish, differed in its farming methods, being cultivated in the way which soil, climate and immemorial experience had proved best. Every district had its particular abundance, the bleak lands as well as the fine. From sandy Norfolk came the enormous turkeys—"the grand Norfolkian holocaust" that at Christmas smoked round Elia's nostrils from a thousand firesides. The stony fields round Bridport were blue with hemp and flax. Salisbury Plain and the Dorset uplands were cropped and fertilised by immense flocks of sheep: "it is the extensive downs in its vicinage," explained the Weymouth guidebook, "which produces the sweetest herbage and gives a peculiarly fine flavour to the mutton." And all over England the folded sheep, fed from the turnip-root, made it possible to grow good crops on marginal lands otherwise too light to bear them: on the Wiltshire downs Cobbett counted four thousand hurdled on a single acre.

The golden creed of "Hoof and Horn," use and return, was the firm and, as it seemed, unalterable base of the country's wealth. The meadows that fed the suckling ewes and lambs in spring yielded hay by midsummer; and, when the corn was cut, the stubble kept the pigs. A Yorkshire squarson—for the very priests were farmers —recorded as the crown of a holiday tour the spectacle of a hundred and twenty shorthorns tethered and fed where they stood in open sheds on successive crops of vetch, mown grass, clover and tares from fields manured by the straw they had soiled. The yields of such rotational agriculture, judged by the standards of other lands, were amazing. The Isle of Wight, with its fine wheat crops, pastures stocked with Alderneys and downs bearing vast flocks of sheep, grew seven times more than its inhabitants consumed. At Milton in the Vale of Pewsey, where three thousand five hundred acres produced annually three thousand quarters of wheat and six thousand of barley and the wool of seven thousand sheep, as well as eggs, milk and poultry, Cobbett reckoned that every labourer raised enough food to support from fifty to a hundred persons.

Necessity acted as a spur. A fast-rising population, which for a generation had been cut off by war from foreign supplies, needed ever more grain, meat and ale and was prepared to pay for it. Landlords and farmers, sowing root crops and clovers, liming, marling and draining, carrying the plough and hurdled sheep to the hills, reclaiming moor and marsh, breeding ever fatter livestock, and pursuing husbandry as a high science, had obtained from the soil the utmost output of which it was capable. The productivity of Norfolk doubled in two decades, largely through the genius of one of its squires, Coke of Holkham, who, working in a smockfrock like a labourer, first taught himself to farm and then taught his tenants. The heaths to the west of London, the haunt from time immemorial of highwaymen, were turned into the finest market gardens. New methods were constantly being tried; horses superseded oxen in the plough, thrashing machines the flail, and drills broadcast-sowing, turnips and swedes eliminated the bare fallow of the past and fed the livestock in winter. "Everyone," wrote a foreigner, "has planted or is planting his thousands or millions of timber trees, has his flocks, talks of turnips, cloves and lucerne, drains and enclosures." Scott took greater pride in his compositions for manure than in his literary ones and boasted that his oaks would outlast his laurels.

This wonderful performance was achieved by organic farming without injury to the permanent capital of the soil. Its object was not to seize the maximum profit from sales against costs in the minimum time, but to secure over the years the highest possible increase from soil, plant and beast. The goal was the productive fertility of the land rather than the immediate saleability of particular crops in relation to costs: output per acre instead of output per wage-earner. The farming was multi-, never mono-cultural, and much of the all-pervading plenty arose from by-products like the snow-white ducks of the Vale of Aylesbury. "Whenever cows are kept, so must pigs," wrote a country gentleman, "or the profit of buttermilk and whey will be lost." The finely thatched roofs of the cottages and barns were made from the combed straw left over by the threshers. When timber was cut, a temporary shed was erected round it so that every piece could be worked for the exact purpose for which it was suited, without leaving a splinter on the ground.[1]

. . . .

The value of farm land soared with its use. In the decade between Trafalgar and Waterloo Lord Aberdeen's rents doubled. Arable land in the Wye Valley, which in the seventeen-eighties had sold for ten pounds an acre, was letting by 1814 at forty shillings and selling at thirty years' purchase. In the Lothians of Scotland, formerly the poorest of western European countries, rents rose more than fourfold in a generation. In the Vale of Festiniog, where embankment had been carried out by the gentry, rents had gone up from seven shillings to three guineas an acre, in parts of Essex from ten to fifty shillings, in Berkshire and Wiltshire from fourteen to seventy shillings. At the summit of the boom in the last years of the war land could scarcely be bought at all.

No class had ever enjoyed such riches as the English landed gentry. "I have no occasion to think of the price of bread and meat where I am now," wrote Jane Austen from Godmersham; "let me shake off vulgar cares and conform to the happy indifference of East Kent wealth!" In Cheshire alone there were fifty landed estates of from £3000 to £10,000 a year, with a purchasing power

[1] Bamford II 21, 260; Bewick 8, 155; Clapham I 15-19; Cobbett, *Rural Rides* I 19-21, 24, 49, 87-9, 108; II 363-6; Lord Coleridge 223-4; *Cranbourn Chase* 47, 65-7; Daniel VII 36; Eland 50, 64, 97-101; Ernle 190-223, 225; Fowler 241; Grote 19-21, 24; Hamilton of Dalzell MS. 151-6; Howitt 109-11, 125; Lamb VI; 480; Lockhart IV 263-4; Mitford, *Our Village* 32, 104-5; Newton 184-8, 195; Paget Brothers 180-1, 271-2; Lady Shelley I 38; Simond I 13, 170-1, 181-2, 195, 206, 209, 216, 239, 330-2; II, 54, 72, 75-6, 223, 242, 245, 291; Smart 138-50; Wansey 22.

equivalent to an untaxed income of nine or ten times as much in present money. The greatest of all commanded revenues larger than those of reigning continental princes; in July, 1813, the United States, then at war with Britain, was unable to borrow as much money as more than one English nobleman could raise on his private credit. The Duke of Northumberland's annual rental was over £150,000; the owner of Berkeley Castle's £180,000. Four-fifths of the House of Commons and almost the entire hereditary personnel of the House of Lords were landowners. Such was the respect for landed wealth that Englishmen felt reluctance in entrusting political power to any man without it; Creevey, a radical Whig without birth or means, wrote with contempt of Canning and Lord Wellesley as "fellows without an acre," comparing them with his own Party's princely leaders, "the Earl Grey, . . . the Russells and the Cavendishes and all the ancient nobility and all the great property of the realm."

As one travelled the country one saw that illimitable wealth: "farmhouses in sight everywhere, . . . large fields fresh ploughed black and smooth, others ploughing, always with horses, never with oxen; farmers riding among their workmen, great flocks of sheep confined by net-fences in turnip fields, meadows . . . of the most brilliant green." At the autumnal sheep fair at Weyhill more than a quarter of a million pounds changed hands annually to be borne home by plaided shepherds or their top-booted, blue-coated masters who gathered over the "ordinary" in the White Hart. At Falkirk Fair a tenant of Lord Egremont's bought twelve thousand head of cattle with £30,000 Bank of England bills carried in his pockets. A man who could raise prize bullocks or grow outsize turnips did not need a pedigree; in their passion for agricultural improvement the English even forgot to be snobs. After local ploughing competitions and cart-horse trials the worthies of a whole county, gentle and common, would dine together to discuss over roast beef and October ale the methods they had successfully pursued. The Duke of Bedford's or Coke of Norfolk's annual sheep-shearing were events as important as the Derby or the meeting of parliament. Coke's rustic palace, Holkham, became a place of pilgrimage that rivalled Walsingham in the age of faith: the interminable drive, the triumphal arch, the lakes, the woods, the obelisk, the distant view of the sea, the overawed Norfolk church peering through its modest cluster of trees, the exquisite changes of autumnal leaf as the shooting parties, in green and buff and brown, moved like regiments across the landscape, the coverts with never-ending partridges rising out of wastes of sand bearded with stunted corn, and, all around, the wilderness flowering like a garden.[1]

All this abundance, though directed by landlords and farmers applying the knowledge gleaned from the great agricultural experiments of the past three generations, was founded on the plentiful labour of an hereditary race of husbandmen bred in the cumulative lore of centuries. In a single field in East Lothian a traveller counted forty-eight reapers; near Bury St. Edmunds he saw ten ploughs turning at the same hedge. In haymaking time squads of labourers moved from tract to tract, leaving the fields cleared behind them, the mowers going before with their scythes, the haymakers following. There were gangs of boys to pull the charlock and keep the land clean, and women to pick stones, weed, reap and glean.

These skilful, simple and generous-hearted men, with the gaunt bony frames, slow gait and stolid, patient eyes, followed husbandry in all its branches, including wood-cutting, hurdling, thatching and sheep-shearing. Their industry was prodigious. They worked from first light till dusk; in a day a good dibbler would sow a bushel and a peck, and a mower cover two acres. They wasted little or nothing; a reaper with his sickle would cut the ears of corn with so short a straw that scarcely a weed found its way into the sheaf. In their spare time—often only achieved after a walk of

[1] "This is probably the only country in the world where people make fortunes by farming. A farmer who understands his business becomes rich in England with the same degree of certainty as in other professions, whilst in most countries a farmer is condemned by the nature of his trade to be a mere labourer all his life." Simond I, 174. See Aberdeen I 30; Arbuthnot I 12; Austen II 243; Clapham I 223; Creevey, *Life and Times* 55; Cobbett, I 49, 97-8; Dixon 241-1, 248-52; Dudley 211; Ernle 195-223; Farington VII 174; Hamilton of Dalzell MS. 151-4; Howitt 88-106; Newton 107-8; *Paget Brothers* 179-81; Shakerley MSS.; Smart 153-4; Toynbee 92; Woodward 87.

several miles home—they kept pigs and bees and cultivated their gardens, those long irregular slips with gooseberry bushes, neatly tended vegetables and flowers, which Cobbett thought distinguished England from the rest of the world; "we have only to look at these gardens to know what sort of people English labourers are."[1]

While their husbands and fathers toiled in the fields, the wives and children at home added their own contribution to England's wealth. They worked at the loom, made lace, buttons, string, netting, pack-thread and gloves, and plaited straw into a thousand useful and beautiful shapes. In season they tramped into the woods or orchards to gather fuel, nuts and fruit, or worked in gangs in the hay and harvest fields. In the pasture lands the unmarried women watched and milked cows, going out in traditional fashion with cans balanced on their heads and wooden milking-stools in their hands. Their younger brothers, in patched round smocks, took service on the farms at eight or nine years of age, learning their fathers' lore and working as long as their elders. For all their hard usage they seemed healthy and happy—"wild, nimble, glee-some beings," as Bamford, looking back, remembered: the "open, spirited, good-humoured race" of Mary Mitford's village, with brown and ruddy cheeks and merry eyes, always ready for a bird's nesting or a game of cricket, "batting, bowling and fielding as if for life" at the end of twelve or fourteen hours' field labour.[2] They grew up to be farmers' boys or "chaw-bacons"—bucolic, round-faced, hardy—the "clods" of whom the county regiments were made which held the ridge at Waterloo. With their grey slouch hats, bright neck-cloths and ribbons and proverbial pitch-forks, they could be seen in the aggregate at the hiring fairs in the county towns or at the traditional farm feasts of harvest and sheep-shearing.

The farm labourer's work was supplemented by a host of rustic

[1] Cobbett I 81; Clapham I 199-201; Eland 21, 70-1, 127-8; Grote 22-3; Howitt 107-18; Mitford, *Our Village* 7-8, 14, 43, 65; Newton 188; Simond I 181, 184; II 86, 293.

[2] Witnesses as temperamentally unlike as Mary Mitford, William Howitt, Samuel Bamford the handloom weaver and Mrs. Grote of East Burnham, wife of the famous radical, paint the same picture from close personal observation in four different counties. So do the great water-colourists.

craftsmen. The drover with his lacquer-back curry-comb, the swearing carter, the shepherd with his dog and crook and eye watchful for tick, foot-rot or blow-fly, the wood-cutters, sawyers, hurdlers, spoke-choppers, faggoters, rake and ladder-makers of the forest lands, the village blacksmiths, saddlers, tailors, wheelwrights, masons, carpenters, glaziers, millwrights, carriers, shoemakers and pedlars who kept the rustic economy self-sufficient, were part of an army many times larger than Wellington's and without which his could neither have been recruited nor maintained. Many were craftsmen of exquisite quality, like Miss Mitford's humble neighbour, "famed ten miles round and worthy all his fame," whom few cabinet-makers, even in London, surpassed. England's wealth rested on the fact that they were able and willing in their lifetime of unresting work to do so much in return for the food, clothing, shelter and modest comfort which in all ages, whatever the nominal money-level of wages and prices, remains the reward of manual labour. The nation which employed them received for their keep a *per capita* return in skill and industry probably greater than that enjoyed by any other in history.

Outside their homely circle, yet auxiliary to it, were the independent *tirailleurs* of the industry—the vermin-catchers with their skin caps, gaiters and leather bags, the samphire and herb-gatherers of the cliffs and moors, the twine-makers of the Derbyshire caves, the hurdle-makers of Cranborne Chase and the bodgers of the Chilterns, the dog-breakers and gamekeepers, understrappers and wild rovers who were all to be found labouring in their place and season. These, too, were masters of their crafts, like the rat-catcher in the *Romany Rye* who described his trade as the best in the world and the most diverting and one that was likely to last for ever. So were the raggle-taggle gipsies—makers of saucepans and basket-weavers—encamped with their ponies and beautifully painted caravans in the dingles and grassy rides. "Can you," ran their song,

> "speak the Romany tongue?
> Can you make the fiddle ring?
> Can you poison a jolly hog
> And split the stick for the linen string?"

A grade higher in the national economy were the yeomen—
the men who worked and owned, whether by freehold or copyhold, their own land. They ranged from the great Norfolk yeoman, ninety years old and worth £90,000, whom Borrow remembered riding into Norwich in a white corduroy suit and snuff-
coloured greatcoat, to the "smock-frock farmer" who entertained
the Romany Rye on a holding of two acres cultivated with four
kinds of grain—wheat, barley, peas and beans—and whose garden,
pollinated by bees, was as full of scents as an orange grove. Such
men knew how to keep themselves and their families self-sufficient,
quartering their lands in husbandly rotation and manuring them
from the cow, mare, foal, sow and poultry that filled their little
yards, fortressed round by hayrick, beanstack, wheatrick and
orchard. They followed the plough and carted muck like labourers,
while their wives handled the churn, pressed curd in cheese-pan,
boiled whey, salted and turned cheese, fed calves, geese, turkeys
and fowls, and, seated on a stuffed sack, jogged weekly to market,
bringing up their children in the process and starching flounces and
shirt-frills for their richer neighbours. On such holdings the whole
family worked without cessation but enjoyed liberty and a share of
the good things they created. They were most numerous in the
unenclosed north, where the "statesmen" of Westmorland and
Wensleydale lived in grey mossy stone houses on the hillsides;
" to this day," wrote Bewick, recalling them in old age, "I can see
their broad shoulders and their hardy sunburnt looks." Historically
speaking, the yeomen were fast declining, but in 1815 between a
quarter and a fifth of England's farmlands was still owned and
cultivated by them. Their greatest contribution was the immense
quantity of poultry, ducks and geese they kept on the commons
and marginal lands; Cobbett saw ten thousand on a single common
between Chobham and Farnham. What they did not eat themselves they sold to feed the nearest town, setting up their standings
of butter, eggs, poultry and vegetables in the market place. Like
their neighbours, the cottage labourers, they also kept pigs fed on
household waste and surplus milk products.

With the agricultural changes which were uprooting them, the
yeomen were yielding to the large tenant-farmers who paid the

rents that supported the aristocratic splendour and display of the English capital and country-houses. Some of these farmed a thousand or more acres, employed sixty or seventy labourers and kept hunters and banking accounts—a thing almost unknown on the continent. They laid out lawns and shrubbed gardens before their substantial farmhouses and had their daughters taught the piano. They would sometimes pay more for a prize-bull or blood-stallion than their fathers had handled in a year. Such a one was Thomas Bates of Halton, later of Kirklevington, who laid the foundation of his herd of shorthorns in 1810 with a cow bought for 185 guineas. To their landlords, though not always to their labourers, they seemed fine fellows "who talked of beef and ate pudding and drank like true-born Britons." Ruddy and broad of beam, in their blue tailcoats, kersey small-clothes, top boots and waistcoats of crimson or yellow swansdown, they represented the very substance of the England of their time; John Bull himself in his hour of thriving. "Everything prospers with him," wrote Mary Mitford, "money drifts about him like snow. . . . There is a sturdy squareness of face and figure and a good-humoured obstinacy, a civil importance. He never boasts of his wealth or gives himself undue airs; but nobody can meet him at market or vestry without finding him the richest man there." The same observer drew the greatest farmer of them all, as she remembered him in the closing years of the war at his massive red house at Botley by Bursledon river. "I never saw," she wrote, "hospitality more genuine. . . . There was not the slightest attempt at finery or display of gentility, and everything was in accordance with the largest idea of an English yeoman of the old time. They called it a farmhouse and . . . everything was excellent, everything abundant —all served with the greatest nicety by trim waiting damsels." The garden was full of wonderful wall-fruit, Indian corn, Caroline beans and water-melons, and glowing in the autumn sun with pyramids of holly-hocks and masses of China-asters, cloves, mignonettes and ger-anium. Over all towered Cobbett himself, tall, stout, sunburnt, with his good-humoured face and never-tiring activity, rising at dawn to mow the lawn with a giant's sweep and rewarding the first of his children downstairs and at work in farm or garden with

the coveted title of lark of the day and the privilege of making his
mother's nosegay.

· · · · · · · · · ·

In one of his outbursts against the social changes that were
destroying the England of his youth Cobbett declared that, though
no theologian, he loved any religion that gave men plenty to eat
and drink. In this he spoke for his country. The English ate as
though eating were an act of grace; the very sick were prescribed
beefsteaks and port. They ate more than any people because they
grew more. A Hampshire farmer at his wedding dinner fed his
guests on fare all raised from his own land: beef, fowls, a gammon
of bacon and a sucking pig, a green goose, river-fish, plum-pudding,
apple-pie, cheese-cakes, custards, home-brewed beer, home-made
wine and sillabub. From the wholemeal bread baked at home
according to some immemorial family recipe to the oysters which
the seamen of the Ratcliffe Highway ate with such relish on their
holidays, the English enjoyed the best of everything. Their seas
afforded harvests as rich as their fields; the submarine plants round
their shores sustained the world's finest eating fish, and cross-
Channel passengers, wind-bound off the Kentish coast, would
borrow lines from the captain and fill their baskets with whiting,
mackerel and gurnet.

England's fat cattle were among the wonders of the age. On
feast days the roast beef of Old England was eaten with musical
honours, and legislators rounded off debates in Bellamy's kitchen
at Westminster with beefsteaks broiled over a clear, strong fire and
served hot, juicy and tender. Borrow thought that nothing in
nature surpassed a leg of Welsh mutton, "rich but delicate, replete
with juices derived from the aromatic herbs of the noble Berwyn
and cooked to a turn." The verdure that raised such meat produced
also the butter and cheeses, the delicious draughts from the can
which the Manchester handloom weavers bought on Sunday
rambles from their loves, the milkmaids of Hoolswood and Gerrard-
hey, the curds and clotted cream which Mother Hundrell, the
Devonshire milk-woman, gave little Thomas Cooper and of which
he used to dream in hungrier years. "Then we went to the dairy,"

wrote a young Englishwoman, "so fresh and cool and clean—glittering with cleanliness, overflowing with dreamy riches! And there I had the greatest enjoyment of my whole day, the printing with my own hands a pat of butter."

Every part of the island had its peculiar delicacies: Norfolk dumpling, Lincolnshire acelet and collared eel, Oxford John, Dee salmon, Pegwell Bay shrimps, Banbury cake, Mansfield gooseberry pie, Isle of Wight crabs, and the great regional cheeses—Stilton, and Cheddar, Cheshire, Double Gloucester, Blue Vinney, Lancashire Leigh, York, Colwick and Wensleydale. It was not surprising that bulging veins, mottled noses and what was politely termed a full habit were common among the English upper and middle classes. Statesmen, judges, merchants, poets, all engaged in the national vice of stuffing; when Coleridge dined with a rich friend in the victory summer of 1814, it was on turbot, lobster sauce, boiled fowls, turtle, ham, a quarter of lamb and cauliflowers, ducks, green peas, a gooseberry and currant pie, a soft pudding, grapes, pineapples, strawberries, cherries, champagne, burgundy and madeira. Charles Lamb, celebrating the glories of roast pig, was writing for a ready public. Even divines shared the ruling passion; Dr. Paley, author of the *Evidences*, always ate everything on the table and finished with a raid on the side dishes which he called skirmishing.[1]

It was not everyone who fared so well. Though agricultural improvements and expanding trade enabled the country to support a far larger population, as London and the factory towns grew the feeding standards of the poor tended to fall. Comparatively speaking, England was growing poorer in food-wealth as she grew richer in other and machine-made forms of wealth. By 1815 it was no longer true, as Defoe had claimed a century earlier, that the English labourer ate and drank three times more than any foreigner.

---

[1] Farington VIII 180; Bamford I 109, 143, 154, 168, 188, 217; II 330; Borrow, *Wild Wales* 47; Brownlow 125; Cobbett, *Cottage Economy* 98; Coleridge, *Unpublished Letters* II 122; Cooper 5; Eland 12, 23; *English Spy* II 98; Fowler I 251; Gronow I, 217-18; Howitt 91-6; Leigh Hunt II 65; Jekyll and Jones 109; Lamb I 35; Mytton 18-10; Newton 122-3; Osbaldeston 30; Raumer III 142-3; Simond I 8, 22, 284; II 35, 169, 242.

Five times during the war, with the Baltic closed to her ships the harvest had failed, and under her dazzling appearance of wealth England faced famine and the shadow of social collapse. Though the rich and middle classes suffered little, those who lived largely on bread were reduced almost to starvation, for the price of grain fluctuated widely. "For two seasons," wrote a poor dyer, "the corn was spoiled in the fields with wet, and when the winter came we would scoop out the middle of the soft distasteful loaf; and to eat it brought on sickness." Such seasons fell with particular severity on the manufacturing districts where the workers, divorced from the land, were dependent on shop prices and where, at the height of the continental blockade, there had appeared a new phenomenon, mass-unemployment, which temporarily deprived whole populations—producing for export instead of subsistence—of the wherewithal to buy. Scarcity prices for grain, too, while benefiting the landlord and farmer, hit, with what seemed a monstrous injustice, the landless labourer in the enclosed villages of the east midlands. For having forfeited his ancient manorial rights, he had lost with them the grain, grazing and firewood which had formerly enabled him, regardless of price and wage levels, to provide his own milk, eggs, poultry and cooking fuel.

Yet in the worst times the dietary of the English had never fallen to the dreadful level of many parts of Europe where periodically starvation and typhus took toll of thousands. Frederic Eden, in his survey of the condition of the poor made during the famine years of 1795 and 1796, analysed the budget of a Leicester wool-comber with two children, who, out of an income of £47 a year, made up of his own and his wife's and elder son's earnings and an £11 grant from the Poor Law guardians, was able to buy weekly ten pounds of butcher's meat, two pounds of butter, three and a half of cheese and about nineteen pints of milk, as well as potatoes, vegetables, tea, sugar and beer. He was not even a particularly industrious man, for he was said to spend several days every month in the alehouse lamenting the hardness of the times. Another case instanced by Eden was that of a Manchester dyer who only earned, with his wife's help, £42 p.a., yet bought five pounds of meat weekly. Even in the workhouses meat usually figured on the dietary three or four days a week. When six Lancashire weavers were consigned by the Home Office to the Cold Bath Fields prison on a charge of treason, they were allowed between them for breakfast six pound-loaves of bread, two pounds of butter, two of sugar and one of tea, for dinner a quarter of pork with vegetables, potatoes and a pot of porter apiece, and for supper cold meat and tea. On another day they were given a leg of mutton weighing thirteen and a half pounds.

Using the measuring-rod of what was customary in his youth, Cobbett reckoned that an English working-class family of five—father, mother, baby, and two growing children—needed daily five pounds of bread, two pounds of bacon, one pound of mutton and a gallon and a half of beer. But though in Kent before the war the farm-worker had enjoyed meat almost daily, in enclosed villages bread, cheese and ale had come to form the labourer's main dietary. In normal seasons there was, however, as much of these as a man could eat or carry with him into the fields. And many cottagers still continued to keep a pig; ham and eggs and "a bit of frizzle" figure with cheering frequency in Bamford's account of his early days of poverty. William Howitt once saw bacon ten inches thick on a farm servant's breakfast, flanked by a peck of boiled beans and a brown loaf the size of a beehive. Country folk still baked and brewed at home; the oven, like the porch and tank, was part of the peasant's birthright. So were the ale brewed in the copper, the mead, sweet and mellow but strong as brandy, made from home-raised honey, the cowslip and other rustic wines distilled from traditional recipes and drunk on special occasions. The old skills and habits were dying out with enclosure, but large numbers of country workers still quenched their thirst on untaxed ale of their own making. And what they bought in the alehouse, if not always wholesome, was at least strong and cheap: an old Buckinghamshire labourer declared he didn't think nothing of no beer if it didn't give him three falls for a shilling. A poor man could drink his skinful; Jack Birt, the Berkshire shepherd in *Our Village*, had a pot of double X placed before his sheepdog, Watch, every evening.[1]

[1] Cobbett I 82. See Austen 27; Bamford I 60, 120-1, 129-30, 152, 157, 208,

In the north the staple food of the poor was oatmeal crowdie, riddle and girdle-cakes, porridge with buttermilk, pease-kail, dumpling, oaten jannocks and barley-bread, butter, treacle and plentiful milk. Thomas Bewick, who grew up among the Northumbrian peasantry, reckoned that, though they lived almost entirely on oatmeal, barley cakes, broth, potatoes and milk, they enjoyed better health than any men he knew. The Duke of Argyll recalled how as a boy he watched the farmhands eating their breakfast with spoons and mugs of horn out of a bowl of steaming porridge as big as a footbath. "I went to rest betimes," wrote Bamford, describing his early dietary, "and rose clear-headed and with a strength and buoyancy of limb that mocked toil and weariness." The same witness has left the picture of a Lancashire weaving family's meals at the beginning of the century: the brown earthenware dish on a low table, the breakfast of boiling water-porridge poured into it from the pan, the children standing round, each with his spoon, oaten-cake and dish of milk, the fatherly blessing before the eager, silent feast; the dinners of crisp-crusted potato pie, dumpling, meat-broth or butcher's meat taken in the same patriarchal fashion, the meat apportioned to each child on a piece of oatcake, the potatoes poured into the central dish from which all helped themselves until it was empty, after which the children stole out to their play munching the remnants of meat and cake. And all the while not a word was spoken.

After the Baltic had been reopened by Nelson's victory at Copenhagen, and again after 1812 until the end of the war, there was a period of full employment and prosperity. "The tables of mechanics," William Howitt recalled, "were heaped with loads of viands of the best quality and highest price; their houses were crowded with furniture, . . . publicans and keepers of tea-gardens made fortunes."[1] Though the peasants in the south—the last to

---

217; II 212, 279; Berwick 73; Clapham I 118, 170-1, 316-17; Lord Coleridge 233-4, Eden 107; Fowler I 25, 251; Gronow II 299; Grote 21; Howitt 115-16; Lockhart IV 194; *Old Oak* 36; De Selincourt II 878; Simond I, 256; II 224; Woodward 9.
[1] For some contemporary accounts of the dazzling appearance of rural pros-

benefit from all this prosperity—tended to be small and rather pale, suggesting to one foreign observer that, for all their neat appearance, they were better dressed than fed, there was about the race an unmistakable air of health and good living; an Italian lady was amazed by the beauty of the adventuresses in the theatres. The country lasses whom Louis Simond saw as he travelled through Lancashire had rosy cheeks, cherry lips, fine shapes and arms red as apples. The carpenter's daughter in *Our Village* was "of square, sturdy, upright form with the finest limbs in the world, a complexion purely English, a round, laughing face, sunburnt and rosy, large, merry, blue eyes, curling brown hair and a wonderful play of countenance."

To those who visited England after the fall of Napoleon there seemed, indeed, about her people an almost insulting opulence. The verminous tatters of the continental peasantry had no part in this tidy countryside; the cottage wives in their grey stuff gowns, woollen petticoats and checked aprons contrasted with the wretched, ragged appearance of the Flemish women that so shocked Dorothy Wordsworth in the Low Countries. Such distress as existed was tucked away out of sight; one had, wrote Simond, who spent two years towards the end of the war studying the country's institutions, to go out and seek it. In sixty miles between Ormskirk and Kendal the only signs of it he could see were a few itinerant paupers—a crippled old man or a widow with a swarm of barefooted children—tramping back to their place of settlement. Their menfolk did not go about in bare feet; except in the north, where the clogs on the cobbles was traditional music, even wooden shoes were regarded as symbols of poverty and popery. What particularly struck one foreigner were the scarlet cloaks and black silk bonnets of the country women in the market towns. "When a class, so inferior, is so well dressed, who can doubt," he asked, "of

perity which England presented to foreign visitors, see Bury, I, 242; Colchester, II, 502; Lord Coleridge, 223-4; Simond, I, 3, 10, 14, 16, 146-7, 201-2, 206; II, 86, 100, 224, 228, 235, 246, 254, 283; Leigh Hunt, *Autobiography*, II, 154; Bamford, I, 94; Lady Shelley, I, 1-3; Washington Irving, *Sketch Book*; Don Juan, Canto X; Wansey, 115.

the prosperity and comfort of the nation to which it belongs?"

Jolly country squires, beautifully mounted, with huge boots, snowy shirt-frills and wide overcoats with capacious pockets; red-faced merchants and farmers in low-crowned, broad-brimmed hats and tail-coats of blue, buff or brown; clergymen and lawyers in black silk gowns; sailors in reefer jackets with mother-of-pearl buttons, straw hats and loose white canvas trousers; mechanics in striped shirts and leather aprons; gamekeepers in green coats and gold-laced hats; drovers in dark green slops with tin vessels jangling at their sides to catch the ewes' "milk of the plains"; farmers' wives and milkmaids wearing combs and earrings, all spoke of the diversity, wealth and cohesion of English society. The field labourer's wear was a straw hat and a round smock frock—blue, tawny or olive-green, but usually white—worn over leggings, breeches and doublet. Beautifully hemmed and embroidered, such smocks were perfectly adapted for out-of-door work; Jane Austen's mother used to wear a green one for gardening. Most Englishmen at their callings dressed in clothes of the stoutest quality; yeomen in fustian coats, corduroy breeches and ribbed worsted stockings, brewers in quilted coats of immense thickness; fishermen in striped jerseys, grey aprons, leather leggings, top-boots and fur-lined caps; firemen in horse-hide lined with leather, quilted with wool and strengthened with metal. A Lancashire handloom weaver's working garb was a green woollen waistcoat with a silk neckerchief, his wife's a white linen mob cap, a cotton bed-gown and petticoat, a striped calico apron and black hose and shoes. A young girl went to the Wakes in a "gown made wi' tucks and fleaunces, new shoon wi' ston op heels, new stokins wi' clocks, a tippet wi' frills o reawnd, manny a streng of necklaces, an a bonnit made by th' new manty-maker, the prattyist at ever wur seen, wi' a skyoy blue underside and pink ribbins." Even servant maids sometimes wore silk on Sundays, when the lanes were full of girls showing off their new pumps, caps and ribbons. And the vagrant gipsies with their scarlet cloaks and bright tents and caravans were as colourful as the cottage gardens. Mr. Petulengro sported a smartly cut coat with half-crowns for buttons, a scarlet and black waistcoat sewn with guineas, stuff velveteen breeches and fur boots, a silver-knobbed riding whip and a high Spanish hat.[1]

English houses impressed foreigners like their food and clothes. Every traveller noted the contrast between the beggars and rural hovels on the continent and the neat Kentish and Sussex villages—"our own land of fair and handsome faces, well-fed inhabitants, richly cultivated and enclosed fields," as Harry Smith, returning from the wars, called it. Village greens with shouting children and fat geese, white-washed cottages grouped round church and manor-house, roses, honeysuckle and jessamine festooned over porch and casement, gardens full of flowers and embowered in trees, gave travellers the impression that the poor lived better than they did. So did the clean-scrubbed floors of the cottage interiors, the gleaming oak and copper, the inns with their neat, sanded parlours and plentiful fare. "This," reported a French American, "is the land of conveniences." After more than a year travelling the country he found, at Barnsley, its first bad inn, and even this, he thought, would have been deemed excellent in France.[2]

In the south the countryman's cottage was generally of stone or brick, half-cast and timber, with a thatched roof and from three to four rooms. It was built of local materials blending with the landscape. The casements, Simond noted, instead of being left open

[1] *Lavengro*, 36, 319-20; Ashton, II, 220-1; Bamford, I, 30, 71, 94, 107, 132, 211-12, 214; II, 56-7,259, 333; Clapham, I, 315-17; Cobbett, I, 17, 43, 53, 81; De Selincourt, *Middle Years*, II, 883; Eden, 108-9; Hill, *Austen*, 177; Howitt, 108, 117, 184; Newton, 166; Pyne, *Costume of Great Britain* (1808); Romany Rye, 44; Lady Shelley, I, 287; Simond, I, 3, 14, 181-2, 184, 226, 256; II, 224, 226, 256, 297.

[2] Ashton, II, 220-1; Bamford, I, 43, 94, 99, 209-11, 214, 219; II, 68-9, 260, 331, 333; Bury, I, 242, 245, 263; II, 15; Clapham, I, 220; Cobbett, I, 43, 61, 81; Colchester, II, 502; Lord Coleridge, 223-4; Cooper, 16, 19-20; De Selincourt, II, 283, 883; Dino, 165; Eland, 12, 19; Farington, VII, 125; VIII, 197; Lady Holland, I, 105, 320; Howitt, 131, 202-3, *et passim*; W. Irving, *Sketch Book*; Jekyll and Jones, 51, 80, 98; *Lavengro*, 2, 330; Leigh Hunt, *Autobiography*, II 153-4; Letts, 65, 211-12; Meidinger, I, 315-17; Mercer, I, 37; Mitford, *Our Village*, 7-9, 14, 16-18, 32, 43, 65, 70-1, 74-5; *Old Oak*, 57-68; *Romany Rye*, 65, 162-3, 175-8; Lady Shelley, I, 287; Simond, I, 2, 3, 10, 12-15, 16, 17, 217, 221-2, 225-6, 256, 297, 338, 354; II, 56, 62, 78, 86, 115, 146, 182, 201, 224, 228, 234-5, 245-6, 251-2, 283, 297; Smith, I, 108, 334-5.

to the weather or stuck up with rags, as on the continent and in
America, were leaded and glazed. In the far north and west, where
far lower standards prevailed, single-room turf-cabins of the continental type were common. Yet even these were usually white-
washed and had casements with gardens and flowers, indicating, a
traveller thought, a remarkable degree of comfort among the
labouring classes. The interiors were furnished with elm and oak
settles, tables and chairs, iron-hooped harvest bottles, pewter and
stoneware utensils, shelves for cheeses, herbs and bunches of yarn,
and on the walls brass bosses, horses' face-pieces and coloured
plumes and streamers. The homes of the better-to-do weavers on
either side of the southern Pennines—daub and timber cottages
with low wooden latches overhanging crystal streams, or stone
houses in rows on the hillsides, with open doors "inviting the
stranger to glance at their neatness, cleanliness and felicity"—usually
had a room in front, a loom-shop behind and two or three sleeping
chambers above, or else a large loft where the family worked. At
Leek the silk workers occupied airy, well-furnished apartments
approached by stairs, with carpets and oil-cloths; Cobbett passing
through Durham and Yorkshire noted the excellence of the miners'
and cutlers' homes. "There were a dozen good rush-bottomed
chairs, the backs and rails bright with wax and rubbing," wrote a
weaver's apprentice of his master's house, "a handsome clock in a
mahogany case, a good chest of drawers, a mahogany corner-
cupboard all well polished, besides tables, weather-glass, cornice
and ornaments and pictures illustrative of Joseph and his brethren."[1]

[1] Howitt 107, 131-3, 202-3; Ann. Reg. 1816, Chron. III; Ashton II 220-1;
Bamford I 43, 94, 99, 209-11, 214, 219; II 33, 68-9, 260, 331, 333; Bury I 242,
245, 263; II 15; Clapham I 28-9, 32-3, 36-7, 230; Cobbett I 43, 61, 81; Col-
chester II, 502; Lord Coleridge 223-4; Cooper 16, 19-20; Daniell I 28-9, 31;
Darvall 31-2; Dino 165; Eland 12, 19, 21-2; Farington VII 125; VIII 197;
Lady Holland I 105, 320; Howitt 107, 132-3, 202-3; W. Irving, Sketch Book;
Jekyll and Jones 51, 80, 98, 100; Leigh Hunt, Autobiography II 153-4; Leslie,
Constable 84; Letts 65, 211-12; Meidinger I 315-17; Mercer I 37; Mitford, Our
Village 7-9, 14, 16-18, 32, 43, 65, 70-1, 74-5; Old Oak 48, 57-68; Lady Shelley I
287; Simond I 2, 3, 10, 12-15, 16-17, 217, 221-2, 225-6, 256, 297, 338, 354; II
56, 62, 78, 80, 115, 146, 182, 201, 224, 228, 234-5, 245-6, 251-2, 283, 297; Smith
I 108, 334-5; Woodward 9.

Where the labourers' homes were neat and those of farmers snug, the houses of the gentry were princely. Almost every parish possessed at least one fine seat on which successive generations of skilled builders, craftsmen and gardeners had been employed by a connoisseurship which scarcely ever lacked taste and a sense of proportion. In most, the impress was classical; the lore of the ancient world and Renaissance Italy had been ransacked by the landowning classes and applied with innumerable insular and local variations, Palladian, Baroque, Rococo and, more lately, Pompeian and Grecian principles being blended with the national genius for diversity and the pastoral background of hill, grove and stream. Others, like the cottages and farms at their gates, were relics of a less sophisticated and purely native culture. Such was the many-gabled black and white mansion of Lady Shelley's Lancashire childhood with the family arms carved in stone over the door, or the old hall at Middleton built of plaster and framework, with its massive beams and black oak carvings and walls hung with matchlocks, swords and trophies of the chase. Many of these older houses had fallen into decay or become farms like moated Parham in Suffolk and Boston Hall in the fens, their rafters exposed, the gilding peeling off the galleries, the vast doors and chests turned to humble rustic purposes, cooking utensils hanging on nails which had held the swords of crusaders, and pigs and chickens ranging the uneven floors. Owing to a new craze for romantic antiquities those that were still lived in by their owners were surprisingly becoming objects of new interest; the house-party in *Mansfield Park* made an expedition to view the beauties of Sotherton, though its improving owner intended to up-root the avenue and modernise the gardens *à la Repton*.

The most impressive thing about England's country houses was their number. They ranged from palaces like Blenheim, Petworth and Castle Howard to unassuming residences of pilastered stone, brick or white stucco little bigger than the houses of the professional classes in the county towns, but set amid the common denominators of park, lawn and drive. They were, above everything else, the distinguishing ornament of the landscape. A gentleman stranded on the road could be sure of shelter under the roof of one of his own kind, where he would find, though with infinite variations, the same classical or Gothic architecture, the same fine furniture of mahogany, walnut and rosewood, the same oriental carpets and china and their English counterparts, the same ancestral worthies in gilded frames flanked by masterpieces or pseudo-masterpieces from Italy and Holland, the same libraries of leather-bound books containing the solid culture of three centuries. And outside would be the cedars, the close-mown lawns, the flower-beds, conservatories and ice-houses, the vistas cunningly blending the artificial with the natural, lawns, park, water merging into the landscape which they commanded and to which they belonged.

Such houses were maintained in flawless order. The Earl of Bridgewater at Ashridge employed five hundred men in his gardens, conservatories and workshops. Nothing was allowed to be slovenly; everything was planned to give the highest possible return in elegance and comfort. The gardens of Jane Austen's Northanger Abbey had countless walls, villages of hot-houses and potting-sheds, and a whole parish at work on them. Nor was the author drawing on her imagination; when she and her mother visited cousins at Stoneleigh Abbey the house was so large that they were unable to find their way about. It had forty-five windows in front, several drawing-rooms, dining-rooms, parlours, galleries and staircases, all hung with velvets, brocades and family portraits, twenty-six bed-chambers in the new part of the building and more in the old. "Every part of the house and offices," wrote Mrs. Austen, "is kept so clean that were you to cut your finger I do not think you could find a cobweb to wrap it up in. In the kitchen garden the quantity of small fruit exceeds anything you can form an idea of. This large family, with the assistance of a great many blackbirds and thrushes, cannot prevent it from rotting on the trees. The ponds supply excellent fish, the park excellent venison; there is a great quantity of rabbits, pigeons and all sorts of poultry. There is a delightful dairy where is made butter, good Warwickshire cheese and cream. One manservant is called the baker and does nothing but brew and bake. The number of casks in the strong-beer cellar is beyond imagination."

In the country house an elaborately graded system existed in which every man and woman had his or her place. At Wentworth Woodhouse seventy sat down every day to dine in the servants' hall; at Blenheim there were eighty house servants and a hundred out of doors. To those impatient of delay and waste of human effort it could be very irritating; Wellington once remarked that he brushed his own clothes and regretted that he had not time to clean his boots, for the presence of a crowd of idle, officious fellows annoyed him more than he could say. To most, however, of the participants in this easy-going, rule-of-thumb English hierarchy the conventions seemed satisfactory enough. Simond found, not only that English domestics were more obliging and industrious than those elsewhere, but that they looked better pleased and happier. If their status was defined towards those above them, it was equally defined towards those below; they might sleep in attics but they lived well and shared the dignity of their masters. There was a decently modulated avenue of advancement that provided for both mediocrity and talent. Mary Mitford's friend, twelve-year-old Joe Kirby, promoted from the farm to the manor house where he cleaned the shoes, rubbed the knives and ran errands, "a sort of prentice to the footman," would, she predicted, one day overtop his chief and rise to be butler. His sisters went into service in the great house at fourteen and stayed till they married, learning there lessons of neatness, domestic skill and respect for quality of all kinds. If deference were a product of English country house life, slatternliness was not. It graded men and women but civilised them. Like the monasteries whose social place it had taken, it made for comfort, culture and order.

Within these stately houses went on a life designed for enjoyment and content. It seemed a paradox that their possessors, as mirrored in their letters and contemporary novels, should have suffered the usual human lot of anxiety, envy, longing and even, sometimes, of despair. Amid furniture "in all the profusion and elegance of modern taste" and the masterpieces of an unbroken civilisation, on lawns shaded by cedars of Lebanon and rolled and scythed till they resembled green lakes,[1] surrounded by avenues,

[1] "The mowing or rather shaving of this smooth surface is done once a week

temples and parks cropped by deer, with terraces for sun and groves and fountains for shade, with walled gardens and hot-houses that poured out a never-ending flow of peaches, nectarines, grapes, melons and pineapples, with coverts full of game, cellars of choice vintages, side-tables of gleaming mahogany groaning with game, hams and cheeses, these elegant, favoured creatures, with the stimulus and wherewithal for the cultivation of every social, aesthetic and learned taste, still contrived on occasion to be bored and out of humour.

Yet, on the whole, as Squire Lambton reckoned a man could do on £40,000 a year, they managed to "jog along." Sitting at the pianoforte in some great sunlit room filled with buhl and ormolu, pier glasses and statues, elegantly *dérangé* sofa-tables from Gillow's fashionable warehouse, Sèvres china, breloques and singing clocks, little Tom Moore would sigh out his enchanting melodies, now gay, now melancholy, to companies of dandy men and exquisitely dressed women. The gentlemen hunted, raced, shot, fished, read, played at billiards, cards and *écarté*, looked after their estates, sat on the Bench, and rode, danced and joined in charades with the ladies; the latter gossiped, sketched, made scrapbooks, embroidered stools, looked at engravings, walked in the gardens and inspected the greenhouses, played with their children in the nursery wings, devoured the novels of Walter Scott or Lady Morgan, constantly dressed and redressed, and displayed their elegant accomplishments to the gentlemen. "Lady Asgill established herself in an attitude with Sir Thomas Graham at her feet," wrote Lady Shelley; "in the next room Lady Jane and Miss Russell at a harp and a pianoforte (both out of tune) played the Creation." At Knowsley, where from June to November there were never less than forty guests, the princely host restricted the gentlemen to five brace of partridges apiece to ensure their return to drive with the ladies in the afternoon, a concourse of carriages and horses parading after luncheon for the purpose. At Woburn breakfast was served from ten o'clock onwards, every guest being furnished,

---

and even twice in warm rainy weather. . . . The grass must be wet with dew or rain and the scythe very sharp." Simond I 154-5.

under the supervision of the groom of the chambers, with a separate teapot at any hour he chose, before parading for the great liveried battues. Here after dinner the "lively, easy young duchess would collect her romping force of girls and young men" and, advancing through an enfilade of half a dozen rooms hung with Canalettos, pelt the gentlemen at their whist with cushions and oranges. And though during the London season the enchanted groves and flowers in the shires wasted their sweetness on the uninhabited air, their owners always returned to them in the end with delight. "Tixhall is in radiant beauty," wrote Harriet Leveson Gower, "all over roses, rain, sunshine and a new fireplace in the hall. I really do love it beyond expression." "After having been at a ball until three o'clock," Lady Shelley concluded her journal of a metropolitan July, "Shelley, Mr. Jenkinson and I drove down to Sutton in the barouche and at nine o'clock we mounted our horses and galloped over that delightful turf. . . . As I breathed this pure air my jaded spirits were restored. I was exalted by a sense of happiness which only those who love and understand the beauties of nature can fully enjoy. . . . From Sutton we rode across country to Maresfield which 'in all its blueth and greeneth' reproached us for our absence. Thank God! I can leave the vanities of London without a sigh and return to my dear home with every good feeling unimpaired!" An English squire wintering in Rome in the first year of peace told a friend that he had seen nothing among its southern profusion equal to Cowesfield House. "Never mind the climate—stay where you are; all their tinsel and show can never be put in comparison with the solids and substantials of England."[1]

[1] *Paget Brothers* 271-2; Arbuthnot 137-8 *et passim*; Austen II 369-70; Bamford II 204, 215; Broughton I, 174; Byron, *Corr.* I 298; Lord Coleridge 241; *Creevey Papers* I 296; Creevey, *Life and Times* 214-15; Farington VIII 17, 98, 141, 143, 301; Gore 57; Harriet Granville I 35, 128-30, 151-2, 197-9, 202-3, 219-20; Gronow II 91; Hill, *Austen* 163-7; Holland, *Journal* I 56; Howitt 1-28; *Lieven Letters* 18-19; Lockhart V 337-9; Mitford, *Literary Life* 26; Newton 24, 93, 159-60; Simond I, 9, 73-4, 154-5, 198-9, 223; II 74, 78, 85, 99, 119; Lady Shelley II 12-13; Willis III, 311.

CHAPTER 6

Land of the Free

COHESION WITHOUT COERCION, wealth without slavery, empire without militarism, such was the spectacle that Britain presented to the world after her defeat of Napoleon. Was the reality behind the splendid façade, the nation behind those proud white cliffs as strong and healthful as it seemed? The great mass of her people, Simond reported, appeared happier and more respectable than any other he knew. The good manners of her country folk, their open, friendly faces, the curtseys of the children on the roads and the raised hats of their elders, bespoke a society against which the waves of egalitarian revolution and the new creeds of envy and infidelity had beaten in vain.

The English plainly loved their country and found inspiration in serving it. They were free as individuals to rule themselves, which made them self-reliant, resourceful and morally, as well as physically, courageous. They had a religion, deeply personal, which enabled them to set a course by conscience and secure the enduring strength of common standards of thought and behaviour. Together these gave them an underlying unity which allowed for almost limitless diversity yet was far more stable than one enforced by a centralised and brittle authoritarianism.

Their belief in freedom was a passion, almost a religion. "'Tis liberty alone," proclaimed their favourite poet,

> "that gives us the flower
> Of fleeting life, its lustre and perfume,
> And we are weeds without it. All constraint
> Except what wisdom lays on evil men
> Is evil."

For the abstract liberty of the mass acclaimed by revolutionary

France they had little use. The fabric of their law had been woven in the course of centuries to sustain that of the individual. The legal protection of his person and property against all comers, particularly against the king's officers, was, even more than parliament, England's distinguishing institution. Parliament itself had been created to ensure it.

For this pragmatic race, hatred of power was an obsession. Even the occasional soldiers posted at street corners to restrain the crowds during the Allied Sovereigns' victory visit in 1814 were denounced as intolerable. Keats at Naples felt unable to visit the opera because of the guards on the stage. "The continual visible tyranny of this Government prevents me having any peace of mind," he wrote, "I could not lie quietly here; I will not even leave my bones in the midst of this despotism." An English lady described how she and her husband, travelling through the dragooned French countryside after the war, chafed at the closed gates and the sentries who paraded the towns.[1]

Such hatred of constraint arose partly from a belief that power corrupted, and that it could not be safely entrusted, untrammelled, to anyone. For this reason the British Constitution was an intricate balance of rights and functions in which it was impossible to say precisely where power resided. The king having in the past tried to monopolise it, the king's powers had been drastically shorn. Though he still possessed great influence and could be a source of grave embarrassment to the Ministers whom he appointed, he could in major matters act officially only through them. His right even to a private secretary was questioned. Yet the Ministers who exercised his former powers were themselves dependent on the good will of parliament. Without the support of a working majority of its members, they could not carry on the business of the country. And parliament itself was a balance of conflicting powers: of rival parties and often rival Houses.

Nor did power reside in the people—that question-begging

[1] Lady Shelley, I, 215. It struck the Frenchman, Simond—even after his long residence in America—as remarkable that at the height of the war visitors to Portsmouth were allowed to pass through the walls and fortifications without being questioned. Simond, II, 247. See also Bury, I, 207; Keats, IV, 112.

abstraction, so dear to the rationalising philosophers of the eighteenth century, in whose name the French had drenched the world in blood. The House of Commons, like the House of Lords, so far as it represented anything definable, represented the interests and property of the country, though not as they were in 1815 but as they had been centuries before when the parliamentary system began. Little more than 400,000 out of the English and Welsh population of ten and a half millions enjoyed a parliamentary vote, and only 4000 out of two million Scots. Nor did the electorate even possess an absolute right to vote. It could be deprived of it by parliament, which if the Crown consented might, as it had done in the past, prolong its own existence. For the English left every parliament free to change the laws as it chose. They would not be bound even by a Constitution.

Only one thing could be said for certain of English politics. No power could be openly exercised without provoking a reaction. The greater the power, the greater the reaction. Even the mob was subject to this law of diminishing returns, since, whenever it went too far, it automatically created an alliance of law-abiding persons against it. England might canonise admirals—their sway was too distant to threaten anyone's liberty—but she never worshipped long at the shrine of any living statesman. Popularity with one faction was certain to arouse the enmity of another; vilification of William Pitt, the national saviour during the war, became the credo of Whigs and radicals for a generation after his death. It was symptomatic of this jealousy of power that the office of Prime Minister had no recognition in law, and that the Cabinet—the inner council of supreme office-holders, who were at once the Government and the managers of the parliamentary majority—was unknown to the Constitution. Its members modestly called themselves "his Majesty's confidential servants." They did not even possess an office or a secretary.

As for bureaucracy, what there was possessed no political power. The Civil Service was purely clerical and was nominated by the statesmen for whom it devilled. These viewed it chiefly as a means of rewarding supporters and providing for younger sons. Walter Scott praised Croker, the Secretary of the Admiralty, for never scrupling to stretch his powers to serve a friend. Such patronage, though valuable for securing Party discipline, was no foundation for a strong executive. Ninety-nine Englishmen out of a hundred viewed with sturdy contempt a bureaucracy recruited by jobbery. The country gentleman who named a litter of puppies, Placeman, Pensioner, Pilferer and Plunderer, was expressing this feeling.[1] Any attempt to increase the size and powers of the Civil Service was certain to be assailed. Even the Foreign Office had a staff of only twenty-eight, including the two Under-Secretaries and a Turkish interpreter. The Home Office consisted of twenty clerks. As every document had to be copied by hand, such administrators had no time for regulating other people's lives.

It was a source of amazement to foreigners that a country so governed, without a regular police and with so small an army, should be so orderly. At Brighton, a town in 1811 of 14,000 people, there were neither justices nor municipality, yet crime was almost unknown and the doors left unbarred at night. The capital, the world's largest city, was patrolled by a handful of police officers and a few hundred elderly night-watchmen. Little Mr. Townsend, the Bow Street "runner," with his flaxen wig and handful of top-hatted tipstaffs, constituted almost the sole force for executing the Government's will. Everything else was left to the justices and parish constables.

Yet the British were not a submissive people. English public schoolboys rose against their masters and had to be driven back to their class-rooms by the military; an attempt to raise the prices of the London theatres provoked the galleries to shout down every play for months and break up the house. Even at royal levees there was so much shoving that the removal of fainting ladies from a "squeeze" was a part of Court routine; when Carlton House was thrown open to well-to-do sightseers after a fête, shoes and frag-ments of clothing were gathered up afterwards in hogsheads. In poorer districts fighting was almost incessant. Simond, staying in Orchard Street, was kept awake all night by Irish labourers having a free-for-all in a slum alley at the back. Above the noise of their rattles he could hear one old watchman calling out to another,

[1] J. E. Austen-Leigh, *The Vine Hunt.*

"If I go in, I shall have a shower of brickbats," and the other replying, "Well, never mind, let them murder each other if they please!"[1]

For the common people, though allowed a licence known to no other country, were, like the poor and uneducated everywhere, quite uninhibited. Nor, for all the deference of the race to rank, did they respect persons. The Chancellor of the Exchequer, when he attended divine service at the Millbank Penitentiary, was bombarded with stale bread by the aggrieved lady inmates. Appalling crimes of violence passed unpunished for lack of police. Lonely turnpike-keepers were robbed and beaten to death; gangs of smugglers and poachers fought pitched battles with keepers and revenue officers. Pickpockets surrounded the doors of the coaching inns for "Johnny Raws from the country," and during fairs and public processions packs of thieves swept through the crowds emptying pockets, snatching purses and even stripping men and women of their clothes. Dusk round London was called footpad hour. Yet the nimbleness and courage of its pickpockets was almost a matter of pride to Londoners. "A man who saunters about the capital with pockets on the outside of his coat," a guidebook warned its readers, "deserves no pity."[2]

A little rough-and-tumble seemed a small price to the English for avoiding the ills of arbitrary power. "They have an admirable police at Paris," wrote Lord Dudley, "but they pay for it dear enough. I had rather half a dozen people's throats were cut every few years in the Ratcliffe Highway than be subject to domiciliary visit, spies and the rest of Fouché's contrivances." The British attitude towards the agents of executive power was instinctively hostile; Stendhal on a visit to London was amazed to see soldiers jeered at in the streets. The Life Guards, who carried printed orders

[1] Simond, I, 89-91. See also Arbuthnot, 144; Ashton, I, 25; Bamford, I, 28, 127, 129, 131, 185, 245-9; II, 67; Bewick, 21-2; 61-2 Gronow, II,; 225-6, 310; Keats, III, 282; Leigh Hunt, *Autobiography*, I, 190 Mitford, *Life*, II, 187; Simond, II, 227-60; Stanhope, 274; Woodward, 466.

[2] Ann. Reg., 1819. Chron. 55; *Diary of Walter Trevelyan*, G. T. Warner, *Harrow in Verse and Prose*, 99. Bamford, II, 64; Colchester, III, 237; *Cranbourn Chase*, 35-7; Fowler, 122-3; Gronow II, 309-10; Lieven, *Private Letters*, 78; Leigh Hunt, *Autobiography*, I, 190; Sydney, I, 122, 210.

to avoid giving offence to civilians and repeatedly showed the most exemplary restraint under showers of stones, were known in the capital as the "Piccadilly butchers." Even the Prime Minister who reaped the glories of Victoria and Waterloo viewed General Graham's proposal for a club for military officers as a threat to the Constitution.[1]

Foreigners could not understand the British attitude to popular violence; it seemed to them like the weakness that had precipitated the Terror. But the people who quietly obeyed their voluntary ring-keepers at a rough boxing match chafed at the least restraint by arms. "The strange medley of licentiousness and legal restraint," wrote a foreigner, "of freedom and confinement—of punishment for what is done and liberty to do the same thing again—is very curious." At first it struck him as irrational, but in the end he decided that it approximated more nearly to natural law than the simpler and more arbitrary processes of other lands. The artificial composition of gardens in England, he noted, like that of her government, abridged only the liberty of doing harm.

As there was no adequate standing Army, police force or bureaucracy to secure property and privilege, the gentry had to preserve these themselves. Having no professional deputies as in more regimented lands to stand between them and those they ruled, they learnt to command respect by force of character, courage and good sense. Instinctive, unreflecting and fearless leadership was a by-product of the country's libertarian laws. It began in boyhood, when future legislators and magistrates took part with the sturdy ragamuffins of the countryside in running, swimming, bird-nesting, riding the wild ponies of the commons, making midnight expeditions, climbing trees, rocks and steeples. They learnt to endure knocks and hardships, to face risks, conceal fear, be quick, bold and adaptable. They acquired, before they inherited wealth and luxury, habits of hardihood such as early rising and cold bathing; John Mytton, with his £20,000 a year, dressed in winter in a thin jacket and linen trousers without drawers, and once stalked wild-fowl all night on the ice stark naked. "Can't I bear pain well," he cried as he lay, skinned and scorched, after a debauch in

[1] Lynedoch, 748-51; Gronow, II, 220; Simond, I, 79, 91; II, 221, 280-1.

which he had set his shirt alight to frighten away the hiccoughs.

From their earliest years Britain's rulers still indulged with passionate intensity in field sports. It gave them, as Walter Scott wrote of his countrymen, a strong and muscular character, saving them from all sorts of causeless fears and flutterings of the heart. Men who rode straight to hounds, shot duck in wintry marches with breech-loaders, learnt as boys to snare and kill wild-fowl, snakes, hares, rabbits, badgers and all forms of game and vermin, and continued to do so, whenever they had a chance, so long as they could walk or stride a horse, were not likely to fail for lack of courage. Their versatility in sport was amazing. The great Master of the Quorn, George Osbaldeston—"little Ossey" or, as he was called later, the "squire of England"—a shrivelled-up, bantam-cock of a man with short legs, a limp, a gorilla chest and a face like a fox cub, excelled at every sport he touched, boxing, pigeon-shooting, steeplechasing, billiards, was one of the six best ama-teur cricketers in the country, rowed for the Arrow club—the forerunner of Leander—beat the famous professional, Barre, at tennis, and kept harriers, gamecocks and fighting mastiffs.

The hunting field played a big part in such education. Under the famous East Midlands masters a new form of foxhunting was superseding the slower and less specialised sport of the past. Its pioneers, establishing a new convention and discipline, were almost as much leaders in their kind as Nelson and Wellington. Their hounds ran from scent to view; "neck or nothing," "a blazing hour," "the pace was too good to inquire," were their watch-words. Their followers—for no man who wished to be respected spared either person or fortune in this pursuit—went like a scarlet streak across the green, enclosed shires. "Throw your heart over and your horse will follow!"[1] the great Assheton Smith used to say. It was a rule gentlemen instinctively applied in time of danger, and to which the people responded.

All Britons admired what they called "bottom." "God don't love those," they were told, "who won't strike out for themselves!"

---

[1] Dixon, 32. See *idem*, 17, 47, 154-63, 166-7; Alken, *passim*; Assheton Smith, *passim*; *Cranbourn Chase*, 42-3; *Creevey Papers*, II, 199-200; Lockhart, V, 81; Newton, 51; Nevill, 38-40; Osbaldeston, *passim*.

Little John Keats, affronted by boy or master, put himself "in a posture of defence"; even the gentle Shelley fought a mill at Eton. Byron used to thrash a pacifically-minded Harrow friend to make him thrash others "when necessary as a point of honour and stature"; he himself fought his way out of the ridicule attached to a club foot by winning six out of seven successive battles. No one but a "game chick" could thrive in this land.

Boxing was the national nursery of manliness. A gentleman was expected to be a "proper man with his fists" and know how "to clear a lane of men" with his "morleys." Thomas Assheton Smith, when Master of the Quorn, after a set-to in a Leicester street with a six-foot coal-heaver, clamped a raw steak on both eyes and sent his prostrated opponent a five-pound note for being the best man that ever stood up to him. Some foreigners landing at Dover were amazed to see a Lord of the Treasury, dispossessed of his Ministerial box by officious Customs men, put himself in a sparring attitude to regain it. Young noblemen took boxing lessons in Gentleman Jackson's rooms in Bond Street or walked proudly arm in arm with the bash-nosed champions of the "Fancy"; an engraving of Tom Cribb was part of the normal furniture of an undergraduate's rooms.

A contest between two "milling coves" was the most popular spectacle in the country. Its finer points were debated, not only by draymen and coal-heavers, but by men of culture; Keats, describing the match between Randall and Turner, illustrated its ups and downs by rapping with his fingers on the window. All England followed the fortunes of its "men of science," those prize specimens of the race who met in the green ring by the river at Mousley Hurst or sparred before the "Fancy" in the Fives Court. The heroes of the ring—Tom Hickman the Gas-Light man, Sutton "the tremendous man of colour," the "Flaming Tinman," "Big Ben Brain," the "Game Chicken," Mendoza the Jew, Belcher "the yeoman," and Tom Cribb, for ten years unchallenged champion of England, were as great men in their way as the Duke of Wellington. What, asked Borrow, were the gladiators of Rome or the bull-fighters of Spain in its palmiest days compared to England's bruisers? With the ring formed, the seconds and bottle-holders in readiness, the combatants face to face, the English were in a kind of heaven. The gladiators, stripped to the waist, walking round each other with their fine, interlaced muscles and graceful strength, the naked fists, the short chopping blows delivered with the swiftness of lightning, the dislodged ivories, the noses beaten flat, the pause between rounds when the "pinky heroes," poised on their seconds' knees, were revived with brandy and water, the crashing blows delivered in the jugular with the full force of the arm shot horizontally from the shoulder, and the game, battered faces under punishment impressed themselves on the memory of the islanders more than all their country's martial victories. "Prize fighting," wrote Pierce Egan, "teaches men to admire true courage, to applaud generosity, to acquire notions of honour, nobleness of disposition and greatness of mind; to bear hardships without murmur, fortitude in reverse of fortune, and invincibility of soul."[1]

Within the framework of law and property the English rule was that a man should look after himself and have freedom to do so. If he failed no one pitied him. It was his own fault; he had had his chance. The islanders had not yet thought out the full implications of this rule; they were to have opportunities for doing so later. But at the time it seemed fair enough; it had the warrant of nature and the law of things. "Fear God," said Isobel Berners to the Romany Rye, "and take your own part. There's Bible in that, young man; see how Moses feared God and how he took his own part against everybody who meddled with him. So fear God, young man, and never give in!" From the time they could stand Englishmen were expected to fend for themselves. There was nothing they valued like spunk. In men, indeed, they respected nothing without it. "Is not this being game to the backbone?"

[1] Boxiana, passim; Assheton Smith, passim; Bamford, I, 28, 127, 131, 185; Bewick, 20-2; Broughton, I, 96; Dixon, 22-7, 151-4; English Spy, I, 152, 338-9; II, 199; Farington, VII, 25; Fowler, 192-5; Gronow, I, 120; II, 79-80, 214-15, 257; Leigh Hunt, Autobiography, II, 85; Keats, III, 282; IV, 304, 323-5; Lavengro, 48, 156-7, 166-9, 207; Leslie, 332; Letts, 212; Life in London, 37, 73, 173, 175; Mytton, passim; New Monthly Magazine, Feb., 1822. W. Hazlitt, "The Fight"; Old Oak, 161-8; Osbaldeston, passim; J. H. Reynolds, The Fancy, 1820; Romany Rye, 98, 131-2, 141-2, 145, 194-5; Simond, I, 125-7; II, 194-8, 227.

asked Walter Scott, when he heard how a boy, punished by three
months in a garret on bread and water for shooting a cat, had
spent his imprisonment hunting rats on a new principle.

.   .   .   .

The religion of a people so libertarian was instinctively Protestant.
An Englishman's home was his castle; he wanted no priest, least
of all a foreign one, to share it. Popery to him was a symbol of
tyranny, absurdity and inefficiency for, since despotism corrupted,
it followed, in his eyes, that those who exercised it in religious
matters must govern badly. An English lady travelling in Switzer-
land declared she could always tell when she was in a Protestant
canton because the roads were passable, the lands well farmed and
the cottages tidy. Jane Austen wrote that she had "a great respect
for Sweden because it had been so zealous for Protestantism." For
cardinals, priests, processions, fastings, penances, "not forgetting
anchorites and vermin," the English had an inexpressible contempt;
the Reverend Edward Stanley at Aix-la-Chapelle was nauseated
by "virgins and dolls in beads, and muslins and pomatum and relics
of saints' beards, and napkins from our Saviour's tomb and mummeries quite disgraceful." The average Englishman thought there
was nothing, however false and horrible, a priest-ridden nation
might not do.[1]

The font of English Protestantism was still the authorised translation of the Bible. With the growth of literacy this great book had

---

[1] In militant Ulster, where English and Scottish Protestantism reached its
apogee, the fanatics of the Orange Lodges on the anniversary of the battle of the
Boyne gave expression to this sentiment in a toast:
"To the glorious, pious and Immortal Memory of King William III, who
saved us from Rogues and Roguery, Slaves and Slavery, Knaves and Knavery,
Popes and Popery, from brass money and wooden shoes; and whoever denies
this Toast may he be slammed, crammed and jammed into the muzzle of the
great gun of Athlone, and the gun fired into the Pope's Belly, and the Pope into
the Devil's Belly, and the Devil into Hell, and the door locked and the key in an
Orangeman's pocket; and may we never lack a Brisk Protestant Boy to kick
the arse of a papist; and here's a fart for the Bishop of Cork!" See also *Romany
Rye*, 16-17, 400; Austen, 238; Bamford, I, 102; Castlereagh, X, 378; De
Selincourt, II, 578; Lady Shelley, I, 252-3, 287, 351-2 Stanley 191; Wilberforce,
II, 322.

become the daily mentor of millions. Every Sunday Mrs. Cooper, the dyer's widow, took down her husband's Baskerville edition of the Scriptures and, turning the pictured pages, recalled for her little son what he had said of each. In country districts the words of the Bible, heard week by week in church or chapel, formed the mould of men's minds. Its phrases strayed into their every-day speech; when Samuel Bamford returned from sea, his father, the weaver, greeted him with the words, "My son was dead and is alive again, he was lost and is found."

Looking back on his experience of the politics of anarchical India and revolutionary Europe, Wellington declared that it was England's religion that had made her what she was, a nation of honest men. By this he meant one in which a majority of men could trust one another and which others could trust. "I would rather sacrifice Gwalior and every other portion of India ten times over," he once wrote, "to preserve our credit for scrupulous good faith."

This insistence on truth and frank dealing had a profound influence on the country's overseas empire and trade. It caused peoples on whom the expansion of the British impinged, if not to like, to trust them. A Bordeaux merchant, on whom a penniless British officer was billeted, offered, unasked, to lend him any sum without security; he had complete faith, he said, in the word of an Englishman. Richard Hotham, the hatter, made it a rule only to sell the best so that every new customer became an old; Samuel Archer, the inventor of imitation pearls, went to extraordinary lengths to prevent his products from being mistaken for the genuine article. Though cheats and knaves abounded as in every society, a bright skein of honesty ran through the nation; a poor Lancashire weaver almost starved on the road from Manchester to London sooner than risk not being in court when his bail was called. Among the Dorset quarrymen the saying "on the word of a Portland man" was as good as a contract.[1]

At the start of the nineteenth century the national Church was

[1] *Sea-Bathing Places*, 500. See also Bamford, II, 254; Bell, I, 184; Bewick, 33, 35-7, 46-7; Daniell, I, 51; Dixon, 66; Moorsom, 272-3; Simpson, 77; Woodward, 86.

still suffering from a surfeit of prosperity. Those rosy-cheeked, homestalled divines, whose faces Charles Lamb thought fragrant with the mincepies of half a century, neither approved of nor were capable of inspiring religious zeal. But the Terror and its military aftermath shattered their complacency and that of their congregations. An age of comfortable rationalism was confronted with the depths of wickedness latent in human nature; there was a Devil after all. The Evangelical revival within the established Church was its reply to the apathy of an over-indulged clergy and the heathen indifference of the neglected poor. It was a spontaneous movement to arouse sluggish consciences and alleviate popular sufferings by personal charity. While England's rulers struck back at the Revolution militant with the sword of Nelson and Wellington, the Evangelicals resisted it at home, under the unofficial direction of Pitt's old friend, Wilberforce, with a flood of Sunday schools, tracts, free bibles, benefit societies, soup and clothing clubs and allotments. In 1811 the *National Society for Educating the Poor in the Principles of the Established Church* was founded; in 1814 the *British and Foreign School Society* for non-denominational Bible-reading. Admiral Cornwallis, the "Billy-go-tight" of the blockade of Brest, refused, like a loyal churchman, to lease his land to a chapel, but gave it to the parish for a church school. While Elizabeth Fry, taking up the work John Howard had begun, strove with love and pity to reform the brutalised prisoners in Newgate—an example followed by the formation of prison committees in every English county town—and Hannah More, De Quincey's "Holy Hannah," closed her life-work of charity with the building of cottages for deserving labourers with large families, young ladies like Jane Austen's sisters occupied themselves in visiting the poor, making them comforts and teaching their children the Scriptures. Cobbett on the way to East Stratton—it was on a Sunday—met a little girl in a camlet gown, white apron and plaid cloak with a prayer book in her hand, all given by the lady of the manor who had had her taught—to his disgust, for he did not like such patronage—to read and sing hymns.

There was nothing new in this; it was the repetition of a recurring pattern in the nation's history. Though its statutory institutions were no longer adequate to the size and energy of its population, its possessing classes and those who, in its infinitely graded society, enjoyed property, status or privilege, felt the obligation to contribute personally to the alleviation of suffering and the elimination of vice, brutality and disease among their poorer neighbours. This sprang partly from their Christian faith and the family life which, in England and Scotland alike, was its base, and partly from the necessity for individual responsibility inherent in a State which refused to tolerate either police or bureaucracy. The English had a talent for fighting fire because they knew that in the last resort there was no one else to put it out but themselves. "What stately edifices," wrote the author of Ackermann's *Microcosm of London*, "arise for the relief of every evil, corporate, moral and intellectual, that afflicts the human species: diseases of every name, accidents of every kind, helpless infancy, friendless youth, decrepid age, moral infirmity and mental derangement, find alleviation, restoration, reception, instruction, support, improvement and renovation . . . within these splendid receptacles."

This was pitching it high; the British possessing classes' treatment of the beneficiaries of their charity was practical but spartan. The dining hall of the House of Asylum at Lambeth was floored with stones, lit by high skylights and fitted with long tables and benches, the fires at either end of the hall being carefully fenced round. Other furniture there was none, but everything was spotlessly clean and the inmates clad in neat white bonnets and tuckers and purple dresses. Here children, deserted or left bereft by their parents, were taught to mend their own clothes, make shifts and table linen, do needlework and perform the business of house and kitchen. They also learnt to read the Bible, write a legible hand and understand the first four rules of arithmetic. At the age of fifteen they were apprenticed for seven years to families approved by the governors.[1]

What was true of London was true also of the provinces. In Liverpool, though only a tenth of the capital's size, there was a

[1] Ackermann, *Microcosm*, III, 119. See *idem*, II, 61-79, 137, 196; Ashton, I, 287; Berry, III, 308; Croker, I, 203; Leigh Hunt, *Autobiography*, I, 283-309; Partington, I, 9, 97-8; Festing, 193; Simond, I, 155-6.

Blue Coat Hospital, a *House of Industry*, a *House of Recovery*, a *Female School of Industry*, a *Seaman's Hospital*, a *Dispensary*, a *Welsh Charitable Society*, a *Ladies' Charity*, a *Lunatic Hospital*, a *Magdalene Society*, an *Institution for restoring Drowned Persons*, a *Strangers' Friendly Society*, a *Society for Bettering the Condition and Increasing the Comforts of the Poor*, a *School for the Indigent Blind*, and a number of free schools, all supported by what was called public patronage. Every village had at least one ancient endowment; at East Burnham in Buckinghamshire there was a free school and a charitable trust with lands and £2600 in the Funds: at Gainsborough two educational foundations, one providing every scholar annually with a blue coat and a cap trimmed with yellow. Though there was little remedial action by the State outside the rather bleak Elizabethan Poor Law—itself, however, unique in a world which still viewed charity as a religious, not a civic obligation—any national or international calamity was sure to provoke among the English a subscription for its mitigation. A fund started after Leipzig by Rudolph Ackermann, the print-seller, to relieve his ruined countrymen in Saxony, was over-subscribed in a few days. The *Association for Relief of the Manufacturing and Labouring Poor* during the Continental blockade had three royal dukes and the archbishop of Canterbury among its patrons. Even the careless Eton scholars competed in charitable contributions "for a poor cad or the widow of a drowned bargee." Most of this spontaneous charity was local; in the severe winter of 1814, for instance, the Quakers of Gainsborough organised a fund for distributing free soups, biscuits, potatoes and herrings to the poor of the town.[1]

For the English based action, not on the State as in France or on the Army, Church or dynasty as in Prussia, Spain and Russia, but on the voluntarily created team. It was hard to think of any object for which there was not some voluntary association. There was a Society for the Prevention of Vice and a Society for the Encouragement of Religion and Virtue; a Society of Antiquaries and a Mechanics' Institute; a Society for the Relief of Foreigners

---

[1] Cooper, 26. See *Fraser's Magazine*, XXXI, 457; Gaussen, II, 353; Halévy, I, 12-13; Ham, II, 168; *English Spy*, I, 35; Daniell, II, 87-93; Newton, 270-1.

and one for the Conversion and Education of Negro Slaves: a Society for Protecting Trade against sharpers and swindlers, and a Society for giving Bibles to Soldiers and Sailors. Almost every corporate national activity, including the Army, was the result of a private contract voluntarily entered into by people of like mind.

Inside such self-chosen associations the English, normally so suspicious of authority, showed themselves astonishingly amenable. At the Beefsteak Club, where even royal dukes served their turn as "boots," members were sworn in with the words, "You shall attend duly, vote impartially, and conform to our laws and orders obediently: you shall support our dignity, promote our welfare and at all times behave as a worthy member in this sublime Society; so Beef and Liberty be your reward!" So long as they were not coerced from above but felt that they were co-operating of their own free choice, the English of all classes were prepared to contribute to their corporate activities a loyalty, enthusiasm and readiness to serve capable of making any institution work. The Czar remarked after his visit to London that the high state to which the English had advanced was the result not merely of their laws and Constitution, but of a temper of mind, a soberness of thought, a habit of reflection, collective and individual, possessed by no other people.

. . . .

The ruling principle of English society was the conception of a gentleman. Good breeding was not merely a mark of social distinction but a rule for the treatment of others. It made few concessions to the ideal of equality; men, it was held, were born to varying lots, and in 1815 one took these distinctions as one found them. But a gentleman was expected to treat his fellow creatures of all ranks openly and frankly, even when it meant sacrificing his interests to do so. A gentleman did not tell a lie, for that was cowardice; he did not cheat, go back on his word or flinch from the consequences of his actions. When Lord Sefton succeeded to his estates he at once settled—and without question—a gambling debt for £40,000 alleged to have been incurred by his father at Crockford's.

A man's reputation as a gentleman was looked on as his most valuable possession. Any action, or even association, incompatible with it was regarded as a stain which must be immediately expunged. This accounted for the extreme sensitivity with which public men reacted to any slight on their honour, vindicating it, if necessary, in some dawn encounter with pistols on suburban common or foreign beach. Pitt, Castlereagh, Canning, Wellington and Peel all risked their lives in this way while holding high office. "How constantly, even in the best works of fiction," wrote a critic, giving his reasons for supposing the author of *Waverley* to be a gentleman, "are we disgusted with offences against all generous principle, as the reading of letters by those for whom they were not intended, taking advantage of accidents to overhear private conversation, revealing what in honour should have remained secret, plotting against men as enemies and at the same time making use of their services, dishonest practices on the sensibilities of women by their admirers, falsehoods, not always indirect, and by an endless variety of low artifices which appear to be thought quite legitimate if carried on through subordinate agents." A gentleman, at his best, was one who raised the dignity of human nature—noble, fearless, magnanimous. When the Governor-General of Canada, the Duke of Richmond, learnt that he was suffering from hydrophobia, he never breathed a word of his impending doom, but performed his social duties with the same calm and dignified bearing to the end. "Throughout the whole of his career," Gronow wrote of Wellington, "he always placed first and foremost, far above his military and social honours, his position as an English gentleman." The founders of Sandhurst laid it down that the professional education of British officers ought to aim at producing, not corporals, but gentlemen. So long as it did so, they knew it would produce the kind of leaders Englishmen would follow.

A gentleman was under an obligation to be generous; he held his possessions, like his life, on terms. The very flies at Petworth, wrote Haydon, seemed to know that there was room for their existence; dogs, horses, cows, deer and pigs, peasantry and servants, all shared Lord Egremont's bounty. If there was anything the

English despised more than a coward, it was a skint. The Duke of Buccleuch in times of agricultural distress left his farm rents un-collected and refrained from visiting London that he might have the cash to pay his retainers; Lord Bridgewater never refused work to any local man, and during times of unemployment increased his Ashridge establishment from five to eight hundred. Captain Sawyer of East Burnham—one of the older school of squires—always allowed his poor tenants as much driftwood and "lop and top" from his plantations as they wanted. Though there were plenty of harsh landlords who rack-rented their estates to finance their ex-travagances, and many more who, absorbed in their pleasures, refused to be troubled, there were thousands of others who, treating their poorer neighbours with kindness and consideration, preserved social distinctions by taking the resentment out of them. Tom Purdy, the Abbotsford gamekeeper, who weekly pledged the laird and his guests at their Sunday dinner in a quaigh of whisky, no more felt a sense of injustice against Walter Scott for being his master than did the latter's dog, Maida. Nor did the page-boy, whose exercise book the great writer regularly corrected.[1]

The ideal of equality which had so intoxicated the French, had as yet made little impression on the British mind. Whenever Squire Lambton, with his £40,000 a year, visited his northern home, the Durham colliers turned out in thousands to draw his carriage. It was injustice and tyranny that this pugnacious people resented, not privilege. "Gentlemen are, or ought to be, the pride and glory of every civilised country," wrote Bewick, himself a radical; "without their countenance arts and sciences must languish, industry be paralysed and barbarism rear its stupid head." Bamford, for all his life of rebellion, wrote with nostalgia of the freedom that had existed in his youth between the gentry and their tenants. "There were no grinding bailiffs and land-stewards in those days to stand betwixt the gentleman and his labourer. There was no racking up of old tenants; no rooting out of old cottiers; no screwing down of servants' or labourers' wages; no cutting off of allowances, either of the beggar at the door or the visitor at the

[1] Mrs. Arbuthnot, *Journal*, 23rd Jan., 1822; Lockhart, IV, 218; Howitt, 56.

servants' hall; no grabbing at waste candle-ends or musty cheese parings." For the English liked the rich to be splendid, ostentatious and free with their money. It was what, in their view, the rich were for.

They liked them, too, to share and excel in their pastimes. "Nothing," the Duke of Wellington declared, "the people of this country like so much as to see their great men take part in their amusements; the aristocracy will commit a great error if ever they fail to mix freely with their neighbours." Sport in England was a wonderful solvent of class distinction. Even foxhunting, with all its expense and showy competitiveness, had still something of a rough democracy about it, at once exclusive and classless, of master and huntsman, groom and whipper-in, dog-stopper and stable boy, meeting day after day on the level of a common love. The coloured prints that depicted its scarlet coats and glossy horses hung in village alehouses as well as manor houses; when the Manchester weavers, true to their country past and oblivious of their proletarian future, went out hunting on the Cheshire hills, Sam Stott, the huntsman, used to treat them to a warm ale and ginger.[1] On the cricket field, too, the conventions of rank were forgotten; the best man was "the hardest *swipe*, the most active *field*, the stoutest *bowler*." "Who that has been at Eton," asked the author of the *English Spy*, "has not repeatedly heard Jem Powell in terms of exultation cry, 'Only see me *liver this here* ball, my young master'?" The game was played by the Prince Regent—before he let down his belly—on his ground at Brighton, by the aristocracy who liked to gamble over it, and by the young farmers and labourers of almost every south country village. At East Burnham, until the sabbatarians stopped it, the common every Sunday afternoon "presented a lively and pleasing aspect, dotted with parties of cheerful lookers-on, with many women, children and old persons." Mary Mitford from her Berkshire cottage window could see two sets of cricketers, one of young men surrounded by spectators, standing, sitting or stretched on the grass, all taking a delighted interest in the game, and the other a merry group of little boys, shout-

[1] Mitford, *Our Village*, 18; Assheton Smith, 21; *English Spy*, I, 28, 72; Grote, 45; *Old Oak*, 132-43; *Sea-bathing Places*, 120.

ing, leaping and enjoying themselves to their hearts' content.

For the English, as Hazlitt said, were a sort of grown children. They loved Punch and Judy and games like skittles and shove-halfpenny, leap frog, blind man's buff, hunt-the-slipper, hot cockles and snapdragon. When Nelson went round the *Victory's* gun-decks before Trafalgar, the men were jumping over one another's heads to amuse themselves until they were near enough to fire. "Cudgel-playing, quarterstaff, bull and badger-baiting, cock-fighting," Hazlitt wrote, "are almost the peculiar diversions of this island. . . . There is no place where trap-ball, fives, prison-base, football, quoits, bowls are better understood or more successfully practised, and the very names of a cricket bat and ball make English fingers tingle." Nothing would deflect them from their sport; when "Long Robinson," had two of his fingers struck off, he had a screw fastened to one hand to hold the bat and with the other still sent the ball thundering against the boards that bounded old Lord's Cricket-ground.[1]

They liked, and honoured above all, what they called "game, bone and blood." It was because their rulers possessed these qualities that, despite all their unimaginativeness and selfishness, they had so little difficulty in ruling them. Most Englishmen were far more interested in dog-fighting, coursing, hunting vermin, fishing and fowling, boxing and wrestling, than in the pursuit of equality or the class war. The man of the age was not the Ben-thamite-philosopher, the radical martyr or the wage-hungry cotton spinner—however important in retrospect—but the sporting type. "Jem Flowers," the Eton boys sang of a local "cad,"

> "baits a badger well
> For a bullhank or a tyke, sir,
> And as an out-and-out bred swell
> Was never seen his like, sir!"

The national norm was "Joey" of the Westminster cockpit—"a

---

[1] W. Hazlitt, "Merry England," *New English Monthly*, Dec., 1825; Bamford, I, 108; Eland, 19-23; *English Spy*, II, 332-3; *Life in London*, 27-8, 145, 180 Haydon, *Table Talk*; Howitt, 495; Strutt, *Sports and Pastimes*, 522-44; *Real Life in London*, I, 81; II, 108n.

small man of about five feet high with a very sharp countenance and dressed in a brown jockey coat and top boots"—to whom Francis Ardry introduced the future author of *Lavengro*. After trying to sell the "green one" a dog, this gentleman expatiated on the future of society.

"A time will come, and that speedily, when folks will give up everything else and follow dog-fighting."

"Do you think so?"

"Think so? Let me ask what there is that a man wouldn't give up for it?"

"Why . . . there's religion."

"Religion! How you talk. Why, there's myself, bred and born an Independent, and intended to be a preacher, didn't I give up religion for dog-fighting. . . . Religion! Why the parsons themselves come to my pit, and I have now a letter from one of them asking me to send him a dog."

"Well, then, politics."

"Politics! Why, the gemmen in the House would leave Pitt himself, if he were alive, to come to my pit. There were three of the best of them here to-night, all great horators. Get on with you, what comes next?"

"Why, there's learning and letters."

"Pretty things, truly, to keep people from dog-fighting! Why, there's the young gentlemen from the Abbey School comes here in shoals, leaving books, letters and masters too. To tell you the truth, I rather wish they would mind their letters, for a more precious set of young blackguards I never seed. . . ."

"You show by your own conduct that there are other things worth following besides dog-fighting. You practise rat-catching and badger-baiting as well . . ."

"Your friend here might call you a new one! When I talks of dog-fighting, I of course means rat-catching and badger-baiting, ay, and bull-baiting, too, just as when I speaks religiously, when I says one, I means not one but three."

One common denominator in particular linked Englishmen of all classes—the horse. The first goal of every boy or girl visiting the metropolis was Astley's circus. The friend who called Charles

Lamb the only man in the country who had never worn boots or sat in a saddle, was only exaggerating. Not that all Englishmen rode well; it was remarked of Wellington, though unfairly, that no conqueror ever combined more victories with more falls. Yet almost every Englishman born within sight of a highroad or a field thought it the height of felicity to be "well mounted on a spunky horse who would be well in front." The English loved horses; O'Kelly, owner of Eclipse, declared that all Bedford Level could not buy him. "When you have got such a horse to be proud of," the ostler told the Romany Rye, "wherever you go, swear there a'n't another to match it in the country, and if anybody gives you the lie, take him by the nose and tweak it off, just as you would do if anybody were to speak ill of your lady!"

"Something slap," a "bit of blood," "an elegant tit," were the phrases with which the English expressed this love. A smart or "spanking" turn-out was, more than anything else, the symbol of national pride; there was no comparison, a visitor to Paris in 1815 reckoned, between French and English equipages; neatness, beauty, finish, lightness, quality, all were on the side of the islanders. "The exercise which I do dearly love," wrote Mary Mitford, "is to be whirled along fast, fast, fast by a blood-horse in a gig." During the first years of the nineteenth century the great coachbuilders of London and the provincial capitals turned out a succession of equipages perfectly adapted for their purposes, from the fashionable landau and deep-hung, capacious barouche to the dashing curricle, tilbury, buggy and gig, and the phaeton "highflyer" with its towering wheels and yellow wings. The most wonderful of all were the mail-coaches built for speed on the new metalled highways, with their blood-horses, bright brass harness, blazoned colours, horn-blowing guards and coachmen with squared shoulders, vast capes, multiple coats and nosegays. Young aristocrats prided themselves on mastering the accomplishments of the professional knights of the road, even to filing and spitting through their teeth; to handle the "ribbons" and be a first-rate "fiddler" was passport to any company.

Supporting the noble institution of the horse was an immense community of grooms and ostlers, of sharp-eyed, wiry little men with bow legs and highlows and many a string dangling from the knees of their breeches, and lads in dirty pepper-and-salt coats and low-crowned hats with turn-up ears. They were members of an *alma mater* of which almost every English lad aspired to be a graduate. Under its splendid clothes and yellow varnished equip-ages Regency England stank of the stable and was proud of it. The fraternity of the curry-comb—that knowing under-world of inn tap-rooms and raffish-looking parties with hats on one side and straws in their mouths—stretched from Dover to Galway. From it sprang the English poet whose mastery of sensuous imagery has only been surpassed by the offspring of the Stratford-on-Avon corn dealer. John Keats was the son of an ostler who married his master's daughter and succeeded him as keeper of a livery stable in Moorfields.

Horse jockeyship, the making of traffic in horseflesh, was "the most ticklish and unsafe of all professions." Coleridge heard a clerical Nimrod at Salisbury boast that he would cheat his own father over a horse. "Then how would you, Mr. Romany Rye," the ostler asked Borrow, "pass off the veriest screw . . . for a flying dromedary?"

"By putting a small live eel down his throat; as long as the eel remained in his stomach, the horse would appear brisk and lively to a surprising degree."

"And how would you contrive to make a regular kicker and biter appear . . . tame and gentle?"

"By pouring down his throat four pints of generous ale . . . to make him happy and comfortable."

The itch for horse-dealing and betting created, like everything English, its institutions. Weatherby's was to the Turf what the Bank of England was to the City, and Tattersall's, "that hoarse and multifarious miscellany of men" below Hyde Park Corner, with its circular counter—a kind of temple to the goddess of chance —and its painting of Eclipse over the fireplace, was the Stock Exchange of the equine world.[1] A little Newmarket quizzing or

[1] *English Spy*, I, 327-9; Dixon, 92-3; *Life in London*, 191; Lockhart, IV, 77, 290, 292; Ackermann, *Microcosm*; *Real Life in London*, 160-5; *Romany Rye*, 187-8, 335; Coleridge, *Miscellanies*, 236.

hocussing was reckoned an essential part of a young gentleman's education for a rough, wicked world. It taught him, in the cant of the day, to keep his peepers open. It helped to give him and his race that strong practical sense—horse sense, they called it—that made them, wherever they went, the lords of the earth.

CHAPTER 7

The Yellow Streak

OF ENGLAND'S TEN MILLION inhabitants at the end of the Napoleonic wars, a million lived in London. From the south bank the city presented a straight, uniform skyline, its roofs crowned with a halo of stone belfries, almost as many, it seemed, as the masts in the river. Above them the cliffs of Wren's vast cathedral carried the eye upwards to a remote golden cross and ball. The dome on which these symbols rode belonged to a different world from the houses below which, shrouded by the smoke of the chimneys, were so close round the temple's base that they seemed to be crowding into its portals. For, if above the level of the houses the city belonged to God, below it Mammon reigned, grudging every foot of ground. Yet the worshippers of God and Mammon alike had observed in their building the rules of proportion and good sense. In all London north of the river there seemed scarcely a house not in keeping with its neighbours.

It was a city built without a plan and yet with a common purpose, not imposed by some grandiloquent king but to serve the needs of a community of merchants who, nursed in a classical tradition, had learnt that, to be free, man must express himself within a framework of order. Controlled since the Great Fire by building acts which laid down the ceiling-heights, types of materials and number of storeys to be used in every class of street, it was at the acme of its ordered and mannered beauty, mellowed by time and still untouched by the hand of the Gothic improver. There were few palaces and large buildings, but street after street of unpretentious, uniform, exquisitely proportioned three- and four-storeyed houses of brown and grey brick, their skylines of parapet, tile and chimney-stack broken only by trees and the white stone of Wren's belfries.

The roadways were mostly straight and, in relation to their height, wide, with flagstoned pavements guarded from the traffic by posts and with wrought-iron railings before the houses. Every house had the same sober, unadorned face of freestone-bordered sash, the same neat white pillars on either side of the pedimented door, the same stone steps over the area crowned by a lamp-post. Only in the beautifully moulded doors and brightly polished knockers, with their lion masks, wreaths and urns, did the English instinct for individuality break through that all-pervading, almost monotonous framework. There, and in the narrow, winding lanes and courts behind the Georgian façade, glimpsed through archways from which came whiffs of laystall and stable and where ragged children swarmed in darkness and cobblers sat at hutches with low open doors.

Between the eye and this classical city lay the source from which it drew its wealth—the river, no longer, as in the reaches below Westminster, given over to purposes of pleasure but lined with wharves, warehouses, timber-yards and manufactories. Spanning it was a bridge dating from the remote past. Its dark camel-back was no longer crowned, as formerly, with houses and shops, but beneath it the stream, narrowed into cataracts, still poured down through arches where wheels sucked water into iron cylinders with a noise like artillery. On either side of the steep slope, crowded with carts and pedestrians, were stone bowers in whose recesses old women sat selling apples and sweetmeats. Below the bridge the sky was dark with masts, and the river almost hidden by the throng of barges and wherries.

Apart from London and the Scottish and Irish capitals there were only two towns in Great Britain, Manchester and Liverpool, with 100,000 inhabitants, and five others—Bristol, Glasgow, Birmingham, Leeds and Sheffield—with over 50,000. At Liverpool, which had taken Bristol's place as the country's first outport, rows of warehouses, eight or nine storeys high, extended for half a mile along the waterfront, where thousands of men perpetually unloaded ships from the far ends of the earth. With its fine residential houses, elegant Grecian buildings, clean broad streets and spreading smoke pall, silhouetted against the Cheshire hills, Richard Ayton, in his

Voyage round Great Britain, thought it the most beautiful town in England after London; it brought to his mind "the country in the pride of its industry and enterprise and under the most striking signs of its wealth, consequence and power."

Everything testified to that wealth and power: the interminable masts in the Thames, Tyne and Mersey, the Chinese, Persian, Parsee and Armenian traders in the Customs House, the Souchang tea that Dorothy Wordsworth wrote for from Rydal to Twinings, the rum with which the abstemious Wilberforce laced his bedtime milk. At the time that Napoleon sailed, a prisoner in a British man-of-war, for St. Helena, wages in the manufacturing districts were higher than they had ever been. Yorkshire woolcombers were earning five shillings a day, coalminers almost as much. Everyone with ambition was borrowing to launch out in new ways; even humble Samuel Bamford, finding work for the handloom so easily procurable, gave notice to his employer and, hiring looms, set up on his own. During the closing years of the war, when Britain was manufacturing for all Europe, a vast working population had been called into existence to supply every manner of article to countries too busy in mutual slaughter to be able to make for themselves.

No one could gainsay the energy with which the British worked to achieve success. At Birmingham, a foreigner reported, no one spoke or thought of anything but labour. The hours of the north country factories ranged from sixty-five to seventy-five a week.[1] The operatives who combed and sheared the cloth of the West Riding worked from four in the morning till eight at night. The London shops closed their shutters at midnight and opened again at dawn. When the first edition of Scott's *Fortunes of Nigel* reached London from Edinburgh on a Sunday—the one day of rest observed by this nation of toilers—the bales were cleared from the wharves by one o'clock on Monday morning and 7000 copies distributed before ten.

Punctuality and dispatch seemed universal attributes. "With habits of early rising," Cobbett asked, "who ever wanted time for any business?" "Sharp's the word and sharp's the action," was the

[1] Smart 196-7.

motto of the great carrier, William Deacon. In this the English resembled their hero, Nelson, who, as he was borne dying from the *Victory's* deck, noticed something wrong with the tiller rope and ordered it, as was his habit, to be put right at once. The founder of W. H. Smith's built up his firm's fortunes by galloping the morning newspapers to catch the out-going mails. Even the postmen went from door to door ringing their bells "with an indefatigable rapidity."

There was something heroic about the energy of the English and Scots. Many resembled Wordsworth, whom Carlyle described as having "great jaws like a crocodile cast in a mould designed for prodigious work." George Stephenson's father looked "like a peer o' deals nailed thetither an' a bit of flesh i' th' inside."[1] A Northumberland pitman of Bewick's acquaintance was so strong that he thought it no hardship to spend his days at the bottom of a pit, breast high in icy water, filling buckets as they were lowered to him. Bewick himself set off at five every morning to walk ten miles to Newcastle, wading through streams and never troubling to change his clothes, even when they were frozen stiff. Even the gentle Charles Lamb, rusticating at Dalston, walked every morning into the Temple to get shaved, while Keats—a consumptive—tramped six hundred miles in a month through the Highlands, rising always before dawn to complete twenty miles by noon. A penniless widow in a little Lincolnshire town made and hawked pasteboard boxes for sixteen hours a day to feed and educate her son; her only respite was an occasional pipe with a neighbour who kept her children by sewing sacks for a factory, whereupon, her son wrote, "the two brave women would go again to work after cheering each other to go stoutly through the battle of life."[2]

[1] Smiles, *Lives of the Engineers* III 17.

[2] Cooper, 8-9, 26-7. See *idem*, 17; Bewick, 3, 35-7, 59-60, 95-7; Cobbett, I, 28-9; Colvin, Keats, 293; Dixon, 66; Eland, 98; Espriella, I, 129; Farington, VII, 175; Hazlitt, "The Letter Bell," *Monthly Magazine*, March, 1831; Lamb, VI, 495, 581-5; Letts, 125, 133-4; Lockhart, V, 170; Lucas, I, 43-4; Simond, II, 77; Smart, 196-7; Sydney, 149; Woodward, 36.

They wasted little. The refuse of the capital was sold to the Essex and Hertfordshire farmers; the scourings of the streets were shipped to Russia to mix with clay for rebuilding Moscow. The great Walter Scott, who, to save cutting up a book worth a few shillings, would spend whole days transcribing passages in his own hand, taught his son-in-law his youthful expedient of sinking his wine into a well in the morning and hauling it up as his guests arrived for dinner. Frugality was the handmaid of industry; the possession of property, saved or inherited, was viewed as the one way a man could become master of his fate and independent.

With energy and frugality went a high sense of enterprise. A nine-year-old Gainsborough boy, having raised fourpence by selling old bits of iron salvaged from the Trent, turned it into a half a crown by begging a lift to Hull, fifty miles away, and returned with a bag of cockles for sale in his native town. From Peg Pimpleface, the costermonger's daughter, driving her donkey-cart round Poplar and Limehouse to sell vegetables from the Middlesex market gardens, to Captain Gordon of Calcutta chartering a vessel to penetrate the sea of Okhotsk and offer British goods to Siberian savages, the English were heroically on the venture. Wherever they went they fended, and expected to fend, for themselves. Simond, going over a West Indiaman, found her cabin hung with pikes, muskets and pistols, and four great guns projecting from the cabin windows. In the same year—1810—he reported that "the light troops of English commerce" were finding entrances to a forbidden continent, consigning their goods in packages which could be carried by hand and making them up to resemble the manufactures of the lands to which they were sent, even to the wrappers and trade labels; in a Leeds factory he saw the name of *Joumaux frères de Sedan* on broadcloth destined for export. A few years later, a clergyman, travelling behind the Allied lines, found all the uniforms of British make and even Prussian soldiers wearing brass lions in their caps. The Flemish burghers whom Dorothy Wordsworth saw after the war had their clothes made in Yorkshire. The very cottons of India were undersold by Lancashire on the banks of the Ganges.[1]

[1] Anderson, 117-20; Bamford, I, 201; II, 86; Berwick, 16-18; Cooper, 24-5;

It was the blast furnaces that had made the armaments that had destroyed Napoleon. With the growing demand for iron—the main sinew of war—and the exhaustion of the south country forests that had fed the old charcoal furnaces and built the nation's wooden ships, steam-power, the invention of a succession of native geniuses, had been applied to the new coke furnaces of the north and midlands. By the end of the war these were turning out between a quarter and half a million tons more than at its beginning. Coke, not charcoal, lit the funeral pyre of the armed Revolution. Simond in 1811 was shown an ironworks in which three hundred men, operating enormous hammers driven by a 120-h.p. engine, produced 10,000 gun-barrels a month. To feed the furnaces and the steam-power engines which inventors and capitalists were evolving in every industry to do with one man's labour what it had needed a dozen to do before, landowners and contractors prospected eagerly for coal and, finding it in abundance, made power-pumps and machinery to mine it and canals and iron-grooved or railed tracks to carry it to their customers.

The British at the time were the most ingenious people on earth. A society that venerated freedom of thought and action, peopled by an hereditary race of skilful mechanics, was a seed-plot for invention. The first suspension bridge in Europe was built over the Tagus in 1812 by a major of the Royal Staff Corps to ensure swift communication between the two wings of Wellington's army. When, in a ship distressed at sea, a match could not be struck to fire the mortar, a young lieutenant was able to produce a bottle of sulphuric acid and a tube, primed with hyperexmuriate of potash and sugar-candy, to effect an instantaneous ignition. The school-boys at Harrow celebrated the retreat from Moscow at "Duck Puddle" with cannon of their own making; Shelley at Eton hired a travelling tinker to help him build a steam-organ which, however, instead of filling the spheres with music, burst and nearly blew up

De Selincourt, II, 883; Lockhart, V, 100, 124; T. Moore, *Diary*, 3rd April, 1823; Pyne, *Picturesque Views*, Plates III, VII; Simond, I, 243; II, 77; Stanley, 185, 192; D. Walker, *General View of the Agriculture of the County of Hertford* (1795), cit. Ernle, 191; Woodward, 369, 444.

his tutor's house. Later, residing in Italy, he interested himself in building a steamer.

Lads of humbler parentage, heirs of generations of fine craftsmen, finding their ingenuity sought after and rewarded, applied themselves to the evolution of new technical processes. Smiles' *Lives of the Engineers* is a saga of miraculous achievement wrought out of the native genius and character of a succession of Scottish and English country lads: Rennie, the millwright's apprentice, who drained the Lincolnshire Fens and built docks and iron bridges; weavers and machinists like Crompton and Thomas Johnson who, backed by their employers, made lonely Lancashire the economic corner-stone of the world; the engineers, Bramah—a village carpenter's boy—Maudslay, Roberts and Whitworth; Trevithick, the Cornish giant, and George Stephenson, the Northumberland collier's son who laid the foundations of the railway age. Steam-power to raise water and coal, and drive engines, ships and vehicles, eliminating the horrors of windbound voyages and such winter exposure on coach tops as killed Keats; gas to light streets, shops and houses; safety lamps to prevent explosions in mines; water-closets instead of foul-smelling privies; wooden legs with elastic springs to reproduce the motions of nature, and pull-over bar-room taps, umbrellas and waterproof hats, patent folding carriage-steps, automatic cheese-toasters, chairs that sprang out of walking-sticks and braces to keep up trousers, were all, in their different modes, manifestations of the tireless British will to tame nature for amenity and social betterment and grow rich in the process.

So were the ingenuities of the scientists—

"The varied wonders that tempt us as we pass,
    The cow-pox, tractors, galvanism and gas"—

who, voyaging ahead of the practical possibilities of their age, were laboriously charting new courses for the future: young Faraday, the Newington Butts blacksmith's son, at his work on electricity; Dalton studying the combination of the elements and determining atomic weights while teaching mathematics at half a crown an hour; Sir Humphry Davy, who invented the safety lamp for miners in the year of Waterloo and thrilled fashionable audiences with his chemical discourses at the Royal Institution in Albemarle

Street. It was part of the same revolutionary urge that threw up in philosophy a Rousseau, in politics a Robespierre, and in war a Napoleon. Being a practical people, the English and Scots made their contribution to it in a utilitarian form. By doing so they did more to transform the material world than any of the other aspirants of the age. And through their philosophers—Hume, Adam Smith, Ricardo, Bentham—they evolved a new science, political economy or economics, to explain how that world operated.

Improved transport was the first condition of this revolution. The unlettered Derbyshire millwright, James Brindley—who with James Watt, the Greenock-born contriver of the expansive use of steam, was, in his humdrum, practical way, the British counterpart of Rousseau—conceived the revolutionary idea of making canals independent of rivers on a nation-wide scale. He and his fellow engineers created radical, man-made waterways, straight and easily navigable, to take the place of God's, controlling water-levels, tunnelling mountains and bridging valleys with aqueducts. Before and during the war, more than three thousand miles of such waterways were built, enabling coal, iron, timber, pottery and other heavy goods to be carried to any part of the country as easily and as cheaply as by sea.

At the same time the character of road travel was transformed. Before the war, even on the main trunk roads, postilions had had to quarter ceaselessly from side to side to avoid huge pools of water and ruts deep enough to break a horse's leg; as late as the winter of 1797-8 the highway from Tyburn to Oxford was from a foot to eighteen inches deep in mud. The genius of two Lowland Scots, Telford, a Dumfriesshire shepherd's son, and McAdam, provided the country, during the first quarter of the nineteenth century, with smooth-metalled highways built on the principles of Roman science. Their engineered gradients, culverts and bridges raised the speed of post-chaises and coaches from four or five to ten and even twelve miles an hour. The cost of such travel remained heavy; an inside ticket from London to Liverpool cost four guineas without tips and meals. But the gain to traders and men of money was immeasurable. Commerce and finance were given the speed and certainty required to control the fast revolving machinery of

Britain's new industrial production. The mail-coaches, with their chocolate-coloured panels, scarlet wheels and melodious horns, became the national timepieces. Such was their regularity that all along the roads men set their clocks by the "Nimrod," "Regulator" or "Tally-ho."[1]

. . . .

Year in, year out, the ships of maritime Britain carried her trade abroad, sailing from her estuaries under great wings of white sails, with manufactured cottons, woollens, hardware and cutlery, guns, wrought copper and brass, refined sugar, linens, lace and silks, saddlery and tanned leather, pottery, china clay, ironware, coal and rock salt, and returning with raw cotton from the United States, timber from the Baltic, wine from France, Sicily, Portugal and the Atlantic islands, sugar, rum and mahogany from the Caribbean, tea and spices from the East Indies, cod from the Newfoundland fisheries. There was no place within reach of flowing water where Britons did not venture and set up shop or factory. Some of them, out-distancing Marco Polo, traded broadcloth and shalloons for tea at the far ends of the earth with pigtailed Chinese. For England did not only enjoy her unrivalled sense of elegance and comfort; she exported it. From Wedgwood's famous factory at Etruria in Staffordshire went out the wares—"neat, strong and beautiful"—which were famed all over the world. In every good inn from Paris to St. Petersburg, it was said, travellers were served on English ware.

For four miles from London Bridge to Deptford the forest of masts was almost continuous. Often there were two thousand sea-going ships lying in the river—more than four times the number a century before. Newcastle, Liverpool and Sunderland, the next largest ports, had between them almost as many. Bernadotte,

[1] Dixon, 61, 72; Fowler, 216-17. See Ashton, II, 230; Austen, II, 423; Clapham, I, 59, 92-7; Creevey, *Life and Times*, 115; De Quincey, *Autobiographical Sketches*; Ernle, 203-5; Farington, VII, 97; VIII, 270; Hammond, *Rise of Modern Industry*, 75-79; Klingender, 13; Lockhart, V, 86; McCausland, 18-19, 23; Mitford, *Our Village*, 63; Nevill, 143-8, 153-4; Newton, 21, Simond, I, 17, 184, 201-2; Smart, 28-9; Sydney, I, 53-6, 58; Woodward, 4.

crossing to Sweden in 1810, saw more than a thousand British merchantmen in the Belt convoyed by six men-of-war. The annual value of imports had risen during the war from nineteen to thirty-two millions, of exports from twenty-seven to fifty-eight millions. "What are we to think of this trade," wrote a foreigner, "of which a whole immense city could not contain the stock and is merely its counting house. . . . The mind forgets that the immediate object is sugar and coffee, tobacco and cotton, and sees only a social engine which rivals in utility, in vastness of operation as well as wisdom of detail, the phenomena of nature itself."

The principal article exported was now manufactured cotton. In Glasgow alone there were more than forty mills employing over two hundred workpeople apiece; Dale and Owen at the great New Lanark Mills—though this was exceptional—employed as many as sixteen hundred. Flax and worsted spinning were following the example of cotton, though weaving in all branches of the textile trade was still mainly done "out". But the steam-power loom, first set up in Manchester in 1806 as the rival of the handloom, was already proving a godsend to manufacturers trying to capture the markets which Britain's naval victories had opened. Three years after Waterloo two thousand power-looms were in operation; thereafter their numbers doubled every other year, rising during the 'twenties to astronomical figures.

The quality of the goods exported, and the integrity and dispatch with which British traders met their customers' demands, earned prodigious dividends. So did the ownership of land in the new industrial areas. The rent-roll of the Shakerleys, a typical Lancashire and Cheshire landed family, rose during George III's reign from £3000 to over £30,000 p.a. A traveller, passing through the Vale of Clwyd in the last year of the war, was shown the house of a formerly poor clergyman who enjoyed an income of £75,000 from a copper mine discovered on a barren piece of land of which he was part owner. Vast underground estates of coal and iron-ore, worthless a generation before, were transformed by the use of steam-power into properties bringing their proprietors rents and royalties transcending even those of high farming, and still greater fortunes to the thrusting, able men who developed them. The

Bridgewater Canal, which cost £200,000 to build, returned an annual profit of £100,000; the thirty-nine original proprietors of the Mersey and Irwell Navigation Company received their capital back in interest every other year for half a century. The first Sir Robert Peel, a dispossessed yeoman's son who invested in a few of the early spinning jennies, left nearly a million sterling. A Bristol merchant, worth at the beginning of the war under a thousand pounds, possessed half a million when Farington met him at its conclusion.

• • • • • • • •

One saw that wealth displayed in the west end of the capital, with its mile after mile of splendid mansions, wonderful clothes and horses, liveried servants and glittering barouches and landaus; in the new Edinburgh—a paradise, it seemed to contemporaries, of order, light and neatness—which had risen near Calton Hill, away from the crooked closes and stench of Auld Reekie; in the county towns with their crescents and railed squares aping London's West End, their exquisitely windowed shops and classical assembly rooms and fine ancestral residences, where the less metropolitan-minded county families spent the winter season for balls, local business and race meetings; in the watering places, Bath and Tunbridge Wells of the mannered past and Cheltenham and Leamington of the dashing present, where the well-to-do flocked as much for pleasure as health. At Bath, wrote Pierce Egan, all was bustle and gaiety, "numerous dashing equipages passing and repassing, . . . the shops capacious and elegant, . . . libraries to improve the mind, musical repositories to enrich the taste, . . . and tailors, milliners of the highest eminence in the fashionable world to adorn the male and beautify the female." In the Pump Room bands of music played almost continuously while the crowds promenaded. Elsewhere, along the sea coast, remote fishing villages were turning overnight into watering places of a new kind, with elegant villas, piers, assembly rooms, libraries, theatres and bathing boxes where the genteel, and moneyed would-be genteel, could enjoy "aquatic gratification." The greatest of these was Brighton, which, with its royal palace, its half-hourly coaches to the capital, its immense promenade, its fashionable domes, bow windows and cupolas, was a kind of miniature West End by the sea.[1]

The dominant desire of all classes was to "cut a dash"; to show "style," to be "elegant." From Lady Londonderry going to a ball so covered with jewels that she could not stand and had to be followed round with a chair, to the poor Edinburgh widow who pinched to be buried in a coach and six surmounted with black plumes and followed by carriages and hired mourners, the British were increasingly becoming martyrs to display. "The necessity of acquiring, not merely the real necessaries and comforts of life, but the means of living in style, a certain inveterate habit of luxury, inexorable vanity," wrote Simond, "answer in England the same purpose as the conscription in France; and the fondest mother thinks as little of resisting the one as the other." To this universal principle of activity, though he doubted whether it secured private happiness, he attributed the country's strength, seeing it drive each generation as fast as it reached manhood into the Army, Navy, East and West Indies, and, he might have added, the Bar, the counting-house and factory.

Almost everything the English rich did served the ends of style. It created both the external beauty whose survivals—houses, streets, gardens, parks, vistas, furniture, china, silver—still linger on into our own age, and the commercial, colonial, and industrial wealth that the Victorians both enhanced and exploited. It filled London and Brighton, Cheltenham, Leamington and St. Leonards, and the new suburbs of every ancient city with tree-lined avenues and Grecian and Pompeian crescents and terraces of white stucco with railed and green-painted *jalousies*, and fine assembly rooms, and Gothic lodges and cottages *ornées*. It spread itself across the country-side, adorning it with park-walls, crested gates and castellated lodges, with Ionic arches and obelisks and Corinthian pillars, with metal turnpike roads traversed by beautiful equipages harnessed in all the pride of the loriner's art, with silver trappings and coloured housings

[1] Ashton, I, 134-4; Bury, I, 99; Clapham, I, 8-9; Creevey, *Life and Times*, 115; Daniell, I, 79; *English Spy*, I, 285, 305; Farington, VIII, 197, 201, 260; Leslie, *Constable*; *Sea-Bathing Places*, passim; Hill, *Austen*, 104-5; Simond, I, 266; Sydney, I, 39.

and outriders in yellow and scarlet jackets. It filled the houses of the gentry with showy, lovely, and sometimes not so lovely, furniture, with buhl and bronzes and damask hangings, with great glasses and embroidered stools and rosewood tambour-frames; with Italian paintings and native portraiture, now reaching its high evening in Lawrence and Raeburn; with engravings and aquatints and the lovely art of the miniaturist; with Athenian marbles rescued by wealthy connoisseurs from the lime-burners in the pasha-ruled, robber-haunted Ægean.[1] At Powderham Castle, according to the guide-book, the music-room was adorned with marbles and *bassi-relievi*; the chimney-piece represented Apollo and the Muses and was copied from the sarcophagus of Homer.

Everyone who could afford it—and many who could not—was engaged in rebuilding and improving and emparking; "my prodigious undertaking of a west wing at Bowhill," wrote the Duke of Buccleuch, "is begun." Owners of ancient country houses, inspired by Repton's book on landscape gardening, were talking, like Henry Tilney in *Northanger Abbey*, of foregrounds, distances, second distances, side-screens and perspective, lights and shades. At Mamhead, Lord Lisburne's seat in Devonshire, the old error of torturing nature by raising gardens with terraces and making ponds and fountains on the sides of hills was corrected, we are told, and the ground restored—with infinite expense and labour—to its pristine natural beauty, with varied prospects of sea, river and the country. At Knowsley, Lord Derby's new dining-room, paid for by the rising wealth of Lancashire, measured fifty-three feet by thirty-seven, with an immense Gothic window at one end and two huge church-like doors at the other; "Pray," asked a guest, "are those great doors to be opened for every pat of butter that comes into the room?" At Fonthill the interior was like a Gothic cathedral,

---

[1] Among them the Elgin marbles. "There is not a classical nook," wrote Simond, "unexplored by these restless wanderers—they dispute with each other for the remains of Greece and Egypt, purchase antique marbles for their weight in gold, pack up and ship home a Grecian temple as other people would a set of china." Simond, II, 148. See *idem*, II, 64-6; Mrs. Arbuthnot, *Journal*, 10th April, 1822; *Sea-Bathing Places*, 217, 246-7, 286, 336-7, 447-8; Harriet Granville, I, 130; Gronow, I, 90-1; Hill, *Austen*, 40-2; Lockhart, IV, 337; McCausland, 22-4, 66; Lady Shelley, I, 48-9; Simond, I, 337; Wansey, 116.

only larger, fitted up with crimson and gold, with statues in every niche and immense gilded and jewelled boxes for relics. In the vast pseudo-medieval castle—a thousand feet in length with avenues radiating for miles in every direction—which the seventh earl of Bridgewater employed Wyatt to build in place of the older Ashridge, the central staircase, flanked with statues by Westmacott, rose to nearly a hundred feet, and the walls—a shrine to victorious aristocracy—were covered with immense pictures of the Allied triumphs at the close of the Revolutionary wars. The orangery was a hundred and thirty feet in length, and the conservatory, with its eleven Gothic windows, almost as long, and in the chapel, where daily services were held and two chaplains maintained, the elegance and snobbery of Regency England reached an almost sacred apogee. "The perforated oak screen which divides it from the ante-chapel; the mighty wrought Gothic ceiling, the windows filled with beautifully painted glass," the house's contemporary historian wrote, "demand our particular notice. . . . The Pulpit and the Reading-Desk are well placed, opposite to each other, and somewhat elevated"—a delicate compliment to the deity—"above . . . the richly carved canopies . . . which form the seats of the Earl and Countess of Bridgewater. Beneath these stalls are the seats for servants. . . . In this chapel was preached, in November, 1817, the first sermon by the Chaplain of the Earl of Bridgewater, who had had the honour of compiling the pages of this history."[1]

The assured, unquestioning snobbery of the rich which sprang from all this seemed as unalterable as the great palaces which housed them. The very approach to a nobleman's house was surrounded with an aura of respect; at Castle Howard visitors—for most of these places were open to gentlefolk on stated days—were expected to alight and respectfully walk the last half-mile through an avenue and deer-park. An American staying at Gordon Castle wrote of the delightful consciousness that, whichever way the duke's guests drove, the horizon scarcely limited their host's domains. "The ornamental gates flying open at your approach, miles distant from the castle; the herds of red deer trooping away from the sound of wheels in the silent park; the stately pheasants

[1] H. J. Todd, *History of the College of Bonhommes at Ashridge*, 1823.

178

feeding tamely in the immense preserves; the stalking gamekeepers lifting their hats in the dark recesses of the forest—there was something in this perpetually reminding you of privileges." When Harriet Granville and her husband stayed by themselves at Trentham, six servants waited on them at dinner, while a gentleman-in-waiting and a housekeeper hovered round the door in case they should express any wish. Too often noblemen, building their lives on such deference, surrounded themselves with a horde of sycophants—led captains, toady dandies and semi-professional wits—who obscured for them both their duties and interests; the fat, pasty-faced chaplain at Castle Howard scarcely dared give an opinion on the weather lest his patron, Lord Carlisle, should disagree.

The rich had become almost too rich for reason. Lord Alvanley, whose dinners were said to be the best in London, had an apricot tart on his table every day of the year and, when his *maître d'hôtel* expostulated at the expense, sent him to Gunter's, the confectioner, to buy up his entire stock. At one fashionable breakfast-party the strawberries alone cost £150. The whole world, wrote a foreigner, was ransacked for the wealthy Englishman's dinner: Périgord pie and truffles from France, sauces and curry powder from India, hams from Westphalia and Portugal, caviare from Russia, reindeer tongues from Lapland, olives from Spain, cheese from Parma, sausages from Bologna. "To live expensive and elegant" had become the end of existence; Lord Grey said he would not dress Lady Londonderry for £5000 a year. Her very handkerchiefs cost fifty guineas the dozen; a guest at Wynyard complained of being unable to sleep because the lace on the pillows and sheets so tickled his face. No one had any use for what was old-fashioned; everything in the *haut ton* had to be new, to use the Corinthian slang, "prime and bang up to the mark." A colonel of the Guards used to give Storr and Mortimer, the Regent Street goldsmiths, £25 a quarter to furnish him with a new set of studs every week during the season.

The acme of perfection, the *summum bonum* of style, was the dandy. The bright glories of the past were beginning to fade a little; even blue coats and brass and gold buttons were going out in London and being replaced by a sober black and white. But the quality of the cloth and the elegance and fit of the tailoring were superlative. A dandy was a formidable figure—the wide-brimmed glossy hat, always new, the spotless, white-starched cravat so tight and high that the wearer could scarcely look down or turn his head, and was for ever pulling it up and running his fingers along the bottom of his chin; the exquisitely cut coat worn wide open to display the waistcoat of buff, yellow or rose and the snowy embroidered cambric shirt; the skin-tight pantaloons or "inexpressibles," gathered up into a wasp's waist and bulging like a succession of petticoats under the stays; the fobs, jewels, chains and spotless gloves; the whitethorn cane—a hint of the broad acres that sustained the type—the wonderfully made boots whose shine rivalled the cuirasses of the Life Guards. Hoby, the famous bootmaker at the top of St. James's Street—a Methodist preacher in private life—told the Duke of York that, if Wellington had had any other bootmaker, he could scarcely have won his victories. The blacking of tops was a high art and mystery: two rival advertisers in a West End street, each holding up a varnished boot on a pole, claimed, the one, that his was the best polish in the world, and the other that it was so good that it could be eaten. Beau Brummell, asked for the secret of his, replied that it was made from the finest champagne.[1]

These bucks or swells—some of whom in youth had shared the friendship of the Prince Regent—ruled the world of fashion from their favourite vantage point in White's bow window. Their court was bordered on the north by Oxford Street, on the east by Bond Street, on the south by Pall Mall and west by Park Lane, but their influence extended far beyond its borders. Byron rated Brummell's importance above Napoleon's. When, after bringing the Regent's soft muslin, bow and wadding neck-piece into contempt by appearing, to the amazement of the town, in a stiff collar, this remarkable man fled overseas from his creditors, he left his secret as a legacy to his country, writing on a sheet of paper on his dressing-table, "Starch is the man!" The long morning hours spent by his disciples with their valets completing their toilets; their sublime lounge

[1] Gronow I 271-3; II 52-3.

with every eye upon them down Bond Street, St. James's or Pall Mall; their exquisite French dinners; their invariable habit of being imperturbably late for every appointment; their condescending appearances at the great summer evening parades in Kensington Gardens or Hyde Park; their extravagant gambling and love of play; their generosity and occasional surprising kindnesses and unshakable self-confidence, were as much part of the England of the time as the fat cattle in the shires and the thoroughbreds on the turnpike roads.[1]

They shared their empire with the great ladies who controlled the *entrée* to Almack's assembly rooms and the balls and routs of high society. As evening fell the streets of London's West End became filled with an endless stream of wonderful carriages, each with its eyes of flame twinkling in the darkness. As with a sudden flurry of horses each drew up at its destination, the tall liveried footmen leapt down and set up a great rapping on the door. From six to eight, and again from ten till midnight, the noise of the wheels in cobbled Mayfair, Simond wrote, was like the fall of Niagara. The houses were lit from top to bottom; the windows from the streets framed a concourse of nodding feathers and stars under chandeliers, while gaping crowds stood at the doors and powdered, gold-laced footmen lined the steps. Every night in the season there were a dozen or more of such assemblies, in which there was seldom any room to sit, no conversation, cards or music, nothing but glittering clothes and jewels and lights, shouting, elbowing, turning and winding from room to room, vacant, famous, smiling or evasive faces, and, at the end of an interval, a slow descent to the hall where the departing guests, waiting in their orders and diamonds for their carriages, spent more time among the footmen than they had spent above with their hosts. "To the Duchess of Gloucester's rout," Cam Hobhouse wrote in his diary, "where was all London, and

[1] One of the greatest of all, "King" Allen, had shown remarkable energy and courage in the battle of Talavera. Gronow, II, 86. See Byron, *Letters and Journals*, II, 128; *Corr.*, I, 142; Broughton, II, 177; Lamington, 5-7; *English Spy*, I, 330-1; II, 218; Farington, VIII, 238; Harriet Granville, I, 158; Gronow, I, 52-3; II, 1-2, 58-9, 86, 238, 252-3, 268-9, 271-3, 294; T. Moore, *Fudge Letters*; Nevill, 169; Newton, 246-7; *Real Life in London*, I, 42; Lady Shelley, I, 53, 64.

such a sight as was never seen. The Duke of Wellington and three Lord Mayors there; spent the night hustling to get the Misses Byng and Lady Tavistock to her carriage." Lady Shelley, who was also present, mentioned that she was nearly squeezed to death and that many cried out in alarm: "the Duke of Wellington, who was standing half-way up the stairs, called out to the ladies below that there was not the slightest danger, but the pressure was so great that many of them fainted. More than sixteen hundred persons had been invited to a house which is not capable of holding more than six hundred."[1]

There were breakfast parties in pastoral mansions among the Middlesex meadows and Surrey woods, water parties in carpeted boats with bands and delicately coloured awnings and Gunter's choicest suppers, *fêtes champêtres* in the gardens of aristocratic palaces, masqued balls and music assemblies and dances where, after endless quadrilles and suppers in which every delicacy was served under Grecian lamps and festoons of exotics, white-gowned, high-bosomed graces relaxed, blushing in the arms of tight-pantalooned cavaliers, in the sensational new German dance, the waltz. There were parades on summer evenings and Sundays in Rotten Row and Kensington Gardens where, through clouds of dust, hundreds of wonderful horses passed and repassed carrying with them the great world in taffeta, feathers and lace, uniforms, quizzing-glasses and curving top hats. There were musical parties—it was the era of the young Rossini—when gifted young ladies vied over harp and harpsichord with singers "in the public line," and nights at the opera in the Haymarket when Catalini's piercing voice drowned chorus and orchestra and, behind the red curtains of the boxes, all that was most brilliant and luxurious in the world congregated, with jewels, bare shoulders and orders blazing under the light of thousands of candles, while, in the libertarian manner of

[1] Broughton, II, 15, 98; Lady Shelley, II, 12. See also Mrs. Arbuthnot, *Journal*, May 31st, 1822; 3rd July, 1823; Lamington, 19; Harriet Granville, I, 28, 140-2, 152-4, 205, 210; II, 80-1; Gaussen, I, 355; Gronow, II, 268-9; Holland, *Journal*, I, 65, 128, 152, 128, 152, 167-8, 173, 256, 332, 264-5; Leslie, *Constable*, 114; Lieven Letters, 18, 112-14, 47-8, 125-6; *Life in London*, 20-1, 234-46; Mitford, *Life*, 1, 80; Moore, *Byron*, 291; *Paget Brothers*, 186-7; *Real Life in London*, II, 148; Simond, I, 26-8; II, 250.

England, frail ladies plied their trade in the galleries, and footmen tradesmen and sailors whistled, howled and cracked nuts. There were other nights at the ballet when, as Vestris sang or Angiolini danced, even society forgot for a moment to admire itself:

"While Gayton bounds before th' enraptured looks
    Of hoary marquises and stripling dukes:
    Let high-born lechers eye the lively Presle
    Twirl her light limbs that spurn the needless veil;
    Let Angiolini bare her breast of snow,
    Wave the white arm and point the pliant toe;
    Collini trill her love-inspiring song,
    Strain her fair neck and charm the listening throng."

There were *petit-soupers* and gay expeditions to Vauxhall:

    "when the long hours of public are past
    And we meet with champagne and a chicken at last,"

and *recherché* dinners when Luttrell or Rogers talked, and unforgettable evenings when Moore sang. "It is not singing," wrote Lady Charlotte Bury after a summer night in 1819, "there is none of the skill of the mere mechanic in the art; it is poetry—the distinct enunciation, the expression, the nationality of his genius—when heard, delighted in, and never to be forgotten."[1]

Yet, though elegant and cultivated, society could often be stupid and vacant. At a dinner party at Lambton, in a dining-room hung with massive chandeliers and dark-coloured, heavily gold-fringed curtains resembling palls, thirty of the best-born people in England sitting at a long narrow table, the malicious Creevey recorded, ate in such a solemn silence that it might have been the Lambton family vault and the company the male and female Lambtons buried in their best clothes in a sitting position. Usually the conversation of the *haut ton* was of the emptiest kind, and concerned, except for politics, with dress, social precedence and scandal. "Shall I tell you," wrote Creevey from Middleton, "what Lady Jersey is

[1] Bury, II, 201-3. See Austen, II, 140; Broughton, I, 94; Byron, *English Bards and Scotch Reviewers*; Lord Coleridge, 204; Croker, I, 66; *English Spy*, I, 164; Gronow, II, 120-3, 297-8; Lamington, 19; Leigh Hunt, *Autobiography*, I, 137-8, 142; *Real Life in London*, I, 16, 19; Lady Shelley, I, 64; II, 58; Simond, II, 198.

like? She is like one of her numerous gold and silver musical dickey birds that are in all the showrooms of this house. She begins to sing at eleven o'clock and, with the interval of the hour she retires to her cage to rest, she sings till twelve at night without a moment's interruption. She changes her feathers for dinner, and her plumage both morning and evening is the happiest and most beautiful I ever saw. Of the *merits* of her songs I say nothing till we meet." There was, as Jane Austen wrote, a monstrous deal of stupid quizzing and commonplace nonsense talked, but scarcely any wit. What there was of it lacked spontaneity; in the *salons* where the conversation of the rival wits "raged," it was often tedious: famous talkers like Rogers, Luttrell and Sydney Smith spent as much time preparing their *mots* as a fine lady her toilet. Scott, in London for a few weeks, longed to be back at Abbotsford, away from fine company, champagne, turbot and plovers' eggs; it was all very well for a while, he wrote, but it made one feel like a poodle dog compelled to stand for ever on its hind legs. Its conventions, though less tyrannical than those of a German Court, were rigid and oppressive; a young man of talent who aspired to a place in society had to spend half his time leaving cards and paying calls. To settle the precedence of going in to dinner required the tact of an ambassador and the pedantry of a herald.

There was a universal sense of straining. "I see her," wrote Harriet Granville—herself a snob of finer, more gossamer texture —of Lady Shelley, "with a sort of hoisted-up look in her figure, tight satin shoes, a fine, thick plait of hair, bloodshot eyes, parched lips, fine teeth and an expression of conscious accomplishments in her face." The little set who under the dictatorship of the vulgar, haughty, indefatigable beauty, Lady Jersey, managed the dances at Almack's had introduced, Cam Hobhouse thought, something new into English life: a rigid narrow pride as stupid as it was inhuman and uncharitable. "It is not fashionable," wrote the Countess Lieven, "where I am not." Stendhal, who visited London in 1821, found society divided like the rings of a bamboo, every class aping the manners and habits and striving to emulate the expenditure of the class above. The universal desire to get into a higher circle and keep out intruders vitiated it; people did not enter it with the desire of being agreeable but of being on the defensive against those less modish. Fashionable life at all levels was becoming a fearful hierarchy. Lords who kept open house for their county neighbours cut them in London; clubs and even provincial sub-scription news-rooms black-balled surgeons and estate-agents on the grounds that they did not admit professional men and servants. Gronow described a rich parvenue hostess who excluded from her parties in Portman Square everyone without a title. Strangers entering Stephen's Hotel, the haunt of fashionable officers and men about town, used to be stared out of countenance by the waiters. An English family whom Thomas Campbell met on the Continent, reduced by some accident to the *diligence* and fearful of compro-mising their dignity, preserved throughout the two days' journey a sullen, timorous silence, never exchanging a word with either their English or French fellow-travellers. Good-humoured England was becoming what Borrow called "gentility crazy." "The com-pany are mostly of the superior ranks of society," a guide-book assured its readers, "the lower orders of the community not having as yet intruded themselves into Southend." The feeling penetrated the very gaols; at Horsemonger Lane a warder told Leigh Hunt that his prison was not fit for a gentleman, since a person not used to "low people" could not be expected to share their accommoda-tion. Snobbery permeated even the ranks of radical reformers; "Orator" Hunt, staying at a York hotel during the Peterloo trials, sent down a servant to tell a weaver's wife who wanted to shake his hand, that he was not at home. "The same contemptible feeling of classism, the curse of England," wrote Bamford, "existed among the witnesses; there were the 'broad cloth' and 'the narrow cloth' ones, the rich and the poor, and the former seldom sought oppor-tunities for inter-communication with the latter, but rather shunned them."[1] Even the hunting-field was contaminated. "These hounds

[1] Bamford, II, 204, 247-8. "It filled the working classes with a fierce contempt and hatred for every one wearing a decent coat." It later explained Karl Marx. See also Ashton, II, 63; Broughton, II, 186-7; Bury, II, 108; Campbell, II, 252-3; Chancellor, 51; Creevey, I, 14, 296; Dino, 110; Harriet Granville, I, 45, 112; Gronow, II, 221, 303; Howitt, 78-80; Leigh Hunt, *Autobiography*, II, 2; Lieven Letters, 25-61; *Life in London*, 148; Johnny Newcome, 160; New-ton, 51, 226, 235; *Real Life in London*, I, 245; *Romany Rye*, 419; *Sea-*

please me," wrote the Rev. Benjamin Newton, "as they are attended by gentlemen, not farmers."

Under the influence of this restless competitiveness class feeling was turning into a religion. To seem "genteely connected," to boast a pedigree and titled relations was the supreme aim; "it is to have the crest," wrote Jane Austen after the purchase of a Wedgwood dinner service. Even those whose self-esteem seemed in little need of such buttressing competed furiously for precedence; the owner of Stowe, with a dukedom and half Buckinghamshire, christened his son Richard Plantagenet Nugent Bridges Temple. The feudal fuss at times was almost intolerable. When the Duke of Atholl's heir was born at Alnwick—his mother's home—no bells were rung in the castle for a month, the servants were put into list shoes and the Duke of Northumberland forwent his daily exercise for fear of disturbing this precious offspring of two ducal houses. Even clerics treated Debrett like the bible; an Oxford tutor is alleged to have prefaced a rebuke to a pupil: "The friendship I have for my Lord, your father, my respect for my Lord Bishop, your uncle, and the peculiar situation in which I stand with my Lord God!"

One of the disastrous effects of this epidemic of snobbery was to destroy the unity of the nation's educational system. The grammar schools, which had formerly recruited leaders for Church and State from all ranks, lost their upper-class pupils to those establishments which, abandoning their local connections, took boarders at high fees and became called, with the English genius for illogicality, public schools. They mixed the older aristocracy with the new commercial and professional classes, but segregated both from the children of the poor. At the same time the country gentry ceased to send their sons to the university colleges which drew their revenue and scholars from their own shire and sent them instead to colleges where only the rich and titled were welcome. As a result, even though academic reform began to stir the surface of their eighteenth century sloth, the universities ceased to be what

Bathing Places, 443-4; Lady Shelley, I, 37, 308, 359; II, 39; Stendhal, *Memoirs of an Egotist*, 71.

their name implied. They became, instead, finishing schools for a class. "You're a man of family," a college tutor is reported to have said to an idle pupil, "I'm a man of family: call it a literary transaction between two men of fashion!" Bamford thought it symptomatic that high walls were everywhere rising round rich men's gardens in place of the green sod ramparts and hawthorn hedges of friendlier days. Christian England was unconsciously falling a prey to the worst of all heresies: the worship of Lucifer and Mammon. Without birth or money a man was nothing; his only hope was to pretend he possessed them. Haydon, having run short of cash on a journey, flung his last sixpence to the porter at the coach stage so that it rang on the pavement; "unused to such a present for looking after luggage," he related, "he bowed and thanked me so much that all the passengers saw it, and so without sixpence in my pocket I got as much respect all the way home as if I had £100." A bit of straw on a lady's petticoat, implying that the wearer had been forced to resort to a hackney coach, could set a room of fine people tittering. The effects of this disease were insidious. To be poor, since it was a mark of inferiority, was a matter for shame and to be hidden. It was this that caused Foscolo, the Italian patriot, when he visited England as an exile to write, "The English are a humane people, but will have nothing to do with one who wants bread. . . . Poverty is a disgrace which no merit can wipe off. . . . Indigence would render Homer himself despicable in their eyes."

It was here that the nemesis of the contemporary passion for elegance lay: so admirable when it had arisen spontaneously from a widespread love and craving for beauty, so dangerous when it became an obsession, driving men of all classes to a heartless, competitive extravagance. Like every social virtue it had become vitiated in the end by the faults of human nature and transformed from a blessing into a curse. It was at once the motive force and temptation of the nation: the stimulus and peril. It was increasingly attended by vanity, greed and covetousness, and by the uncharitableness to which these gave rise. It reduced even good men from Christians to cads. It ceased to occur to gentlemen that there was anything ignoble in speaking of those socially beneath them with contempt. "I never saw more ridiculous figures," wrote Fox's great-nephew after a levée, "tailors and haberdashers were among them." "King" Allen, the dandy, used to call his bankers his tradesmen, and the Benchers of Lincoln's Inn resolved that writers in the Press were unfit to be called to the Bar. "Mr. Powlett," a country clergyman noted in his journal, "would not go to any place to dine where Mr. Claridge was invited because he was a steward; how soon Mr. Powlett seems to have forgotten that he is the son of a country attorney!" Lady Shelley's father was so disgusted at seeing a rich cotton spinner secure the best turbot at the local fishmonger's that he left his town house at Preston in a passion and never returned. She herself was unable to enjoy a fête at Geneva because some vulgar English were looking on, and felt a strong prejudice against Peel on account of his birth. Even so choice a spirit as Mary Mitford could not escape the infection and wrote contemptuously of sitting next to the grocer's wife, jammed in between brewers and bakers and tailors and corn dealers. When the Prince Regent joined his servants at a Pavilion supper party, the Opposition Press made high jest at royalty condescending to "cooks, scullions, dish-washers, lick-trenchers, shoe-blacks, cinder-sifters, candle-snuffers, etc." A great poet like Wordsworth, a man whose life was dedicated to the contemplation of the eternal, could write of the disgrace—he was of yeoman stock—his brother had incurred by marrying his young housekeeper: "a connection with a servant, and that one his own."[1]

Across the elegant surface of the national wealth ran a yellow streak. The cad—showy, heartless, deceptive and bouncing—was a special product of the Regency; the Regent himself was one. So, for all his genius, was the most famous poet of the age, Lord Byron, who corresponded facetiously with the mother of the man he had cuckolded about her daughter-in-law's indiscretions. The dandies insulted their social equals and were offensively rude to their inferiors; a set of men, a contemporary recalled, who arrogated to themselves the right of criticising the entire universe, who never condescended to laugh, always looked hazy after dinner and

[1] De Selincourt, *Middle Years*, II, 612. See Holland *Journal*, I, 141; Mitford, I, 110-11; Newton, 89; Shelley, I, 3, 8, 236; II, 17; Woodward, 28, 541.

sneered at everyone and everything. The air—the manner—the *je ne sais quoi*—of a Corinthian's quiz, "the curled lip of contempt and the eye, measuring, from top to toe, his companions" became the glass of fashion at which young England dressed itself in the self-indulgent years after Waterloo. His imitators were "the smokers, jokers, hoaxers, glass-cockers, black-legs and fancy fellows of the town," the Corinthian Toms, Jerry Hawthorns and Hon. Tom Dashalls who figure with such gusto in the blackguard pages of the journalist, Pierce Egan, and who became a vogue towards the end of the first quarter of the century. Their motto was to be ripe for any spree, by which they generally meant any frolic that involved others in trouble. It was the result partly of too much food and drink, and, with the growing upper-class substitution of snobbery for religion, of too little sense of responsibility. Lord Barrymore, driving home from a midnight revel in his highflyer phæton, cracked half the windows—"fanning the daylights," he called it—on either side of Colnbrook high street with his whip.

The older ideal of a gentleman was being obscured by one that, though based on elegance, high vitality and courage, was both competitive and calculating: "*an out and outer*, one up to everything, down as a nail, a trump, a Trojan, . . . one that can patter flash, floor a charley, mill a coal-heaver, come coachey in prime style, up to every rig and row in town and down to every move upon the board from a nibble at the club to a dead hit at a hell; can swear, smoke, take snuff, lush, play at all games and throw over both sexes in different ways—he is the finished man!" Bamford, tramping through Oxford, was told in an alehouse that the undergraduates were courageous fighters, generous remunerators and profuse spenders, all of which the company allowed to be gentlemanly qualities, but that, in intercourse with those beneath them, they were arrogant, wilful and capricious and prone to lay on too hard when they got the upper hand. A heartless disregard for the feelings of others was the hallmark of the "blood." It was con-sidered a joke to crowd timorous passers-by off the pavement, to throw a drunk in a dunghill, drop a live coal on a sleeper's head, rob a blind man of his dog and swear in the presence of ladies and clergymen. "What d'ye think of that for a lark, eh?" cried one of the type relating his evening at his parson brother's. " 'Keep it up—keep it up, d—— me,' says I, so I sets down to the table, drank as much as I could—then I mix'd the heel-taps all in one bottle and broke all the empty ones and rolled home in *prime and plummy* order, d—— me!"[1]

This notion of gentility had dangerous consequences when applied by the flashy sons of the rough, upstart employers and money-makers of the cotton and mercantile towns. Some Lancashire weavers' wives after Peterloo, who, wearied out on a tramp over the Pennines, boarded the York stage-coach, were greeted with coarse abuse by the young Manchester sparks aboard, and, when they sought protection from the coachman and guard, were ridiculed by these obsequious snobs. Below such "gemmen" were the stable-boys, cadgers, pugilists, horse-croppers and raffish hangers-on of the sporting world, with their cheap cigars, hats askew and hands in pockets, swearing obscenely at street corners or hanging about dog-pits or public houses making up their betting-books.[2]

Gambling—reckless and showy—was the crowning vice of the rich idler. Clubs like Crockford's and White's, with their exquisite furnishings and princely food and service, drained away more than one great estate and drove gentlemen to courses which damaged both their honour and their country. Lord Sefton—an upright and kindly man—after losing a small fortune at Brooks's, recouped himself, like others, by an enclosure-bill at the expense of his poorer neighbours. Sometimes the play at these establishments would continue for two or three days before the infatuated gamblers broke up. At Crockford's, during the parliamentary session, supper, cooked by the great *chef*, Ude, was served from midnight till five, every delicacy and drink that could gratify the most fastidious taste being provided without charge.[3] It was the

[1] *Real Life in London*, I, 35, 90-1, 128; *English Spy*, II, 217, 219-21, 234.

[2] Bamford, II, 210-11, 220-1; Byron, *Corr.*, I, 132-3; *English Spy*, I, 143-5, 247; II, 217-21, 234; Gronow, I, 227; Leigh Hunt, *Autobiography*, II, 173; *Life in London*, 35, 128; McCausland, 59-60; *Real Life in London*, I, 3, 26, 90-1 n.; Sydney, I, 131.

[3] Those who chose, however, would throw a ten-pound note on the play-table at the end of the session and leave it there. Lamington, 11-12. See Lord Coleridge,

green hazard table and the croupiers in their white neckcloths that maintained the club and made the fortune—more than a million pounds—of the old fishmonger who owned it. Humble men copied the vices of their betters; during the peace celebrations in Hyde Park the dicing tables in the gambling booths were continually surrounded by multitudes. In Dartmoor the poor perverts, shunned by their fellow prisoners and living apart under a monstrous king of their own choosing, gambled away their very clothes and food until they were left starving and naked.

185-6; Ashton, I, 356-7; *Creevey Papers*, 36; D'Arblay, IV, 44-5; *English Spy* I, 332-6; II, 13; Greville, I (Suppl.), 48-9; Gronow, II, 10, 81-6, 92-4, 282; Moorsom, 27; *Paget Brothers*, 177; *Real Life in London*, I, 196.

CHAPTER 8

The Naked and Outcast

IN SPITALFIELDS, once a village of pleasant gardened houses built by Huguenot silk-weavers, one saw the reverse of the London of elegance and splendour that the free institutions and the vigorous habits of the English had created. Here 50,000 workers, cut off from direct access to the raw materials of their labour and dependent solely on wages and the fluctuations of distant markets, were crowded in conditions of squalor which worsened as ever more newcomers poured into the place, its stately homes become over-crowded tenements, its mulberry trees cut down and gardens obliterated by mean dwellings, its rustic lanes transformed into unpaved and sewerless streets. In these nightmare extensions of London to the east and beyond the river, and in the rookeries and foetid courtyards that huddled behind the haunts of fashion and commerce, pallid, diminutive-looking men, women and children dragged out their crowded existence amid heaps of garbage. The only cheerful places in such abodes of misery were the gin or "blue ruin" shops. Here were the characters of low life that Corinthian Tom and Jerry Hawthorn, in their resolve to drain the last dregs of metropolitan pleasure, found revelling by night: Tinker Tom, dirty Suke, boggle-eyed Jem and Billingsgate Moll, full of fire and fury defending herself with her fish basket, African Sall, flashy Nance and Bet, the ballad singer, "rolling her peepers for a new fancy man"; the cadgers and flat-catchers of the "Holy Land" enjoying their "peck and booze" after their eleemosynary labours; the lascars, jack-tars, coal-heavers, dustmen, women of colour and remnants of once fine girls, who jigged together at "All Max"—that "bit of life" at the east end of the Town—where the reckless could drown their miseries in "Daffy," "Ould Tom" and "Stark Naked."

Half the customers of such places lived outside the law. The thieves' kitchen was the natural flower of the London slum. The world of Fagin and the Artful Dodger did not spring from Dickens's imagination. Neither did the "stout, broad-shouldered, sturdy chested man"—with the broad-skirted green coat with large metal buttons and the pale, scared woman and emaciated children waiting for him outside the tap-room—who, as Bill Sikes, matriculated from burglary to murder. "We never calls them thieves here but prigs and fakers," the old apple-woman on London Bridge told the author of *Lavengro*. "If you have any clies to sell at any time I'll buy them of you; all safe with me; I never peach and scorns a trap!" There were parts of the town like Tothill Fields and Seven Dials where by tacit agreement neither watch nor Bow Street runner ordinarily entered. In these "flash cribs," or "infernals," thousands of thieves and their female "pals" lived in ancient tumbledown houses and narrow courts reeking with ordure. Across their horizons lay the shadow not of Paul's cross but of the Newgate gallows and the gibbet. The most popular of London spectacles was a hanging; then the underworld, drunk on gin and horrors, shouted itself senseless as Jack Ketch, the hangman, cut down the lifeless bodies.[1]

In the capital the slums crowded behind the grander houses, out of sight—though not always out of smell—of their owners. They were still what they had been in the Middle Ages, fever-ridden haunts of vice and wretchedness: a maze of alleys and lanes fading into the unwholesome vapour that always overhung them, of dirty, tumbledown houses with windows patched with rags and blackened paper, and airless courts crowded with squabbling women and half-naked children wallowing in pools and kennels. The improvements effected by eighteenth century humanitarians were constantly counteracted by the influx of newcomers from every part of the kingdom who created new slums that

[1] Ashton, *Old Times* 246-7; Bamford I 67; II 130-2; Cooper 9-10; Dixon 50; *English Spy* I 338; *Fraser's Magazine* XXXI (1843) 335-6; *Lavengro* 194-5, 289-91; Lucas I 45; Newton 94; *Life in London* 181, 207-31, 225-8, 271-3; *Real Life in London* I 295; II 128-30; Sydney II 175; F. Warner, *The Silk Industry*.

spread even farther eastwards into the Essex and Kentish meadows, leaving a string of low, dingy towns on either side of the Thames.

In the manufacturing districts vice and destitution lived, not in juxtaposition with respectability and splendour, but far removed from them. Most of the steam-factory towns were situated on wild heaths and moors in scantily populated neighbourhoods little influenced by gentry or clergy. In these settlements, doubling in size every five or six years, with their filth, noise and perpetual inflow of new inhabitants, the old framework of society, built round church, manor-court and the village democracy of constable, way-warden and overseer, had broken down completely. Here only the law of the jungle held. Just outside Birmingham, capital of the Midland hardware trade, was a squalid manufacturing village known as "Mud City" whose inhabitants were the terror of the neighbourhood. Passing through Nottingham a few years after Trafalgar, the wife of one of Nelson's captains described with horror the drunken, riotous rabble that careered all night outside her inn.

These manufacturing towns, or rather overgrown squatters' villages—now spreading fast around the new steam factories, iron works and mines of the Midlands, South Lancashire, Clyde and Tyne—were astonishing phenomena. As travellers approached them through the encircling mists, they heard the rumbling of wheels and the clang of hammers, and saw long rows of furnace fires. Pückler-Muskau's picture of Birmingham serves for all: flame and smoke belching from diabolical chimneys, factories larger than palaces with every window blazing through the night as men made goods and weapons for the destruction of Bonaparte, and, gleaming above the lurid town, the spires of ancient churches silhouetted in the moonlight. Classically-minded young ladies, passing through such places, were reminded in their journals of "the realms of Plutus."[1]

[1] Wynne III 343. The author of *A Guide to all the Watering and Sea-Bathing Places* (1815 ed.) 349-51, thought Birmingham "a wonderful town, the houses well built, the streets . . . broad and well-paved and the spirit of industry so universally predominant that scarcely a child is unemployed." See Bamford II

For success in discovering new forms of livelihood was uprooting growing numbers from the country's traditional life. Though many thrived in that freer society, many more, the old props gone, went to the wall. Those swept into the slums of the capital or the squatters' towns around the steam factories could transmit to their children only a memory of the Christian traditions and influences among which they grew up. A generation after Waterloo a third of Manchester's children attended neither church, chapel nor school. The stony places in which the dispossessed took root tended inevitably to make hard, cruel, reckless men and sluttish, depraved women.

Competition was the condition of English economic life. The end of competition was increased wealth and liberty for the individual. The virtues which made for success in it were largely those which had given England victory in battle and which were engendered by the free and Christian society in which the more fortunate of the English grew up. But the end of life was imperceptibly ceasing to be the pursuit of those virtues and was becoming instead the property and prestige which those virtues had created.

Nor were the qualities which made for such success—energy, faith, resource, happy co-ordination of body and mind—equally engendered in all. English liberty, with its educative virtues, depended for its operation on the institution of property. Without it the boasted freedom of the individual had little real existence. A man without property, a man of straw, could preserve neither his own freedom nor that of others. He could be incarcerated for debt, pressed, in time of national emergency, into the Navy, or, lacking the wherewithal to hire a substitute, called up for wartime service in the Militia. If the local justices feared he might become a charge on the poor rates, he could be forcibly removed to the parish of his birth or "settlement." Even *habeas corpus* could not avail without the wherewithal to fee a lawyer: "an Englishman unless he can lay his hands on £25," wrote Stendhal, "is an outlaw." In a country where tyranny was held in universal detestation

333, 335; Hammond, *Rise of Modern Industry* 221-32; Letts 127, 129-30; Newton 25-6; Simond I 278; II 76, 79, 83; Lady Shelley II 41; Smart 249-51.

and the right to liberty regarded as every man's birthright, the poor were at the mercy of the petty bully—the greedy employer, the embezzling tradesman or jerry-builder, the pawnbroker and usurer, the corrupt beadle or constable. There was no national organisation to enforce order and justice; only twenty clerks at the Home Office. That and hanging! The substitute for a police force was the hundred to one chance that even the least offending malefactor might finish on the gallows. There were over two hundred capital offences; a man might hang for chipping the balustrade of Westminster Bridge or impersonating a Chelsea pensioner. It was because the sanctity of property seemed so important to the English—the sheet-anchor of all independence and virtue—that in 1810 the House of Lords rejected Romilly's bill for exempting petty larceny from the death penalty. A man who stole five shillings' worth of goods from a shop counter, it was held, was undermining the structure of a free society. As, however, the English were a humane and Christian people in their private relationships and instinctively reacted, when personally confronted with it, from the harsh reality to which their principles gave rise, the chief result of the bloodthirsty rigour of the laws with which they defended pro-perty was to ensure the acquittal of the majority of petty male-factors, judges and juries refusing to inflict death for such trifling offences.

It was the essence of all economic activity in England that it was uncontrolled. Everything was left to individual enterprise. The very gardens in the new seaside resorts were laid out by speculating gardeners who recouped themselves by charging for admission and selling fruit and flowers. A service that was worth no one's while to provide—that did not offer profit to someone—was regarded as an activity not worth providing. Even the cleansing of the streets was left to the self-interest of men like Dickens's golden dustmen who filled the suburbs with vast piles of stinking, fly-haunted rubble and manure which, regardless of their neighbours' amenities, they kept for sale to farmers and road contractors. Fire-fighting was left to insurance companies; London had to wait a generation after Waterloo before even its parishes were allowed to maintain a fire engine. All monopolies, it was felt, especially State monopolies, were bound to be inefficient and corrupt. "An individual," wrote Walter Scott, "always manages his own concerns better than those of the country can be managed."

Apart from the means of defence the State owned nothing; the very ministers of the Crown regarded the official papers that passed through their hands as private property. Foreigners commented with surprise on the inadequacy of the public buildings; the benches and chairs in the London parks were invariably disfigured or destroyed. Even the royal arbours in Kensington Gardens were scribbled over with dirty rhymes. The cascade in Hyde Park below the Serpentine was blocked with duckweed and decaying branches; a large part of the metropolitan water supply—though the cost of a single week of the war could have supplied an aqueduct from the Surrey hills—was drawn from canals in which the poor washed or the Thames into which the sewers flowed.

If London was badly off in public services, other places were far worse off. There were towns of ten thousand inhabitants which did not possess a post office or a postman. Their sanitary condition, a doctor reported, was like that of an encamped horde.[1] Birmingham—a city of 100,000 people and the fourth largest in the kingdom—was without even a charter and was administratively a mere agglomeration of squatters' dwellings, growing ever more congested and anarchical. Local government was a harlequinade; there were more than 250 municipal corporations in England and Wales and 15,000 parishes, and almost all corrupt. No one, except the very poor, showed the slightest respect for their authority or the antiquated regulations they feebly tried to enforce. Simond's first impression of England was the sight of the Falmouth beadles on a Sunday, in old-fashioned silver lace and cocked hats, trying to compel a Quaker to shut his shop, which reopened the moment they had gone.

In such a society scarcely anything was planned. Man was left

[1] Hutchins, *Public Health Agitation* 64; Bury I, 252; Clapham I 36-7; *English Spy* I 191; Fremantle I 46; Hammond, *Town Labourer* 44; *Rise of Modern Industry* 153; Letts 123-5; Lockhart IV 74; Partington I 27-8; Raumer III 142; *Sea-Bathing Places* 349-51, 429, 437; Smart 245-9; Woodward 4, 41, 46, 432, 441, 448.

free to act as and when it seemed fit to him to do so. In the hurly-burly of this untrammelled individual activity it was difficult even to unveil a statue or open a bridge without someone being crushed or killed. When Kean, the great actor, visited Liverpool a woman was trampled to death in the gallery; the king's brother, the Duke of Cambridge, taking his bride for a walk in Kensington Gardens, had to set her with her back to a tree to prevent her being smothered by the crowd. In the manufacturing districts, where the controlling forces of custom, Church and ancient neighbourhood were lacking, English anarchy reached Homeric heights. When Messrs. Hole, Wilkinson and Garthside's new sheets were set out on the Manchester warehouse floor, the country drapers fought for the pieces with their fists.[1]

For here in the industrial north and midlands was revolution—one more permanent and, to those who could comprehend its effect, more terrifying than any wrought by mob or guillotine. A whole society was being transformed by the impact of whirling wheels and grinding machines, while the nation's traditional leaders far removed from the wild moors, mosses and lonely valleys where the revolution was being enacted, stood aside and let it take its course. The new mechanical processes in weaving and spinning cotton, wool, flax and silk, in smelting iron, mining coal and making pottery, in harnessing steam power, the manufacture of tools and the transport of goods, were creating a life of a kind hitherto unknown, where craftsmen and mechanics, instead of working as semi-independent manufacturers in their rural homes, crowded round large-scale factories as the wage-earners of employers with the capital to buy and maintain machines. The old domestic craftsman was a countryman, not only living within sight of the fields but frequently owning a stake in them. The competition of steam power either drove him, starving, from his home to seek employment in a factory town or turned his surroundings into one.

In the industrial districts the whole appearance of the countryside was changing. In south Lancashire and north-east Cheshire, in the

[1] Bamford I 227; *Ann. Reg.* 1815, Chron. 71, 91; Partington I 139; Lady Shelley II 15.

West Riding, on Tyneside and Clyde, on the Warwickshire and Staffordshire heaths, the landscape was growing black, the villages were turning into towns and the towns were running into one another. Lady Shelley, after a journey in the west midlands, wrote of "that disagreeable, cold and manufacturing county which for twenty miles smokes from a thousand steam engines, so that at night the whole country from Birmingham to Wolverhampton appears to be on fire": "all the shining jewels of this wondrous cave," another traveller wrote of Sheffield, "shrouded in smoke and glaring red fire." In Burslem the smoke was so dense that the potters had to grope their way to work.[1] A traveller from Rochdale to Manchester in the year after Waterloo found the houses as thick as in the environs of London, and "smoke and trade and dirt" everywhere. The trout streams were being poisoned by dye-vats and the valleys studded with smoke-stacks; the willows and hazels of the Irk blackened and laid waste, the groves of birch, wild rose and rowan and the green hills with the classical names and haunting rustic deities—Babylon Brow and Stony Knows—desecrated by money-grinders.

The character of economic relationships was changing with the appearance of the countryside. The weaver, spinner, stockinger, working in his own cottage with the help of his family and, perhaps, an apprentice, owning or hiring his own tools and selling the finished article to a capitalist wholesaler in the nearest town, from whom he also obtained the raw materials of his trade, was being superseded by the proletarian factory worker operating expensive power-machines owned by others and owning nothing himself but his labour. With every advance of the technological revolution the control of the capitalist over the conditions of work tightened. Before the end of the war the East Midland hosiers were letting out frames to stockingers in the Leicestershire and Nottinghamshire villages at thirty per cent per annum of their capital cost. Workmen who, rather than pay such rentals, tried to buy their own

[1] Wedgwood, *Staffordshire Pottery and its History* 65; Bamford I 60, 71, 168, 223; II 50-3, 80-2, 115, 86, 333; Clapham I 36; Darvall 24; Hammond, *Town Labourer* 46; Klingender 42; Newton 25-6; Lady Shelley II, 41; Simond II 76, 83.

machines, found themselves shut out from both raw materials and markets. If they could not sell their wares promptly, their families starved. The decent hosier's standards were constantly forced down by the price and wage-cutting of his less scrupulous rivals. So were the good craftsman's.

This process of transformation had still a long way to go. There were at least a quarter of a million handlooms in the country at the time of Waterloo. On market-days three thousand domestic clothiers rode into Leeds, Bradford and Huddersfield to sell their wares: "at Hathersage," wrote Bamford, "we heard the sound of a shuttle and my wife said we were getting near home." The "weaver's trade" was as much part of the English tradition as husbandry or seamanship; when the poet Blake wished to explain the mystery of life, he wrote that joy and woe were

"woven fine

A clothing for the soul divine."

In 1811 four-fifths of the Midland stockingers' frames were scattered in more than two hundred and fifty villages with an average of twenty-two stockingers apiece, each operating three or four frames. Yet whenever markets dried up and competition intensified— during the Continental Blockade and American War, and in the more sustained deflation that followed the peace—the undercutting of the machines and of the capitalists who exploited them forced down the living standards of domestic workers and drove increasing numbers from their traditional life. In the trade depression of 1811/12 the average family earnings of Nottinghamshire silk workers dropped by a third, and the wages of Bolton cotton weavers fell to five shillings a week. Though a recovery always followed, each successive slump took its toll of independent "manufacturers"—a word which was ceasing to denote a crafts-man and becoming applied solely to employers.

. . . .

It was a tragedy that at the moment when the introduction of labour-saving machinery effected this social revolution, the pre-vailing economic philosophy should have been so fanatically opposed to any protective regulation of conditions of employment. There were many regulations on the statute book dating from Stuart, Tudor and even medieval times, but the political economists, who since the time of Adam Smith had monopolised the ear of Parliament, held them in contempt. Even where they were not repealed, they were becoming a dead letter. The idea of regulating men's morals and social behaviour for their own good ran counter to the whole spirit of the age. Jeremy Bentham, father of utilitarian radicalism—the creed of every progressive for the next quarter of a century—maintained that all law was evil, since law was an infraction of liberty, and devoted his well-endowed life to exposing the unreason of past legislation. To him, as to the great seventeenth century Whig merchant, Josiah Child, the laws of England were "a heap of nonsense compiled by a few ignorant country gentlemen." Every intelligent man subscribed to Burke's dictum that the chief inlet by which oppression entered the world was by one man pretending to determine the happiness of another. "The right of the State to interfere to prevent a man from injuring himself," wrote the economist, Nassau Senior, "supposes that the legislator knows better how to manage the affairs of an individual than the man does himself."

The effect of this theory could be best seen in places where the new industrial workers lived. In the first two decades of the century the population of Manchester increased from 94,000 to 160,000, of Bolton from 29,000 to 50,000 and of Lancashire from 672,000 to 1,052,000. The houses were put up by jerry-builders as cheaply as possible, with bricks so thin that neighbours could hear one another speaking, with roofs and floors supported by planks, without water pipes or drains. In the sinister, sunless city beside the filthy Sheaf, whose forges, set against the bleak Derbyshire hills, made the world's finest cutlery, Bamford and his wife Mima were driven from their inn by the bugs which swarmed off the dirty walls and bedding. Fever caused more deaths in the industrial towns every year than Wellington's armies suffered in the Peninsular War. Thousands, particularly where the Irish "bog-trotters" congregated in search of subsistence, lived in foetid cellars and airless courts. Within a few months of their migration from a moorland village to Manchester, Bamford's entire family was stricken down by typhus.

In all the steam-engine towns—"oppressive, smoky, noisy, riotous"—the creation of wealth and the perpetuation of poverty went hand-in-hand. In the vicinity of an inexhaustible supply of coals in South Wales the mouldering remains of Neath Abbey were populated by the families of the workmen employed in the neighbouring copper-smelting works. Obsession with external display was wholly lacking in the industrial districts. Despite the vast scale on which manufactures were conducted, the power and perfection of the machines, the capital invested on them, nothing was spent on appearance. The factory buildings were shabby and ugly, and added at different times without attempt at design or reference to convenience or beauty. Industrial capital was only employed in the creation of new capital. The sole end of all activity was profit. Success or failure turned on not spending sixpence more than was necessary.

Unfortunately the end was too narrow for the purposes of a continuing communal life. Cotton manufactory and coal mining —the trades on which England's new wealth was principally founded —were inherently unhealthy. The one confined men, women and children for long hours in hot, vitiated, humid air which clogged the lungs with floating particles of cotton; the other banished them from the daylight. Accidents with primitive, unfenced machinery were common; Pückler-Muskau saw workers with thumbs crushed into formless lumps of flesh. They were even more frequent in the mines, where explosions, floods and landslides engulfed whole companies of colliers. Half the workers in the Cornish copper mines, Ayton was told when he visited them in 1814, suffered from tuberculosis. Every year increased the numbers employed in the mills, mines and foundries; every year their surroundings grew more squalid, insanitary and hideous. And every year machines exerted a greater tyranny over men's lives, forcing them to work yoked to automata which neither wearied nor rested.[1]

[1] In one Manchester factory any spinner who was sick and unable to find an adequate substitute had to pay six shillings a day for wasted steam. Hammond, *Town Labourer*, 20.

The early cotton-spinning mills, driven by water power, were mainly operated by child-apprentices hired from poor-law overseers. Situated in the lonely upper reaches of Pennine rivers, there was no other way of staffing them. Steam power transferred the mills to large centres of population—generally in the neighbourhood of coal mines—where a plentiful supply of unskilled labour could be obtained, often from the families of skilled artisans who, being thrown out of work by machine competition, were forced to let their wives and children enter the factories. The process was exploited with ruthless realism. "When a manufacturer," wrote Walter Scott, "wishes to do a particular job he gathers one or two hundred weavers from lanes, streets and garrets without the slightest attention to character or circumstances or to anything but that they have ten fingers and can drive a shuttle. These men are employed perhaps for a fortnight and then turned off, the employer knowing no more or caring no more than if they were so many old pins or shuttles."

Few of those who, by the power of employment, controlled this new society had been trained to lead or had been responsible for anyone save themselves and their families. They had been educated only for their craft, of which they were usually past-masters. Many were decent and kindly men, like the Manchester counterpane and bed-quilt manufacturer for whom Bamford worked at the beginning of the century, or his successor, who read prayers to his family and apprentices every Sunday night, and whose wife nursed the latter through their illnesses. Peter Dixon, the "Druid's" father, who had a cotton mill in Shaddongate, Carlisle, visited his workpeople in their homes, looked after the sick and taught their children in Sunday school. Simond was much struck by the good nature and politeness of the large Birmingham industrialists round whose works he was escorted in 1811.

Yet most factory owners were small men, little removed in upbringing or education from those they employed. They sprang from a rough, primitive, passionate folk who loved fighting, hard drinking and simple, sensual pleasures. They had been uprooted from the pastoral communities of their forbears whose standards and beliefs they had either forgotten or repudiated as irrelevant in the wider world of clanging machinery and smoking chimney. With great virtues of energy, courage, native shrewdness and industry, they were mostly thrusting, ambitious, ruthless types who succeeded because they were. As the machinery in which they had so boldly invested undercut their rivals and drove them into their factories, they found themselves in possession of great public and personal power. They used the former with little thought for the national good and the latter in pursuit of further wealth or the gratification of low, ignorant pleasures.

Under such circumstances the relations between employer and employed were bound to deteriorate. The old handloom weavers who worked for Messrs. Broadbent of Manchester would rest after their tramp from their moorland homes on the seat thoughtfully provided for them before having a friendly check-up with the firm's "putter-out," neither party trying to drive a hard bargain because of the other's necessities; perhaps afterwards buyer and seller would sit down together to a friendly glass of ale and a pipe at the "Hope and Anchor." Often in such old-fashioned firms, Bamford records, the master would take his men home to dine with his family on broth, dumpling and baked pudding. But as machinery came in, the gap between capitalist and artisan widened. The snobbery that vitiated the society of the well-to-do, vitiated that of the industrial town. A man who worked with his hands, being increasingly prevented by the cost of machinery from becoming more than a wage-earner, was looked down on by those who enjoyed the increase wrought by the machines he tended. Hereditary skill counted for less and less as mechanical power took the place of craft. Phrases like the "lower orders," the "swinish multitude," "the rabble," became habitual to men and women who felt themselves to be a different species from the poor toilers whose grandfathers and fathers had been the equals of their own. The filthier the workers' surroundings, the more deadening and brutalising their conditions of labour, the more savage and pagan they grew and the more a race apart—a different and potentially hostile nation within the body politic. "Their conduct on a Sunday," a witness reported of juvenile cotton workers, "is such that females as well as men insult their well-behaved superiors in the street, and that to a degree that well-behaved, discreet gentlemen, even if they meet the factory people, will, if possible, go on the other side of the street to avoid them."[1]

This breach within the nation was allowed to develop and widen because the ruling class had been taught by the economists that the pursuit of self-interest was the key to national well-being. To buy at the cheapest and sell at the dearest was the commandment which in economic matters was taking the place of the original ten. Any restriction on what was called "free" bargaining was repugnant to progressive, or as it was then called, "enlightened," opinion. An Act of 1802, which confined—at least in theory—the hours of poor-law apprentices in water-driven cotton-mills to twelve hours a day, was not re-enacted to cover the steam-power factories which by the end of the war had almost completely taken their place. A Bill to make it do so, introduced in the year of Waterloo by a humane spinner, Sir Robert Peel—father of the statesman—was allowed to drop. Kindly employers, whose hearts were touched by the sufferings of children in their mills and in those of their harsher competitors, and who sought restrictive legislation to render humanity compatible with solvency, were able to do little against such a combination of solemn belief and self-interest. The nation which had repudiated the Slave Trade now accepted as inevitable a new and still more paying form of slavery.

The miracle of mechanical production had impressed sensitive contemporaries with such awe that they had temporarily lost their critical faculty. "It is impossible," wrote a visitor to Glasgow in 1810, "to see without astonishment those endless flakes of cotton, as light as snow and as white, ever pouring from the carding machine, then seized by the teeth of innumerable wheels and cylinders and stretched into threads, flowing like a rapid stream and lost in a tourbillon of spindles. The eye of a child or of a woman watches over the blind mechanism, directing the motions of her whirling battalion." The sight of gangs of maimed and exhausted children trailing daily into the factories and mines that supported

[1] Evidence of George Gould, fustian merchant, cit. Hammond, *Town Labourer* 162. See Bamford I 106-11, 251; Woodward 6, 40.

England's new industrial wealth caused kindly and cultured men no astonishment, only a defeatist fatalism. In the great cotton manufactory at Lanark, employing 2500 hands, mostly children who had started work at the age of seven or eight, the hours were from 6 a.m. till 7 p.m., followed by evening school from 8 p.m. to 10 p.m. Some of the children's homes were close to the factory, but others, whose parents lived a mile away, had the additional advantage of a healthy night and early morning walk; they could be distinguished, visitors were told, by their brighter colour. The long hours—in some places they were as many as fifteen a day for six days a week—were regarded as essential to enable manufacturers to compete against undercutting and secure the markets without which their employees might be thrown out of work and starve. Viewed in this sense, the labour that crippled children's limbs, rotted their lungs and stunted their minds, could be defended as a blessing, a means of preserving them from famine. Some supporters of the system went further, seeing in the children's ceaseless activity an inspiring spectacle. "They seemed," wrote one employer, "to be always cheerful and alert, taking pleasure in the light play of their muscles—enjoying the mobility natural to their age. . . . It was delightful to observe the nimbleness with which they pieced the broken ends as the mule-carriage began to recede from the fixed roller-beam, and to see them at leisure, after a few seconds' exercise of their tiny fingers, to amuse themselves in any attitude they chose till the stretching and winding-on were once more completed. The work of these lively elves seemed to resemble a sport in which habit gave them a pleasing dexterity."[1]

This philosophy accorded perfectly with the requirements of those who, needing ever larger sums for their competitive and showy society or for the enlargement of their businesses, accepted the under-nourishment and degrading surroundings of their fellow countrymen as an inevitable dispensation of Providence. It received its intellectual justification from the works of a clergyman named Malthus who contended that population automatically outran sub-

[1] Andrew Ure, *The Philosophy of Manufactures*, 1835. See Bamford I 111; Farington I 134; Gomm 311-12; Peel I 259-62; Woodward 11; Simond I 278.

sistence, nature's ruthless but beneficent law being to preserve the economy of the world by eliminating surplus mouths and hands by starvation. "We are bound in justice and honour," he wrote, "formally to disclaim the *right* of the poor to support. To this end I should propose a regulation to be made declaring that no child born from any marriage taking place after the expiration of a year from the date of the law should ever be entitled to parish assistance. ... A man who is born into a world already possessed, if he cannot get subsistence from his parents on whom he has a just demand, and if the society does not want his labour, has no claim of right to the smallest portion of food and in fact has no business to be where he is. At nature's mighty feast there is no vacant cover for him."

It was a proof of the extent to which educated and humane Englishmen were bewildered by the immense rise in the population —since 1750 it had almost doubled—and alarmed by the French Revolution, that they accepted, and even with a kind of melancholy enthusiasm, this doctrine from a professor of the Christian Church —himself a most kindly and reasonable man. If a natural law of increase made vice and misery inevitable for millions, there seemed no need for the ruling and possessing classes to reproach themselves for the increase of vice and misery which attended their own enrichment or to waste money trying to remedy it. It was like the fall of leaves in autumn.

In this matter the poets were wiser than the statesmen. Southey, the poet-laureate, denounced it as "a technical sophism and a physical assumption as false in philosophy as detestable in morals," and Coleridge, in his rambling but prescient talk—delivered as from some lofty height from which he descried, invisible to all eyes but his, the course of human folly and frailty for a century ahead— remarked that if society disclaimed all responsibility for the starving, the latter would reply that in that case they had no duties towards it and might take by force what was denied by humanity. Such arguments, however, made little impression on anxious ratepayers forced to alleviate the growing pauperism caused by the wage-policy of manufacturers and farmers.

In the international sphere Britain's rulers had resisted the revolutionary claim that the strong possessed a natural right to ignore the mutual obligations of law. Yet in the economic sphere the same rulers, despite unavailing protests by the poor and in defiance of their country's historical tradition, accepted the revolutionary thesis that men had a right to enrich themselves without regard to social obligations and the continuing claims of the community. In England the legatee of the supremacy of natural right—the untrammelled liberty of superior energy and brain—was not the soldier of fortune, but the thrusting, broad-shouldered condottiere of commerce and finance. He, too, like Napoleon, regarded the world as his oyster and ravaged and exploited as he conquered. Such men made themselves rich and their country economically strong, but they uprooted and rendered millions wretched in the process. And to them was left, in accordance with the revolutionary doctrine that the pursuit of private gain must automatically enrich the community, the almost unfettered control of the ordinary Englishman's home, surroundings, food, health, and conditions of labour.

Such a theory of society made for a new kind of mind. Commerce was growing stricter, stingier. Charles Lamb, a clerk of the London trading company that had conquered India, wrote of "this mercantile city and its gripple merchants," and related how his employers, like the Bank of England, had cut down the old saints' days' holidays almost to nothing. No longer, he told his correspondents, could he pass their letters through the Company's bag; the directors, "rascals who think nothing of sponging upon their employers for their venison and turtle and burgundy five days in a week to the tune of five thousand pounds in a year, now find out that the profits of trade will not allow the innocent communications of thought between their underlings and their friends in distant provinces to proceed untaxed." So, too, in deference to the new outlook—cold, calculated, remorseless—his fellow clerk, Tommy Bye, coming into the office a little hazy one morning after an evening's debauch, found himself summarily dismissed after twenty-seven years' service. "Clerk's blood, damn 'em! my brain, guts, skin, flesh, bone, carcase, soul, time is all theirs," Lamb wrote, half in jest, but also in earnest, "the Royal Exchange, Gresham's Folly,

hath me body and spirit!" The apostles of Mammon were warming
to their business, shutting up growing numbers of their fellows in
factory and counting-house away from the fresh air and sunlight.

·   ·   ·   ·   ·   ·   ·

It was not only in the towns that man suffered on a cross of
economic necessity. Between 1796 and 1815 more than eighteen
hundred enclosure Bills were passed, four hundred more than in the
previous forty years. In no other way could the supply of home-
grown food—and none other was available—have kept pace with
the population. Growing numbers of husbandmen who had enjoyed a small but vital stake in the land—a strip or two in the parish
arable fields, pasture on the common for a few ragged cattle, pigs
and geese, the right to gather manure and fuel—found themselves
deprived of them. Unable to face the initial costs of legislation, fencing and drainage involved in enclosure, they were forced to sell
their compensatory allotments to their richer neighbours. Those
who possessed only squatters' rights on the manorial commons or
waste received no compensation at all. Men with an hereditary
talent for dealing with soil and beasts were requited with payment
in a medium in whose use they had neither skill nor experience.
As often as not, they spent it in the alehouse. Henceforward they
and their children had no resource but that of the wages they earned. They ceased to be peasants and became proletarians, without
security and therefore without liberty.

The rich welcomed the changed status of the rural poor because
it made them easier to discipline. "The land," wrote a Scottish
agriculturalist, "is divided into a limited number of great farms,
and the tenants, men of capital and intelligence, are enabled to give
the best effect to the virtues of the soil, and the great body of the
people live quietly under them as farm servants and hired labourers,
having no care but to do their own work and receive their wages."
The more profitable farming became and the more eager the rich
to buy, the greater became the temptation of the poor to sell. Every
year the amount of land in well-to-do hands increased. It was
leased from them at high rents by a new race of tenant farmer who,

operating under almost ideal conditions, with expanding markets, rising war-prices, and cheap and abundant labour, could afford to operate on a far bigger scale than their fathers.

Having no stake in what he raised, the farm labourer in an enclosed village gained nothing from its increased price. On the contrary, having to buy most of his family's food, he was doubly the loser. Though his wages rose during the war, they did not rise as quickly as prices. The inflationary rise began for him at the wrong end, with the proceeds of labour instead of its reward. At the same time his family's supplementary earnings from domestic handicrafts were being reduced or eliminated by the growing competition of machines. And the farmhouse where the young unmarried labourer had formerly boarded with the homely family of his yeoman employer became the residence of a finer kind of farmer, whose sons hunted and whose daughters played the piano and who could not be bothered with the board of farm domestics. Many of the smaller farmhouses disappeared altogether in the engrossment of farms which followed the enclosures. The landlords and their new tenants, Cobbett wrote in 1821, stripped the land of all shelter for the poor. Simond earlier noted the same phenomenon; the countryside swarmed with gentlemen's houses and opulent farms, but the dwellings of the real poor were hard to discover. Among the roofless ruins of Valle Crucis Abbey he saw peasants and their children squatting with pigs and poultry. "The poor are swept out of the way," he wrote, "as the dust out of the walks of the rich."[1]

Before enclosure the chief source of hired agricultural labour had been the smallholder or commoner, who devoted two or three days a week to looking after his own land and worked on that of a richer neighbour for the remainder. Though the latter was now becoming the peasant's sole support, the farmer who employed him, being in an advantageous bargaining position—for a man with a hungry family cannot stand on terms—was slow to raise his wages.

---

[1] "The labourer who sows and does not reap sees abundance all around him, creates it and does not partake of it." Simond I 172-5. "Shall we never cease to make him a miserable being, a creature famishing in the midst of abundance?" Cobbett, I 592.

During the war with Revolutionary France the rapidity with which prices had rocketed under the triple stimulus of war, increased urban population, and a bad harvest had caused the Berkshire magistrates, meeting at Speenhamland in 1795, to take a fatal decision. Instead of enforcing a minimum wage—a measure which, though empowered to take, they shirked out of deference to the new economic teaching—they fixed a basic rate of subsistence, based on the fluctuating price of corn and the size of the family, and authorised a grant in aid to all who were being paid less than this by their employers. By thus subsidising wages out of rates they pauperised the labourer and robbed him of self-respect.

Many magistrates had followed their well-intentioned example. Not only were farmers countenanced in their reluctance to pay an economic wage, but poor-rates rocketed out of all proportion to the incomes of the smaller ratepayers, who had thus become saddled with part of the working costs of their richer neighbours. The decent employer was taxed to subsidise his unfair competitor and —since no man with savings could qualify for relief—the thrifty husbandman to maintain the unthrifty. By 1818 the annual national contribution to poor-rates, little more than £700,000 in 1750, had risen to nearly eight millions. More than a fifth of the rural population of England and Wales—Scotland had no poor-law—was in receipt of some form of parochial relief. Thousands of small husbandmen, faced by rate-demands beyond their means, were also driven into the ranks of the landless workers and became themselves a charge on the rates. The poor-laws, wrote Malthus, had created the poor they assisted.[1]

The labourer's suffering was aggravated by the increasing rigour with which the game laws were enforced by landowners obsessed with the new mania for vast battues and game-bags. A parliament of game-preservers, in the south of England at least, was banishing the peasant from the sports of his fathers. Men whose families were hungry and who saw pheasants, hares and partridges swarming in

[1] Simond I 225. See *idem* 229; II 295. It was a system, said Southey, which converted the peasantry into the poor. See also Darvall II 46; De Selincourt II; Dicey 101; Ernle 308-12, 327-8; Hammond, *Village Labourer* 104; Porter 88, 90; Smart 137-9; Woodward 431.

every wood around them, could not resist the temptation of going
out at night with gun and net to fill the pot or reap the rewards—
far higher than their wages—offered by the agents of the London
poulterers. When caught, they received short shrift from magistrates, who in this matter, so close to their hearts, could be utterly
ruthless. By a savage act of 1816 a man caught at night in an enclosure with instruments for trapping game could be sentenced to
transportation by two magistrates, one of whom might be the
injured property owner, while a blow, struck or even threatened
in a poaching fray, could be punished by the gallows. The war
between poachers and gamekeepers reached a terrible crescendo in
the agricultural depression after the Napoleonic wars. Hundreds
were killed or maimed in pitched battles in the woods or by the
spring-guns and mantraps with which the more ignoble landlords
protected their property and pleasures.[1]

Old England was tightening into neat-hedged and gated fields
and high-walled parks; the sense of property was running mad and
cruel. Though many landlords and farmers maintained the old
kindly, paternal relations with those who worked on their own
farms and gardens or lived in their immediate vicinity, others, in
their absorption in fashionable and sporting pleasures, increasingly
left the management of their estates to professional intermediaries.
The way in which bailiffs and land-stewards whittled away or
ignored ancient rights was bitterly resented. In the unenclosed
manor of East Burnham, bought in the early years of the century
by the great Whig family of Grenville, the latter's agent claimed
an absolute rather than a manorial property in the soil, contemptuously refusing to fulfil the lord's duties of ringing pigs and
maintaining fences and selling the peat, wood, turf and sand from
the common to non-parishioners. At Middleton Lord Suffield's
steward broke up the village bowling green and turned it into a
burial ground, because he could not keep its rustic frequenters in

---

[1] "Nothing would induce me to put up boards threatening prosecution or
cautioning one's fellow-creatures to beware of man-traps and spring-guns."
Walter Scott, 8 Jan., 1825. Lockhart V 399. See Cobbett, *Rural Rides*, I 110-11;
Coupland, *Wilberforce*, 428-9; *Cranbourn Chase* 35-7, 39-41; Green, *Stendhall*
183; Hammond, *Village Labourer*, 187-206; Woodward 439.

"respectful bounds." As he passed through Savernake Forest, Cobbett noted how many small farms had been swallowed up to add park after park to Lord Ailesbury's domain.

"Hence, yeoman, hence!—thy grandsire's land resign;
Yield, peasant, to my lord and power divine!
Thy grange is gone, your cluster'd hovels fall;
Proud domes expand, the park extends its wall;
Then kennels rise, the massive Tuscan grows,
And dogs sublime, like couchant kings, repose!
Lo! 'still-all-Greek-and-glorious' art is here!
Behold the pagod of a British peer!"[1]

At the time of Waterloo the social cataclysm which befell the English peasant was far from universal. In the north, where the competition of the industrial towns for labour kept up wages, its effects had been comparatively little felt. And everywhere the sufferings of the poor, in this tremendous and little understood revolution, were modified by the decency and kindliness of thousands of worthy men and women, whose sense of duty to their fellow-beings remained unaffected by opportunities of self-enrichment or by the new philosophy of *laissez faire*. Yet, while the horizon had lifted for the rich and strong, beckoning to an illimitable future of wealth and opportunity, for the poor it was darkening. The rulers of Christian England were blind to the changes which these new opportunities of enrichment were bringing to their poorer countrymen. They only saw the new, neatly-hedged fields and smoking chimneys and the rising revenues of their estates and of the Exchequer. They failed to see the hopelessness and hunger of the peasant deprived of his stake in the land and of the produce that had sustained his family. They failed to comprehend the agony of once independent countrymen imprisoned in the discipline of the factory and surrounded by the hideous squalor of the industrial town, or the mentality of children who grew up among these gloomy phenomena knowing no other. There was some excuse for their incapacity to realise the social consequences of the Industrial Revolution. There was less for their failure to understand the tragic social transformation being wrought

[1] Ebenezer Elliot, *The Splendid Village* (1833).

by the agricultural revolution at their park gates. They knew that
by its means more food was obtained for their country and more
rent for themselves. They turned a blind eye to its inability to
produce the free and contented men and women who were the
main source of England's wealth.

CHAPTER 9

Early Victorian Metropolis

BY THE TIME of Queen Victoria's accession in 1837 the population of London had risen to two millions—twice as many as at the end of the Napoleonic wars. It was now by far the largest and richest city in the world. Stretching from Shadwell and Wapping in the east it extended along both banks of the Thames as far as outer Chelsea and Battersea: thence a double line of villas ensconced among trees and large gardens continued almost to Hampton Court. For the first time in its history it was venturing away from the river; houses, skirting the new Regent's Park, strayed into the fields and farms of Primrose Hill where children still gathered the flowers which gave it its name. Everywhere bricks and mortar were rising: the removal of the Court from St. James's to Buckingham Palace had stimulated an outburst of building on the marshy fields and market gardens of Pimlico, soon to be renamed after its Cheshire owners, Belgravia. The red brick of which Wren and his successors had re-created London after the great fire was giving place to white and potentially grimy stucco:

> "Augustus at Rome was for building renowned
> And of marble he left what of brick he had found;
> But is not our Nash, too, a very great master,
> He finds us all brick and leaves us all plaster."

Looking down from the top of the Duke of York's Column on an early summer day of 1842, the eye lighted on a jumble of old houses and red-tiled roofs mingling with the foliage and blossom of Spring Gardens. Along the Mall the trees still straggled anyhow, unregimented into their modern rows, while cows thrust their horned heads over the wooden palings of Carlton House Terrace. Trafalgar Square was building on the recently cleared site of the old Royal Mews, where untidy advertisement-pasted hoardings concealed the stump of Nelson's slow-rising column, and the Percy lion, with its straight poker tail, roared defiance above the Tudor brick palace of the dukes of Northumberland. Farther afield loomed the great Pantechnicon in Belgrave Square, and Apsley House, with its world-famous inhabitant and its ferruginous shutters defying reform and revolution, standing solitary against the country setting of Hyde Park. Beyond lay Kensington village and the first rising mansions of Bayswater. Southwards towards the river were the Abbey and the long straight line of Westminster Hall, but Barry's Houses of Parliament were still only rising from the scaffolded ashes of old St. Stephen's. Opposite that empty spot stood the eighteenth century houses of Bridge Street and Westminster Bridge; beyond tall chimneys, bespeaking the industrial employments of the dwellers in the Lambeth and Southwark suburbs, and the virgin heights of woody Penge and Norwood.[1]

This city, multiplying itself in every generation, was still governed on the rustic model of its own past. Side by side with the medieval Lord Mayor and Corporation were three hundred parish and other authorities, mostly vestries, whose functions overlapped in the most inextricable manner and whose members, self-elected or holding office for life under no less than 250 Acts of Parliament, interpreted democracy in their own jovial way by almost ceaseless entertainment at the public expense. The hammering and plastering that daily enlarged London's circumference went on without control or interference: except for the new west-end squares which Cubitt was raising for the Marquis of Westminster, the small speculating builder built as he felt fit. Nobody had time or money to plan: there were no broad avenues or boulevards; the town, free from continental fortifications, grew outwards not upwards and on the principle that the best place to build was the nearest available space. The brand-new suburbs which housed the City clerks over the former village pastures and gardens of Islington, Hoxton and Camberwell, were monotonous agglomerations of mean streets

---

[1] The bird's-eye view described in this paragraph is based on a large-scale folding engraving in the opening volume of the *Illustrated London News*, the world's earliest illustrated newspaper, first published in 1842.

and terraces, marked by pathetic Cockney attempts at gentility and country ways of living wherever there was room for a vine, a carpet-sized flower garden or a fanlight over the narrow hall.

That was the new London; it was still overshadowed by the old. Past the great white invitations to "Try Warren's" or "Day and Martin's Blacking" and the castellated summer houses and villas of the outer bourgeoisie, the traveller entering London felt the shock and heard the roar of the cobblestones and saw elm trees and winkle stalls giving way to continuous lines of houses and gas lamps. The narrow streets through which the coaches and drays forced their way were thronged with the human material from which Dickens and Cruickshank derived their inspiration. Women in fringed shawls and straw bonnets, pock-marked and ragged beggars and pickpockets, clean-shaven and tightly-stocked young men with mutton-chop whiskers and tall fluffy beaver hats, clerks, also crowned with the universal stovepipe, flowing inwards to the counter or back to suburban villages—"proceeded by a ripple of errand boys and light porters and followed by an ebb of plethoric elderly gentlemen in drab gaiters"—and, as one reached the fashionable squares and roadways of Mayfair, a wealth of coloured and gilded liveried servants with stuffed white calves, cockaded hats and gold aigulets, emulating prize cattle in their rotund solemnity. These not only mixed with the crowds on the pavements and appeared sunning themselves at innumerable doorways but flowed majestically along the streets at a higher level, as they sat red-nosed on the draped boxes or stood erect with tall silver-crowned canes on the swinging platforms of crested coaches. And behind the double doors of the great houses of Grosvenor Square and Piccadilly were their brethren, the hall porters, sitting in vast hooded chairs, sometimes with a foot-rest and a foaming tankard as witness of their master's absence in the country.

These were the rank and file of the private armies of the privileged, sleeping in truckle beds in tiny dusty attics or dark basement pantries but sharing their master's glory and living on the cream of the land. At the great routs of high society and at the levées of St. James's, the populace crowding about the flambeau-lit doorways could see them in all their magnificence, enacting their well-

217

rehearsed parts in the cavalcade of the last age in which the English rich expended their wealth on public pageantry instead of on personal comfort. The bedizened flunkeys and the elegant, disdainful beings they attended never lacked spectators: a nimbus of ragged wide-eyed urchins, sometimes jeering, always half-admiring, attended them wherever they went—gamin school and spawn of the true Cockney with his love of splendour and his delight in derision.

Here the ages mingled—the past and the future. The great country houses of Piccadilly behind their high stone walls, ignoring London and dreaming of the shires from which the rosy country-bred lords and legislators who governed England hailed, were washed by the ceaseless tides of the London of commerce. Jogging past those tall brocaded windows, the fathers of the Forsytes sat crowded and upright within or sprawled, long-legged and check-trousered, on the narrow knife-edged roofs of the little sixpenny buses that, driving a resolute way among the crested barouches, chariots and landaus of the fashionable west-end, plied between the Bank and outer Paddington and Brompton or the "Yorkshire Stingo" close by leafy Lisson Grove. At the back, straw in his mouth and ribaldry on his lips, stood the outrageous cad, loudly touting for passengers against the conductors of rival machines and pushing his clients through the narrow door into his hot, swaying straw-strewn pen.[1] There they sat, six aside on the dirty plush cushions, glaring suspiciously while their thoughts ranged ahead of the steaming horses on schemes of money-making which never troubled the fine pates of the great lords and ladies whose residences they were humbly passing. For in the first days of the young queen new England was on the make and old England was on the spend. The nation's growing wealth offered scope for both.

At the time the battle between the vigorous young England of the future and the antique pomp and stately polity which it was

---

[1] In May 1842 the stipendiary magistrate at the Marlborough Street police court, in sentencing the conductor of one of Powell's Brentford omnibuses for an assault on a passenger, "observed in very indignant tones that it was necessary to protect the public and females in particular against the ruffianly conduct of omnibus conductors." *Illustrated London News* I 46.

to supplant was still undecided. The foundations of the old world looked firm and brassy, the busy vulgar confusion of the new rootless and evanescent. The teeming legions of the money-makers were there on sufferance: back in the shires from which they or their fathers came, they paid the common immemorial tribute to the lords of hereditary status and acre. Down in his native Wessex by the sea, superior Dosset, master of London bricks and mortar, touched his cap with his yeoman cousinry to the squire of Lulworth or Osmington. Here in London he fought for a footing in a crowded hurly-burly from which status was lacking for all but the richest. Even for his place in the omnibus—the advancing chariot of democracy—he had to rise betimes and struggle: for, in the race for money, many were called and few chosen and the prize was only to the assiduous, the pertinacious and the thrifty. In 1837 London boasted only 400 narrow, three-windowed, two-horse buses and 1200 dirty hooded gigs or cabs, with a total carrying capacity of less than ten thousand.

Other public conveyances there were none. The river, whose scourings the tides could no longer cleanse, had ceased to be the city's waterway: the watermen who had ferried the generations of the past between the stone stairs were dying out. Mostly London tramped over the cobbles to its labour, nearly a hundred thousand pedestrians daily crossing London Bridge. In those narrow crowded streets Shanks's pony generally proved the swiftest mount: with long swinging strides the Londoner covered his morning and evening miles and went abroad for country rambles after his midday Sunday dinner. The studious Macaulay thought nothing of walking for recreation from his chambers in the Albany to New Cross or riverside Greenwich.

It was a London that still had a country appetite. It ate not because it wanted vitamins but because it was hungry. At midday the new London sat down in a steaming panelled chop-house—at "Cock", "Rainbow" or "Cheshire Cheese" and many a humbler horse-box hostelry—to devour steaks, joints, chops and porter, cheese, potatoes and greens, usually with hot spirits and water to follow. Off liver and bacon at 10d., a pint of stout at 4½d., potatoes, bread, cheese and celery one could dine very comfortably for

2s. and leave a pile of coppers for that loquacious piece of old England, the waiter. Men whose immediate forbears had been hale and hearty farmers would think nothing of tackling at a sitting a boiled leg of mutton with carrots, turnips and dumplings, black pudding of pigs' and sheeps' trotters, tripe and faggots and pease pudding. In their appetites the gentry were at one with the rising commercial classes: at Lord Grey's house Creevey sat down with five or six others to a luncheon of two hot roast fowls, two partridges, a dish of hot beefsteaks and a cold pheasant, and to a "double" dinner of two soups, two fishes, a round of beef at one end of the table and a leg of mutton at the other with a roast turkey on the sideboard, followed by entrées of woodcocks, snipes and plovers, with devilled herring and cream cheese to lay the last despairing stirrings of appetite. Dinner was followed, after due time allowed for the gentlemen's port, by tea, and, where late nights were in contemplation, by the supper tray—Melton pie, oysters, sandwiches and anchovy toast with sherry, bottled stout and Seltzer-water and the usual mahogany case with its four cut-glass decanters labelled Rum, Brandy, Whisky, Gin. The London poor, few of whom tasted butcher's meat more than once a week, had to content themselves with envying the well-filled forms and rosy faces of their betters.

The poor—the flotsam and jetsam of casual labour and the ne'er-do-wells, who lacked the status and solider fare of the skilled artisan class—were becoming an increasing problem in that great city, and the bigger it grew the more of them there were. The magnet of wealth seeking more wealth drew them from the dissolving world of status and the hedgerow, and from the old trades which the new were paralysing. To house them the jerry-builders worked ceaselessly, raising innumerable straight streets of plain two-storied houses with slated roofs, the cheapest that could be built. Here, and in the regions where older and grander buildings had decayed to verminous tenements, they lived and died and multiplied, for despite filth and cholera and typhus life proved stronger than death. Even the down-and-outs and the homeless urchins, sleeping in their thousands under the arches of the Adelphi and Waterloo Bridge, lived.

Many of the worst slums jostled the dwellings of the rich and the haunts of fashion. There were rookeries of thieves and prostitutes under the very noses of the lawyers in the Temple and the legislators in Westminster, and close behind the fine new plate-glassed shops of Regent and Oxford Streets the urban poor squatted in worse than farmyard filth and squalor. But few troubled much about the poor who were left to the Vestries and Providence: everyone was too busy making money or spending it. Only sometimes a wretched creature, rising from the shadowy recesses of London or Waterloo Bridge, would mount the parapet and, sliding into the water, take swift dramatic leave of a world that knew small pity for failures.

Strangely contrasted, the life of rich and poor yet mingled. In Tothill fields, the scholars of Westminster took almost daily part in gigantic battles against gangs of young roughs from the adjoining slums. And the street walkers on their promenade from Temple Bar to Westminster Hall knew more of the good and great who ruled the aristo-democracy of England than the good and great would have cared to admit. Many of the traditions of the Regency died hard, paying tardy deference to the more squeamish and frugal morals of the money makers. Fine gentlemen of the shires, accustomed of ancient use and lusty living to take their pleasure of the willing wives and daughters of their tenantry—and no one, in their estimation, the worse in thought or fact—kept dual establishments in town: a house in Portland Place or Berkeley Square for family and *haut ton* and a pretty box for some charmer, promoted from ballet or millinery shop, in one of the little Chelsea or Brompton squares that were ever rising on the sites of the western market gardens. At night the young bucks and their hangers-on would assemble at the Cavendish or some neighbouring Piccadilly hostelry. When the white damask was strewn with empty jugs of Château Margaux and broken decanters of port, they would sally out to wrench off the knockers and bell handles of Sackville Street and Vigo Lane, make merry with the blackguard democracy of the London underworld on comic songs, roast kidneys, cigars and gin and water in the smoky haunts of Leicester Fields and the Haymarket, and finish the night in riotous harmony amid the dishevelled Cyprian delights of the Piccadilly Saloon or at Vauxhall Gardens, watching the fireworks and the dances in the Rotunda from a leafy grotto and lingering long into the morning over sliced ham and a bowl of arrack with the nymphs of the place. The sleepy turnpike men on the bridge and the newly-formed metropolitan police, in their tall hats and clumsy belted coats, treated such privileged revellers with respect so long as they kept their amusements from assuming too dangerous a shape. The "Peelers" had been brought into the world not to molest but to protect property and its owners. For on the untrammelled use of property, it was held, the nation's liberties depended.

Though a rough natural democracy governed by an aristocracy and landed gentry was still, as in the preceding century, the English model, with plenty of scope for folk who wished to be free and easy, the shades of a more prim and decorous age were already falling. The new police and new passion for making laws had begun to trace on the nation's ruddy face the sober lineaments of a more formal society. In Oxford Street the first wood blocks had taken the place of cobbles, and in the larger thoroughfares the stone posts on the pavements were being crowned with spikes to discourage the urchins of the streets from their interminable leapfrog. The day-long music of the London street cries was beginning to grow fainter.

Within the club-houses of Pall Mall and St. James's, a new life for the rich, based on decorum and silent comfort, was taking the place of the noisy gambling and drinking of the unregenerate past. By 1837 there were twenty-five of these great institutions from behind whose windows warm men with broad acres or money in the Funds could sit over their *Quarterly* or *Edinburgh Review* and watch a safer and remoter world than their fathers had ever known. Here the old and the new were already learning to mingle, and the successful man of commerce who had negotiated the terrors of the black ball might hope to strike an acquaintance with the quieter sort of lord or squire. There was even a special club dedicated to Reform with the most famous chef in London installed among tin-lined copper pots and gas ovens to teach old England the way to live after a new French model.

At night the march of progress was symbolised by the lighting of the London streets. Gas lighting had come in a couple of decades

back and was now being slowly extended from the main thoroughfares into the courts and alleys of the older London that besieged
them. The great gasometers rose like fortresses above the drab rows
of working-class dwellings, and from dusk till dawn the flaring gas
jets made a peculiar humming that was the musical background to
the nocturnal activities of the Londoner. Judged by modern
standards the light they gave was dim and little diffused: to our
rustic forefathers it seemed a prodigious illumination. Yet four
years were to elapse before the main road from Hyde Park Corner
to Kensington was lit by a single lamp.

The essential services of life were still supplied to the Londoner
after a country model. Donkeys carried vegetables to Covent
Garden, and colliers or "Geordies" brought their "best Wallsend"
from Tyne and Wear by sail: a prolonged west wind could cause
a fuel shortage in the capital. And the wintry streets were perambulated by tall-hatted coal-heavers peddling their wares. Here, too,
the old cries of London were still heard: in winter, crossing-sweepers
sat by braziers to gather toll of familiar clients for keeping their
pitch clean. In her rough white cottage in Hyde Park opposite
Knightsbridge, old Ann Hicks sold gilt gingerbreads and curds and
whey and took her modest toll, won by half a century of prescription, of park brushwood and hurdles to make her fire. In the
Bayswater road one could watch haymakers in the open fields to
the north: a little farther on, where the gravel Oxford turnpike
fell into Notting Dale, the pig-keepers who supplied the London
hotels squatted in rustic confusion. In the cellars of Westminster as
well as in the suburbs Londoners still kept cows: the metropolis's
milk supply was mainly home-made with, so it was hinted, liberal
assistance from the pump. And on any Monday morning herds of
cattle were driven by drovers armed with cudgels and iron goads
through the narrow streets to Smithfield: pedestrians were sometimes gored by the poor beasts. In Smithfield, Tellus kept his
unsavoury rustic court: a nasty, filthy, dangerous country Bastille
in the heart of London and a great offence to sensitive and progressive persons. Vested interests defended it stubbornly against
all assaults: the new satirical weekly, *Punch*—founded in 1841—
depicted a proprietary alderman taking his wife and family for a

walk there. "Oh! how delicious," he declares, "the drains are this morning!"

How rustic London still was could be seen from its summer greenery. The west-end was full of trees and green squares. The fields were half-a-mile away from Buckingham Palace and Grosvenor Square, and snipe were occasionally shot in the Pimlico marshes. In St. James's Park long rough untrimmed grass ran down to the water's edge, and there were no railings to keep people from wandering on it. Sometimes on wintry evenings the scarlet of a huntsman's coat could be seen in the fading light ascending the slope of Piccadilly or entering the Albany courtyard. In Chelsea, where the old brown roofs and twisted high chimneys of the houses almost tumbled into the unembanked river, the sage Carlyle rode down eighteenth century lanes to improve his digestion. Here on Saturdays would come bowling by many "a spicy turn-out and horse of mettle and breed," with the little liveried top-hatted tiger swinging on the footboard behind and his gay bachelor master smoking his cheroot and flicking his whip as he sped to his riverside villa, with its fairy-like grounds, cellar of recherché wines, pictures, statues and "many a gem of vertue."

There was a pastoral quality about the Londoner's amusements. The great summer regattas on the Thames between London Bridge and Hammersmith were attended by paddle steamers with brass bands and boats full of fluttering flags and pretty girls giggling in the sunlight under painted awnings, while the banks were thronged with runners and riders and convivial parties watching from the festooned balconies and gardens of riverside pubs. At Putney Fair were Fat Ladies and Learned Pigs, much "firing of cannon, jollity, shouting, jangling of street pianos and popping of ginger beer," and many a pull at Finch's ale. Every Whit Tuesday the Cockneys went *en masse* to Greenwich, cargo after cargo going down the river singing and cheering and devouring stout and sandwiches, to sample the traditional delights of the great fair—its rows of booths hung with dolls, gilt gingerbreads and brandy balls, its raree-shows and performing pigs, its giants and its dwarfs. Here 'prentices and shop boys pushed about with whistles, penny trumpets, false noses and rolled twopenny scrapers—in sound simulating tearing material

—down the backs of their elders. And the park was filled with young people and hoydens—playing at kiss-in-the-ring, riding donkeys, or, more simply, tumbling head over heels down the hill.

For though London was the greatest city in the world its people still had their roots in the country or were separated only by a generation or two from country ways. They were scarcely yet sophisticated. The poorer streets were frequented by gigantic brown dancing bears led by picturesque, seedy-looking Italians. Barry, the clown at Astley's Circus, went down the Thames in a washing tub drawn by geese, and a lady rider at Vauxhall could draw all London. For children the chief sights of the town were the Tower, the Elgin Marbles and Mr. Cross's Surrey Zoo, recently moved from the old Royal Mews to make way for Trafalgar Square. Here in the grounds of Walworth Manor lions and tigers perambulated in a circular glass conservatory more than a hundred yards wide and a giant tortoise carried children on his back. Another popular treat was the Panorama. At the Colosseum on the east side of Regent's Park one could view the Fire of London with canvas scenery and fireworks and the Alps with a real Swiss and a real eagle. Athens and the Himalayas were also shown for a shilling— "the Ganges glittering a hundred and fifty miles off, and far away the snowy peak of the mountain it rises from." A little later a new Royal Panorama was opened in Leicester Square, where scenes from England's contemporary colonial wars were presented in the manner of a modern newsreel. The battle of Waterloo—the chief title-deed, with Trafalgar, of an Englishman's innate superiority to all foreigners—was a permanent exhibit.

For sport the well-to-do Londoner affected the pastimes of squires and farmers. Cricket was already established at Lord's suburban ground and was played vigorously in top-hats: but shooting parties, steeplechases, hunting with the Queen's, the Old Berkeley or the Epping Hunt, and fishing up the river were far more widely patronised. At Richmond the well-to-do merchant and shopkeeper, arrayed in top-hat, white tie and long tail-coat, would sit in a punt of a Saturday afternoon perched on a chair with rod and line, dining afterwards at the "Star and Garter" and calling on the way home at the pastrycook's to buy his wife sixpennyworth of Maids of Honour. The old Chelsea bun house, the ale-house standing solitary in the Kensington road between Hyde Park Corner and the royal gardens, the ox that was roasted whole in the park on Coronation Day, were all reminders that the capital of a great empire had not wholly shaken off the village. So were the established bad characters who frequented its shady gambling-houses and saloons, the imitation bucks and dandies, the bankrupts, bullies and half-pay captains who still, in the last age before the railway came in, sometimes emulated Macheath and Turpin by robbing the benighted traveller in Epping Forest or on the Surrey heaths. On an execution morning at Newgate one saw the rough old London of the landless squatter—greasy, verminous and grimy—gathered outside the gaol; ribaldry, coarse jokes, reckless drinking and unashamed debauchery continued uproariously until the chimes of St. Sepulchre's striking eight and the tolling of the prison bell brought a momentary hush as the prisoner mounted the steps and the sickly jerk of the rope gave the signal for an unearthly yell of execration. For countrymen deprived of their land and status soon degenerated.

So rough and ill-disciplined was that London that until Home Secretary Peel had established his metropolitan police in 1829, St. James's Park had been patrolled by Household Cavalry. Some still living could remember the terrible week when in 1780 the mob, emerging from its filthy lairs in the cellars and crazy tenements of Blackfriars and St. Giles's, had surrounded parliament and all but burnt the capital. When in the winter before her coronation the little queen, with pretty pink cheeks and pouting mouth, drove behind her emblazoned guards through the streets, the crowd gaped but scarcely a hat was raised or a cheer heard. "The people of England," wrote Greville, "seemed inclined to hurrah no more." Even at Ascot in the following summer only a few hats were raised as the royal barouche drove down the course.[1]

---

[1] This chapter is based, not only on contemporary books and literature, but on contemporary illustrations and, in particular, on early volumes of the *Illustrated London News* and *Punch*—two wonderful sources for a reconstruction of social life lacking for earlier periods.

CHAPTER 10

Green Pastures

THERE WERE MANY in that age who thought England was driving to a republic. For a hundred and fifty years the innate English loyalty to the monarchic principle had been undermined by the iconoclastic Whig contempt for royalty and its pomps and gewgaws, by a race of foreign rulers on the throne and, during the last four decades, by the vagaries and indecorums of the royal family. These had reached their climax in 1821 in the spectacle of a stout vulgar and hysterical German queen vainly attempting amid the plaudits of the mob to force an entry into the Abbey at the coronation of her adulterous and bigamous spouse. Though the dignity with which the young Victoria bore her part in the ceremonies of coronation in the summer of 1838 did something to stir deeper and latent national instincts, the general feeling was expressed by William Dyott when he wrote, "A very young queen coming to the throne of this mighty empire (just eighteen years of age) brought up and subject to the control of a weak and capricious mother, surrounded by the parent's chosen advisers . . . gives token of unpropitious times to come."

A sovereign sat on the throne and went through ancient forms, but an aristocracy governed. The real rulers of England were still the greater squires. In Lord Melbourne's Whig Cabinet of 1835, eleven out of fourteen members were lords or the sons of lords: in its Tory successor of 1841, nine. Yet, though until 1832 a magnifico like the Duke of Buckingham could return a dozen members to the House of Commons, after the Reform Bill of that year the landed magnates no longer controlled the urban franchise. A new political power had come into existence—the voters of Britain's growing industrial cities.

Not that the £10 householders enfranchised in 1832 constituted a revolutionary body. They were a respectable, and to those of superior station who troubled to approach them rightly, an even deferential body, as Macaulay, deprived of Lord Lansdowne's rotten borough of Calne by the Reform Bill, discovered when he contested Leeds in the same year. "My leading friends," he wrote to his sister, "are very honest, substantial manufacturers. They feed me on roast-beef and Yorkshire pudding: at night they put me into capital bedrooms; and the only plague which they give me is that they are always begging me to mention some food or wine for which I have a fancy or some article of comfort and convenience which I may wish them to procure." As a result of a brief period of furious agitation an electorate of 300,000 had been discreetly widened into a slightly less submissive one of 800,000. The new electors like the old continued to return men of substance to the House of Commons. The wealth, power and culture of an ancient and complex community were still represented by those who possessed them.

For another two generations, therefore, the House of Commons remained an exclusive club. A number of northern manufacturers and eccentrics with radical hobby horses were tolerated with humorous or contemptuous resignation by the well-groomed majority, who viewed them as they would have viewed the few odd slovens and cranks at a fashionable public school. The House was a place where the gentlemen of England sat or lolled at their ease, with feet stretched out before them, arms akimbo, and top hats tilted over their eyes or pushed comfortably to the back of their heads while papers and blue books were strewn idly on the floor before them. When, as often happened, the course of debate flowed languidly, many would stretch themselves out on the benches and sleep or watch the familiar proceedings of their House with half-closed eyes, some face downwards, others with legs in the air. Honourable members could not see anything incongruous in such a method of conducting their business: the House was as much their property as their own library or club, and to have questioned what they did there would have been the highest presumption. Only within the last few years had the right of the public to read first-hand reports of its debates in the press been tacitly admitted by the provision of a press gallery.

The gentlemen of England carried their downright and frank assurance into the administration of public affairs. "Goose! goose! goose!" wrote Palmerston across a diplomatic despatch. The great Foreign Secretary treated what he regarded as the literary lapses of his country's representatives abroad like an outraged schoolmaster: one received back a despatch with an injunction that it was "to be re-written in blacker ink," while another was forbidden to use the un-English gallicism "corps diplomatique" and reminded that the expression "to resume" did not mean "to sum up" or "to recapitulate" but to "take back." "Sentences," he wrote on another occasion, "should . . . begin with the nominative, go on with the verb and end with the accusative."[1] Such men were accustomed to leave no doubt as to what they meant in the minds of those they ruled.

In this they represented, not inadequately, the people of rural England whose homely lands gave them their titles and wealth. They were rough and ready in their ways, brave and independent. At Oxford sporting undergraduates, in ancient rooms lined with pictures of prize-fighters, race-horses and dogs, would amuse themselves by opening a cageful of rats for their terriers to worry. Young noblemen had their pet prize-fighters: every village its "best man" who had won his title in some homeric contest with his predecessor. There were no Queensberry rules and men fought with their bare fists. A "mill" brought all the neighbours running to see fair play and courage: afterwards the combatants were usually ready to be friends. There was something intensely good-humoured about that open-air, fighting England. It was rough but it was healthy. Borrow has left a picture of an old prize-fighter, his battles over, keeping open house in his "public" down Holborn way, "sharp as winter, kind as spring . . . There sits the yeoman at the end of his long room, surrounded by his friends. Glasses are filled and a song is the cry, and a song is sung well suited to the place; it finds an echo in every heart—fists are clenched, arms are waved, and the portraits of the mighty fighting men of yore,

[1] H. C. F. Bell, *Lord Palmerston* I 261.

Broughton and Slack and Ben, which adorn the walls appear to smile grim approbation, whilst many a manly voice joins in the bold chorus:

> " Here's a health to old honest John Bull,
> When he's gone we shan't find such another,
> And with hearts and with glasses brim full,
> We will drink to old England his mother."

The independence of the national type matched its pugnacity. For all the deference of traditional England to its superiors, it was a deference strictly based on established right and custom. It yielded little to claims based on anything else. A man owed certain duties to Church, State and society to be performed according to his station: when they had been fulfilled he owed no others. Lord Palmerston, in attendance as Foreign Secretary at Windsor Castle, rode as befitted his office beside her Majesty's carriage: when, however, she embarked on Virginia Water he did not accompany her but left the royal barge to row about in a dinghy, not choosing to miss his daily exercise. The skilled craftsmen of Birmingham disposed of their hours of labour in a similar spirit: when they had earned enough, they would take a day or even a week off to drink. Even the clerks of the Bank of England—though the new powers were fast taming them[1]—insisted on their ancient rights of private trading and of receiving tips from clients, kept shops and pubs and drank spirits in office hours. For according to the old English reckoning a man who did his duty had a right to do it as he pleased.

Any interference by the State not established by prescription was viewed with abhorrence. A magistrate told some poor pavement vendors, arrested by an officious policeman for selling water-cress in Marylebone High Street, that they had as good a right to sell their wares as other people to dispose of anything else. When Income Tax, abolished after the Napoleonic Wars amid the loudest cheering ever recorded in the history of the House of Commons, was reintroduced in 1842 at 7d. in the £, it was regarded as an almost intolerable inquisition which struck at the freedom and privacy of every respectable Englishman. "Private affairs must be

---

[1] Their traditional holidays, forty-two a year, were reduced in 1834 to four. *Early Victorian England* I 178.

divulged," commented a newspaper, "private feelings outraged—malicious curiosity gratified—poor shrinking pride, be it never so honest, humbled and put to the blush—deceit and the meanness of petty trickery, encouraged in evasion—and much appalling immorality spread with the abandonment of truth. Many a gentleman will sicken over the forms he has to bear with; and many a tradesman will become either ruined or a rogue."

The more rustic the scene, the stronger this almost exaggerated passion for independence. Fred Bettesworth, farmer's boy, wishing to see the world, left a master with whom he was perfectly happy without a word and waited on Staines Bridge till he found a carter to give him new employment. A year or two later, sooner than be tied, and feeling he had "a kind o' roamin' commission," he left another master and tramped forty miles into Sussex to see the country. Every summer for many years he did the same. In the villages of Whittlebury Forest almost every householder was a poacher: a decade or two back when the gamekeepers of the enclosing lords had failed in the face of local opinion to make an arrest for nutting in the forest, the whole village of Silverstone turned out armed with staves to repel the Bow Street runners in pitched battle and assert their ancient privileges. A yeoman farmer of the same place left a sum of money to cover his grave with spikes pointing upwards, swearing that he had never been trodden on when alive and would not be when dead.[1]

In most villages the Church was still the centre of communal life, its Sunday service, with its gathering of the rustic hierarchy, churchyard gossip and interchange of news, the chief social event of the week. Until the old string and brass choirs were superseded by the new-fangled organs and harmoniums the village played as great a part in communal worship as the parson. Standing each Sunday in the west gallery these rustic instrumentalists, with their copper key-bugles, trombones, clarinets, trumpets, flutes, fiddles and bass viol, represented a folk tradition older than squire or clergy. Yet for all their tenacious clinging to old forms and ritual—"it allus has bin sung an' sung it shall be"—the string choir was doomed and the conservative democracy of the English

1 *Old Oak* 34.

village with it. It was suppressed by the reforming vicar just as the landed peasantry of the old unenclosed parish had been by the re- forming squire a generation or two before.

Already in many villages the established Church had lost its hold. Pluralism, though recently abolished by ecclesiastical re- formers, had long accustomed country folk to the spectacle of neglected churches,[1] perfunctory services and clergymen who seemed more interested in foxes and sometimes in the bottle than the cure of souls. Christian zeal among humbler folk was by 1840 more often to be found among the Methodists and in the Baptist and Independent congregations of the older nonconformity. Of a somewhat primitive and uncritical kind, made up in fervour and homely force what it lacked in subtlety, it had a stimulating effect on the Establishment, provoking a strong rivalry between "Church and King" and "Dissent." To the adherents of the former the "Methodies" were "long eared 'uns,"—ignorant and cantan- kerous fanatics—while to the Methodists, churchgoers seemed little better than damned. Yet even the most enthusiastic adherent of the meeting-house usually preferred to be buried like his father in the churchyard.

The dying flame of the old Faith still burnt brightly at the traditional festivals of the Christian and pastoral year. At Christmas the mummers came round to hall and farm-house with their age- long drama and unchanging characters—

> "A room, a room, for me and my broom,
> And all my merry men beside,
> I must have room and I *wull* have room
> All round this Christmastide."

On Oak Apple Day the inns were decorated with oak boughs and the village lads wore oak apples in their button-holes and cried "Shickshack" to those who wore none. There were morris-dancers in duck trousers and white ribboned shirts and handkerchiefs at Whitsun, and the summer Sunday school treat when the gifts of home-brewed wine were divided by the teachers into two classes,

[1] Edward Fitzgerald always wore his thickest greatcoat in church as the fungi grew in such numbers about the communion table. *Letters and Remains of Edward Fitzgerald* I 119.

the less alcoholic to be drunk by the children and the stronger by themselves when the children had gone to bed. Many villages had their annual feast—a relic of the old pagan Whitsun Ale—when the lads and lasses out on service came home, the travelling fiddler appeared, the inns were crowded and the feast ale tapped. At Abbot's Bromley in Staffordshire on the first Monday after September 4th, the Deer Men with their hobby horses danced the Horn Dance in painted reindeer heads and ancient costumes of red and green. In May, at the Furry Festival at Helston, any person who would not join the dance and remained at work was set astride a pole and carried to the river there to leap or compound in cash:

> "Where are those Spaniards
> That made so great a boast, O?
> They shall eat the grey goose feather,
> And we will eat the roast, O!"

On Christmas Eve in the villages of the New Forest libations of spiced ale were poured out to the orchards and meadows: at Huddersfield the children on their wassailing bore evergreens hung with oranges and apples:

> "We are not daily beggars
> That beg from door to door,
> But we are neighbours' children
> Whom you have seen before.

> "Call up the butler of this house,
> Put on his golden ring;
> Let him bring us a glass of beer,
> And the better we shall sing."

And after service on Christmas morning in many parts of the north country the whole people ran through the streets crying—

> "Ule! Ule! Ule!
> Three puddings in a pule,
> Crack nuts and cry Ule.'

At Polebrook, Northamptonshire, during the last days of April, the May Queen and her attendants gathered posies in the meadows and begged the loan of ribbons, handkerchiefs and dolls from their neighbours to carry on garlanded hoops round the village to a song

that came out of the depths of antiquity. In other places they
sang:

"The life of man is but a span
It flourishes like a flower,
We are here to-day and gone to-morrow,
And are dead in an hour.

"The moon shines bright and the stars give a light
A little before it is day,
So God bless you all, both great and small,
And send you a joyful May."

All this spoke of a culture founded not on courts and cities but
on the green fields and growing earth. When the parish bounds
were beaten the whole community attended in witness of its existence: the beer-laden wagons, the rough practical jokes, the unchanging rituals and chants were the shrew-bread on the altar of Christian
neighbourhood. A diary-keeping parish clerk records these homely
pieties: "Stopt on the mount in the lane and cut X cross, put
Osgood on end upon his head, and done unto him as was necessary
to be done by way of remembrance . . . Old Kit Nation was
turned on end upon his head and well spanked in the corner of
Northcroft and upon the Wash."[1]

So, too, ancient schools and charities kept alight beacons lit by
bygone piety. The Bluecoat boys of Christ's Hospital passed
through the London streets in the belted gown of Edward VI's
England and in the knee-breeches and shining shoe-buckles of that
of George I; the children of the parish school of St. Botolph's
Bishopsgate still wore silver badges and muffin caps. At Eton,
under elms planted in the days of Charles I, the boys, celebrating
the martial heroes of antiquity, kept the old feast of Montem—the
tenure by which the college held its domains. Few could see
unmoved the heroic pageantry of the Trooping the Colour or the
great annual spectacle of six thousand London charity children
assembled under the dome of St. Paul's, singing with that "honest
old English roughness that no man need feel ashamed of" while
their eyes shone with the thought of the feast before them. As,

[1] W. E. Adams, *Memoirs of a Social Atom* I 54-6.

after the prayers, thousands of glossy aprons fell simultaneously, it seemed to one watching like the fall of snow.

It was not only its own traditions that England commemorated, but those of the two great peoples of the ancient world—the Hebrew and the Greek. Those who stood Sunday after Sunday in the parish church identified the songs and faith of Zion with their own rustic life. The manger in which Christ was born stood in the byre where the friendly beasts of the field crowded on wintry nights: the green pastures into which the Good Shepherd led his flock were the meadows of home. Men who could not write their names but whose memories were unimpaired, knew every collect in the prayer book by heart and were as familiar with the bible names as with those of their own fields. So for the more sophisticated the images of the classics were superimposed on those of their own England: an Eton boy recalled his first May Day walking by Fellows' Pond through a half-Grecian haze, "the fairies tripping in rings on the turf, the dryads tempted out of their barken hiding-places, the water-nymphs making high festival on the silver flood."

Knowledge of the classics was still a universal passport. It opened the doors of intellectual society. On that solid foundation of common effort and allusion the culture of a gentleman rested. Statesmen quoted Latin in the Commons and even on the hustings; and busy men of the world found relaxation in the evenings or on holiday in re-reading the pagan authors whom they had first encountered at school or college. Macaulay defined an independent scholar as one who read Plato with his feet on the fender. In the characters of the ancient world such men recognised themselves, their own failings and virtues; "I am reading Plutarch's lives," wrote Edward Fitzgerald, "one of the most delightful books I have ever read: he must have been a gentleman." Sometimes the incongruity of it struck them with a glow of pleasure: "think," wrote one, "of the rocococity of a gentleman studying Seneca in the middle of February, 1844, in a remarkably damp cottage." The pleasure once acquired never deserted them, and death found them with their thumbed Homer or Horace by their side. An English poet who had grown up with the century, crossing Lake

Garda on a summer's evening, put into his native verse the innate
love of his generation for the classical learning of his youth:

"Row us out from Desenzano, to your Sirmione row!
So they row'd, and there we landed—'O *venusta Sirmio*'—
There to me thro' all the groves of olive in the summer glow,
There beneath the Roman ruin where the purple flowers
    grow,
Came the *'Ave atque Vale'* of the poet's hopeless woe,
Tenderest of the Roman poets, nineteen hundred years ago,
'Frater Ave atque Vale'—as we wandered to and fro
Gazing at the Lydian laughter of the Garda Lake below
Sweet Catullus' all-but-island, olive-silvery Sirmio!"

The great country houses with the classical colonnades and
porticoes, and their parks recalling some gentle Sicilian or Thracian
scene, were a natural setting for these gentlemen scholars. Their
library walls were lined with the golden volumes of two centuries
of English and more of classical thought and learning: the child
who grew up in those stately rooms knew, subconsciously, that he
was heir to the ages. Even when, as often happened, the eldest son
abjured books for the superior charms of horse, rod and dog, it
was almost certain that one or other of his numerous younger
brothers would acquire in the freedom of his father's library the
scholarly tastes that he would carry with him into a wider world.

Such houses were still the headquarters of England's chief industry,
agriculture. From their estate offices a great national interest was
directed. One saw it on market day in any country town—the
countrywomen's stalls and baskets spread about the roadway, the
gentry and tenant farmers in their John Bull top-hats, loose open
frock-coats, vast collars, white waistcoats and breeches and heavy
top boots. One saw it, too, in the great fairs that sprang up annually
throughout the countryside, where a whole neighbourhood of
peasant and farmer folk would assemble to buy, gossip and junket
and when those who wished to be hired for service for the coming
year proudly carried the symbols of their trade—the carter his whip,
the milkmaid her pail and the cook her ladle. The lads or lasses
hired received a shilling as testimony of acceptance and stuck a
ribbon in cap or hair in honour of the bargain. "I took the shilling,

put a bit of ribbon in mi' hat to show as I were hired like 'tuthers,"
said an old farm labourer recalling the days of his strength and
pride, "and went and spent the rest of the day at the pleasure fee-ar."
And as night fell and the drums and bugles outside the painted, lit
booths sounded over lonely down and far watching valley, the
rustic fun waxed fast and furious. A national industry was relax-
ing.

If the apex of the agricultural community and of its ordered
industry and culture was the country house, its basis was the
cottage. Of the 961,000 families engaged in agriculture in 1831,
686,000 were now those of labourers who worked the land for
others. Yet if deprived of his former stake in the land, robbed of
his share in the dwindling wild food supply of the countryside by
Game Laws and of a market for the products of his domestic handicrafts by the machines, the peasant still clung to his hereditary
standards and virtues. An intense confidence in his skill and capacity
for work sustained him through a life of hardship—that and his
feeling for the land he tended. Love of the soil, love of food— 'beeacon wi' fat about three inches thick, that's the tackul!"—pride in
his own strength and skill—"I eeant very big but I can carry a
sack of whait ur wuts or beeans wi' anybody"[1]—and unshakable
integrity and conservatism were the attributes of the English peasant.

"Wurken an the land is lovely wurk," was the ungrudging
verdict of an old Buckinghamshire labourer after a life of ceaseless
labour, "and in mi time I wurked furteen and fifteen hours a day,
but that was afuur the machines come about. We sowed by hand,
ripped by hand, and threshed wi' the thraiul. It was lovely wurk,
and that was how it done when I was a young man. We used to
dibble the sayd in, and I a' dibbled many a aiacre of wheeat, beeans,
wuts and barley. Sometimes we used to sow bradcast. At harvist
we cut wi' a sickle." At times the same witness spoke in the language
of poetry of his feeling for the land:

"Some people think they can git summit out a nauthing—but
they can't, and nivver wull. All me life I a noaticed that land
wi' no dress gis very poour craps—short straa, little eeurs, and
little kurnuls; but land well dressed always gis good craps—

---

[1] H. Harman, *Sketches of the Bucks Countryside* 23.

long straa, long eeurs, and big kurnuls: and I nivver yit sin big
eeurs wi' fat kurnuls an thin short straa, and nobody else
nivver did. When carn is sold by weight, and it better to taiak
a peck out a the sack, than put a peck in? That's the difference
atween good and bad farmin'. You must a cleean land, plenty
a dress, and plenty a laiabour to git the' increeas and, when ye
a got these, the increeas comes.[1]"
Such a man when his time to die came could look round on an
entire countryside which he had helped to cultivate.

Higher in the economic scale than the labourer was the smallholder. He still represented a substantial element in the rural community. With the village craftsman—a numerous class—he constituted the social and moral backbone of the parish. In 1831 one
countryman in three possessed some stake in the land. One in seven
worked his own land without hiring labour. Such a man—often
a yeoman who held his tenure for life—was still the standard rustic
Englishman.

Yet the yeoman type was disappearing. It was too conservative
to compete successfully with the more ruthless and greedier values
set by urban and industrial commerce. And the tendency of
landlords was to allow the old tenures for life—a rustic economy
based not on accountant's statistics but on the rhythm of the human
heart—to expire when they fell in. In their place they offered
annual or determinable leases. The number of lifehold properties
and copyholds of inheritance was every year diminishing.

The older, smaller type of squire was also departing—killed by
the violent fluctuations which followed in the wake of the Napoleonic wars and by the rising standard of social expense set by rich
neighbours. But he was still to be found in considerable numbers
in the remoter parts of the country—particularly in Devonshire,
Wales and Clun Forest, in the Fens, and in the Yorkshire and
Cumberland dales. Like the old hero of Scawen Blunt's poem he
liked the hunting of the hare better than that of the fox, spoke in
dialect, dined at six and spent his evenings over a long pipe and a
tankard in the village inn. The pride of his house was the gun-
room which he called his hunting parlour. In white breeches and

[1] H. Harman, *Buckinghamshire Dialect* 110-11.

buckled shoes, fawn-coloured leathers, tight double-breasted, brass-buttoned, bright blue coat, buff vest and low top hat—for he inclined to the "old Anglesey school of dressers"—he was still an essential part of the English landscape.

To him and his kind, defying the sombre black of the encroaching towns, that landscape owed at least a part of its enchantment. The lovely primary colours of the English past that to-day only survive in the dress uniform of the Guards and the huntsman's coat shone in front of the vivid greenery of May or glowed through the mists of autumn. So, too, long afterwards when England had grown drab and urban, old men recalled with a thrill of pleasure the sight of the coaches, thirty or forty a day in any fair-sized main-road town: "the dashing steeds, the fanfaronades on the horn, the scarlet coats of the coachmen and the guard."

Down by the coasts the country looked out on the sea. In white Jane Austen houses along the Solent one could see through the vistas in the trees the great battleships with their bellying sails and the stately West Indiamen "sailing between worlds and worlds with steady wing." Here was the watery highway from which the new England drew its ever-expanding wealth, with clippers bringing tribute from Pagoda Bay and the far ends of the earth, and the rough, passionate sailors whom coastwise England bred, singing as they pulled on the ropes how soon they would

"be in London city,
Blow my bully boys blow!
And see the girls all dressed so pretty,
Blow! boys, blow!"

Such men, by modern standards, lived lives of almost indescribable hardship, spending years afloat before they set foot on shore and, cleaned out by a single gargantuan and open-handed debauch, signing on again a few days later for another voyage. They were ready, like their fathers who fought under Nelson, to dare and do almost anything, and the safety and wealth of England rested on their rude, unconscious shoulders. For them the great shipbuilding yards on the Thames still turned out wooden ships of a quality unmatched throughout the world, made by men who had learnt their craft—part of England's hereditary wealth—from their forbears. "His father's name before him was Chips, and his father's name before him was Chips, and they were all Chipses."

Pride in craftsmanship and skill handed down the generations were the attributes that made the products of English manufacture sought and honoured throughout the earth. Except for cotton, no textile had been radically transformed by machinery before 1830; wool-combing was still governed by skill of hand, as was the hardware industry of the midlands and the cutlery of Sheffield. The old trades were still more extensive than the new: at the time of the Reform Bill there were more shoemakers in England than coal-miners. The unit of industry was small: apprentices frequently lived with their employers over their own workshop, and every craftsman might aspire to be a master. The 200,000 brick-layers, masons, carpenters, house-painters, slaters, plumbers, plasterers and glaziers who made up the close corporation of the building trade, the serge and cloth workers of the West Country, Gloucestershire and East Anglia, the bootmakers of Northampton, the blanketers of Witney, the chair-turners of the southern Chilterns and the cabinet-makers and clock-makers of almost every country town were—for all the threat of the new machines to their employ-ment and standards of living—men with a status in the country based on personal skill and character.

So were the rural handicraftsmen—blacksmiths, wheelwrights, carpenters, millers, cobblers—the fishermen and sailors of the coast towns and the engineers who were coming into existence to make and tend the new machines of steel and iron. North of the border in Lanarkshire, a French traveller found the Scottish craftsmen the best educated in Europe, "well-informed, appreciating with sagacity the practice of their trade and judging rationally of the power of their tools and the efficiency of their machinery."[1] Pride in his home was the hall-mark of the independent British artisan: the Handloom Weavers' Commissioners' Reports of 1838 spoke of the midland weavers' cottages as good and comfortable and much superior to those of the surrounding agricultural labourers, with a solid dower of clocks, beds, chests of drawers and prints. Within was cleanliness, good order and fine frugal cooking.

[1] Baron Dupin, *The Commercial Power of Great Britain* (1825) II 237.

Such a man, wrote Engels, in the changing world of 1844, "was no proletarian; he had a stake in the country, he was permanently settled and stood one step higher in society than the English workman of to-day." He and his like "did not need to overwork; they did no more than they chose to do, and yet earned what they needed." They were rooted fast in their own soil, had faith, home and love. They were freemen, for within their narrow bounds they had freedom of choice. "But intellectually, they were dead; lived only for their petty private interest, for their looms and gardens, and knew nothing of the mighty movement which, beyond their horizon, was sweeping through mankind. They were comfortable in their silent vegetation and but for the industrial revolution they would never have emerged from this existence, which, cosily romantic as it was, was nevertheless not worthy of human beings." For to the pure but rootless intellect of the German radical, Engels, they scarcely seemed human such.[1]

In the letters of Edward Fitzgerald one sees that green England sunning herself in her immemorial peace—"the same level meadow with geese upon it, . . . the same pollard oaks, with now and then the butcher or the washerwomen trundling by in their carts." "I read of mornings the same old books over and over again, walk with my great dog of an afternoon and at evening sit with open window, up to which China roses climb, with my pipe while the blackbirds and thrushes begin to rustle bedwards in the garden." "We have had," he wrote on another occasion, "glorious weather, new peas and young potatoes, fresh milk (how good!) and a cool library to sit in of mornings." Down in his native Suffolk this gentle patriot found the heart of England beating healthily: whenever he returned from sophisticated London he was amazed at "the humour and worth and noble feeling in the country." Fishing in "the land of old Bunyan . . . and the perennial Ouse, making many a fantastic winding . . . to fertilize and adorn," he stayed at an inn, "the cleanest, the sweetest, the civillest, the quietest, the liveliest and the cheapest that was ever built or conducted. . . . On one side it has a garden, then the meadows through

[1] "In truth they were not human beings." F. Engels, *The Condition of the Working Class in England in 1844*, 3.

which winds the Ouse: on the other the public road, with its coaches hurrying on to London, its market people halting to drink, its farmers, horsemen and foot travellers. So, as one's humour is, one can have whichever phase of life one pleases: quietude or bustle; solitude or the busy hum of men: one can sit in the principal room with a tankard and a pipe and see both these phases at once through the windows that open upon either."

To such a one the changing seasons only brought new contentment—spring, "Tacitus lying at full length on a bench in the garden, a nightingale singing and some red anemones eyeing the sun manfully," and autumn, "howling winds and pelting rains and leaves already turned yellow" with a book before a great fire in the evening. "In this big London," Fitzgerald wrote to Bernard Barton, "all full of intellect and pleasure and business, I feel pleasure in dipping down into the country and rubbing my hand over the cool dew upon the pastures, as it were. . . . I should like to live in a small house just outside a pleasant English town all the days of my life, making myself useful in a humble way, reading my books and playing a rubber of whist at night. But England cannot expect long such a reign of inward quiet as to suffer men to dwell so easily to themselves."

For he knew that it could not last. The portents of change were already blazing in the northern and midland sky. "The sun shines very bright, and there is a kind of bustle in these clean streets, because there is to be a grand True Blue dinner in the Town Hall. Not that I am going: in an hour or two I shall be out in the fields rambling alone. I read *Burnet's History—ex pede Herculem*. Well, say as you will, there is not, and never was, such a country as old England—never were there such a gentry as the English. They will be the distinguishing mark and glory of England in history, as the arts were of Greece, and war of Rome. I am sure no travel would carry me to any land so beautiful as the good sense, justice and liberality of my good countrymen make this. And I cling the closer to it, because I feel that we are going down the hill, and shall perhaps live ourselves to talk of all this independence as a thing that has been."

CHAPTER II

The Cry of the Children

"We have game laws, corn laws, cotton factories, Spitalfields, the tillers of the land paid by poor rates, and the remainder of the population mechanised into engines for the manufactory of new rich men; yea the machinery of the wealth of the nation made up of the wretchedness, disease and depravity of those who should constitute the strength of the nation."

S. T. Coleridge

IN MAY, 1842, four men published a document which profoundly troubled the conscience of England. It was called the First Report of the Children's Employment Commission. It dealt with the conditions of labour of children and young persons working in coal mines. The commission had been set up two years before by Lord Melbourne's Government, largely through the pertinacity of Lord Ashley—the Earl of Shaftesbury's heir—an inconveniently well-connected young Tory of strong evangelical tendencies who had taken up the cause of the north-country factory operatives with an enthusiasm which seemed to some of his contemporaries to border on the hysterical.

Everybody by now knew that the conditions of life and labour in the new factory towns of the north and midlands were rough and primitive. There had always been rough and primitive Englishmen, and in these smoky and unsavoury districts they were on the increase. It was part of the price that had to be paid for the nation's growing wealth. But the revelations of the Commissioners took the country by surprise.

From this document it appeared that the employment of children of seven or eight years in coal mines was general. In some pits they began work at a still earlier age: a case was even recorded of a child of three. Some were employed as "trappers," others for pushing or drawing coal trucks along the pit tunnels. A trapper, who operated the ventilation doors on which the safety of the mines depended, would often spend as many as sixteen hours a day crouching in solitude in a small dark hole. "Although this employment scarcely deserves the name of labour," ran the Commission's report, "yet as the children engaged in it are commonly excluded from light and are always without companions, it would, were it not for the passing and repassing of the coal carriages, amount to solitary confinement of the worst order."

Those who drew the trucks were "harnessed like dogs in a go-cart" and crawled on all-fours down passages in some places only eighteen inches high. Other children worked at the pumps in the under-bottom of the pits, standing ankle deep in water for twelve hours. One who was cited, only six years of age, carried or dragged half a hundredweight every day up a distance equivalent to the height of St. Paul's cathedral.

What struck the conscience of early Victorian England with especial horror was the fact that girls as well as boys were employed in these tasks. Naked to the waist, and with chains drawn between their legs, the future mothers of Englishmen crawled on all-fours down tunnels under the earth drawing Egyptian burdens. Women by the age of 30 were old and infirm cripples. Such labour, degrading all who engaged in it, was often accompanied by debauchery and sickening cruelty: one witness before the Commission described how he had seen a boy beaten with a pick-axe. Lord Ashley in a speech in the Commons mentioned another whose master was in the habit of thrashing him with a stick through which a nail had been driven: the child's back and loins were beaten to a jelly, his arm was broken and his head covered with the marks of old wounds.

Here was something never contemplated by Church and State. "We in England," wrote a leading journal, "have put ourselves forward in every possible way that could savour of ostentation as champions of the whole human race; and we are now, on our own showing, exhibited to the world as empty braggarts and shallow pretenders to virtues which we do not possess. . . . We have listened to the cries of the slave afar off, but we have shut our ears to the moaning of the slave at our feet." When Ashley, striking while the iron was hot, rose in the Commons a month later to introduce a Bill excluding all women and girls from the pits and boys under thirteen, he found himself almost a national hero.

Yet there was nothing new in what the Report revealed or Ashley described: these things had been going on for years. They had been defended, as they were defended on this occasion by honourable men with all conscientiousness on the grounds that they were the unavoidable result of the laws of supply and demand. The more the population increased and the greater the consequent suffering of the poor, the more incumbent it became on those who governed to refrain from any interference with economic processes. For it could only end in calamity. The most one could hope for, in the view of the professors of "the dismal science," was that the poor should be fed at all. Hardships suffered by them in the course of obtaining food were in reality blessings in disguise, since without them they and all mankind would starve.

This fatalistic attitude towards industrial suffering was bound up with the high hopes which had been formed of human nature by the idealists of the eighteenth century. It was this that made it so formidable. The age of reason had seen the birth of a belief that challenged the older notion of revealed religion and morality. By the light of the untrammelled mind, man would be able to attain to perfection. Only two things were necessary: that he should observe natural law and be freed from every antiquated shackle, superstition and custom that prevented him from following his will according to the light of his own reason. In France this theory, preached by philosophers and later accepted as a social truism, had resulted in the storming of the Bastille, the Declaration of the Rights of Man and the Revolutionary and Napoleonic armies. In sober commercial England it had taken a more prosaic form. Expounded for more than half a century by a rich and respectable philanthropist of genius, the promotion of "the greatest happiness of the greatest number" had become the faith of most "enlightened" English reformers. It was Jeremy Bentham's belief that that happiness could most readily be realised by the free exercise on the part of every individual of enlightened self-interest. Freedom of contract was the necessary pre-requisite of the utilitarian creed.

The early factory reformers—a little minority of humane men, several of them millowners like the first Sir Robert Peel—had concentrated their efforts on regulating the worst abuses of indentured child labour in the cotton mills. Later they were able to extend their tentative reforms to what was ironically termed "free" child labour and to other branches of manufacture. But the only reforms they could smuggle on to the Statute Book were of the most rudimentary kind, such as the prohibition of the employment of children under nine in cotton mills and the limitation of hours of labour for young persons under sixteen to twelve a day. Even these were avoided in practice. The Factories' Inquiry Commission of 1833 showed that many manufacturers were still employing children of six and seven and that the hours of labour were sometimes as high as sixteen a day. Flogging was regarded as a necessary part of the process of production. Harassed parents, with their eye on the family budget, accepted all this as inevitable and even desirable: many fathers acted as sub-contractors for the employment of their own children. And humane and kindly men regarded as inevitable the spectacle of women with blackened faces and tears coursing down their eyes as they dragged their loads up pit ladders, of work-dizzy cotton spinners mangled in the shafts of unfenced machinery, of workhouse children rented by frugal-minded overseers to rough north-country millowners who treated them like beasts of burden. They treated them worse, for while only a fool would maltreat his horse, a manufacturer could always replace crippled or prematurely senile human workers by further supplies of cheap labour that cost him nothing but their keep.

Nor did such reforms as there were keep pace with the growth of the system. The victims of the factory—at first only an insignificant fraction of the population—increased by leaps and bounds. Every year new inventions widened the scope of machinery, offered new opportunities for growing rich and forced more hungry craftsmen to seek employment for their wives and children in the factory towns. What had hitherto been a localised evil became a national one.

During this period of transition from cottage to factory labour, the course of nature was reversed. The breadwinner was left idle in the home, the wife and her little ones driven by want to the mill. In 1833 the cotton mills employed about 60,000 adult males, 65,000 adult females, and 84,000 young persons of whom half were boys and girls of under fourteen. By 1844, of 420,000 operatives less than a quarter were men over eighteen and 242,000 were women and girls.

The result was appalling. A wife who worked twelve or thirteen hours a day in a factory had no time to give to her children who grew up, in Engels's tragic words, like wild weeds. Put out to nurse with some half-savage creature for a few pence a week until old enough to become wage-earners, they learnt nothing from their mothers of the arts of domestic life and little of its charities. The home to which they returned at night, after their labours often too weary even to eat, was an untended hovel. The machines to which they hurried back before dawn never tired as they did. In the country which had abolished slavery and was vig-orously opposing the slave trade in every corner of the world, "strappers" were kept to flog drowsy factory children lest they dropped asleep at their work, and groups of pallid mites could be seen supporting each other home as they dragged their limbs up the dark cobbled lanes of the Lancashire and Yorkshire valleys.

Many were crippled for life: few grew to mature and healthy manhood or womanhood. Long, monotonous and unnatural working positions resulted in permanent curvature of the limbs. Whole families went about with crooked legs or twisted shoulders. Knees bent inwards and backwards, ankles were thickened and deformed and spinal columns pressed forward or to one side. Every street had its company of cripples, of prematurely aged and arthritic youths bent double and limping, of hag-like girls with deformed backs and hips. Constitutions were permanently enfeebled: long hours in hot, damp, crowded rooms and foul and vitiated air left debilitated bodies and listless minds. The factory population of Lancashire and the West Riding was discoloured and stunted and seemed more like some ill-fated race of pigmies than normal human beings. A Leeds surgeon testified that but for the constant new recruits from healthy country stock, the race of mill-hands would soon be wholly degenerate.

On no one did the tragedy of factory life fall more heavily than on the old craftsmen class of northern England—the finest artisans in the world. Accustomed to independence, to the regulation of their own hours of labour, to a solid standard of comfort and to the environment of the countryside, they found themselves through causes beyond their ken deprived of their wonted markets, undersold by cheap machine-made wares and finally driven in desperation into the close air and foetid lanes of the new towns where their wives and children could sell their labour. The bottom had fallen out of their world. In a letter to Oastler, the factory reformer, a Yorkshire workman described how a fellow artisan, tramping Lancashire in search of work, had come across an old acquaintance of his in a cellar in St. Helens.

"There sat poor Jack near the fire, and what did he, think you? Why he sat and mended his wife's stockings with the bodkin; and as soon as he saw his old friend at the doorpost he tried to hide them. But Joe had seen it, and said: 'Jack, what the devil art thou doing? Where is the missus? Why, is that thy work?' and poor Jack was ashamed, and said: 'No, I know this is not my work, but my poor missus is i' the factory; she has to leave at half-past five and works till eight at night, and then she is so knocked up that she cannot do aught when she gets home, so I have to do everything for her what I can, for I have no work, nor had any for more nor three years, and I shall never have any more work while I live;' and then he wept[1]

When such simple Englishmen, feeling themselves cheated and lost, turned for relief to their rulers they received little comfort. The new Poor Law—enacted in 1834 to remedy the effects of the Speenhamland system of subsidising wages out of rates—bore the cold impress of the mathematical mind. It was based on the principle that the smaller the burden placed by the relief of poverty on the taxpayer, the greater the country's wealth. Itself a contradiction of the strict letter of that economic law, it adhered as closely to it as was compatible with the traditional English dislike of al-

[1] Engels 145-6.

lowing a man to die of hunger. Outdoor relief, with all its kindly charities, was sternly discouraged: in its place the workhouse, built with sombre economy by the administrative Unions of parishes formed under the new Act, offered to the needy poor the maximum of deterrent with the minimum of subsistence.

It was this austere form of charity that was doled out to the dispossessed weaver, the hungry handcraftsman deprived of his employment and the agricultural labourer who had simultaneously lost his grazing rights on the common and the supplementary earnings of the traditional home industries which the machines had destroyed. To men and women nursed in a kindlier tradition it seemed an outrage that old folk who had laboured all their lives and become destitute through no fault of their own should be torn from their homes, separated from each other's company and herded in sexes into prison-like institutions.

But the economists did not see Labour as a body of men and women with individual needs and rights but as a statistical abstraction. Labour was a commodity of value on which the man of capital, with whom all initiative lay, could draw as the state of the market demanded. And as that market—a world one—was at the mercy of accident and fluctuated unpredictably, a "reserve" of labour was indispensable. In exceptionally good times the whole "reserve" could be quickly absorbed by productive industry: in normal or bad ones, it remained unemployed and subsisted on poor relief or beggary. "At the gates of all the London docks," an East End preacher testified, "hundreds of the poor appear every morning in winter before daybreak, in the hope of getting a day's work. They await the opening of the gates; and, when the youngest and strongest and best known have been engaged, hundreds, cast down by disappointed hope, go back to their wretched homes. When these people find no work and will not rebel against society, what remains for them but to beg? And surely no one can wonder at the great army of beggars, most of them able-bodied men, with whom the police carries on perpetual war." Engels, writing in 1844, reckoned the unused labour reserve in England and Wales at a million and a half or about a tenth of the population.[1]

[1] Engels 86-7.

The economic justification of this was that the factories were giving to the country wealth she had never before possessed and bringing within the purchasing power of the poor articles which had hitherto been available only to princes. The evils inseparable from the system were transitional; the nation had only to be patient, to refrain from palliative and wasteful measures and observe the laws of supply and demand, and all would be well. The general body of the middle class accepted this comforting proposition. "Our fields," declared Macaulay, "are cultivated with a skill unknown elsewhere, with a skill which has extracted rich harvests from moors and morasses. Our houses are filled with conveniences which the kings of former times might have envied. Our bridges, our canals, our roads, our modes of communication fill every stranger with wonder. Nowhere are manufactures carried to such perfection. Nowhere does man exercise such a dominion over matter." Scarcely anyone heeded Coleridge's warning that the price of neglecting human health, breeding and character for the sake of profits would have to be paid with heavy interest in the future. "You talk," he wrote, "about making this article cheaper by reducing its price in the market from 8d. to 6d. But suppose in so doing, you have rendered your country weaker against a foreign foe; suppose you have demoralised thousands of your fellow-countrymen and have sown discontent between one class of society and another, your article is tolerably dear, I take it, after all." The wealth and power of Britain to which the economists and their middle-class disciples loved to draw attention were not merely the result of machinery and the laws of supply and demand. They were based on the skill, discipline, industry and social cohesion of the British people—qualities which they had derived from generations of healthy living and sound social organisation. The early Forsytes, for all their integrity and frugality, never comprehended this and, unknowingly, committed waste on the national estate.

The new England they built was housed not so much in towns as in barracks. These were grouped round the new factories, on the least expensive and therefore most congested model attainable. Since the rate of profits was not affected if their inhabitants died prematurely, no consideration was paid to matters of sanitation and health. The dwellings which housed the factory population were run up by small jerry-builders and local carpenters, back to back and on the cheapest available site, in many cases marshes. There was no ventilation and no drainage. The intervals between the houses which passed for streets were unpaved and often followed the line of streams serving a conduit for excrement.

The appearance of such towns was dark and forbidding. Many years had now passed since the first factories appeared among the northern hills. Now the tall chimneys and gaunt mills had been multiplied a hundredfold, and armies of grimy, grey-slated houses were encamped around them. Overhead hung a perpetual pall of smoke so that their inhabitants groped to their work as in a fog. There were no parks or trees: nothing to remind men of the green fields from which they came or to break the squalid monotony of the houses and factories. From the open drains and ditches that flowed beneath the shade of sulphurous chimneys and between pestilential hovels arose a foetid smell. The only symbols of normal human society were the gin shops. Here on the rare days of leisure the entire population would repair, men, women and children, to suck themselves into insensibility on "Cream of the Valley" or Godfrey's Cordial.

In a terrible passage in one of his novels of the 'forties, Disraeli described such a town. "Wodgate had the appearance of a vast squalid suburb . . . There were no public buildings of any sort; no churches, chapels, town-hall, institute, theatre; and the principal streets in the heart of the town in which were situated the coarse and grimy shops . . . were equally narrow, and if possible more dirty. At every fourth or fifth house, alleys seldom above a yard wide, and streaming with filth, opened out of the street. . . . Here, during the days of business, the sound of the hammer and the file never ceased, amid gutters of abomination, and piles of foulness, and stagnant pools of filth; reservoirs of leprosy and plague, whose exhalations were sufficient to taint the atmosphere of the whole of the kingdom and fill the country with fever and pestilence."

Reality was more terrible than art. Disraeli did not exaggerate but, out of deference to Victorian proprieties, toned down the horror of his picture. The official reports of the royal Health of

Towns Commission of 1845 were more graphic, for they were more exact. In 442 dwellings examined in Preston, 2400 people slept in 852 beds. In 84 cases four shared a bed, in 28 five, in 13 six, in 3 seven, and in 1 eight. The cellar populations of Manchester and Liverpool, nearly 18,000 in the former and more in the latter, were without any means of removing night-soil from the habitations. Even for those who lived above ground water-closets were unknown and the privies, shared in common by hundreds, were generally without doors. A doctor in his report on the Lancashire towns testified:

"I have known instances where the wall of a dwelling-house has been constantly wet with foetid fluid which has filtered through from a midden and poisoned the air with its intolerable stench: and the family was never free from sickness during the six months they endured the nuisance. Instances in which foetid air finds its way into the next dwelling-house are not infrequent. I know an instance (and I believe there are many such), where it is impossible to keep food without its being tainted for even a single night in the cupboards on the side of the house next the public necessary, and where the foetor is offensively perceptible always and oppressive in the morning before the door is opened. In this instance the woman of the house told me she had never been well since she came to it, and the only reason she gave for her living in it was, the house was 6d. a week cheaper than others free from the nuisance."[1]

Such horrors must be seen in proportion: it was only the unprecedented rapidity and extent of their growth which made them seem terrible to contemporaries. There had always been filthy slums in the small, semi-rural cities of the older England; nobody had dreamt of regulating them. Nor was sanitary carelessness confined to the poor of the new towns. Even at royal Windsor the footmen in the pantry suffered perpetually from sore throats until 1844 when more than fifty unemptied cesspits were discovered under the castle. A people still rustic regarded bad drains as a joke in the same category as high cheese and "old grouse in gunroom,"

[1] Dr. Lyon Playfair, Health of Towns Commission. *Report on the State of Large Towns in Lancashire*, 1845.

and even welcomed their stench as a useful warning of bad weather. Yet those of the better-to-do classes who had to pass through the new factory towns found the nuisance there beyond a joke.

In Little Ireland, Ancoats, Engels, seeking material for his great work on the proletariat of south Lancashire, described the standing pools, full of refuse, offal and sickening filth, that poisoned the atmosphere of the densely populated valley of the Medlock. Here "a horde of ragged women and children swarm about, as filthy as the swine that thrive upon the garbage heaps and in the puddles. . . . The race that lives in these ruinous cottages behind broken windows mended with oilskin, sprung doors and rotten door-posts, or in dark wet cellars in measureless filth and stench . . . must really have reached the lowest stage of humanity. . . . In each of these pens, containing at most two rooms, a garret and perhaps a cellar, on the average twenty human beings live. . . . For each one hundred and twenty persons, one usually inaccessible privy is provided; and in spite of all the preachings of the physicians, in spite of the excitement into which the cholera epidemic plunged the sanitary police by reason of the condition of Little Ireland, in spite of everything, in this year of grace, 1844, it is in almost the same state as in 1831."

But Engels encountered worse. Groping along the maze of narrow covered passages that led from the streets of the old town of Manchester into the yards and alleys that lined the south bank of the Irk, he found a courtyard at whose entrance there stood a doorless privy so dirty that the inhabitants could only pass in and out of the court by wading through stagnant pools of excrement. In this district, where one group of thirty hovels housing three hundred and eighty people boasted not even a single privy, the joint founder of modern Communism obtained his famous view of the Irk from Ducie Bridge:

"The view from this bridge, mercifully concealed from mortals of small stature by a parapet as high as a man, is characteristic for the whole district. At the bottom flows, or rather stagnates, the Irk, a narrow, coal-black, foul-smelling stream full of debris and refuse which it deposits on the shallower right bank. In dry weather, a long string of the most disgusting, blackish-green, slime pools are left standing on this bank, from the depths of which bubbles of miasmatic gas constantly arise and give forth a stench unendurable even on the bridge forty or fifty feet above the surface of the stream. . . . It may be easily imagined, therefore, what sort of residue the stream deposits. Below the bridge you look upon the piles of debris, the refuse, filth and offal from the courts on the steep left bank; here each house is packed close behind its neighbour and a piece of each is visible, all black, smoky, crumbling, ancient, with broken panes and window frames. . . . Here the background embraces the pauper burial-ground, the station of the Liverpool and Leeds Railway and, in the rear of this, the Workhouse, the 'Poor-Law Bastille' of Manchester, which, like a citadel, looks threateningly down from behind its high walls and parapets on the hilltop upon the working people's quarter below."[1]

As Engels asked, how could people compelled to live in such pig-styes, and who were dependent for their water supply on this pestilential stream, live natural and human lives or bring up their children as anything but savages? And what kind of posterity was England, in her feverish search for wealth, breeding to preserve and enjoy that wealth? It was a question to which economists gave no answer.

. . . .

If reflection could not teach the intellect that men who inhabited the same country were dependent on one another, germs could. The microbes of infection never acknowledged the economists' law that every man could find and maintain his own separate level. Asiatic cholera in 1831 and typhus in 1837 and 1843 from their strongholds in the industrial towns defied every effort of hastily improvised sanitary police and chloride of lime to dislodge them and threatened to devastate the whole country.

There were other warnings that a nation could not neglect a substantial part of its population without endangering its safety. A sullen and savage proletariat, growing in numbers, was turning against the rest of the community, its symbols and traditions.

[1] Engels 49-50.

Carlyle, with his poet's sensitiveness, felt from the seclusion of his Chelsea study the imminence of some terrible explosion among the northern workers. "Black, mutinous discontent devours them. . . . English commerce with its world-wide, convulsive fluctuations, with its immeasurable Proteus steam demon, makes all paths uncertain for them, all life a bewilderment; society, steadfastness, peaceable continuance, the first blessings of man are not theirs. This world is for them no home, but a dingy prison-house, of reckless unthrift, rebellion, rancour, indignation against themselves and against all men."

In such a soil the orator of social revolution could look for speedy returns. In the year of Victoria's accession a People's Charter was put forward by a small group of radical members of parliament, dissenting ministers and Irish and Cornish orators. It demanded the immediate transfer of electoral power from the middle-class electorate of 1832 to the numerically superior labouring class through universal franchise, the ballot, annual parliaments, the abolition of the property qualification, payment of members and equal electoral districts.

Agitation for the Charter caught on like wildfire in the industrial towns. Arms were called for by excited Celtic orators, and forests of oak saplings were brandished at mass meetings by grimy sons of toil. Stories were whispered about the country of how the master workmen of Birmingham—the savage "bishops" of heathen midland tradition—were manufacturing pikes which, smuggled out in the aprons of Staffordshire chain and nail makers, were being sold to honest revolutionaries at 1s. 8d. a piece or 2s. 6d. polished. Men spoke of kidnapping the wives and children of the aristocracy and carrying them into the northern towns as hostages, of the secret manufacture of shells and hand-grenades and caltrops for strewing in the path of the hated yeomanry. Newcastle was to be reduced to ashes: "if the magistrates *Peterloo* us," the cry went round, "we will *Moscow* England." In 1839 the principal town of Monmouthshire was attacked by miners with muskets and pitchforks. Here and in riots at Birmingham many lost their lives.

The climax came in 1842, the year which saw the publication of the Report on the employment of children in the coal mines. One

of those prolonged and periodic depressions that attended industrialisation had culminated in almost unbearable hardship in the
midlands and north: factories were closing and the families of the
operatives starving. That year the first illustrated weekly appeared
in London and the pages of its earliest issues were full of sombre
pictures of distress in the manufacturing districts. At Burnley,
where weavers were working for 7½d. a day, the Guardians, with a
quarter of the population destitute, were forced to appeal to the
Government for help. Idlers with faces haggard with famine stood
in the streets, their eyes wearing the fierce and uneasy expression of
despair. A doctor who visited the town in June found in eighty-
three houses, selected at hazard, no furniture but old boxes, stone
boulders for chairs and beds of straw and sacking. The whole
population was living on oatmeal, water and skimmed milk.

Revolution was in the air. The workers were talking openly of
burning down the mills in order to enforce a nation-wide strike.
Haggard orators bade starving audiences take cheer, for soon
"Captain Swing" would rule the manufacturing districts. At a
Chartist gathering on Enfield moor near Blackburn, a speaker
announced that the industrial north would soon be marching on
Buckingham Palace; if the Queen refused the Charter, every man
would know what to do.

Across St. George's Channel, Ireland—the mother of many an
English factory operative—starved and rioted. In Ennis the mob
attacked the flour mills; at Cork, wearying of a diet of old cabbage
leaves, it stormed the potato markets. Dear corn—popularly
believed to be the price of the time-honoured Corn Laws which
protected the landowner at the expense of the poor—the new
machines and the middle-class franchise were indicted by bitter and
angry men as the cause of their sufferings. As the uneasy parliamentary session of the summer of 1842 drew to a close, the
authorities reinforced the troops in the industrial areas.

The first rumblings of the storm came from Staffordshire. Here
towards the end of July, the colliers, following a reduction of their
wages to 2s. 6d. a day, turned out and, marching on every works
in the neighbourhood, compelled their comrades to do likewise.
Those who refused were flung into the canals, plugs were ham-

mered out of the boilers and furnaces extinguished. The word went round that all labour was to cease until the Charter had become the law of the land. The markets in the towns of the western midlands were deserted and every workhouse besieged by vast queues of gaunt women and children and idle men.

The explosion came on August 4th at Stalybridge, where the employees of Messrs. Bayley's mill had received notice of a further reduction in wages. The strikers, as though acting on prearranged orders, turned out the workers at every factory in Ashton and Oldham. Next morning they marched on Manchester. For a few noisy hours the main body was held up by a small detachment of police and troops at Holt Town. But other rioters swarming out from the streets on either flank, the authorities were forced to fall back, leaving factories and provision shops at their mercy. At Messrs. Birley's mill, where momentary resistance was encountered, the roof was stormed, every window broken, and two policemen and an onlooker killed. The great "turn out," long threatened by heady orators and whispered among the people, had come at last. On Sunday the 7th the rioting spread to Stockport and other parts of Cheshire. Mills were attacked, bakeries looted and the police pelted with stones. At Preston the mob attacked the military, and several lost their lives. In the Potteries some colliers arrested by the police were rescued by their fellow miners who subsequently stormed the Burslem Town Hall, burnt its records and rate books, and sacked the George Inn and the principal shops. Afterwards the town looked as though an invading army had passed through it.

Work throughout the industrial north was now at a complete standstill. In Manchester all the shops were shuttered and the streets thronged with thousands of workmen who besieged the sidewalks demanding money and food from passers-by. Similar scenes were enacted in almost every industrial town from Leicester to Tyneside, and in western Scotland. At Stoke-on-Trent the mob gutted the Court of Requests, the police station and the larger houses; at Leeds the Chief of Police was seriously wounded, and fatal casualties occurred at Salford, Blackburn and Halifax. The wildest rumours circulated: that in Manchester the police had been cut to pieces with volleys of brickbats; that the redcoats, welcomed by the hungry populace as brothers, had risen against their officers; that the queen who had "set her face against gals working in mills" was ready to grant the Charter and open the ports to cheap corn.

The alarm of the well-to-do classes in the adjacent rural areas was by now intense. In the factory towns of Lancashire 6000 mill-owners and shopkeepers enrolled as special constables to defend their menaced interests. The Government decided to act with vigour. In every northern and midland county the yeomanry were called out, and farmers' sons sharpened sabres on the grind-stone at the village smithy before riding off to patrol the grimy streets of a world they did not understand. Tall-hatted magistrates rode beside them ready to mumble through the Riot Act and loose the forces that had triumphed at Peterloo over the urban savagery their own neglect had created.

On Saturday, August 13th, there was fierce rioting in Rochdale, Todmorden, Bury, Macclesfield, Bolton, Stockport, Burslem and Hanley. At the latter place 5000 strikers marched on a neighbouring country mansion and left it blazing. Hordes of rough-looking men in fur caps carrying clubs and faggots patrolled the squalid unpaved roads around the idle mills; others attempted to hold up the mail and tear up the permanent way on the Manchester-Leeds railway. Next morning, though Sunday, the Cabinet met and issued urgent orders to the Guards and the artillery at Woolwich to hold them-selves in readiness for Manchester. That evening as the 3rd battalion of the Grenadiers debouched with band playing through the gates of St. George's Barracks into Trafalgar Square, vast numbers of working men and boys closed in and tried to obstruct its progress. In Regent Street the crowd became so menacing that the order was given to fix bayonets; all the way to Euston Square Station, which was packed with police, hisses and groans continued. The 34th Foot, summoned in haste from Portsmouth, was also continuously hooted on its march across London.

By the evening of the 16th, Manchester was held by three regular infantry battalions, the 1st Royal Dragoons and artillery detach-ments with howitzers and six-pounders. A few miles away the streets of Bolton were patrolled by companies of the 72nd High-landers. Other troops poured in by the new railroads with such rapidity that the rebellion quickly began to lose its dangerous appearance. All that week the magistrates and police, protected by the military, were busy arresting ringleaders and detachments of rioters, and every main road and railway was watched by mounted constables and dragoons.

After that the insurrection crumbled. Further resort to force was useless. Hunger did the rest. Anger and hectic excitement gave place to weakness and despair. The shops were guarded and, with the mills closed, even the miserable wages of the past year of want ceased. The poor rates in every Lancashire town soared as pale, famished multitudes besieged the workhouses, and ruined householders, unable to pay their rent, abandoned their homes. In November Engels saw gaunt, listless men at every street corner in Manchester, and whole streets of houses in Stockport standing empty.

Gradually the factories reopened and a defeated people crept back to work. The insurrection had failed. Yet, like the Report on the employment of children in coal mines, it had done something to awaken the conscience of England. It had added to pity, fear, and, as is the way with the English in times of trial, a sober resolve to remove the cause of the evil. So long as the rioting continued, worthy and peace-loving folk set their faces resolutely against the rioters. But when it was over they took counsel of their consciences.[1]

Many, particularly the manufacturers and the new middle-class, who had nothing to gain by the protection of agriculture and much by the cheapening of provisions, laid the blame on the Corn Laws. Others, like the country landowners, condemned the inhumanity of the millowners, who retaliated by pointing to the low wages and neglected hovels of the agricultural workers in the

[1] "It is certainly a very dismal matter for reflection . . . that the possessing of . . . all our wealth, industry, ingenuity and that superiority in wisdom and virtue which we confidently claim are not sufficient to prevent the existence of a large mountain of human misery, of one stratum of society, in the most deplorable state both moral and physical, to which mankind be reduced, and that all our advantages do not secure us against the occurrence of evils and mischiefs so great as to threaten a mighty social and political convulsion." Greville, *Memoirs*, Part II Vol II 119-20.

southern counties. As Ashley, the factory reformer, knew to his misery, none were worse than those on the Dorset estate of his father, Lord Shaftesbury. The economists and the statesmen who subscribed to their theories continued to reiterate the importance of non-interference with the laws of supply and demand.

But with the general thinking public the view gained ground that there were limits to the efficacy of *laissez-faire*, where public health and the employment of children were concerned. Sanitary reform and factory regulation began for the first time to be taken seriously. Early in 1843 Ashley was able to carry without opposition an address to the Crown for the diffusion of moral and religious education among the working classes. In the following year a new Factory Bill became law limiting the hours of children under sixteen to six and a half a day and establishing further regulations for the fencing of machinery and the inspection of industrial premises. In the same year a commission on the Health of Towns was appointed. Its Report written by Edwin Chadwick revealed that of fifty large towns examined, only six had a good water supply and not one an adequate drainage system.

Public opinion was by now far ahead of parliamentary action. During the middle and latter 'forties the novels of Dickens, Disraeli and Charles Kingsley, the pamphlets of Carlyle and the poems of Elizabeth Barrett Browning educated the reading classes in the Condition of the People question and stimulated their desire for social reform. Intelligent England had become conscious of the new towns. Even Tennyson turned from his dreams of a remote chivalry to confront the inescapable problem of his age:

"Slowly comes a hungry people, as a lion creeping nigher,

Glares at one that nods and winks behind a slowly dying fire."

The thought of a new generation was crystallised in Ashley's question, "Let me ask the House, what was it gave birth to Jack Cade? Was it not that the people were writhing under oppressions which they were not able to bear? It was because the Government refused to redress their grievances that the people took the law into their own hands."

The urge for social reform was spontaneous and its first fruits were voluntary and unofficial. It took the form of numberless remedial activities of a private or only semi-public nature, from church building and the foundation of industrial schools for the waifs and strays of the urban slums to the "poor peopling" which became so fashionable an occupation for well-to-do young ladies in the late 'forties: it was in this work that Florence Nightingale began her life of voluntary service. All over England and Scotland isolated individuals began to tackle self-imposed tasks, each striving to cleanse his or her own small local corner of the Augean stable. Such were provincial doctors who faced fever and vested interest in a tireless campaign against insanitary conditions, devoted clergymen and nonconformist ministers, city missionaries and temperance workers, and young men and women of comfortable circumstances—often evangelicals or Quakers—who gave up their leisure hours to teach in ragged schools or to organise clubs, sports and benefit societies for their poorer neighbours.

Yet the evil was deeply rooted, and the remedy, for all the energy and enthusiasm behind it, so ill-co-ordinated and tardy that those who prophesied revolution and social chaos might have been proved right had it not been for one overriding factor. The social maladies that provoked revolt were not destroyed though they were henceforward slowly mitigated. On the other hand, while diminishing in intensity, they continued to grow in extent through further urbanisation. Revolution was avoided by extending the area of exploitation. But the very factor which most hastened that process ended the isolation of the industrial areas from the rest of the community. The railways had already been decisive in the suppression of the rebellion: an express train had brought a critical appeal for help from Preston to Manchester, and the Guards had been transferred from London to Lancashire in the course of a single night. Rapid internal communication and a new habit of travel, born of cheap transport, was within a few years to transform England and give her a new unity and orientation.

CHAPTER 12

Railroad and Free Trade

TO TURN OVER the pages of the early volumes of the *Illustrated London News* is to experience a social revolution. The first volume depicts an England that, apart from the capital, is mainly rural— a land of cathedral spires embowered in trees; fairs and markets; fat cattle, gaitered farmers and squires and smocked peasants. Where the manufacturing districts appear they do so as an almost savage *terra incognita*, with rough unpaved roads, grim gaol-like factories and men and women of sullen and brutish appearance. Even here one feels the country has only been occupied by a horde of nomad invaders: on the outskirts of the Manchester of 1842 there were still sloping wooded valleys with girls keeping sheep a stone's throw from the flat slate roofs and tall smoking chimneys.

Yet before the end of the 'forties the scene has completely changed. It is an urban England that is engraved on the crowded page. The stress is now on paved streets, vast Gothic town halls, the latest machinery, above all the railroad. The iron horse, with its towering, belching funnel and its long load of roaring coaches plunging through culvert and riding viaduct, had spanned the land, eliminating distance and reducing all men to a common denominator. And the iron horse did not go from village to village: it went from industrial town to town. The England of Winchester and Canterbury and Chester was a thing of the past. The England of smoking Rotherham and Hull and colonial Crewe had arrived.

This revolution in transport came with an extraordinary rapidity. In 1830, and in most places in 1840, a man who wanted to take a journey did so on the roof of a stage coach. Tom Brown went to Rugby of all places in the old Tally-ho! To travel by the London Tantivy Mail to Birmingham along the macadamised turnpike, a distance of 120 miles, took twelve hours; to Liverpool another eleven. One left London shortly before eight in the morning, changed in the course of ten minutes into the Birmingham-Liverpool Mail at the same hour in the evening, and reached one's destination, bleary-eyed and exhausted, at seven next day.

That was the very fastest travel. And what travelling it was! On a cold, damp, raw December morning one waited in the dark at the posting-house for the Highflyer or Old True Blue Independent coach "coming hup" and, when the muddied, steaming horses drew up in the courtyard, took one's "preference" seat in the hot, suffocating, straw-strewn box. There one sat in cramped darkness for many hours of creaking, lumbering and jolting until the "many-coated, brandy-faced, blear-eyed guard let in a whole hurricane of wind" with the glad tidings that the coach had reached another inn "wot 'oss'd it," where the company was allowed half an hour's grace to dine. The only alternative was to travel on the roof, in dust and glare in summer, and muffled to the nose in a frozen eternity in winter. It had its romantic side, of course, but no man would undertake such travel lightly. And what with the fare of sixpence a mile for inside accommodation, the cost of meals at the posting-inns, and the tips to ostler, boots, guard, post-boy and waiter, it was beyond the means of all but a small minority.

In what seemed to our ancestors only a few years all this was changed. The first tentative steam railway from Stockton to Darlington had been opened in 1825, and the Liverpool and Manchester line had followed in 1830. A year after Queen Victoria's accession there were only 500 miles of operating railway in the British Isles. The first railway boom in 1830-9, following a run of good harvests and financed mainly by provincial money, added another 5,000 miles of projected track. Of these, 1,900 miles were open by the summer of 1843. They included the lines from London to Birmingham, Manchester, Brighton and Bristol.

Once they had got over the first shock of noise, sulphur and speed, travellers were entranced by the railroad. Greville in 1837 travelled in four and a half hours from Birmingham to Liverpool to the races, sitting in a sort of chariot with two places and finding nothing disagreeable about it but the whiffs of stinking air.

His first sensation, he admitted, was one of slight nervousness and of being run away with, but a feeling of security soon supervened and the velocity was delightful. "Town after town, one park and *chateau* after another are left behind with the rapid variety of a moving panorama." At every stop all heads appeared at the windows, while the platform resounded with astonished cries of "How on earth came you here?" The most surprising feature of it all, apart from the speed[1] and smoothness of motion, was the wonderful punctuality. It gave to man something of the precision and power of the machine.

At first, of course, until people got used to the idea, there was a certain amount of opposition. Landowners, corporations and venerable cathedral clergy and dons were at pains to keep the vulgar, snorting intruders away from their domains, thus both impoverishing and inconveniencing their successors. Gentlemen resented their noisy intrusion on their parks and huntsmen on their favourite gorses. Poets like Wordsworth thought them hideous, and farmers complained of frightened horses and cattle; keepers of posting-houses, stage coachmen and canal proprietors also naturally hated the puffing billies. "I thought likewise," wrote Jasper Petulengro, "of the danger to which one's family would be exposed of being run over and severely scorched by these same flying fiery vehicles." Such opponents found a doughty champion in the Tory M.P. for Lincoln, Colonel Sibthorpe, who "abominated all railroads soever" and made it his business to oppose every bill for their promotion.

These efforts could not avert the march of progress. The taste for railway travel, once acquired, continued to grow. In 1842 the linking of England by rail was still very incomplete. When a Chartist agitator was arrested in Northumberland for a seditious speech at Birmingham, he was taken by hackney coach to New-castle, by ferry across the Tyne to Gateshead, by rail to Carlisle, by stage coach over Shap Fell to Preston, and thence by what was soon to become the London North-Western Railway to Bir-

---

[1] One "engineer" on the Liverpool-Birmingham line in 1837 reached the rate of 45 m.p.h., for which he was promptly dismissed by his alarmed employers. *Greville Memoirs*, Part II Vol. I 13.

mingham. In this fashion a man could travel from Euston to Glasgow in twenty-four hours—by rail to Fleetwood, by steamer to Ardrossan and by rail on to Glasgow. "What more can any reasonable man want?" asked the *Railway Times*. Yet the reasonable man and the railroad speculators who catered for his needs wanted more.

Of the latter the most famous was George Hudson, the York linen-draper. Under his dynamic and sanguine leadership a railway mania developed that rivalled the South Sea Bubble. During the period of cheap money after 1843 nearly ten thousand miles of new railway were sanctioned by private parliamentary acts. Much speculative money was lost in the process—the sudden slump of 1847 was a minor social calamity—but amalgamation of the smaller and more hare-brained ventures by the larger resulted in ultimate stabilisation. By 1849 the railway system of England had taken on the general form it retained till the second half of the twentieth century.

All this involved a revolution in English life and organisation. For many years the country was covered by armies of "navigators" or "navvies," whom contractors employed to translate the grandiose dreams of the railway projectors and the capital of their shareholders into solid cutting, embankment, tunnel and permanent way. In 1848 nearly 200,000 labourers, many of them Irish, were engaged in this vast task. With their rough habits and speech, high wages—pay day was usually a brutal debauch—and their generous taste in steak, plush waistcoats and whisky, they uprooted ancient ways of living in every place where they encamped. To many of the older skilled workers in the country districts their square-tailed coats of velveteen, their soiled white felt hats and spotted scarlet vests symbolised the "accursed wages of savagery and sin": for the younger villagers their sojourn had an exciting, unsettling quality that in after years caused many to follow them to the great cities along the gleaming lines they had laid.

In 1840 England was still regional in outlook: by 1850 it was national. Save in the remoter shires where there was still no puff of smoke in the valleys to mar the soft horizons, it had become the common lot of an Englishman to live near a railroad. And the new travel had been made accessible to the poorest. In 1845 Gladstone, then President of the Board of Trade in Sir Robert Peel's Conservative Administration, brought in a measure compelling every railway company to run at least one train daily over its system with covered third class accommodation at a penny a mile. Within a few years the receipts of such cheap travel had become almost the most valuable part of the companies' revenue. With the railroad came also cheap coal and cheap food, linking mine, port and countryside to the all-consuming town, and the creation of a vested interest carrying the capital of thousands of shareholders and employing a growing multitude of workers. All these were henceforward dependent on the continued industrialisation of their country.

In other ways England had become more closely knit internally, as well as better connected with the outer world. The first electric telegraph was tried in 1838; eight years later the Electric Telegraph Company was formed to exploit it commercially. Within two years there were nearly 2,000 miles of public telegraph with offices open day and night. Meanwhile the Penny Post, introduced by Rowland Hill in 1840, had led to a far-reaching change in social habit: in three years the weekly delivery of letters in the United Kingdom rose from a million and a half to nearly four millions. Correspondence, hitherto an activity of the well-to-do classes alone, became common to all who could read and write. The prepaid adhesive stamps, affixed to the new paper bags or envelopes which took the place of folded sheets and wafers, were the symbols of a new conception of life, less local and more universal.

So were the trails of smoke that marked every sea-coast horizon. The first British steamboat had been launched on the Clyde in 1811: in the next thirty years over six hundred were built. In 1838 the first iron sailing vessel crossed the Atlantic. Four years later the *Great Western* steamship arrived one June morning in King's Road, Bristol, from New York, having performed in twelve and a half days a passage which until then had normally taken a month. The world of which industrial Britain was the centre was daily growing smaller.

To grasp it she stretched out eager and vigorous hands. History had never recorded such an expansion of wealth and opportunity as came to island Britain in the first half of the nineteenth century: even the golden Spanish discoveries in the Americas three centuries before paled beside it. Exports of unmanufactured iron soared from under 30,000 tons in 1815 to five times as much in 1830, ten times in 1840, and nearly twenty times in 1850. In the first half of the century coal exports were multiplied fifteen-fold. Between 1839 and 1849 alone the exports of mixed wool and cotton fabrics from the West Riding expanded from 2,400,000 to 42,115,000 yards.

In that torrent of opportunity nothing seemed to matter but getting rich. Whoever could do so was honoured: whoever failed was passed by and trampled under foot. In Merthyr Tydfil, where an army of iron-workers lived, sleeping sometimes sixteen in a room, there were no drains, the water supply came from the open gutters, and the filthy streets were unpaved. At the palace of Cyfarthfa Castle a few miles away stood, in Mr. and Mrs. Hammond's phrase, "the home and monument of the man who had started life on the road to London with all his fortune in his stout arm and his active brain, and had died worth a million and a half." "Persons in humble life," wrote the editor of the *Mechanic's Magazine*, "should be the last—though, we regret to say, they are the first—to speak disrespectfully of the elevation of individuals of their own class, since in nine cases out of ten the individual is the architect of his own good fortune, and the rise of one man by honest means furnishes a ground of hope to all that they may by a proper exertion of the powers which Nature has given them be equally successful."[1] It was the model which the early Victorian moralist held out to his countrymen. Self-help seemed almost divine.

Of all avenues to individual wealth—as well as to misery, pauperism and degradation—the chief was cotton. In the late eighteen-twenties Britain imported annually an average of 100,000 tons of cotton, ten years later of 200,000 tons, and in 1849 of nearly 350,000 tons. Cotton came to represent nearly a third of the nation's trade. It seemed to many that the national centre of gravity

[1] C. Wilkins, *History of the Iron, Steel and Tinplate Trades of Wales*.

must shift from London to Manchester. The railways underlined the change. What cotton, in other words Lancashire, needed England could no longer deny.

Even in adversity Lancashire was wont to speak out its mind: and Lancashire with brass in its pocket spoke it loud. What Lancashire needed most was to import and export more cotton. Any policy that tended to check its imports of raw cotton was opposed to its interests. For centuries the policy of England had been based on the protection of the industry on which the health, social well-being and safety of the bulk of its people depended—agriculture. But to Lancashire the Corn Laws which afforded that protection were an impediment and an affront. By restricting imports, they restricted the growth of the industries which manufactured for export and blocked the channel of expanding profits for Lancashire.

What Manchester thought to-day, it was said, England would think to-morrow. As the power of Lancashire grew, a nation-wide campaign was begun for the abolition of the Corn Laws. It enlisted the services of two cotton-spinners of genius, both of whom entered parliament, Richard Cobden and John Bright. They and the sturdy middle-class voters whose interests they championed held that the proper organisation of human society was one in which Britain devoted herself to the production of manufactured goods, and the rest of mankind supplied her with food and raw materials in exchange. The cheaper these, the cheaper and therefore the larger the quantity of goods sold. In this view, the maintenance of duties on foreign corn was a form of national insanity. For they restricted the foreign sales of Lancashire cotton. They could only be explained by the power of monopoly possessed by a handful of selfish and reactionary landowners.

The case for the repeal of the Corn Laws received new strength from the misery of the industrial proletariat and the rural worker caused by industrial change. Both, confronted by the refusal of the authorities to relieve their sufferings, felt a sense of grievance. The fine gentlemen in parliament and the landowners on the Board of Guardians who refused outdoor relief and ignored the promptings of common humanity in the name of *laissez-faire*, themselves enjoyed a protection that was the antithesis of *laissez-faire*. In the

shape of a tax on food, protection wore its most odious and therefore most vulnerable form. Wages being low and employment
uncertain, the obvious remedy was to remove the impost and
cheapen the workers' bread. In 1846, impelled by and using as
pretext a dreadful famine in Ireland caused by failure of the potato
crop, Sir Robert Peel overrode the objections of his Tory supporters
and repealed the Corn Laws.

Though the repeal of the Corn Laws failed to do more than
temporarily relieve Ireland, whose starving population continued
to fall[1] and, in despair, to emigrate, Cobden's triumph and Peel's
apostasy—as his followers called it—were attended in England by
an unexpected return of industrial prosperity. Trade recovered,
demand grew brisk, and the capital laid down in machines began to
yield quick returns. At the same time the new railways cheapened
the cost of provision, clothes and fuel. Though the repeal of the
Corn Laws made little immediate difference to the price of wheat
—which in normal seasons remained much the same until the building of the American prairie railways in the 'seventies—Protection
formally abandoned with the repeal of the Navigation Laws in
1849, became a lost cause. Free Trade was accepted by all. The
"hungry 'forties" were over.

With this revival of prosperity came in 1849 the rush to the gold
diggings in California. Two years later more gold was found in
Australia. Both America and Australia were able to increase their
imports of British goods with gold payments. In 1852 there was
more gold in the Bank of England than had ever been there before.
Money was plentiful, interest rates low and everyone had more
to spend.

With improved transport and increased purchasing power, the
capitalist organisation of industrial society entered on a new and
vaster phase. The unexploited markets of Asia and the newer
continents became accessible to the manufacturer. A golden era
dawned for south Lancashire, the West Riding, Tyneside, Staffordshire, the Clyde and South Wales. Industrial Britain was becoming
the workshop of the world. The opportunity of the greater capitalist
was at hand.

[1] It fell from eight millions to under five millions by the end of the century.

As he grasped it, and trade began to boom, the lot of the worker improved also. Employment expanded, and the larger firms which wider markets created had no need, with their larger turnover, to resort to such petty economies and merciless conduct as their predecessors. Wages tended to rise, hours of labour to fall, and the worst abuses of truck, sweating and child labour to diminish. Ashley's—now Lord Shaftesbury's Ten Hours' Bill and other measures incompatible with the strictest letter of *laissez-faire* found their way on to the statute book. The country, pleased with its growing prosperity, felt at last that it could afford them.

. . . .

England was not a revolutionary country at heart. Given a modicum of bread and beer and a little liberty and leisure to enjoy himself, the sweating toiler in the classic island home of the proletariat proved astonishingly good-humoured. In August, 1848, the year of revolutions, a middle-class writer in a popular journal noted in rhyming couplets how—

"Townward from Richmond, at the close of day,
Two of us were on foot returning straight,
We having dined—the fact 'tis meet to state—
A pleasure van there passed us on the road,
Which bore of honest folks a goodly load;
Holiday makers of the class and rate
Of working people, by our estimate.
The party was obstreperously gay;
Slightly elate, it may have been, with beer.
Joining in chorus as they roll'd along,
'We won't go home till morning,' was their song.
We hailed those revellers with a gentle cheer;
And 'Ah! that that truly British strain,' said we,
'Is livelier than, *Mourir pour la patrie.*'"

Despite the sufferings of the factory operative and the slum-dweller, there was something incorrigibly jolly about England. If it was given the chance to be, it was fundamentally healthy, kept its pores open and its heart kindly and merry. It did so when it could, even in the new towns. With the passing of the Factory Act in 1850 and the legal enforcement of a Saturday half-holiday, the week-end habit began and, as wages increased, the supply of cheap amusement arose to cater for the demand. It was often of a vulgar, garish, sodden kind: there was much drunkenness and often a good deal of brutality. But at its core was an invincible love of good fare and of sport. In Lancashire and the West Riding, gala days, wakes and feasts emptied the mine and stopped the wheels of the mill at customary times every summer. Excursion trains, packed with pale-faced workers and their families with bands, banners and bottled beer, descended annually from the cotton towns on Rock Ferry and Blackpool: it was close by the cheap ferry from Liverpool to the Cheshire shore that Nathaniel Hawthorne in 1853 saw a working man pulling from his pockets oyster after oyster "in interminable succession" and opening them with his pocket-knife. There was whippet-racing and pigeon-flying for miners and scarlet-vested railway navvies, horse-racing of a rough kind on the Yorkshire and Lancashire moors, wrestling, boxing, quoits, bowls, and cricket and football of an order more democratic and vigorous than any that would be officially recognised to-day. In London the working-class population affected the open-air gardens where in the summer families could eat, drink and be merry at little expense. Vauxhall, sinking rapidly lower in the social scale, lingered on until 1859; Cremorne in Chelsea, founded by a uniformed Prussian baron in 1830, proffered fireworks, cascades, balloon ascents, bad music, rather indecorous dancing, alfresco theatrical entertainments and polar bears in white cotton trousers to very mixed company; and there were pleasure gardens at Chalk Farm, Hackney, Hoxton, the "Eagle", Islington, the "Red House", Battersea, and many another suburban resort. In all this, partaking of the village from which it had sprung, the proletariat of urban England showed how little its heart was in ideological abstraction. It was difficult to make it class conscious. It just wanted to be comfortable and jolly and have a good time. Its class anthem was not the *Marseillaise* but the popular song whose roaring refrain went:

> "And damn their eyes
> If ever they tries
> To rob a poor man of his beer!"

CHAPTER 13

Palmerston's England

THE UNIT OF NATIONAL life in mid-Victorian England was the family—the sacred nursery of the individual. The wealth and power of the British empire grew in ratio to the size of this homely unit. The first half of the nineteenth century saw the population increasing more rapidly than ever before, not because more children were born but because, thanks to advances in hygiene and medical science, more survived. Between 1841 and 1861 the population of England, Scotland and Wales rose from seventeen to twenty-three millions. Not only in working-class homes but in those of the upper and middle-class, large families were the rule. The queen herself had nine children: a judge of the High Court twenty-four. Strangers admitted to the sacred circle of the home would usually find their hostess in the family way and be greeted by the spectacle of a flock of little boys running off to hide and little girls running out to peep. Often the children would mount in yearly steps from the baby at the breast to the grown youth of nineteen.

Around that holy of holies centred a life of the strictest regularity and order. Paterfamilias, for all the love he bore his family, was an awe-inspiring figure, infallible in his judgments and irreproachable in his whiskers and moral conduct: his wife—a few years before a slender and clear-complexioned girl—"a housekeeper, a nurse, a sitting hen," as a distinguished French critic saw her, "broad, stiff and destitute of ideas, with red face, eyes the colour of blue china, . . . spreading dresses, . . . stout masculine boots, . . . long, projecting teeth."

In the more prosperous families the boys would start work early with a tutor and at eight or nine leave home for the rough republic of one of the great boarding schools which were constantly expanding and multiplying to train new rulers for a growing commercial empire. Here sensitive children from rich and sheltered homes would rise in the small hours of the morning to light fires and boil water for their majestic seniors, sweep rooms, run errands and do the meanest chars, endure flogging and bullying without a murmur, and sleep at night in noisy, crowded dormitories subject to influences which would have made their mothers and sisters swoon.

In contrast, the lives of girls in well-to-do families were often sheltered to an extent that cut them off from the roots of life. The men were trained to make wealth: the women to transmit and form part of it. They were regarded as the chief measure of a husband's or father's opulence and social dignity: their elegant accomplishments, their delicacy and chastity were sources of male pride and satisfaction. As girls they were taught to play the piano, draw, dance, make wax flowers and bead-stands and do decorative gilding and crochet work. That a man's womenfolk should be able to devote themselves to occupations so materially useless was a tacit tribute to the labour and self-sacrifice that had gone to the making of the wealth that sustained it. "Oh yes, mum," said the cook in *Punch* of the squire's bride, "she's a perfect lady, mum. Don't know one j'int o' meat from another, mum."

On a simpler and more spartan scale the family life of the north-country manufacturer followed that of the lawyer in Kensington and the banker in Bayswater. Often he still lived on the premises of his own works in the shade of the smoke and within earshot of the hammering that created his wealth. In other cases he had moved out to one of the suburbs of gardened, gothic villas that were growing up on the outskirts of places like Manchester and Birmingham. His daily round and social habits were less leisured than those of the Londoner: he still went to the mill at six, dined in the middle of the day and went early to bed after a hot meat supper and family prayers. Sometimes his working day would last sixteen or more hours. He sent his sons into the works in their early teens instead of to public school and college which, he held, unsettled the mind for commercial pursuits.

Though many of those engaged in trade were men of cultivatino —buyers of pictures and founders of public libraries and colleges—

the bulk of the provincial merchants tended, like their richer Forsyte brethren in London, to be Philistines, valuing all worldly things by the sterling standard, ignoring and despising art and having little truck with intellect which they left to the leisured and endowed landed gentry. The spiritual side of their natures would have been stifled but for their feeling for religion. This was like themselves: downright, undiscriminating and practical. Its dominant note was a militant Protestantism, which comprised a great readiness to criticise, a strong sense of self-righteousness, a very real respect for integrity and sound moral conduct, and an unreasoning distrust of the Pope and of all foreign fal-lals. It found vigorous expression in the busy, black-coated, white-tied unction of Exeter Hall—where middle-class opinion was ceaselessly mobilised in favour of missionary, pacifist and humanitarian ventures, all of a strongly Protestant trend. Its antithesis was the Puseyite movement which, spreading out from Oxford—still the home of lost causes—was filling long-neglected, sober Hanoverian parish churches with painted chancels, niches, candles, altars, Popish-looking rails to keep off the profane laity, and painted windows bearing the idolatrous image of the Virgin Mary.[1]

This apparent drift to Rome aroused all the Protestant pugnacity of the British people. In 1850 an attempt by the Pope to create English metropolitan titles for Catholic bishops all but brought down the Government, who were suspected of being lukewarm in their opposition to this outrageous act of "invasion." Mobs processed through the streets of quiet provincial towns, smashing Catholic shop windows, tearing up chapel railings and bearing effigies of the offending Pope and his cardinals (previously exhibited in some local tailor's window) to the bonfire. In his public letter repudiating what *Punch* described as "an insolent papal brief," the Premier, Lord John Russell, assured an anxious nation that "no foreign prince or potentate will be permitted to fasten his fetters upon a nation which has so long and nobly vindicated its right to freedom of opinion, civil, political and religious. . . . I will not bate a jot of heart or life so long as the glorious principles and the

[1] "I wanted Oliver and his dragoons to march in and put an end to it all." *Letters and Literary Remains of Edward Fitzgerald*, I 180.

immortal martyrs of the Reformation shall be held in reverence by the great mass of a nation which looks with contempt on the mummeries of superstition." This, and a great deal more like it, was the kind of language the serious middle class of the eighteen-fifties liked to hear. To still its honest fears the Government brought in an Ecclesiastical Titles Bill, as a "slap in the face"—it was little else—"to papal aggression." There was an eternal child in the English heart, and a little make-believe, so long as it was kept out of business hours, was necessary from time to time.

There was no make-believe in the piety of the English middle-class home. Occasionally tyrannical and more than frequently oppressive—for the English seldom did things by halves—it was none the less the central core of life for a great body of men and women who represented between them the major portion of the wealth, power and activity of the world. It gave them regularity of habit, a rule of sober conduct that made them invincible in their narrow achievement and a certain intensity of purpose that lent dignity and even beauty to their otherwise monotonous and ugly lives. Over the frieze of one of the chief London banks were written the words, "Lord direct our labours"; the very railway terminuses provided bibles chained to reading-desks for the waiting business man to consult.

In his *Notes on England*, published in 1861, the Frenchman, Taine, drew a picture of the head of an English family conducting prayers in the sheltered bosom of his household. "On Sunday evening he is their spiritual guide, their chaplain; they may be seen entering in a row, the women in front, the men behind, with seriousness, gravity, and taking their places in the drawing-room. The family and visitors are assembled. The master reads aloud a short sermon —next a prayer; then everyone kneels or bends forward, the face turned towards the wall; lastly, he repeats the Lord's Prayer and, clause by clause, the worshippers respond. This done, the servants file off, returning in the same order, silently, meditatively; . . . not a muscle of their countenances moved."

One saw the full intensity of that spirit of worship on the Sabbath. The English kept this day holy and unspotted from the world: that is to say, they did no work on it, avoided travel, attended church

or chapel and stayed at home. Here the family virtues were inten-
sively cultivated. An old man who once taught the writer of this
book has recalled his childhood's Sunday round in mid-Victorian
days. At eight the elder children breakfasted as a Sabbath treat
with their parents, and after breakfast and family prayers settled
down quietly until it was time for chapel over some special illustrated Sunday magazine: *Good Words, The British Workman, The
Band of Hope, The Sunday Magazine*. These works were not quite
as heavy reading as their titles suggested, for, interspersed with
moral sermons and excerpts from the Scriptures, were serial stories
by approved writers which, published elsewhere, might have been
set down as frivolous and pernicious novels but which, between
sacred covers, took on an almost privileged guise. In the afternoon
the programme of devotional reading and instruction was repeated:
a missionary narrative read aloud by mother after dinner, Sunday
school in the nursery conducted by a nurse, a Bible lesson from
father at four, family tea followed by hymns, evening chapel for
the elder children and family prayers again after supper.[1]

Such was the kind of day of which Macaulay was thinking when
he appealed in parliament for proper week-end leisure for the
factory worker. "We are not poorer but richer because we have,
through many ages, rested from our labour one day in seven. That
day is not lost. While industry is suspended, while the plough lies
in the furrow, while the Exchange is silent, while no smoke ascends
from the factory, a process is going on quite as important to the
wealth of nations as any process which is performed on more busy
days. Man, the machine of machines, the machine compared with
which all the contrivances of the Watts and the Arkwrights are
worthless, is repairing and winding up, so that he returns to his
labours on the Monday with clearer intellect, with livelier spirits,
with renewed corporal vigour." He certainly needed it in that age
of strenuous endeavour. Gaining so much from the Sabbath rest
itself, the respectable middle class, whose votes now swayed the
legislature, naturally wished to assure the same blessings for the
rest of the population. It was prepared to use its political power to
enforce them.

[1] Somervell 14-17.

Sunday observance was one of the salient peaks of the mid-Victorian scene. On that day over a busy nation there fell an awful calm. Any attempt to relieve it was met by the full terrors of the canalised English forces of moral righteousness. In 1856 an effort was made by certain scholarly aristocrats to open the National Gallery and the British Museum on Sunday. The storm this aroused in a House of Commons assailed by all the propagandist powers of Exeter Hall caused them quickly to withdraw. A proposal in the same year to provide Sunday bands in the dreary Manchester and Salford parks met with a like repulse.

At midnight on Saturday—a noisy drunken evening in any working-class district—all movement and sound suddenly ceased. As Big Ben's new clock chimed its last stroke a solemn hush announced that the Sabbath had begun. Next morning the food shops opened for a few hours, but at eleven, the time for divine service, every shutter went up. For those with large houses and affectionate families, the quiet scene had a familiar and reassuring air; to those who lived in tiny tenement rooms and had no playground but the drab streets it was less pleasing. Taine, visiting England in 1860, found the prospect almost more than he could bear:

> "Sunday in London in the rain: the shops are shut, the streets almost deserted; the aspect is that of an immense and a well-ordered cemetery. The few passers-by under their umbrellas, in the desert of squares and streets, have the look of uneasy spirits who have risen from their graves; it is appalling."

The virtuous middle class had the franchise: the working-class majority had not. It was the middle class, therefore, that enforced the new urban English Sabbath in conformity with its own frugal virtues. But there was one point on which the rough majority insisted: Jewish Sabbath or no, it would drink when it pleased. Beer and gin, and plenty of them, were the unspoken price with which the busy Gradgrinds and Bounderbys reconciled the proletariat to the social chaos and vacuum of *laissez-faire*. When, in 1856, an evangelical peer brought in a bill to close the pubs on the Lord's Day, the church parade of high society in Hyde Park was interrupted for three successive Sundays by an angry multitude who booed every rider and carriage on the first Sunday, pelted them with showers of turf and stones on the second, and on the third made the few daring survivors ride for their lives till the police, in long lines, raining blows on rioters and spectators alike, cleared the park. After that the bill was withdrawn and the pious aristocrat left the country.

At midnight on Sunday the Sabbath gloom lightened. The respectable classes, replete from their devotional exercises and anticipating an early start to the new week of labour and lawful gain, slept the sleep of the just. But the dancing saloons and the all-night haunts of vice in the metropolis turned on their lights and began to revel again openly.[1]

This was of a piece with the national taste. England kept its more austere moments with great solemnity and decorum, but it liked to do itself well and knew how. The Forsytes carried their love of good living from the country to the town, and with their new wealth, were the better able to gratify it. They loved to take the summer steamer to Blackwall or Greenwich and dine in Lovegrove's great room or at the "Ship" or "Trafalgar" off piled plates of whitebait, salmon and India pickle, spitchcocked eels and stewed carp, followed by roast duck and haunch of mutton, tarts and custard, iced punch, hock, champagne and port, while the river shimmered in the rays of the setting sun and the white sails passed against the twilight. Toasts, pipes and good stories rounded off the feast, and singing in the train all the way home, and a draught of soda and a purge of pills before negotiating the stairs to join one's sleeping partner.[2]

They did themselves as well at home. The merchantry and the semi-commercial professional classes were making money hand over fist and they disposed of it, partly in ever growing investments but partly in comfortable living. They spent little on splendour, art and travel: they left these to the aristocracy and gentry. They concentrated on dinner parties. In this there was much competitive expenditure. A man and his wife measured their status by the weight of their table silver—vast épergnes, massive salvers, tureens and

[1] Francis Wey, *A Frenchman sees England in the Fifties* 250-6.
[2] *Punch* XVII 102.

candlesticks—the fineness of their table damask, cut-glass and china, above all on the quantity of dishes served. Vast saddles of mutton and sirloins of beef, whole salmons and turbots, interminable courses of potages, fishes, removes, entremets and removes of the roast, were helped out by vegetables boiled in water, pastries and enormous Stilton and Cheshire cheeses. The wines followed each other in equal profusion until the table was cleared for further orgies of dessert, preserved fruits, nuts, port, madeira and sherry. All this suggested to a foreigner that the race would eat itself to a standstill. Taine reckoned that to the one and a half sheep consumed in a year by a Frenchman, an Englishman ate four.

The circumference took its standards from the centre. The larger industrial towns were beginning to evolve a social life for the well-to-do modelled on that of the metropolis, with their own clubs, fashionable places for promenade and recreation and assembly and ball-rooms. In Liverpool, the most aristocratic city of the industrial north, the merchant princes wore white cravats and evening dress coats on Change, and in Manchester's Athenaeum and at its world-famous Hallé concerts, first established in 1848, well-to-do Quakers could be seen soberly conversing in broad-brimmed hats, neat grey or mulberry-coloured coats, frilled shirts and knee breeches. The urban sporting world, familiar to the twentieth century, was beginning to take shape: the I. Zingari was instituted in 1845 and a regular All England cricket eleven began to play a few years later, travelling the country in billycock and checked shirt and arousing widespread enthusiasm for the game, soon to bear fruit in the first county matches. Rugby football was also evolving from a local into a national sport, with its own customs and rules: the famous Blackheath Club was founded by a little group of old Rugbeians and Blackheath boys in 1858.

For though England was turning urban and the old field sports could no longer suffice, the strong national love of pleasure re-asserted itself as soon as the first rush for wealth was over. A new form of recreation, first tentatively essayed at Weymouth, Scarborough and Brighton in the days of George III, found especial favour with the well-to-do merchant and professional classes. The annual seaside holiday had the supreme advantage of catering for the whole family, and its healthful properties gave a fillip to business. Many London families emigrated for the summer to Margate, the bread-winner coming down the river for the week-end on Saturday night on the "husbands' boat." The place was already an institution before the middle of the century, with its trim houses and spired church, its famous pier and fishermen, arbours and seats, its old ladies in deck-chairs and gentlemen in straw hats, and its rows of horse-drawn bathing-boxes and bottle-nosed bathing women wading through the water in great bonnets.

Though newer resorts of quality like Folkestone and Hastings were winning favour, Brighton was still the first seaside town in England with many survivals of its Regency heyday, including "old, wicked-looking gentlemen with thin faces, long noses and quaint hats who had drunk Regent punch with King George the Fourth at the Pavilion." These mingled, a little incongruously but in the English mode, with demure young ladies in curls and bonnets, armies of children in jackets and knickerbockers, and fanatic-looking preachers in tall hats and white ties who attempted to hold prayer meetings on the beach. The normal costume of the seaside holiday-maker was a loose-fitting check suit and a bowler. It was fun, after days in counting-house and office, to stroll along the windy pier—where the French were periodically expected to land—and watch the gulls and fishing-boats and the old salts in jerseys and straw hats, to dine off turtle and strawberry ices at Mutton's, to drive in an open fly from one cliff to the other, eyeing the "galls" as they passed to and fro in their crinolines and parasols before the rows of dazzling white houses with green blinds and sun-blistered verandas, to hear the fisherwomen hawking their prawns with shrill "Yeo Ho's!" and, in the cool of the evening, to listen to the Negro melodists singing "I would I were in Old Virginny" and the band playing the Overture to *Zampa* or the March from *Athalie*.

Even Victorian decorum relaxed a little by the seaside. Monsieur Wey, a Frenchman of delicacy, noted with astonishment how bathing took place in full view of a front swarming with idlers of both sexes: at Brighton men bathing alone went into the water stark naked. Never, he wrote, would he forget his bathe there in 1856. It was on a Sunday at the time at which worshippers returned from church. He had been assigned a cabin in which to undress. It was a wooden construction on wheels placed at the water's edge with its steps half-submerged. He committed himself to the waves. When he was ready to return a fearful thing happened. Three ladies, a mother with her daughters, settled themselves on camp stools in his direct line of approach. They seemed very respectable females, and the girls, he noted, were both pretty. There was no possibility of reaching his cabin without passing in front of them. They each held a prayer book and watched him swimming about with serene unconcern. The Frenchman's feelings can be imagined. To give them a hint without offending their modesty he advanced cautiously on all fours, raising himself by degrees as much as decency permitted.

English notions of propriety were always hard for a foreigner to appreciate, for strict as they were, they seemed founded on no principle and were often a matter of words. A Frenchman noted that the more respectable islanders would sooner die than mention the human posterior by name, yet in mixed company would roar with laughter at the story of the lady who said she had plenty to sit on but nowhere to put it. Mr. Roget in his famous *Thesaurus* of English words and phrases, published in 1852, classified all concept and matter except the human body, which was discreetly scattered about the book, the stomach concealed under the general title of "receptacle," the genitals under that of production. Yet physical rough and tumble, often of the crudest kind, was the essence of the national humour.

For unlike the older territorial aristocracy to which in its power and wealth it was already beginning to give tone, the new English middle class was only half civilised, and its advance in manners, rapid as it was, could not keep pace with its fortunes. The moment it relaxed its puritanical decorum, the rude native Adam, so full of rustic nature and vitality, emerged. In its pleasures urban England still smacked of the earth. When it went on the spree, it left its prudery at home. It sat top-hatted, eating devilled kidneys, drinking *aqua vitae* and joining in the roaring choruses of the smoky Cider Cellar in Maiden Lane: it kicked up its flounces and heels and stamped them on the ground in the rhythmic surge of the polka.

All the vulgarity and vitality of the nation burst out in such annual institutions as the Christmas pantomime, when even the family split its sides in uninhibited and unashamed laughter at the gargantuan jests and antics of the Dame and goggled its eyes at the tight-laced, broad-bosomed ample-flanked, Principal Boy. The pantomime had full licence to be coarse, and respectable fathers and mothers who took their families to revel in its rich spectacle would have been gravely disappointed had it been otherwise. The crowded house rocked at the broad jests, gaped with delight at the tinsel scenes in which fairies and genii floated before ethereal landscapes of gold, crystal and diamonds, and uproariously applauded the brutal, noisy but good-humoured parody of the harlequinade.

To see Victorian England really enjoying itself, no spectacle compared with the Derby. With the growth of London it had become the chief sporting event of the year. On the way to Epsom all the world mingled, fours-in-hand with rakish young gentlemen smoking cigars and wearing check trousers and muslin shades on their top-hats; ladies with parasols in open carriages; crowded family brakes; pearl-buttoned costers in donkey carts; cabs, barouches, droskies. Everyone was laughing, chaffing and shouting, with only a single thought and destination. The windows and balconies of the mellow, shaded Georgian houses along the road to the Downs were alive with smiling faces, the walls were crowned with cheering schoolboys, and on every village green stood groups of pretty girls with new ribbons and finery fluttering under the tender, sun-kissed leaves of the chestnut trees. Every girl who acknowledged the waving hands and kisses blown to her was greeted with a cheer. Among the sweet-williams and Canterbury bells sat old gentlemen at their cottage doors smoking long pipes and giving as good as they took from the wags on the passing brakes. At each successive turnpike there was a jam, and here and at the roadside pubs the noise was like all England speaking at once.

On the course itself the colours of the rainbow, and many more crude, mingled. Round the carriages and coaches barefooted, hungry-looking beggars, gipsies and children swarmed seeking food. The world of fashion and the workaday City rubbed shoulders with comic Negro singers, hucksters selling trinkets and red-haired Scottish lassies dancing to the sound of bagpipes. On vehicles overlooking the course sat jolly old boys from 'Change or counter in top-hats with side whiskers, high stocks and massive gold chains suspended across monumental waistcoats, drinking champagne out of long glasses and eating game pie, sandwiches and melon. Behind them were painted booths and bookies' stands, and all the fun of the great day—boxers and banjoes, thimble rigs and knock-em-downs, shooting and archery galleries, skittle alleys and dirty, bright-coloured, bawling vendors of every kind.

Towards evening, when the races were over and swarms of carrier pigeons had borne their news of triumph or disaster into every corner of England, the carnival entered on its final stage. Bacchus and the old Saxon gods of horn and mead seemed to have descended on to the packed, twilit downs. The astonished Frenchman, Taine, tried to describe the scene:

"Twenty-four gentlemen triumphantly range on their omnibus seventy-five bottles which they have emptied. Groups pelt each other with chicken bones, lobster-shells, pieces of turf. Two parties of gentlemen have descended from their omnibuses and engaged in a fight, ten against ten; one of them gets two teeth broken. There are humorous incidents: three men and a lady are standing erect in their carriage; the horses move on, they all tumble, the lady with her legs in the air; peals of laughter follow. Gradually the fumes of wine ascends to the heads; these people, so proper, so delicate, indulge in strange conduct; gentlemen approach a carriage containing ladies and young girls and stand shamefully against the wheels; the mother tries to drive them away with her parasol. One of our party who remained till midnight saw many horrors which I cannot describe; the animal nature had full vent."

A drunken land at times the old fighting England of the urban 'fifties was: the right to empty his can of beer whenever he pleased was the first clause of Magna Carta which the Englishman took with him from the country to the town. In 1850 Manchester, with its 400,000 inhabitants, had 475 "publics" and 1,143 beer houses. Every night the eternal revelry would begin outside their flare-lit

doors: the tip-tapping of the wooden clogs, the tangled hair and
dirty, sodden faces swaying, swinging and leaping to the music
of fiddle or seraphine. In the casinos or music saloons, where a
man might pay 2d. or 3d. for admission, eat apples and oranges
and afterwards sup on tripe and trotters, drink and harmony went
hand in hand, as, amid a strong flavour of gin, corduroy and
tobacco smoke, the rough audience joined in the chorus of the latest
music-hall ditty. On Saturday night, after the workman's weekly
pay had been taken, it was a revolting sight for a sensitive man to
witness the ghastly scenes at the tavern doors. Drunken women
by the hundred lay about higgledy-piggledy in the mud, hollow-
eyed and purple-cheeked, their ragged clothing plastered with
muck.[1] Occasionally one would stagger up to fight or beat off
some whimpering wife come with her bedraggled babes to seek a
drunken husband before the coming week's housekeeping money
was all spent.

For though the worst days of hunger, destitution and low wages
were over, and the industrious, frugal artisan, like the resourceful
manufacturer, was enjoying better times, the more the nation
became industrialised, the more squalid became the background of
the bulk of its people. The greater towns—several of them now
nearing the half-million mark—were still organised on the parish
model that had sufficed when they were half rural: that is to say
they were without efficient local government, sanitation or communal amenity. Even the capital was indescribably filthy. Here,
as everywhere else, the rate of expansion had outgrown the civic
institutions and organisation of the past, and the result was pandemonium. London was increasing at the rate of 2,000 houses a year.
Efforts of public-spirited individuals to cleanse it were always
defeated by the flow of fresh immigrants from Ireland and the
country. Even the new fashionable districts of Belgravia and
Pimlico were unpaved and almost without illumination. Footmen
carried lanterns at night in front of their masters, and the highway
down the centre of Eaton Square was a sea of ruts with islands of
brickbats and rubbish.

For the new London as it grew outwards rose on the muck of

[1] Wey 117-18.

the old. Its Medical Officer of Health, in a report issued in 1849, described the subsoil of the City as "17 million cubic feet of decaying residuum." Belgrave Square and Hyde Park Gardens rested on sewers abounding in the foulest deposits which blocked the house drains and emitted disgusting smells, spreading purulent throats, typhus, febrile influenza, typhoid and cholera among the well-to-do and their servants. As late as the middle of the century a summer's evening walk by the waters of the Serpentine sometimes ended in fever and death brought on by the morbid stench of the stream-borne drainage of Paddington. Even the queen's apartments at Buckingham Palace were ventilated through the common sewer: and a mysterious outbreak of fever in Westminster cloisters led to the discovery of a mass of old cesspools from which 500 cartloads of filth were subsequently removed. Many of the busier streets were ankle-deep in horse-dung.

If these were the sanitary conditions among which the prosperous lived, those of the workers can be imagined. Off Orchard Street, Portman Square, a single court 22 feet wide, with a common sewer down its middle, housed nearly a thousand human beings in 26 three-storied houses. And the passer-by, pursuing the course of Oxford Street towards Holborn, was favoured by the sight and whiff of a narrow, winding, evil-smelling lane lined with hovels, through the open doors of which could be seen earthen floors below the level of the streets swarming with pallid, verminous, crawling human animals. "Is it a street or kennel?" asked *Punch*,

> "foul sludge and foetid stream
> That from a chain of mantling pools sends up a choky steam;
> Walls black with soot and bright with grease; low doorways,
>   entries dim;
> And out of every window, pale faces gaunt and grim."

In Wapping the courtyards were deep with filth in which incredibly ragged and often naked children crawled seeking for vegetable parings and offal among the refuse. In Bethnal Green there were 80,000 inhabitants living under almost completely primitive conditions. Until the first parliamentary Sewer Commissioners in the middle 'fifties laid down over fifty miles of underground arterial drainage and pumped out millions of cubic feet of nauseating sludge, almost every street was barricaded against overflowing sewers. London that had become a city such as the world had never before seen was still governed like a village. *Punch* depicted the Court of Aldermen guzzling at one of the great traditional feasts, while King Death, with folded arms and socket eyes, gazed down on his henchmen, the spectres of Carbonic Acid Gas, Miasma, Cholera and Malaria, who took their toll of gaunt, ragged humans amid arched sewers and slime.

As for the state of the river into which all this unmastered nastiness drained, it beggared description. Its shores were rotten with "guano, stable dung, decaying sprats, and top dressings from the market gardens." In the hot summer of 1858 the stink became so foul that there was talk of removing parliament. In a famous cartoon England's leading comic journal apostrophised Father Thames as a filthy old man dragging up dead rats from a liquid, gaseous mass of black mud and dying fish.

> "Filthy river, filthy river,
> Foul from London to the Nore,
> What are thou but one vast gutter,
> One tremendous common shore.
>
> All beside thy sludgy waters,
> All beside thy reeking ooze,
> Christian folks inhale memphitis
> Which thy bubbly bosom brews.
>
> . . . .
>
> And from thee is brewed our porter,
> Thee, thou gully, puddle, sink!
> Thou vile cesspool art the liquor
> Whence is made the beer we drink."

The water supply of three million people was polluted. Not till the establishment in 1855 of the Metropolitan Board of Works—forerunner of the London County Council—did the evil begin to abate.

Not only inertia and a certain native spirit of muddle, untamed by the discipline of established leadership, but the selfishness of vested interests operated to keep mid-Victorian London dirty and unhealthy. Two scandalous examples were the state of Smithfield which, reeking with the carcases of half a million beasts slaughtered annually in the heart of the City, stood a ten years' siege by the sanitary reformers—and the privilege of intra-mural burial still claimed under ancient charters by private dynasties of citizens. These suicidal rights, automatically repeopling the piled-up church-yards, continued unabated until 1852. This was all part of the intense and traditional individualism of England: up to 1851 any-one could open a slaughtering yard.

So too in the narrow crowded streets pandemonium was long permitted in the sacred name of liberty. The drivers of the 2d. buses, growing in numbers as well as in girth, raced each other through the City while their stripe-trousered "cads" or conductors ran shouting beside them, sometimes almost dragging unwilling passengers into their vehicles. The pavements were blocked with long, rotating files of wretched men encased in huge quadrilateral sandwich boards, and the narrow streets with advertising carts towering ever higher like moving pagodas in the attempt to over-shadow one other. Vans stuck fast between the stone posts that still served to mark the footways: vendors of vegetables with wheel-barrows and ragged organ-grinders paraded the cobbled gutters. In the national mania for turning everything to money-making the very paving-stones were scrawled with injunctions to buy so-and-so's wares. Bill-stickers were allowed to cover every vacant wall and hoarding with advertisements; beggars, their clothes caked with a layer of phosphorescent grime, to exhibit their sores and destitution. Within a stone's throw of the heart of London, Leicester Square, formerly the home of great artists, was a "dreary abomination of desolation." In its centre a headless statue, perpetually bombarded by ragged urchins with brickbats, stood in a wilderness of weeds frequented by starved and half-savage cats.

. . . .

It was a good England for the healthy and successful: a fearful one for the weak and inefficient. Yet, for all the horrors of its growing towns, the nation had enough of vigorous country blood in its veins to make light of its cancers. It stood four-square to the world with a confident smile on its good-humoured, pugnacious face, ready to take on all-comers. Its wealth was growing day by day, its ships sailed triumphant and unhindered on every sea, the beauty, order and peace of its countryside were the wonder and admiration of every foreigner who visited it. The loveliness of that Miltonian landscape, the prosperity of its rose and ivy-covered cottages, the strength and assurance of its thriving farms and lordly parks and mansions blinded the indulgent eye to its darker corners. There was so much to love in England—those wonderful oaks and green lawns, the sleek, lowing cattle, the smoke curling up from cottage chimneys in a mysterious and blended sea of tender verdure, the strong, kindly men and women who were so at home among its familiar scenes. One just took this strong-founded, dynamic island of contradictions for granted and accepted it as a whole.

It was fitting that the chosen leader of such a land should be Lord Palmerston. With his jaunty mien, his sturdy common sense, his straw between his lips and his sobriquet of Cupid, the game old man was the idol of mid-Victorian England and the embodiment of everything for which it stood. From 1855 until his death at the age of 81 in 1865, he was continuously Prime Minister, with one short break in 1858-9 when the discredited protectionists under Lord Derby and Disraeli had a brief spell of minority office.

The last of the aristocratic Whigs of the tradition of the "Glorious Revolution," "Pam" represented the Liberals in his contempt for obscurantist mysticism and the Tories in his hatred of doctrinaire reform. For ten years he kept a fast-changing Britain in a political backwater and ruled, not by the magnetism of ideals nor the machinery of party organisation—for he had neither—but by sheer personal popularity. Nothing could shake his hold on the British people. They loved him for his brisk contempt for foreign ways and threats, for his English balance, for his unshakable individualism, for his courage and assurance—"an old admiral cut out of oak, the figure-head of a 74-gun ship in a Biscay squall." They delighted in his sporting tastes, his little jokes—"it is impossible to give the Shah the garter: he deserves the halter!"—even his little scrapes: a rumoured affair at the age of 78 with a clergyman's wife on the eve of an election brought from the lips of his opponent, Disraeli, who understood his countrymen, a hollow, "For God's sake don't let the people of England know, or he'll sweep the country!" That familiar figure—the tilted white hat, tight-buttoned coat, cane, dyed whiskers—riding down Piccadilly before breakfast or rising to jest or bluff away an awkward situation in the House, gave the English confidence. It was just so that they liked to think of themselves, boldly confronting a world of which they had somehow become lords.

The spirit and health of this old man sprang from the same sources as the nation for which he stood. Palmerston directed the course of a commercial empire from his house in Piccadilly. But when he needed recreation he rode in white trousers across the green fields to the wooded Harrow Hill of his schooldays or went down for the vacation to his native Broadlands in Hampshire. So it was with England. Since the 'forties John Bull had donned the sober civic wear of the towns, abjured horse for train, and settled down to work at lathe or ledger among the chimney pots. But his strength still derived from the countryside of his fathers in which, for all his new absorption in money-making, his heart lay. "Home, sweet home," the Englishman's favourite song, pictured not a tenement building but a country cottage. London was only an encampment from which all who could afford it fled so soon as the Season and parliamentary session were over, when the blinds were drawn, the hotels left empty and the clubs asleep.

"In France," a French traveller wrote, "we live in the towns and go to the country. The Englishman resides in the country, where his real home is. There he keeps his treasures, and pride of race and station is given full play." Here the rural gentry, still untouched by commerce and living on the cultivation of the classical and leisured past, had its strong roots, sending out its shoots into the professional and administrative life of the nation and empire. At the back of the educated Englishman's consciousness in the 'fifties lay always the thought of the country house and the green shires: of slow talk of acres and timber, of bullocks and crops, of sport by covert-side and river, of sitting in the saddle among the blackthorn bushes, of the smell of the gun-room, meadow hay and hot leather, of dining out at the full moon, of archery parties and croquet on smooth lawns, of familiar names and faces and childhood's remembered scenes repeated in the churchyard on Sunday mornings after service, when countrymen met their neighbours among the mounds beneath which their fathers slept.

Somewhere in the 'fifties the urban population of England began to exceed the rural. But agriculture remained the great central productive industry of the country, excelling in importance and influence even cotton. The competition of the new wheat-growing lands overseas had still to be developed: free trade spelt cheap and abundant raw materials for the manufacturer but not yet unlimited imports. Despite the ceaseless rise in population, not more than a quarter of the country's wheat was imported and very little of her oats and barley. The urban worker had more in his pocket, and he spent it on the products of the English farmer. During the Crimean War wheat prices rose, averaging 74/8 in 1855—a figure not to be equalled till 1917—and fluctuating for many years around 50s., or 10s. a quarter more than they had been in 1850. The nemesis of Free Trade was not yet. The middle of Victoria's reign constituted a golden age for British agriculture, when capital was cheap and plentiful, markets expanding and improvements profitable for landlord and tenant farmer. Employing more than a million skilled workers and supporting the richest aristocracy the world had seen, it gave bread to seventeen millions and meat to the whole population.

Those were the days when the Earl of Ladythorne sat at the covert-side like a gentleman in his opera stall, thinking what a good thing it was to be a lord with a sound digestion and plenty of cash, when tenant farmers built conservatories and planted ornamental trees, and young ladies in flowing skirts and jackets and little feathered caps played croquet on ancient lawns or gossiped over "hair brushings" in rooms once habited by Elizabethan statesmen and Carolean divines. The great parks with their noble trees slumbered in the sunlight of those distant summers; children, born heirs to the securest and happiest lot humankind had ever known, rode and played in their shade never guessing that in their old age they would see the classic groves felled by the estate breaker and the stately halls pulled down or sold to make convalescent homes for miners or county asylums.

The age of the small man was almost done. But there were still nearly 100,000 men farming holdings of less than fifty acres without hired labour. The agricultural worker was ill-paid and without a real stake in the country, but his wages, which averaged well under 10s. a week in the south in 1850, touched 11s. in the early 'sixties and 13s. in the next decade. He had his garden, a wife who could bake his bread, and many small perquisites—harvest money, beer or cider in the field, occasional firewood and gleanings. So long as he was healthy—and his life kept him so—he was happy. Old Jas Dagley of Gawcott, Bucks, who with his low forehead, eagle eyes, powerful nose and jaw, and stern trap mouth, looked like Gladstone, paid £2 a year rent for his cottage, never wanted for good wholesome food in all his long life of thrift and labour—"plenty a vegetables the whool yeeur roun and a flitch a beeacon . . . alwiz hangin' up in the kitchen, and plenty a rabbuts round the meddurs"[1] —worked on his allotment every night when his day's work was done and boasted that he had never missed a feast in any one of the villages about, and that he had once carried a nine-gallon cask of ale in a sack on his broad shoulders for three miles.

Strength and endurance were still the virtues that England, rustic or urban, prized above all others. In April, 1860, on a lovely spring morning, Tom Sayers, the English champion, met Heenan, the American, known to the fancy as the Benicia Boy, on the edge of a wood near Farnborough to fight for the championship of the world. For weeks in every town and village in the land men and women had canvassed the chances of the event, and the police, fearing a fatal casualty in those days of timeless contests and bare fists, had forbidden the fight and kept close watch on the would-be combatants. But where there was a will there was a way; old England was not to be disappointed. On the night before the great day every tavern and public-house in London remained open all night until the word went round where the trains to the secret ringside were to start.

[1] H. Harman, *Sketches of the Bucks Countryside* 17.

Sayers was thirty-four, stood five foot eight, and weighed ten stone twelve. His American challenger was eight years younger, stood five inches taller and weighed thirteen stone. In the opening rounds the Englishman was knocked down repeatedly, only to rise smiling for more. The blood poured down his brown, tanned face which shone in the morning sun as though it had been carved of old oak. For two hours after his right arm was broken by a terrific blow of Heenan's he fought on, and, when the police broke through the exultant crowd into the ring, the English champion, giving as good as he took, was still undefeated.

CHAPTER 14

Men of Property

To a foreigner visiting England for the first time in the 'sixties and 'seventies, there seemed something terrifying about its energy and power. "Every quarter of an hour," wrote Taine of the entry to the Thames, "the imprint and the presence of man, the power by which he has transformed nature, become more visible; dock, magazines, shipbuilding and caulking yards, stocks, habitable houses, prepared materials, accumulated merchandise. . . . From Greenwich the river is nothing but a street a mile broad and upwards, where ships ascend and descend between two rows of buildings, interminable rows of a dull red, in brick or tiles bordered with great piles stuck in the mud for mooring vessels, which come here to unload or to load. Ever new magazines for copper, stone, coal, cordage, and the rest; bales are always being piled up, sacks being hoisted, barrels being rolled, cranes are creaking, capstans sounding. . . . To the west, rises an inextricable forest of yards, of masts, of rigging: these are the vessels which arrive, depart or anchor, in the first place in groups, then in long rows, then in a continuous heap, crowded together, massed against the chimneys of houses and the pulleys of warehouses, with all the tackle of incessant, regular, gigantic labour. A foggy smoke penetrated with light envelopes them; the sun there sifts its golden rain, and the brackish tawny, half-green, half violet water balances in its undulations striking and strange reflections. . . ."

For over this vast city had fallen a perpetual pall. The classical pillars and ornaments of the churches and larger buildings were half hidden under soot: the naked Achilles in the park, tribute to the Iron Duke, was almost black. Even the dripping trees and foliage were grimy. It was like Homer's Hell—the land of the

Cimmerians. "The vast space which in the South stretches between the earth and sky cannot be discovered; . . . there is no air, there is nothing but liquid fog."[1] Tall chimneys cast a shroud of smoke between earth and sky: the Thames ran no longer blue and sparkling but rayless under the grimy bridges. The summer's trip to Greenwich—joy of many generations of Londoners—was no longer a thing of delight; the trees on the Isle of Dogs had begun to give way to ugly factories and mean houses, and the yachts and pleasure boats to belching steamers and strings of coal barges. Even the time-honoured ministerial Whitebait Dinner was soon to be abandoned: men had less leisure than before for the graces and amenities of life.

The complete absorption of the English urban middle classes in the pursuit of wealth was both impressive and terrifying. The old talkative, hail-fellow-well-met London was yielding place to one more sombre and self-contained. Men went silent and absorbed about their business: "faces do not laugh, lips are dumb; not a cry, not a voice is heard in the crowd; every individual seems alone; the workman does not sing; passengers travelling to and fro gaze about them without curiosity, without uttering a word."[2] They were on the make, each man pitting his strength and cunning against his neighbour and seeking not to make things for the joy of making or to win the applause of his fellows, but to amass sufficient wealth to keep himself and his family in time of need. Their perpetual nightmare was the fear of poverty. Unredeemed by the neighbouring field sports of the countryside and cut off by the factory smoke and the high walls of the houses from the cheerful sun, the life of the streets was not to be borne without wealth. Those who had won it by their sweat and struggle dreaded to lose it: "to have £20,000 in the funds or cut one's throat" was their unspoken thought. Those without it were driven back, as the fields receded, into a life ever more drab and uninviting. Taine noticed how many working-class faces wore a starved, thwarted look: hollow, blanched and spent with fatigue. In their patient inertia they reminded him of the old "screws" in the cabs standing in the rain.

[1] Taine 6-8, 10.   [2] Wey 5.

In the world of the new city, property was the breath of life: without it men and women shrivelled and died. Save for murder, offences against property were more severely punished than those against the person. A barman and a glazier for stealing 5s. 4d. were sentenced to five years' penal servitude: a hideous assault on a woman with child was expiated with six weeks' imprisonment. Against the supreme right of commerce even–duty as it came to be regarded–nothing was held to weigh: social amenity, happiness, beauty. Whatever did not contribute to this one great commercial object was neglected. In the British Museum in grimy Bloomsbury the greatest masterpieces of human sculpture stood covered with dust on filthy floors in a neglected yellow hall that looked like a warehouse.

No one protested, for the English townsman had come to accept such a state of affairs as the natural order. On the railways, the second-class carriages were without upholstery; in the third the windows were unglazed and the floors never swept. Men had no rights but those they paid for after process of free bargain with their fellows. Not even, it seemed, the right of life for, though accidents were frequent, the railways directors kept the doors of the carriages locked while trains were in transit lest any passengers should escape without paying for their tickets.

Business was business: wherever English commerce reigned the phrase was sufficient to explain and justify almost every terrestrial happening. A man must abide by the law: he must keep his bond: he must deliver the goods he had promised or pay the forfeit. From that, there could be no challenge: Shylock was entitled to his pound of flesh. He had earned it by his industry, skill and integrity. In the innumerable little grimy brick houses between the Tower and St. Paul's, whose modest brass plates bore names famous throughout the world, the sons of millionaires arrived each morning with the punctuality of their own clerks to transact business and later bought their mutton chops and threepenny loaves in a Cheapside tavern for their Spartan midday meal. Only when they went home in the evening to Portland Place or Grosvenor Square did they indulge the princely tastes to which their hard-earned wealth entitled them.

Such men were resolute in purpose: iron when anyone crossed their strong intent. Taine on his visit observed their kind closely:

"When at eight o'clock in the morning, at the terminus of a railway, one sees people arriving from the country for their daily avocations, or when one walks in a business street, one is struck with the number of faces which exhibit this type of cold and determined will. They walk straight, with a geometrical movement, without looking on either hand; without distraction, wholly given up to their business, like automatons, each moved by a spring; the large, bony face, the pale complexion, often sallow or leaden-hued, the rigid look, all even to the tall, perpendicular, black hat, even to the strong and large foot-covering, even to the umbrella, rolled in its case and carried in a particular style, display the man insensitive, dead to ideas of pleasure and elegance, solely preoccupied in getting through much business well and rapidly. Sometimes one detects the physiognomy of Pitt—the slight face, impassive and imperious, the pale and ardent eyes, the look which shines like the fixed gleam of a sword; the man is then of finer mould, yet his will is only the more incisive and the stouter; it is iron transformed into steel."

Under the pressure of the claims of money-making, the character of the English middle class was changing. It was growing sterner, narrower in sympathy since too much sensibility weakened the will. The new kind of public school which Arnold of Rugby had made the model for England catered for those who needed hardening: the virtues it bred were reticence, regularity and rectitude, above all self-reliance. An English boy of the mid-Victorian age if he was short-sighted was not expected to wear spectacles.[1] If he was cold he was not expected to wear a great coat. His heart and senses were put on ice: from the first day he was chucked into the lonely maelstrom of a great boarding school he was taught to keep a stiff upper lip. For the highly sensitive or affectionate child this stern schooling was hell: in self-defence boys learnt to keep their emotions to themselves, if possible to eliminate them. In

[1] Arthur James, Earl of Balfour, *Chapters of Autobiography*, 7-8.

France, Taine reflected, happiness depended on affection; in England on having none.

Boys brought up in this way were like young bull-dogs in their teens: tough and tenacious, sometimes ferocious, unconquerable. Being discouraged from excessive feeling, the average product of the public school could feel little sympathy for the classical authors whose works he laboriously and mechanically translated and parsed: he preferred organised games. From this time dates the start of the decline in English upper-class culture and classical learning. Save at a few schools like Eton and Winchester, where much of the older and freer tradition lingered, the scholar of an earlier age was to become the despised public-school "swot," the solid lad of brawn and muscle the hero. This made little difference to the object of the new public school, which was the training of character for a competitive world, and was as well effected by the harsh discipline of the dormitory and the football ground as by the Greek syntax.

At the universities the early discipline of the public school was relaxed. Here the freer and more liberal model of the past was retained: a gentleman was encouraged to choose his own life and tastes and to be a scholar if he chose. But the harm as well as the good of the public school system was already done. The average lad from Harrow or Rugby came up to Oxford or Cambridge what his school had made him. If, as still frequently happened, he came from a cultivated home or had an exceptionally brilliant teacher, he might have wide sympathies and genuine love for learning. More normally he cared for nothing but sport which he pursued in the academic groves with the same zest as on the Sixth Form Ground or Old Big Side. He had character, integrity, energy —the qualities needed for worldly success. But his emotional and intellectual development were stunted. For that reason he fell the more readily into the unthinking worship of material attainment that was the fault of his age. The poor prize-man of the schools might still be the talk of the Upper Common Room; on the long benches of Hall the man acclaimed was the "Blue" and the "blood" with money to burn.

The commercial type created by the conditions of the urban

middle-class homes and academies that had not yet attained public school status—the nursery of Matthew Arnold's "Philistines"— has been drawn by John Galsworthy in *The Forsyte Saga*. It valued strength, order, above all things property: it despised weakness, subtlety, width of sympathy. It was redeemed by its native boyishness and by a certain inherent kindliness. But to a foreigner its superficial appearance was not congenial: these English merchants with their stiff, big-boned frames and repressed, self-contained faces looked stupid, frigid and unfeeling, caring for nothing but money and the animal pleasures of the chase and table. There seemed to be too much roast-beef in them. Sometimes they were lean, gaunt and awkward; more often they ran to fullness of flesh, brick-red faces and apoplectic tempers; Taine met such a one in the train going to the Derby—"large ruddy features with flabby and pendant cheeks, large red whiskers, blue eyes without expression, an enormous trunk, noisy respiration."[1]

For those with gentle blood, with family traditions and connections, and the status afforded by a university degree, there was employment in the civil and military services of the Crown, in the empire and the learned professions. For the great majority commerce was the one sure road to the desired goal of private wealth, security and comfort. With the rapidly expanding population and with improved transport—supported by British sea-power and arms—opening ever new markets in lands overseas, the opportunities for growing rich were enormous. Between 1850 and 1872 the annual exports of Britain, almost doubling themselves every ten years, increased from £90,000,000 to £315,000,000.

A walk through the central districts of London revealed that wealth. A circumference of nearly a mile round the country-like parks of the west-end was being filled by large six or seven-storey houses, mostly built in the Italianate style, for the residence of the upper middle merchant and professional classes. "Paris," Taine reported, "is mediocre compared with these squares, these crescents, these circles and rows of monumental buildings of massive stone, with porticos, with sculptured fronts, these spacious streets. . . . Sixty of them as vast as the Rue de la Paix; assuredly Napoleon III

[1] Taine 50.

demolished and rebuilt Paris only because he had lived in London."
Such great houses needed establishments of seven or eight servants
apiece and could not be supported by incomes of less than £2,000
or £3,000 a year: yet scarcely any were empty. They were the
homes of "carriage-folk"—of families who kept private carriages,
whose numbers by 1856 ran into five figures.

The great summer afternoon parade in Hyde Park between four
and six revealed Victorian society in all its glory: the long unbroken
stream of brilliant equipages and lovely horses between Cumberland
and Albert gates, the fine ladies with their glaring coloured silks,
crinolines and parasols gossiping and quizzing under the chestnuts,
the Dundreary-whiskered gentlemen with their white top-hats
and silver-topped malacca canes, who leant over the iron railings
of Rotten Row to chat with elegant, long-skirted, veiled equestrians
or lolled on the fashionable grass slope by Lancaster Gate. To a
poor man who had ventured into the park at such an hour amid
all this splendour, the spectacle might well have seemed to represent
the wealth of the entire world assembled in the persons of a few
thousand fabulously favoured creatures in this little space of English
earth. Taine recorded that if one took a cab from Sydenham,
where the re-created Crystal Palace stood, one could travel for five
continuous miles past houses representing an annual outlay of
£1,500. In this feast of property the professional as well as the
commercial classes had their share. While a professor at the Sor-
bonne had to content himself with the equivalent of £500 a year,
the head of an Oxford or Cambridge College could look for
several thousands. The headmasters of Eton and Harrow, the poet
Tennyson and the novelist Thackeray all enjoyed incomes of
£5,000 or more. And successful lawyers and doctors made far
more in days when income tax stood at 7d. in the pound. Yet
even their comfortable emoluments paled into insignificance when
set against the princely incomes of the great industrial manufacturing and engineering masters of the north. The Fairbairns,
Hawthorns, Kitsons, Platts, Stephensons, Whitworths constituted
a new millionaire aristocracy of effort whose title deeds of wealth
and power were their own revolving wheels of iron.

This commercial aristocracy looked far beyond the boundaries of the little misty island which their works and warehouses enriched. There was scarcely any place on earth capable of trade where their representatives were not established. In distant Shanghai and Hong Kong one met the English merchant princes of the China trade, men of almost fabulous wealth made out of tea, silk and opium. Every year the tea-clippers—the fastest sailing ships ever made by human hands—took part in the famous race from Foochow to London river to win the £600 bonus for the first cargo of the season to reach the English market. John Masefield in his *Bird of Dawning* has drawn the picture of one coming up the Channel, her three months' voyage done, and of the rough, simple men who manned her. Galsworthy's Jolyon Forsyte, the elder, is the counterpart of Captain Trewsbury: the City merchant of taste and flawless integrity with his great house in South Kensington and his fastidious ways, whose palate for tea was a byword.

Since the repeal of the Navigation Act in 1849, the lovely ships that carried the tribute of the world to the cliffs of England sailed, under many flags. Yet most of them, including the best, were owned and built by Britons, for free trade if it took privileges from the merchant marine with one hand gave with another since it stimulated interchange of sea-borne merchandise. With the absorption of her chief shipping rival, the United States, in a long and exhausting civil war during the early 'sixties, Britain had things very much her own way at sea for three halcyon decades. The new iron ships, triumphs of the marine engineering works of the Clyde and Tyne, of Birkenhead and Belfast, were beginning to come into their own: the *Great Eastern*, the famous iron leviathan, 700 feet in length and 80 in beam, was launched at Millwall in 1858. Yet two years later not more than a tenth of the merchant service of the United Kingdom was steam driven. In that year the country's sailing tonnage reached its zenith. These proud masterpieces of timber and canvas, cleaving the ocean "with mainyards backed and bows of cream and foam" were the key to Britain's commercial and industrial supremacy. They were recognised as the élite of the sea in every port of the earth.

This art and skill and the wealth that sprang from it rested in the last resort on the British command of the seas. During the late 'fifties and early 'sixties fear of the French Empire under Louis Napoleon had recalled an island race immersed in moneymaking to the necessity of looking to its moat. After the Crimean War a period of naval reorganisation began which, quickened by a panic over the new French strength in ironclads, culminated in the launch of the 9,000-ton iron frigate, *Warrior*, the fastest and most powerful ship in the world. It was the first of a new fleet of iron-hulled, armoured, screw-driven ships armed with muzzle-loaders, the latest product of Armstrong's, and capable of blowing the old three-decker navies of the past out of the water. This mighty force —the strongest single unit of ordered power in the nineteenth century world—was supported by a secondary fleet of unarmoured wooden frigates and corvettes and by naval bases in all the seven seas—a standing terror to the slaver and pirate.

Out of all this sprang great comfort for the English possessing classes. Peasants toiled in distant China and Ceylon to fill the teapots of rich old ladies in Lancaster Gate, naked Malay boys laboured to draw up pearls from the bottom of shark-infested seas, and trappers fought with bears in the frozen snows of Hudson Bay to send home furs and hearthrugs. As they grew rich the hardy English surrounded themselves with costly comforts, the elder generation of the Forsytes because they valued the outward forms of the wealth for which they had laboured so hard, the younger because they were growing accustomed to them. Soft pile Brussels carpets, thick padded settees and ottomans, elaborately-carved tables of polished mahogany and rosewood with marble tops, enormous gilt mirrors flowed in a never-ceasing flood out of the factories and warehouses and fashionable furniture emporiums into the spacious houses of Kensington and Bayswater, Edgbaston, Stockport and Everton until even their great rooms seemed crowded out with these heavy symbols of tribute. A cultured foreigner staying in an English house in 1861 was amazed by the furniture of his bedroom —the entire floor carpeted, a strip of oilcloth in front of the washstand, matting along the walls; two dressing-tables, a swing looking-glass, a great bed covered with the whitest and softest of tissues, three pairs of candles, two of them in a writing-table, porcelain extinguishers, wax matches, paper spills in pretty holders, pin-cushions. The most intimate piece of furniture in the room was a miracle of elaborate ingenuity, made of the finest mahogany and marble: the washstand was furnished with a large and smaller jug for hot and cold water, two porcelain basins, a dish for toothbrushes, two soap-dishes, a water-bottle with a tumbler and a finger glass with another. In addition there was a large shallow zinc bath, and a towel-horse in the cupboard with several towels of different sizes. A servant visited the room four times a day to see that all was in order.

When an Englishman of the upper middle order travelled, the same observer noted, he carried so many glasses, opera-glasses and telescopes, umbrellas, canes and iron-tipped sticks, overcoats, comforters, waterproofs and wrappers, dressing-cases, flasks, books and newspapers that it seemed astonishing that he should ever have set out under such a burden at all. Every year the English with their all-conquering Midas touch sank deeper under the weight of their own possessions. From the queen on her throne, who, in the course of her reign accumulated a vast museum of objects, each acquiring with usage attributes of an almost sacred kind and possessing its own hallowed and unalterable place in one or other of her palaces, to the thrifty and well-to-do artisan who filled every inch of wall space in his cottage with engravings, keepsakes, mementoes, grandfather clocks, samplers and photographs, and kept apart a special airtight compartment named the parlour for the display of more treasured pieces of furniture and *vertu*, the nation seemed to have gone mad on property. As ever with the English and the object of their heart's desire, it became invested with a semi-religious and mystical quality. Since the pursuit or retention of wealth was for the time being the first end of their single-hearted lives, that which wealth bought was worthy of worship. The drawing-room furniture, the silver and best china in the safe, the contents of the maternal jewel case, were the sacred vessels on the altar, and a visit to the banker or solicitor was conducted with a solemnity like going to church.

From this arose tragic consequences. Poverty in other lands was regarded, as it had been in England in the past, as part of the eternal human lot: to be pitied, to be avoided if possible, to be relieved or ignored according to a man's nature or temperament, but not to be despised. It was a share of humanity's bitter heritage, like sickness, tempest and death. But in London and urban England in which the making of wealth had been elevated into a moral duty, poverty hung its head for shame. It crept out of sight into that new phenomenon of industrialisation—the working-class district in which no man of wealth or position lived. The new East End of London with its miles of mean, squalid streets covering an area greater in extent than any continental city, was something of a portent in the world. It was not for nothing that the scholar Marx was studying economic phenomena in the British capital.

Here lived the poor—not merely the respectable artisans but the countless broken outcasts of the industrial system. These were pallid and gin-sodden; their ragged reeking clothes, which had passed through many phases of society in their long, declining history, were so vile that they left a stain wherever they rested: they stank. They herded together in bug-ridden lodging houses and rotting tenements: they slept under railway arches and on iron seats on the new Victoria Embankment. They were the "submerged tenth," the skeleton at the rich Victorian feast, the squalid writing on the whitened wall.

They were not merely congregated in the "darkest London" of Charles Booth's later survey: they were to be found in every place where the untrammelled march for wealth had broken down the old world of status and social morality. They were living testimonies of that against which Coleridge had warned his country—trespasses on "its own inalienable and untransferable property, the health, strength, honesty and filial love of its children." Across the lives of the rich and comfortable, of all who inherited or had acquired established property they passed like a remote shadow: to the remainder of their countrymen, especially to the lower middle-class and the skilled and respectable artisan, they were a terrible menace whose horrid existence it was almost impossible to shake from the mind. Their pale, degraded, beseeching faces and dripping rags were a reminder of what unemployment, sickness or any lapse from the straight and narrow path of social integrity might bring: like wraiths they rose out of a precipice into which every man without property might at any moment of his life fall. More than any other cause, they account for the almost fanatic desire of the Victorian of all classes to acquire and retain property.

"I recall," wrote Taine, "the alleys which run into Oxford Street, stifling lanes encrusted with human exhalations; troops of pale children nestling on the muddy stairs; the seats on London Bridge where families, huddled together with dropping heads, shiver through the night; particularly the Haymarket and the Strand in the evening. Every hundred steps one jostles twenty harlots; some of them ask for a glass of gin; others say, 'Sir, it is to pay my lodging.' This is not debauchery which flaunts itself but destitution—and such destitution! The deplorable procession in the shade of the monumental streets is sickening; it seems to me a march of the dead. That is a plague-spot, the real plague-spot of English society." Once down in that mire there was no rising again. The sordid round of drink, debauchery, violence, punishment, incompetence and hideous destitution never ceased. "The great social mill crushes and grinds here . . . the lowest human stratum."

CHAPTER 15

The Old Kent Road

"Knocked 'em in the Old Kent Road."

Albert Chevalier

IN THE REFORM BILL of 1867 Disraeli, with a minority Government, added a million voters to the electoral roll, roughly doubling it. By providing a dual vote for education and property he had sought to make the franchise a reward rather than an indiscriminating right, "to be gained by virtue, by intelligence, by industry, by integrity" and exercised for the common good.[1] He wanted to see the working man a partner in the constitution rather than its arbiter. But his Party held office on sufferance, and his device for restoring an older and more English basis of representation than a purely numerical one was sabotaged in committee. The bill created a democracy of heads of houses, of men with some stake, however small, in the country, but its weakness in its author's eyes was that it gave too much ultimate power to mere numbers. It was in Lord Derby's phrase "a leap in the dark." And the direction it took suggested further leaps into deeper darkness before long.

The first general election fought on the new register gave the Liberal party a six years' lease of power. But, as Disraeli had prophesied, the interests of artisans and middle-class utilitarians were not necessarily the same. The latter wanted to restrict the functions of government and leave the ring clear for the individual with talent and industry. The workers on the other hand needed protection against the economic excesses of the individual. As soon as they realised the power which the vote had given them, they began to demand it. They leant not towards the classic liber-

[1] Monypenny and Buckle II, 144.

alism of *laissez-faire* but towards that social reform which Disraeli had preached since his Young England days and which Shaftesbury and the factory reformers had fought for against the utilitarians. Gladstone's programme of civic emancipation, Irish Church disestablishment and administrative reform therefore made little appeal to them. After a few years of Liberal rule the country became surfeited with change. The sun of "the Peoples' William" waned: that of "Dizzy," the inspired Jew boy who had "climbed to the top of the greasy pole," rose. In 1874 for the first time in 33 years the Conservatives obtained a parliamentary majority.

The date marked the dividing line between the utilitarian legislation of the middle half of the century and the collectivist or socialist legislation which thereafter increasingly took its place. Since the collapse of the Chartists the working-class movement had been silently gathering momentum. In every town where skilled workers were assembled, Trade Unions had made their appearance. The quiet years of widening trade and employment helped their growth, giving them cohesion, tradition and financial reserves. Local consolidation was usually followed by amalgamation on a national scale. The first great national Union, the Amalgamated Society of Engineers, was founded in 1851 with the fusion of over a hundred local trade societies. In the next fifteen years its membership of 12,000 more than doubled. With its many imitators it fought against piece-work, overtime, victimisation and the employment of unapprenticed men, survived early attempts of impatient employers to destroy it by lock-outs and taught a hostile bourgeois world to tolerate and fear, if not to respect it.

To the middle-class citizen in his top-hat and castellated home, the Trade Union was something of a bogey—a secret and treasonable society threatening mob violence and plotting confiscation and revolution. In popular repute its path was attended by a succession of outrages: explosions, stones and broken glass, striking mobs intimidating honest Britons out of their property and right to work as they pleased. None felt this more strongly than the progressive radicals of the north. "Depend upon it," wrote Cobden, "nothing can be got by fraternising with Trade Unions. They are founded upon principles of brutal tyranny and monopoly. I would rather live under a Bey of Algiers than a trades committee."[1]

The law, reflecting middle-class opinion, treated the Unions with suspicion. Judges, who still regarded them as combinations in restraint of trade, refused to protect their funds from the defalcations of dishonest officials. A Trade Union was an association to coerce individuals and limit their profits. It was therefore viewed by a generation educated in *laissez-faire* principles as injurious. It was only tolerated because it was impossible to prevent it.

Though those brought up in the principles of Bentham tried not to see it, everything that was happening in the crowded urban world which individual enterprise had created was minimising the importance of the individual and raising the power of the herd. The sturdy pupil of self-help, who by his devotion to his individual interests had created a thriving industrial unit employing 5,000 workers where only fifty had worked before, had unconsciously called into being a community whose common hopes and interests must presently clash with his own. For though the more he prospered the more they mutiplied, the more they did so the more certain became their ultimate triumph over himself. So soon as they realised that their opportunity of happiness lay not in their action as individuals, in which being poor and ill-educated they were powerless, but in their collective strength, their final victory was certain.

In his great work, *Capital*, first obscurely published in 1867 "amid carbuncles and the constant dunning of creditors", Karl Marx demonstrated the course events were taking. He saw that with its ever-increasing scale of operations capitalism was digging its grave. The evolution of a society which put its faith in figures was predestined. "While there is thus a progressive diminution in the number of capitalist magnates . . . there occurs a corresponding increase in the mass of poverty, oppression, enslavement, degeneration and exploitation; but at the same time there is a steady intensification of the wrath of the working class—a class which grows ever more numerous and is disciplined, unified and organised by the very mechanism of the capitalist method of production. Capitalist monopoly becomes a fetter upon the method of pro-

[1] Morley, *Cobden* I 299.

duction which has flourished with it and under it. The centralisa-
tion of the means of production and the socialisation of labour
reach a point where they prove incompatible with their capitalist
husk. This bursts asunder. The knell of capitalist private property
sounds. The expropriators are expropriated."

To Marx's logical, academic but violence-loving mind the
inevitable end was revolution. Divorced by his circumstances and
temperament from the contacts of normal life and society, this
morose prophet never grasped the nature of the people whose
commercial institutions he studied with such brilliant and prophetic
insight. He failed to see that in an ancient country like England,
with its strong social character and representative institutions,
revolution would be deflected into smoother channels.

The change that Marx predicted happened. But it took place in
so unexpected a way that nobody, not even Marx, realised that it
was happening at all. The utilitarians' thesis, which suppoited
laissez-faire, involved the extension of the vote to the poor man.
He used it to obtain legislation to offset his disability in contractual
power. In England the passage of the second Reform Bill, and not
the shouting proletarian crowds and the blood-bath of the ex-
ploiters, marked the end of unlimited freedom of contract and
therefore of *laissez-faire*.

The new direction was first set by Disraeli's Government in the
latter 'seventies. In the course of five years this Administration of
rich hereditary peers and landowners passed legislation which,
though little noticed at the time, struck at the roots of the Ben-
thamite thesis that the individual should be left free to enrich himself
as he chose. Factory acts were extended and consolidated and the
hours[1] and conditions of labour codified. The process of private
enclosure was reversed—though too late to save more than a frag-
ment of what once had been public property—and the conversion
of common land forbidden unless it conferred a public as well as a
private benefit. By the Public Health Act of 1876 the interests of
the individual were first subordinated to the requirements of public
sanitation. Defending a policy of "*sanitas sanitatum, omnia sanitas,*"

[1] Limited by an Act of 1874 to 56 hours a week, 10 on five weekdays and 6 on
Saturdays. See Dicey, *passim.*

Disraeli replied to the attack of those who declared that he was reducing statecraft to an affair of sewerage; that "to one of the labouring multitude of England, who had found fever always to be one of the inmates of his household, who had, year after year, seen stricken down the children of his loins on whose sympathy and support he had looked with hope and confidence," it was "not a policy of sewerage but a question of life and death."

The same Government introduced an Artisans' Dwelling Bill, empowering local authorities to demolish insanitary dwellings and replace them by houses built expressly for working men. The measure was not compulsory but only permissive. It was no more than a tentative beginning: a mere drop in the still rising ocean of slum. Yet its ultimate effect was revolutionary. For it revived, in however dim a form, the ancient ideal of the State as the guardian of the people's homes.

Behind all this legislation lay the silent voting power of the workers. In 1874 there were returned to the House of Commons two men who were to be the pioneers of a mighty army. Even at the time Alexander Macdonald and Thomas Burt, the first two working-class M.P.s, were something of a portent among the landed squires and thriving manufacturers at Westminster. Burt was Secretary of the Northumberland Miners' Association, which, by helping to establish that the occupants of colliery houses, though not paying rates direct, were entitled to voting rights like the compound householders in the towns, had secured a majority of pitmen in the constituency of Morpeth. These representatives of the sons of toil tended at first to vote with Disraeli's "gentlemen of England" rather than with his opponents. Macdonald told his constituents in 1879 that the Conservative party had "done more for the working classes in five years than the Liberals in fifty."

For the old Jew, now nearing his end, for all his absorption in duchesses and oriental splendour saw in the working man, with his native prejudices and conservative instincts, an ally against the levelling utilitarian forces he had fought all his life. By redressing injustices he sought to end the fatal gulf between the "two Englands" which he had perceived in his youth and still—though it was almost thirty years too late—hoped to bridge. His Administration's labour laws were an attempt to do so. The common law, dating from an age when status was fixed and the workman given security of tenure by the State, treated breach of contract by an employer as a civil offence and that of his workman as criminal. The application of *laissez-faire* to commercial relationships had long made this distinction grossly unjust. By an act of 1875 Disraeli ended it by placing the workman on the same legal footing as his employer. In the same year he righted a still greater grievance of industrial labour against the law. Though the ancient doctrine of "conspiracy" had been modified by an Act of 1825, the Courts still refused to accord Trade Unions full legal status. Their funds were unprotected against breaches of trust by their own employees and their officers criminally liable for certain actions carried out in the course of their duties. By a new Act of 1875 Trade Unions were given the protection of the law. The mere fact of association to defeat an employer was freed from criminal taint. It could only be indicted as a conspiracy when it constituted what done by a single person would have been a crime.

By this change in the law "peaceful" picketing became permissible if unaccompanied by violence or threat of violence—though, as the upshot proved, it still remained open to judges to take such a view of "intimidation" as to constitute all picketing "unpeaceful." Not until the Trades Disputes Act of 1906, passed by a Liberal Government which had repudiated *laissez-faire* for full-blooded collectivism to win working-class support, did the Trade Unions establish the privileged position they sought.[1] To a believer in great national institutions, preserving by their trusteeship undying liberties and rights, it was a position to which a Trade Union was entitled. To a middle-class lawyer, nursed in the tenets of Benthamism, it was not. For several decades after the second Reform Bill the struggle continued between *laissez-faire* and the new socialism of the great towns *laissez-faire* had created.

It was often for the early leaders of labour a cruelly hard one. They had to do their public work in their spare time and finance it

[1] Reversing the decision of the judges in the Taff Vale case, it freed Trade Union funds from liability for damages committed by its members in the coures of strikes.

out of their wages. The pioneers of the Dockers' Union met "like conspirators hatching a second Guy Fawkes plot in a gloomy cellar with only the flickering half-lights given by tallow candles thrust into the necks of pop bottles." In the 'eighties the members of even the executive council of so famous a union as the Amalgamated Society of Engineers—at least two of whom in after years became cabinet ministers—used to receive one shilling and sixpence a night for their direction of the leading Union of the time and think themselves lucky to get it. Trades Union leadership in those days was less a career than a vocation. It was sometimes a martyrdom.

For this reason, and because of the wrongs from which their class had suffered and was still suffering, these pioneers of a still inconceivable future were often politically embittered. The good-humoured rank and file in pub and music hall, on the beach at Blackpool or the racecourse at Aintree, troubled their heads little about past history or future proletarian aspirations. But their leaders and the earnest young men studying under immense difficulties in public libraries and Mechanics' Institutes[1] who were to be their leaders in the next generation, were painfully aware of the fact that they and their class had not had a square deal.

Yet, with the vote in the workman's wallet, time was on their side. They felt that they had only to open the eyes of the wage slaves, teach them to combine and use their latent strength with discipline and loyalty to obtain their share of the kingdom. The prejudices against them—the malice and victimisation of employers, the biased use of the civil arm and even the military in time of strikes, the snobbery and class treachery of the workers themselves—were not so strong as the social impulse of the exploited to combine or perish. Whenever times were hard the men the Unions battled for, who were oblivious of their efforts when employment was regular and beer and bread plentiful, were reminded of how much still remained to be won before there could be any security

---

[1] The Working Men's College in London was founded by the Rev. Frederick Denison Maurice in 1854, with a voluntary staff of middle-class "Christian Socialist" sympathisers who included Ruskin, Tom Hughes—author of *Tom Brown's School Days*—Lowes Dickinson, Ford Madox Brown, Dante Gabriel Rossetti and Edward Burne Jones.

for themselves and their dear ones. Without the Trade Union there could be only loss of hearth and home and starvation for the workman who lost his job, and worse for the family of the man crippled or killed by accident in the course of his employment.[1]

Neither the error and human frailty of leaders nor the folly and shortsightedness of the rank and file could halt the steady march of organised labour. In 1880 the Trade Union Congress only represented 600,000 members: by 1892 the figure had doubled. It was not only for advances in wages that the older Unions fought, but for recognition as the sole representatives of the workers in all negotiations with employers. They demanded a share in the direction of their labour. To the fury of the old-fashioned capitalist, to whom freedom of contract meant freedom of choice for the master and obedience for the man, the new Trade Unionism sought to abolish overtime and regulate piecework. It went further. It used the worker's vote to appeal over the head of the employer to a parliament now dependent on that vote, for legislation to enforce its demands. At its annual Congresses, begun in 1866, the T.U.C. instructed its members to press parliamentary candidates for such reforms as an eight-hour day, compulsory compensation for injured workers, the limitation of shop hours, new factory regulations, further amendment of the law of conspiracy and the abolition of child labour. It also demanded free elementary education, land for allotments in country districts and the appointment of working men to the Bench.

Organised labour in these years sought more than the protection of the skilled worker. As Cobden had prophesied in the hungry 'forties, the triumph of *laissez-faire* had brought enhanced prosperity

---

[1] "Life was cheap in those days. It was by no means an uncommon thing to see the maimed and sometimes the dead being brought up from the dock bottom. . . . I remember two cases in our gang. George Washington, a smith's striker, fell into the dry dock one foggy night on his way home and was found at the bottom half dead in the morning. Jim Platt, a machinist, had his back nearly broken by the fall of a loose plank from the workshop roof. The result was the same in both cases—patched up in the hospital and then death after a year or two of lingering pain at work. But compensation was never thought of."—G. N. Barnes, *From Workshop to War Cabinet*, 34.

to many workers. The skilled artisan had taken his share, however small, in the increased prosperity of his country. He had enjoyed good wages, untaxed and plentiful food, long continued employment, cheap transport and amenities—municipal parks, libraries, galleries and concerts—such as his father in a grimmer age had never known. In many cases he had been able to put away money, insure against old age and sickness, even to buy his own home. The utilitarian State had given him opportunity and he had taken it.

But the skilled artisan in employment was only a part of labour. For if *laissez-faire* postulated the successful workman growing rich like his master through his own thrift and industry, it also necessitated a residue of unskilled labour to meet the fluctuating demands of a competitive world. This the capitalist used in good time and discarded in bad. Such a system multiplied the wastrel, the diseased and the ne'er-do-well. It multiplied their inefficient and unhappy posterity. The statistics of the economist showed the profits of unrestricted competition. The slums of the industrial cities revealed its wastage.

It was no part of *laissez-faire* that the successful should burden themselves by helping the failures. The only economic place for the weak was the rubbish heap. It was at this point that *laissez-faire* always clashed with the English temperament. The middle-class employer in the rarefied privacy of his sanctum might—in the interests of a higher wisdom—suppress his inherited feelings of charity and kindness. But the working man, who had never heard of *laissez-faire*, could not. He never even tried. For he was nothing if not sentimental, and under his corduroys beat a heart full of English instincts and prejudices. One of them was an incorrigible desire to help the underdog.

It was from such a motive, unreasoning and unscientific, that English socialism sprang. Abroad socialism followed more logical channels: the brand that Karl Marx was preaching to his fellow Germans and to embittered and excitable French and Russian comrades was of a severely practical kind. There was nothing that Marx despised so much as an underdog. He merely wished to use him and his misery to destroy the capitalist system. But it was precisely because they wished to help the underdog that the English

Socialists were Socialists at all. Men like William Morris and Arnold Toynbee devoted their lives to the working-class movement because their sense of justice and kindliness was affronted by the sickening misery and cruelty of a great reserve of unskilled labour like the East End of London. They did not wish merely to use the underdog but to tend and cherish him, just as they wished not to exterminate the bourgeois but to convert him. The University Settlement, then first taking shape, was a characteristic product of both these wishes. And in their dreams for the future the early English Socialists sought a gentle Christian paradise after their own kindly middle-class hearts. Morris's *News from Nowhere* published in 1890 is as far removed from Marx's *Capital* as the Gospel of St. John from the Book of Judges. "I know," said its author of a working-men's procession, "what these men want: employment which would foster their self-respect and win the praise and sympathy of their fellows, and dwellings which they would come to with pleasure, surroundings which would soothe and elevate them; reasonable labour, reasonable rest. There is only one thing that can give them this—Art."[1]

Haranguing in his gentle voice on Eelbrook Common and looking in his blue serge reefer jacket like a cross between a farmer and a sea captain, this lovable, and to the Marxist mind, incurably futile old poet, and his proletarian prototype, John Burns, were the life and soul of English socialism. Their object was to save the underdog from sweating and exploitation by organising him like his comrades, the prosperous artisans of the skilled Trade Unions. During the recurrent trade depressions of the 'eighties they organised vast processions of unemployed—of the unwanted and starving army of *laissez-faire* capital. One of these, on "Bloody Sunday," November, 1887, became part of English history. Long drab companies of pallid ragged men, marching behind red banners and bands of antiquated instruments, converged in defiance of the police from the outer slums on Trafalgar Square; here they were repeatedly charged by massed constables with drawn batons until hundreds of skulls were cracked and bleeding. It was the first

[1] Speech delivered at Burslem, 13 Oct 1881, cit. R. H. Gretton, *A Modern History of the English People* 64.

glimmer of the red light that threatened social explosion. "No one who saw it will ever forget the strange and indeed terrible sight of that grey winter day, the vast, sombre-coloured crowd, the brief but fierce struggle at the corner of the Strand, and the river of steel and scarlet that moved slowly through the dusky swaying masses, when two squadrons of the Life Guards were summoned up from Whitehall."[1] Afterwards two of the leaders, John Burns and the chivalrous Cunninghame Graham, were taken into custody.

The red light was not unheeded. Two years later the selfless pioneers of the British Socialist movement won a great triumph. In August, 1889, several thousand labourers in the London Docks struck work. Such men were the poorest of the poor—the flotsam and jetsam of the water-side. They were unorganised, despised even by their fellow workers, without hope or craft. They slept in the fo'c'sles of empty ships and subsisted on scraps of mouldy biscuits left over by their hard-bitten crews, were subjected by sub-contractors—often more brutes than men—to work with rotten plant and defective machinery and left to perish in crippled destitution and misery when their limbs had been mangled in some squalid accident on the dock-side. In the frantic competition for freights, they could scarcely ever look for more than two days' continuous employment. But stirred by the new spirit among their downtrodden kind, they now made the unheard of demand that their labour should be hired at not less than four hours at a time and at a uniform rate of 6d. an hour. It was rejected by dock-owners who relied on the poverty and stupidity of the poor derelicts they exploited to ensure their defeat. But the sullen resolve of the men, fanned to anger by the fiery eloquence of one of their number, Ben Tillett, and sustained by the growing sympathy of the public, proved stronger than the familiar weapon of starvation. For two months the docks remained closed. Then the dockowners gave way. Not only was "the docker's tanner" won, but a great Union of "unskilled" labour—the Dock, Wharf and Riverside Labourers' Union—had been founded.

Yet by itself Trade Unionism was not enough. In a society seeking profits through world trade and based on economic

[1] J. W. Mackail, *Life of William Morris* II 191.

fluctuation, an army of surplus labour was inescapable. Under the existing system its periodic unemployment was attended by the extreme of destitution and degradation. This hard rock of unorganised poverty was a constant threat to the Trade Union movement. In the highly-skilled trades, the aristocrat of labour could present a solid front to the capitalist aggressor. But elsewhere the employer could always count on the amorphous mass of starving poverty from which to draft non-Union or "free" labour into his factories and so break a strike. The bitterness of Union feeling against the "blackleg"—generally some poor down-and-out in need of a meal—and the sullen insistence on the rightfulness of peaceful picketing sprang from this.

Before labour could secure its full rights the working class as a whole needed to be redeemed from extreme poverty and given self-respect, knowledge and *esprit de corps* through better housing, education and, above all, some sort of living wage. Organised Labour could not stand erect so long as it rested on the social morass of the submerged tenth. State action was necessary to give the workers' organisations—Trade Unions and co-operative societies— a secure field of operation. Otherwise the capitalist, with his constant recourse to new machinery displacing skilled men by unskilled, might beat them in the end.

It was the recognition of this that inspired the foundation in 1885 of the Fabian Society. It began as a little group of youthful radicals —drawn mostly from the middle-class—who had repudiated the *laissez-faire* tenets of utilitarianism but who retained the utilitarian's contempt for the inefficient and illogical. One of the members was a young, red-haired Irishman named Bernard Shaw who about this time electrified a conference of intellectuals and highbrow politicians by reading a paper to prove that the landlord, the capitalist and the burglar were equally the enemies of society. The Fabian thesis was that before social revolution could be achieved, the educated leaders of society must themselves be brought to see the necessity of revolution. In a law-abiding country like England mob oratory and emotional appeals to mass violence could never succeed. The capitalist state was not to be stormed but gradually occupied by a process of infiltration.

This was the policy of "permeation." The Fabians were encouraged to seek membership of every society—Liberal, Tory or Labour, Christian or atheist—that would admit them and there secure by the arts of persuasion and lobbying the adoption of socialist measures. Especially were they to seek to permeate the Opposition, since by its very nature parliamentary Opposition is inclined to be revolutionary and always seeking to overturn the Government.

The Fabians pinned their faith to an extension of legislative action. They announced that "the era of administration had come." The state was to be socialised through its own machinery. Instead of concerning themselves with such questions as free trade, retrenchment, Church disestablishment and the abolition of the House of Lords, the Fabians were to concentrate on free education, municipal trading, the provision of state-aided houses and small holdings and the graduated taxation of incomes and estates. They were not to dictate but to throw out suggestions. Nothing could have been better adapted to the spirit of the time or the character of England.

Fabianism went with the tide of contemporary thought. The Benthamites had long emphasised the sanatory qualities of reforming legislation supported by an incorruptible and centralised bureaucracy and inspectorate. As a result of their teaching, Liberals had purged the civil service of corruption in the name of utility and reason. An efficient administration, subject to a parliament increasingly taught to regard itself as a legislative rather than a debating assembly, was now to be applied for a purpose which its utilitarian sponsors would have viewed with horror—"the practical extension of the activity of the State." The weapon the utilitarians had forged was to destroy economic utilitarianism.

For only the State's intervention could now redress the State's neglect. The only remedy for the evil of *laissez-faire* seemed to be to repudiate *laissez-faire*. For many years past, great teachers like Ruskin and T. H. Green at Oxford had impressed on younger consciences the ideal of social responsibility. A new generation of educated men and women was now growing up whose minds were contemplating the necessity of solving the problems created by a century of industrialism.

But it was too late to undo what *laissez-faire* had done. In fifty years its hold on English thought had transformed the face of society. By 1881 seventeen and a half out of twenty-six millions were living in towns: by 1891 twenty-one millions out of twenty-nine millions. Eager Americans visiting Britain in the 'eighties and 'nineties looked in vain in the city streets for the hordes of rosy, golden-haired, blue-eyed children whom they had been led to expect in the Anglo-Saxon island. The national type, already affected in London by the constant influx of cheap foreign labour, was growing smaller and paler. Bad teeth, pasty complexions and weak chests were becoming British traits.

Capitalism had created the proletariat, and the proletariat was not a theory but a fact. It could not be destroyed or ignored: it could only be transformed by education and improved urban conditions. Education and municipal reform were the themes of the hour. "We must educate our masters," Robert Lowe had declared before the passing of Disraeli's Reform Bill. The older ideal of education based on religion and the teaching of hereditary crafts in the home had vanished with the migration into the towns. Only the most rudimentary instruction in reading, writing and arithmetic had as yet taken its place. The great mass of the nation was illiterate. In 1869 only one British child in two was receiving any education at all. Of those, more than half were being taught in schools maintained by the Church of England, which together with other denominational and voluntary schools had for some time been in receipt of small Government grants-in-aid.

In 1870 William Edward Forster, a Quaker member of Gladstone's first Liberal Administration, introduced an Education Act, setting up compulsory Local School Boards to provide secular elementary education for all children between the ages of five and thirteen[1] not already provided for by denominational schools. The cost was met partly out of State grants and rates and partly out of parents' fees. Owing to jealousy between the churches, the principle was laid down that all grant-aided education should be unsectarian. By this means religious teaching inspired by conviction was virtually

---

[1] The school-leaving-age was raised to 14 in 1900 by a Conservative Government which in the previous year established a national Board of Education.

ruled out. It thus came about that the idealism of future generations, founded on a secular State education, differed from that of the old, which still derived from the Christian ethic.

Forster's Act affected little more than half the children in the country. It was unpopular with working-class parents who resented the limitation put on the family earning capacity by school attendance. Yet its underlying principle served the ends of organised Labour, not only by bringing cheap education within reach of the workers but by its indirect check on the competition of juvenile labour and its tendency to raise adult wages. A strong demand arose, therefore, to extend its scope. In 1876 a Conservative Government tightened the obligations of parents and in 1880 a Liberal Government made them universally compulsory. In 1891 another Conservative Administration dispensed with fees and made elementary education free for all. Thus both parties acknowledged the collectivist principle that the rich should be compelled to contribute to the education of the poor.

The insignificance of the contribution could not alter the significance of the principle. Once established, the pressure of electoral numbers was sure in the end to do more. Because of the normal Anglo-Saxon indifference to the claims of intellect, the advance of State education was at first deliberate rather than rapid. But the figures speak for themselves. In 1870 the total grant out of revenue towards national education was £912,000. By 1888 it had risen to £4,168,000. By 1905 it was nearly £11,000,000 and the contribution from local rates another £7,000,000. At the turn of the century London alone was paying a million a year or £28 per child—almost the equivalent of a contemporary farm labourer's wage. After the Liberal triumph in 1906 school medical services were established and public funds afforded for feeding necessitous children. To an old Chartist, who fifty years before had paid 6d. a week for his fees at a night school, the new policy appeared one of "coddling." "It is well to educate the people," he wrote, "but the tendency of much of the School Board policy of the day is to pauperise the people. Yet School Boards ought, above all things, to beware of undermining the independence of the individual."[1]

[1] W. E. Adams, *Memoirs of a Social Atom* II 109-10.

In municipal administration the collectivist advance was even more striking. Within a generation a vast new vested interest, officially subordinated to the general will as expressed in local and parliamentary elections and controlled by salaried public servants, had sprung into existence in the island dedicated to the sanctity of private wealth. Parliamentary powers of collective control and ownership, and sometimes of monopoly, were sought and obtained, at first by the greater cities, later by the counties and smaller urban areas. The Local Government Act of 1888 established elective County Councils with control of local affairs and taxation. In that year London achieved its County Council—presently to revolutionise the life of its poorer inhabitants. The services of communal life, which individual effort had failed to give to the vast urban agglomerations it had created, were supplied step by step by local authorities. They were paid for out of rates and loans charged on rates. The first successful flotation of municipal stock was made in 1880 by the Liverpool Corporation. By 1896 the local government debt of the country was already 200 million pounds. Only fourteen years later it was three times greater.

The first services performed by the new local authorities were lighting, paving, and cheap transport. By far the most important were education and housing. In nothing had *laissez-faire* achieved so much and so badly as in housing. It had built homes for millions of new factory workers, not to endure but to perish. The vital attribute of a home is that it should be permanent. The principle of the jerry builder was to make as quick a profit as possible on as large a turnover for as little expenditure of labour and money. The houses went up fast enough but they did not last. They were not meant to.

They were built in rows and usually back-to-back—poky, hideous, uncomfortable and insanitary. The last thing that was thought of in making them was the convenience of the occupant. Except in the granite towns and villages of East Lancashire and the West Riding many were so flimsy that they swayed with the wind and their walls so thin that their inmates were traditionally reputed to be able to hear their neighbours making up their minds. Frequently such houses were erected by the companies that employed their occupants. This was particularly so in iron and coal districts where there was little alternative employment. A man who lost his job lost his home. The rents were "kept back" from the weekly wages. The feeling of security and the pride of ownership which home should foster in a free man were lacking.

It was due to the slowly-growing realisation of at least some of this by the comfortable classes, many of whom were now encountering slum conditions at first hand in their "settlement" work, as well as to the galloping deterioration that had by now begun in the earlier industrial dwellings, that a Royal Commission on the Housing of the Poor was set up by Gladstone in 1884. It was, most significantly, presided over by the Prince of Wales. Its interim report published a year later proposed a preliminary purchase at a statutory price of three old prison sites for housing estates. This, in itself, was a most important modification of utilitarian principle since it recurred—in however tentative a form—to the old medieval ideal not of a market but of a "fair" price. It was the first sign of recognition of a new, or rather a very old, ideal of government.

The Housing of the Working Classes Act of 1890 which embodied the main part of the recommendations of the Royal Commission stemmed if it did not reverse the rising tide of slum-dwelling. It created new powers of buying and demolishing insanitary houses, opening out congested alleys and culs-de-sac and building new dwellings on their sites. In practice, until tightened up by increased powers of government inspection and the growing force of organised working-class opinion, the Act was frequently evaded or perverted. Representation on local councils was usually confined to the smaller capitalists who alone had both the time and the inclination to give to municipal work: all too often they were prompted by the opportunities afforded of serving their own interests. Jerry builders were apt to pack Health and General Purposes Committees in order to frame—and what was worse supervise—the bye-laws about building and sanitation which parliament had intended to control them. And the purchase of land for building purposes was often preceeded by elaborate and shady manoeuvres by those who were— according to democratic notions—supposed to represent and protect the people but who used the machinery of democracy to exploit them further.

Yet, as the theory of social responsibility increasingly haunted the minds of the educated minority, a process characteristically English took place. The larger and better-established capitalists— and above all their sons—began to devote themselves to the service of the public they or their forbears had fleeced. They did so without hope of further profit and out of a sense of *noblesse oblige*, gained more often than not at the new public schools which, since Arnold of Rugby's days, had opened their gates and their ideology to the commercial classes. A new type of public man arose—provincial, aggressive and democratic in method and appeal—whose interest lay neither in foreign policy nor parliamentary debate but in the extension of municipal services. Living on the private wealth acquired or inherited under *laissez-faire*, they were able to throw their entire energies into the work of mitigating the evils wrought by *laissez-faire*. These new, and to their individualist fathers' way of thinking, heretical radicals were still iconoclastic towards the older notions of privilege and decorum. But though they resented the power of the landed aristocracy and lost no opportunity of humbling it, they were no enemies to the capitalist and manufacturer. The very inroads they made on *laissez-faire* practice helped to maintain the prestige and opportunities of their class by appeasing the social unrest of the masses. The most famous of these local radical reformers was Joseph Chamberlain, the dapper young hardware merchant with orchid, monocle and the terrible republican sentiments who became mayor of Birmingham in 1873 at 37, and President of the Board of Trade in Mr. Gladstone's second Administration in 1880.

In all this the domestic history of Britain during the last two decades of the nineteenth and the first of the twentieth century constituted the first act of a great revolution. During these years a vigorous capitalist, and less vigorous but still powerful aristocratic, England were converted to an elementary socialism whose basis was that the weak and inefficient should constitute a first charge on the strong and able. The pioneer activities of a humane and intelligent minority of their own members contributed to that conversion. But the real driving force came from the superior votes of the urban workers which, by a third Reform Act in 1884, had been reinforced by those of the county householders.

The ruling classes did not consciously admit their conversion, for they were unaware of it. And their struggle against it, like all English struggles, was grudging and tenacious. But, while denouncing the name of socialism which they believed to be synonymous with mob plunder and the bloody destruction of their homes and altars, they allowed socialist principles to inspire their laws and, in an illogical, piecemeal and incomplete way, they increasingly applied socialist practice. For the void in the great industrial towns that their fathers' search for wealth had created left them no alternative. The more the towns grew the more it clamoured to be filled.

. . . .

The English working man, even after a century of factory labour, did not take readily to aggregate conceptions of himself. He did not want liberty as a member of a class: he wanted it as a man. An official bossing him about was no less a tyrant in his eyes because he was vested with popular authority. The English proletarian was a contradiction in terms: economically a wage slave, he was still spiritually and in his own eyes a freeman. He was easily "put upon" but did not readily brook interference. His fists and his tongue were always quick to assert his independence.

The love of liberty came out in his phrases, in his jokes, in his invincible, half-blasphemous, ironical commentary on the ups and downs of his harsh life. His "'Ere, who d'yre think yre a'getting at?" his "Tell us anuvor, guvnor," like his jokes about mothers-in-law and old gentlemen slipping on banana skins, were part of his protests against interference and pompous power. He refused to part with his humour, his right to grumble, his right to what little liberty the wage struggle left him to go about his private business in his own way. Not clearly understanding how he had been cheated of his birthright—home, status and privilege—he was yet aware of the dignity of his descent. He knew himself to be as good as any man, and better.

Robbed by the machine of pride and pleasure in his work, he still kept inviolate his right to take pleasure in his liberty. His most precious possession was his right to enjoy himself in his own way. On Hampstead Heath or Hackney Marshes on a bank holiday one saw him at his most uproarious, expressing himself in cockney carnival: costers in all their pride of pearls and feathers, frolicsome young women with tambourines singing and making unblushing advances to jolly strangers, old parties with bottles of stout and jests for every passer-by, side-shows and booths with giants and dwarfs, nigger minstrels and performing dogs. So in the trains from Stepney to Highbury one might in the course of half an hour's journey encounter a lad playing airs on a fiddle, an old man beguiling his journey with an accordion and a chorus of young workmen singing in unison. By being jolly and having a good time when the occasion offered, the English poor reminded themselves and the rich men they served that Jack was as good as his master and that freedom was his birthright.

One saw industrial England at its roughest and freest in any town where seamen congregated. In the Ratcliff Highway in the 'eighties and 'nineties almost every house was a tavern with a dance hall at the back where a steam organ kept up perpetual revelry. The whole place resounded with music, the shouting of drunken sailors and their bright-scarved girls, the clatter of the steam organs and the strumming of nigger minstrels. But any poor street on frequent occasion presented the same scene in miniature: a German band, a dancing polar bear, a visit from the Salvation Army or a band of morris dancers could bring the population of every crowded house into the street. Most poor districts had their quota of barrel-organs, whose owners, having finished their day's work in wealthier parts, could generally be prevailed upon to oblige with a tune to which the whole street stepped it on the flags. A wedding was always the occasion for the hire of a barrel-organ for the day and for continuous music from the time of the bridal couple's return to the adjournment of the company to the nearest "boozer." Only a fight—a common occurrence—could bring the harmony to a stop.

The supreme embodiment of the surviving character of the

English working people was the music hall. Here art held up the mirror to nature. Springing spontaneously out of the sing-song of the upper tavern room and the old out-of-door gardens of the artisan of the pastoral past, it became for a space of time a British institution. Its morality was to make the best of a bad job: its purpose to make every one free and easy. Performers and audience, under the genial and bacchanalian presidency of the chairman, with his buttonhole, his mesmeric eye and his town crier's voice, combined in expressing their own individuality. At the old South London, whenever there was a hitch in the programme, the chairman, "Bob" Courtney, glittering with false diamonds and laying aside his glass and cigar, would rise to sing his traditional song, "Britannia's Voice of Thunder," while the whole audience kept time, drowning singing and even big drum with an equally traditional refrain of "good old Bob! Bob! Bob! Bob!" Its songs, circulating in succession among the entire population—"Champagne Charlie," "Lardi-da," "It's all done by kindness," "How's your poor feet," "What ho! she bumps," "Pretty Polly Perkins of Paddington Green," "Ask a policeman," and "Knocked 'em in the Old Kent Road"—were vernacular, irreverent, democratic, yet intensely individualistic, as of a nation of disinherited, cheery aristocrats, and arose from deeply felt experience: they were the English answer to the lot which had befallen the English worker. They told a man, in rousing chorus, to "paddle his own canoe," "to cling to his old love like the ivy," and to fill himself up with "beer, beer, glorious beer," bade Tommy make room for his uncle, and the nation put the foreigner in his place:

"I'd wake men from their torpor, and every foreign pauper
That helps to make the sweater rich and wages always low,
I'd send aboard a ship, Sir, for an everlasting trip, Sir,
And a chance give to the English if I only bossed the show."

Such rough songs spoke of unchanging virtues: of courage and cheerfulness in adversity, of loyalty to old "pals," of constancy to home and wife. There is no ballad more English than that which Albert Chevalier wrote for his cockney impersonation of the old London workman philosophising over his pipe on the faithful wife of his youth:

"We've been together now for forty years,
And it don't seem a day too much,
Oh, there ain't a lidy living in the land
As I'd swop for my dear ole Dutch."

Above all the music hall expressed the English passion for liberty:
the English desire, so hard to translate into the life of the factory,
to follow the current of one's own nature and be true to it by being
free. What was, however bad it seemed, had to be and was therefore, in a humorous way, good, since man being free could turn his
necessity to glorious gain. So the fat woman, the grace and opportunity of youth gone for ever as it was for most of her audience,
would stand up, mountainous and undeterred, and, announced by
the leering chairman as "your old favourite, So-and-So," send her
steam-roundabout voice pulsating through the thick pipe and cigar
smoke:

"I weigh sixteen stoney O!
I'm not all skin and boney O!"

So, in a more studied and perfect expression of the inner soul of a
great people who had lost everything but its cheerfulness and
courage, Marie Lloyd in a later age, when the old music hall was
dying, would sing, a vinous old female, moist-eyed, wandering
but invincible:

"My old man said, Follow the van
And don't dilly dally on the way!
Off went the cart with the home packed in it,
I walked behind with my old cock linnet.
But I dillied and dallied, dallied and dillied,
Lost the van and don't know where to roam.
I stopped on the way to have the old half-quartern,
And I can't find my way home."

It was to the people whose life this vulgar, proud and humane
art represented that the Socialist offered his collectivist remedy.
He assumed, not without the justification of logic, that the English
working man was already a proletarian slave and that he would be
only too willing to band himself as a nameless comrade in the
great army of his class against the rich and privileged. But this
was not so. The downtrodden wage-slave did not think of himself

as such. All the while that the socialist propagandist was telling him of the proletarian heaven, he was dreaming of the day when a rich unknown cousin would die in Australia or the horses he so hopefully and religiously backed each week would bring him a fortune and he would be able to have a house and a garden of his own and go to race meetings and cricket matches every day instead of working with his fellow proletarians in the factory.

Thus it came about that the first missionaries of the new socialist religion were treated with derision by the rough, unbelieving multitude. They were denounced as atheists, anarchists and republicans, as liars and quacks who offered "sum'at for nothing." Their meetings were frequently broken up amid rude noises. In those days it was the Socialists who were heckled by the local toughs and practical jokers, not the Tories. England was so accustomed to being governed by well-spoken gentlemen in top hats that the spectacle of an avowed Socialist going down to the House of Commons in a check cap with a brass band blaring at his side profoundly shocked many humble men and women. Working men were at first exceedingly suspicious of members of their own class who sought to enter parliament as if they were toffs and were always ready to listen to any malicious charge, however wild, of peculation or self-seeking brought against them. Their creed was regarded, in pubs and other places, where sound men congregated, as laughable if not lunatic. In the 1895 election—a Conservative triumph—only one working man held his seat, and every one of the twenty-seven candidates put up by the virgin independent Labour Party suffered defeat at the polls.[1] It was not till the great Conservative rout of January, 1906, when the rising tide of collectivism swept an almost revolutionary Liberal government into power that a Parliamentary Labour Party took its place as a permanent force in politics with a solid bloc of 51 seats and a strength sufficient to sway the course of legislation.

Even many of the Trade Union and Co-operative Society leaders —often stalwarts of the local Tory working mens' club—regarded

[1] The Party Chest for the Election totalled only £400. Ardent supporters pawned their watches, Sunday suits, accordions and fiddles.—Sir James Sexten, *Agitator*, 145.

the new socialism with disfavour. It was too highbrow and foreign for their shrewd liking[1]: too far removed from the familiar tastes and prejudices of the simple men they represented. Had those who represented the larger forces of organised capital been a little more sympathetic towards their Labour *vis-à-vis* instead of treating them, as they too often did, as impertinent inferiors who had forgotten their place, the intellectual socialist movement might well have died still-born.

Yet a new spirit was abroad. For just as the first translation of the scriptures spelt out by unlettered zealots lent wings to an earlier English revolution, so the education of the board school helped to carry a new conception of life into the homes of the people. To cater for the needs of this new class of reader, a halfpenny press made its appearance, jejune, snappy, sensational. The first in the field was the radical *Star*—the "twinkle, twinkle little star" of the late 'eighties and 'nineties. It had many imitators. Those who controlled this revolutionary power might differ in politics and educational purpose, but the circulation of their papers and the advertisements from which they drew their profits depended on their giving to the million what the million wanted. Being obscure it wanted flattery and, being poor, a share of the pleasures of the rich. The cheap newspaper gave it the one and fed its appetite for the other. It promised that a time was coming when the hungry should be filled with good things.

For the intelligent young worker, to whom State education had given the key to the world of books and new ideas, and to whom the pub and the humorous philosophy of his class were insufficient solace, the background of life—even though it was already vastly improved—was dreary and uninspiring. As Joe Toole remembered, it was that of the street corner, the smell of the tripe-works, the clatter of clogs, the street brawls, short commons, the pawnshop

---

[1] "Much daring, I went one night to speak at the Battersea branch of the Social-Democratic Federation where I was so belaboured with words about exploitation, bourgeois and others of learned length and thundering sound just then imported from Germany that I . . . determined to go no more to Social-Democratic Federation Branches. And I never have. G. N. Barnes, *From Workshop to War Cabinet* 42.

and the cries of women giving birth to new citizens.[1] The usual lot was to start selling papers after school hours at eleven, borrowing 4½d. to purchase thirteen with a hope of making 2d. profit for each bundle sold. Three years later the scholar left school to plunge into a battle for life which took the form of constantly changing casual labour—sweeping floors or streets, holding horses' heads for commercial travellers, laying tram tracks, storekeeping, running errands and monotonous machine-minding sometimes for ten hours at a stretch. All these occupations were "blind alley"; the weaker brethren never climbed beyond them out of the ruck of the unskilled. Between jobs one stood at the corner of the street or scoured the shop windows for a notice of "Boy Wanted." In such a start to life there were constant temptations: the skylarking, chi'iking gang of boon companions who slipped imperceptibly from practical joking into petty larceny on sweet shops and battles with sticks and broken glass; the pubs to which a boy became accustomed from his earliest years, the racecourse and the bookie at the street corner. Later came the long losing battle with poverty, undernourishment and insecurity, the home with the verminous walls and broken window-sashes in the crowded dirty street, the risk of accident and maiming, and the certainty sooner or later of "slack times" and unemployment with the sickening tramp from factory gate to gate, the days of idle, hopeless hunger, the rot of body and soul and the dread of the workhouse at the end of that bitter road.

It was to those whom this dreary heritage inspired to bitter anger that the new socialism made its initial appeal. Behind the solid structure of Trade Unionism and the brittle façade of the intelligentsia fermented the spirit and fervour of a new religion. During the quarter of a century that preceded the first world war, socialism was preached through the crowded cities of Britain as Methodism had been preached in the eighteenth century and Puritanism in the seventeenth—as a salvationist crusade. Into the drab lives and starved minds of the industrial masses came a new message of hope and righteousness, uttered on evangelist platforms by ardent believers with red ties and flashing eyes: that poverty and injustice

[1] J. Toole, *Fighting Through Life* 20-1.

could be abolished by State action. The little handful of the elect who gathered in the north-country market square after some crushing electoral defeat to sing Carpenter's Labour hymn, "England, arise! the long, long night is over," were like the grain of seed which grew into a great tree.

Among the younger generation of the workers there were many who read more seriously. Henry George's *Progress and Poverty* sold in thousands, and Blatchford's *Merrie England*, published at 6d. in 1894, in tens of thousands. The latter's humble *Clarion*, issued under many difficulties, made proselytes wherever the factory chimneys and slated roofs marked the abode of the toiling masses. For humbler minds the new gospel was preached in its simplest and most appealing form. The bloated capitalist with his white top-hat, his gold watch-chain and his money-bags, was the Devil who sucked the blood of the workers. The upright young Socialist with his Union ticket and his Fabian pamphlet in his pocket was the pioneer of a new and better world, ready for martyrdom if need be but never for compromise with the evil spirit of greed which kept the virtuous proletariat in chains. In a more sophisticated way this point of view was broadly adopted by a whole generation of middle-class writers and artists who, appalled by the accumulating evils of *laissez-faire* industrialism, carried the message of socialism into their art. Generous youth at Oxford and Cambridge and newer centres of learning thrilled at the gospel of apocalyptic hope: the schoolmasters, journalists, clergymen and civil servants of the future went out to their labour consciously or unconsciously imbued with the teaching of Socialists of genius like Shaw and Wells.

Yet the advance of Socialism was nearly always anticipated by the premature retreat of the individualist. Before the vanguard of the red revolutionaries reached each successive barricade the capitalists were already receding. Many of the demands of organised Labour were granted by Liberal and Tory politicians—quick to sense the changing wind of electoral favour—long before its Socialist representatives were in a position to enforce them. Successive Employers' Liability Acts limited and largely abrogated the old legal doctrine of common employment. Under pressure from the Unions the scope of the Factory Acts was steadily extended.[1] The Workmen's Compensation Act of 1897 made an employer theoretically liable for all the risks of his workers' employment. Charity, now invested with the prim pince-nez of the statistical bureaucrat, was restored to its former place as a civic obligation. The stigma of pauperism was removed and those in receipt of poor law relief were admitted to the franchise. Labour Exchanges were established at the expense of the taxpayer to help find work for the unemployed. Small holdings were provided for agricultural labourers.

The Socialist principle that the State as the ultimate owner of all property had the right to tax capital as well as income was admitted by the imposition of death duties in Sir William Harcourt's Liberal budget of 1893. Fourteen years later, Mr. Asquith introduced the distinction between earned and unearned incomes and a new impost on very rich men called super-tax. In order to finance a nation-wide scheme of old-age pensions and other "rare and refreshing fruit for the parched lips of the multitude," the new levy was extended to all incomes of more than £5,000 a year by the Liberal Chancellor, David Lloyd George. To modern minds such modest measures of working-class amelioration, now taken for granted, may appear trifling. To a Liberal of the 'sixties they would have seemed a revolutionary interference with the laws of supply and demand and a half-way step to wholesale confiscation and Communism. To many old-fashioned persons like the Conservative die-hard peers, who sacrificed the powers of their own House in a last desperate attempt to stay the new electoral will, they seemed so even in 1910.

For the underdog it was a far cry from the socialised industrial England of Lloyd George's budgets to the grim commonwealth of liberty to survive or perish of the mid-nineteenth century: from the omniscient government inspector, the statutorily enforced closing hours and half holidays, the working-class housing estate with its bathrooms and gardens to the "young ladies" of Madame Elise's dressmaking establishment with their fifteen hours' working day and airless, fever-stricken dormitory, the filthy, ragged child

[1] Within a few years of bringing the dockers within the scope of the acts, the number of dock accidents was halved.

crossing-sweepers sleeping under the Adelphi arches, and the days when W. E. Adams, tramping through Salford in search of work, found at Peel Park with its museum and free library an almost solitary example of municipal enlightenment.

Looking back in 1923, one whose whole life had been passed in the service of the Labour movement which had raised him from a poor apprentice's bench to a Privy Councillorship and a seat in the Cabinet, made an attempt to sum it all up. "I have seen many lands," he wrote, "but none as good as my own. I have mixed with many peoples but found none with so large measure of fellow feeling or sense of fair play. I have seen freedom broadening down to the class in which I was born and bred and which I have tried to serve. When I was young, working folk were uneducated and unenfranchised. They were poor and dependant and their working days were bounded by age and want without concern by the State which their labour had enriched. Now they have at least a modicum of education, they are politically as well as industrially organised, and although there is still unemployment and, in too many instances, fear of want, yet these grim problems are being tackled with greater knowledge and more humane feeling than ever before. I take the present signs and tokens as indications of better things to be."[1]

All this was true. The good man, looking back on his life of struggle and seemingly miraculous achievement, knew how much greater were the opportunities of the young workers of the new age than were those of the old. But the young who had never experienced the full fury of the storm of *laissez-faire* merely knew that they were born into a world of mean streets, monotonous labour, cramping poverty and narrowing uncertainty. They inherited from the past, not only elementary and secondary schools, labour exchanges, and Council houses, but bad digestions, uninspiring surroundings and the instability of a commercial system based not on human welfare but on profits. They were better off than their parents, but they were not satisfied with their lot. For their instincts, as well as the professional preachers of discontent, told them that something was still lacking.

[1] G. N. Barnes, *From Workshop to War Cabinet* 295.

List of Abbreviations Used in Footnotes

Aberdeen. Lady Frances Balfour, *The Life of George, Fourth Earl of Aberdeen.* 1923.
Ackerman, *Microcosm of London.* 1808-10.
Add. MSS. Additional MSS. British Museum.
Ailesbury. Thomas Bruce, Earl of Ailesbury, *Memoirs,* 2 vols. 1890.
Alken. H. Alken, *The National Sports of Great Britain* (1903 ed.).
Anderson. J. A. Anderson, *Recollections of a Peninsular Veteran.* 1913.
Ann. Reg. Annual Register.
Arbuthnot. *Journal of Mrs. Arbuthnot* (ed. F. Bamford and Duke of Wellington). 1950.
Ashton. John Ashton, *Social England under the Regency.* 1890.
Assheton Smith. Sir J. Eardley-Wilmot, *Reminiscences of the late Thomas Assheton Smith* 1860.
Aubrey. Aubrey's *Brief Lives* (ed. O. L. Dick). 1949.
Austen. *The Works of Jane Austen* (ed. J. Bailey). 1927.

Bamford. S. Bamford, *Passages in the Life of a Radical* (ed. H. Dunkley). 1893.
Baxterianae. Reliquiae Baxterianae (ed. M. Sylvester). 1696.
Bell. G. Bell, *Rough Notes by an Old Soldier.* 1867.
Bell, *Fire.* W. G. Bell, *The Great Fire of London.* 1920.
Bewick. *Memoirs of Thomas Bewick written by himself.* 1924.
Blundell. M. Blundell, *Cavalier.* 1933.
Boxiana. P. Egan, *Boxiana.* 1818-1822.
Bramston. *Sir John Bramston, Autobiography of.* 1845.
Broughton. Lord Broughton, *Recollections of A Long Life.* 1909.
Brown. *Thomas Brown, The Works of,* 3 vols. 1707-8.
Brownlow. Countess of Brownlow, *Slight Reminiscences of a Septuagenarian.* 1867.
Bury. Lady Charlotte Bury, *The Diary of a Lady-in-Waiting* (ed. A. Francis Stewart). 1908.

C.S.P.D. Calendars of State Papers Domestic (1660-81). 1866-1922.
Campbell. W. Beattie, *Life and Letters of Thomas Campbell.* 1949.
Castlereagh. *Memoirs and Correspondence of Viscount Castlereagh.* 1850-3.
Chamberlayne. Edward Chamberlayne, *Angliae Notitia.* 1671 ed.
Chancellor. E. Beresford Chancellor, *Life in Regency and Early Victorian Times.* 1926.
Clapham. J. H. Clapham, *An Economic History of Modern Britain.* 1926.
Clark. G. N. Clark, *The Later Stuarts* (Oxford History of England). 1934.
Cobbett. Cobbett's *Rural Rides* (ed. G. D. H. and M. Cole). 1930.
Colchester. *Diary and Correspondence of Charles Abbot,* Lord Colchester. 1861.
Colquhoun. P. A. Colquhoun, *A Treatise on the Commerce and Police of the River Thames.* 1800.
Cooper. *The Life of Thomas Cooper written by himself.* 1879.
Cosmo. *The Travels of Cosmo III, Grand Duke of Tuscany.* 1821.
Crabb Robinson. *Diary of Henry Crabb Robinson.* 1869.
Cranbourn Chase. W. Chaffins, *Anecdotes and History of Cranbourn Chase.* 1818.
Creevey. *Creevey's Life and Times* (ed. John Gore). 1934.
Creevey Papers. The Creevey Papers (ed. H. Maxwell). 1903-5.
Croker. *The Croker Papers* (ed. L. J. Jennings). 1884.
Cunningham. W. Cunningham, *The Growth of English Industry and Commerce,* Pt. II. Modern Times, 6th ed. 1917-19.

LIST OF ABBREVIATIONS

Daniell. W. Daniell, *A Voyage Round Great Britain*, 8 vols. 1825.
D'Arblay. *The Diaries and Letters of Mme. D'Arblay* (ed. A. Dobson). 1904.
Darvall. F. O. Darvall, *Popular Disturbances and Public Order in Regency England*. 1935.
Defoe. Daniel Defoe, *Tour* (ed. G. D. H. Cole), 2 vols. 1927.
De Selincourt. *The Letters of William and Dorothy Wordsworth, The Middle Years* (ed. E. de Selincourt). 1937.
Dicey. A. V. Dicey, *Law and Public Opinion in England* (1914 ed.).
Dino. *Memoirs of the Duchesse de Dino* (ed. Princesse Radziwill). 1909.
Dixon. J. B. Booth, *Bits of Character: A Life of Henry Hall Dixon*. 1936.
Dudley. Lord Dudley, *Letters to "Ivy"* (ed. S. H. Romily). 1905.
Dyott. *Diary of William Dyott* (ed. R. W. Jefferey). 1907.

Early Victorian England. *Early Victorian England, 1830–1865* (ed. G. M. Young). 1934.
Eden. F. M. Eden, *The State of the Poor* (ed. A. G. L. Rogers). 1905.
Eland. G. Eland, *In Bucks.* 1923.
Engels. F. Engels, *The Condition of the Working Class in England in 1844.*
English Spy. "B. Blackmantle". *The English Spy* (1907 ed.).
Ernle. Lord Ernle, *English Farming Past and Present*. 1912.
Espriella. R. Southey, *Letters from England by Don Manuel Alvarez Espriella*. 1807.
Evelyn. John Evelyn, *Memoirs*, 3 vols. 1906.

Farington. *The Farington Diary* (ed. J. Grieg). 1922–6.
Feltham. J. Feltham, *The Picture of London for 1802.* 1802.
Festing. J. Festing, *John Hookham Frere and his Friends.* 1899.
Fiennes. C. Fiennes, *Through England on a Side Saddle in the Time of William and Mary.* 1888.
Fowler. J. K. Fowler, *Echoes of Old Country Life.* 1892.
Fremantle. E. A. Fremantle, *England in the Nineteenth Century*, 2 vols. 1929–30.

Gaussen. A. C. C. Gaussen, *A Later Pepys.* 1904.
Gomm. Sir W. Gomm, *Letters and Journal.* 1881.
Gore. J. Gore, *Nelson's Hardy and his Wife.* 1935.
Granville. *Private Correspondence of Granville Leveson-Gower, Earl of Granville.* 1916.
Grattan. W. Grattan, *Adventures with the Connaught Rangers.* 1847.
Greville. *The Greville Memoirs* (ed. H. Reeve). 1874.
Greville (Suppl.) *The Greville Diary* (ed. P. W. Wilson). 1927.
Gronow. *The Reminiscences and Recollections of Captain Gronow.* 1892.
Grote. *Some Account of the Hamlet of East Burnham, by a late Resident* (Mrs. Grote). 1858.

Halévy. E. Halévy, *A History of the English People from 1815* (Engl. transl.), 3 vols. 1924–7.
Halifax. *Works of George Savile, Marquis of* (ed. Sir W. Raleigh). 1912.
Hamilton of Dalzell MS. Manuscript Journal in the possession of Lord Hamilton of Dalzell.
Harriet Granville. *Letters of Harriet, Countess Granville* (ed. F. Leveson Gower). 1894.
Hatton. *The Hatton Correspondence* (ed. E. M. Thompson), 2 vols. 1878.
Haydon. *The Life of Benjamin Robert Haydon from his Autobiography and Journals* (ed. T. Taylor). 1853.
Hill, Austen. Constance Hill, *Jane Austen.* 1902.
Historical Essays. *Historical Essays 1600–1750*, presented to David Ogg (ed. H. E. Bell and R. L. Ollard). 1964.
H.M.C. Reports of the Historical MSS Commission.
Holdsworth. Sir William Holdsworth, *History of English Law*, 9 vols. 1922–32.
Holland, Journal. *The Journal of the Hon. Henry Edward Fox, 4th Lord Holland* (ed. Earl of Ilchester). 1923.
Howell. J. Howell, *Londonopolis.* 1657.
Howitt. W. Howitt, *The Boy's Country Book.* 1839.

Jekyll and Jones. J. Jekyll and S. R. Jones, *Old English Household Life.* 1939.

Johnny Newcome. *The Military Adventures of Johnny Newcome* (1904 ed.).
Jusserand. J. J. Jusserand, *A French Ambassador at the Court of Charles II.* 1892.

Keats. *The Poetical Works and Other Writings of John Keats* (ed. Harry Buxton Forman). 1883.
King. Gregory King, *Natural and Political Observations upon the State and Condition of England.* 1696.
Klingender. F. D. Klingender, *Art and the Industrial Revolution.* 1947.

Lady Holland. *Elizabeth, Lady Holland to her Son* (ed. Earl of Ilchester). 1946.
Lady Shelley. *The Diary of Frances, Lady Shelley* (ed. Richard Edgcumbe). 1912.
Lamb. *The Works of Charles and Mary Lamb* (ed. E. V. Lucas). 1905.
Lamington. Lord Lamington, *In the Days of the Dandies.* 1890.
Laslett. Peter Laslett, *The World we have Lost.* 1965.
Lauderdale. *The Lauderdale Papers* (ed. O. Airy) 3 vols. 1884-5.
Leigh Hunt. *Correspondence of Leigh Hunt.* 1862.
Leslie. C. R. Leslie, *Memoirs of the Life of John Constable.* 1845.
Letts. M. Letts, *As the Foreigner saw Us.* 1935.
Lieven Letters. *Letters of Dorothea, Princess Lieven* (ed. L. G. Robinson). 1902.
Life in London. P. Egan, *Life in London* (1821 ed.).
Lockhart. J. G. Lockhart, *Memoirs of the Life of Sir Walter Scott.* 1837.
Lord Coleridge. Lord Coleridge, *The Story of a Devonshire House.* 1905.
Lucas. W. Lucas, *A Quaker's Journal.* 1934.
Lynedoch. A. M. Delavoye, *Life of Thomas Graham, Lord Lynedoch.* 1880.
Lysons. D. Lysons, *Environs of London.* 1792-1811.

Malton. T. Malton, *Picturesque Tour through the Cities of London and Westminster.* 1792-1810.
Marlay Letters. *The Marlay Letters* (ed. R. W. Bond). 1937.
McCausland. H. McCausland, *The English Carriage.* 1948.
Mercer. C. Mercer, *Journal of the Waterloo Campaign.* 1870.
Misson. Henri Misson, *Memoires et Observations faites par un Voyageur en Angleterre.* 1698.
Mitford. A. G. L'Estrange, *The Life of Mary Russell Mitford.* 1870.
Moorsom. W. S. Moorsom, *A Historical Record of the Fifty-Second Regiment.* 1860.
Morris. Gouverneur Morris, *A Diary of the French Revolution.* 1939.
Mytton. *Memoirs of the Life of the late John Mytton,* by Nimrod (1915 ed.).

Nef. U.N. Nef, *The Rise of the British Coal Industry,* 2 vols. 1932.
Newton. *The Diary of Benjamin Newton* (ed. C. P. Fendall and E. A. Crutchley). 1933.
North, Roger. *The Lives of the Norths* (ed. A. Jessop), 3 vols. 1890.

Ogg. David Ogg, *England in the Reign of Charles II,* 2 vols. 1934.
Old Oak. J. E. Linnell, *Old Oak.* 1932.
Osbaldeston. Squire Osbaldeston: *His Autobiography* (ed. E. D. Cumming) 1926.

Paget Brothers. *The Paget Brothers* (ed. Lord Hylton). 1918.
Partington. C. F. Partington, *Natural History and Views of London.* 1834.
Pepys. *The Diary of Samuel Pepys* (ed. H. B. Wheatley), 8 vols. 1893-9.
Ponsonby. Arthur Ponsonby, *English Diaries.* 1923.
Porter. G. L. Porter, *The Progress of the Nation.* 1851.
Postman's Horn. Arthur Bryant, *Postman's Horn.* 1936.
Powell. Anthony Powell, *John Aubrey and his Friends.* 1948.
Prideaux. *Letters of Humphrey Prideaux* (Camden Society). 1875.

Raumer. F. von Raumer, *England in 1835* (transl. H. E. Lloyd). 1837.
Rawlinson MSS. Rawlinson MSS, Bodleian Library.
Real Life in London. P. Egan, *Real Life in London* (1905 ed.).

Reresby. *Sir John Reresby, The Memoirs of* (ed. Cartwright). 1875.
Rochefoucauld. *A Frenchman in England* (ed. J. Marchand). 1933.
Rogers. J. E. Thorold Rogers, *History of Agriculture and Prices in England.* 1887.

Savile. Henry Savile, *Letters.* 1857.
Sea-Bathing Places. A Guide to all the Watering and Sea-Bathing Places (1815 ed.).
Shakerley MSS. Manuscripts of the Shakerley family of Cheshire, Lancashire and Denbighshire.
Simond. L. Simond, *Journal of a Tour and Residence in Great Britain during the years* 1810 *and* 1811. 1815.
Simpson. J. Simpson, *Paris after Waterloo.* 1853.
Smart. W. Smart, *Economic Annals of the Nineteenth Century.* 1910.
Smith. *The Autobiography of Sir Harry Smith* (ed. G. C. Moore-Smith). 1901.
Sorbière. S. de Sorbière, *Relation d'un Voyage en Angleterre* 1664 (transl. 1709).
Stanhope. Earl Stanhope, *Notes of Conversations with the Duke of Wellington.* 1888.
Stanley. *Before and After Waterloo, Letters from Edward Stanley* (ed. J. H. Adeane and M. Grenfell). 1907.
Strutt. G. Strutt, *The Sports and Pastimes of the English People* (ed. J. C. Cox). 1903.
Sydney. W. C. Sydney, *The Early Days of the Nineteenth Century in England.* 1898.

Taine. H. Taine, *Notes on England.* 1861.
Teonge, *Henry Teonge, The Diary of* (ed. J. E. Manwaring). 1927.
Thurloe. John Thurloe, *A Collection of the State Papers of,* 7 vols. 1742.
Tipping. H. A. Tipping, *English Homes.*
Toynbee. Arnold Toynbee, *Lectures on the Industrial Revolution.* 1906.
Traill. H. D. Traill (ed.) *Social England.* 6 vols.
Trotter. E. Trotter, *Seventeenth Century Life in the Country Parish.* 1919.

Verney Memoirs, The, 2 vols. 1925 ed.

Wansey. H. Wansey, *A Visit to Paris.* 1814.
Webb. S. and D. Webb, *English Local Government from the Revolution to the Municipal Corporation Act,* 7 vols. 1906-27.
Wey. Francis Wey, *A Frenchman sees England in the Fifties* (transl. V. Pirie). 1935.
Wilberforce. *The Correspondence of William Wilberforce* (ed. R. A. and S. Wilberforce). 1840.
Williamson. *Sir Joseph Williamson, Letters addressed to* (Camden Society), 2 vols. 1874.
Wood. *The Life and Times of Anthony Wood* (ed. A. Clark), 5 vols. 1891.
Woodward. E. L. Woodward, *The Age of Reform* (Oxford History of England). 1938.
Wynn Papers, Calendar of. 1930.
Wynne Diaries. The Wynne Diaries (ed. A. Fremantle). 1935-40.

Index of Subjects

SUBJECT INDEX

Index of Names and Places

345